P9-CMX-025

BARRON'S
BUSINESS
REVIEW
SERIES

Operations
Management

Jae K. Shim, Ph.D.
College of Business Administration
California State University, Long Beach

Joel G. Siegel, Ph.D.
Queens College of the City University of New York

BARRON'S EDUCATIONAL SERIES, INC.

All inquiries should be addressed to:
Barron's Educational Series, Inc.
250 Wireless Boulevard
Hauppauge, New York 11788
http://barronseduc.com

Library of Congress Catalog Card No. 98-27825

International Standard Book No. 0-7641-0510-8

Library of Congress Cataloging-in-Publication Data

Shim, Jae K.
    Operations management / Jae K. Shim, Joel G. Siegel.
        p.   cm. — (Business review series)
    Includes index.
    ISBN 0-7641-0510-8
    1. Production management. I. Siegel, Joel G. II. Title.
III. Series.
TS155.S4535   1999
658.5—dc21   98-27825
                                                          CIP

CONTENTS

PREFACE

This book provides a clear and concise introduction to *operations management,* which involves the planning, coordinating, and executing of all activities that create goods or services. The course *operations management* is offered in a variety of titles including *production and operations management, analysis for production systems,* and *design and engineering of production systems,* at both the undergraduate and graduate levels.

This book is an excellent supplement to those courses. It focuses on the fundamentals and essentials needed to understand how operations strategies are carried out and how they are tackled using new concepts and tools. It illustrates decisions with many solved problems to test and help students reinforce their understanding of the subject. It covers many application-oriented problems that help readers to relate, to integrate, to discover, and, in general, to gain useful insights. Further, many business professionals can benefit from this up-to-date book containing the latest techniques and methods.

The book presents, in an integrated fashion, much of the material covered in the exams leading to professional status as a Certified Production and Inventory Manager (CPIM) or Certification in Integrated Resource Management (CIRM). The CPIM exams and certification are administered by the American Production and Inventory Control Society (APICS). In 1991, APICS also initiated the CIRM program with the intention of establishing the internationally recognized standard for excellence in the field of integrated resource management.

Throughout the text, you are advised to follow the following ground rules to enhance benefits:

1. **Understand the Definitions and Key Points.** Each chapter begins with *Key Terms,* which are discussed throughout the chapter. It is followed, wherever applicable, by *You Should Remember* boxes, which summarize key points.

2. **Study Each Example Over and Over Again.** Be sure to work out each example. This is the key process of learning and understanding the chapter material. Of course, you will be tested with similar problems at the end of the chapter. You will be provided with suggested solutions so that you can check your answers.

3. **Do All Problems.** *Do You Know the Basics* tests your understanding of the main concepts of the chapter. *Practical Applications* test your ability to handle analytical—mostly numerical—problems. Do not fail to do both!

If you stick to this game plan and work at it, you will be assured of enhancing your understanding of *operations management* and be successful in the course. By the same token, business professionals will gain a better understanding of the subject and be able to apply the tools to make informed decisions.

The authors are grateful to Allison Shim for her enormous word processing and editorial assistance.

Jae K. Shim
Joel G. Siegel

1
THE SCOPE OF OPERATIONS AND PRODUCTION MANAGEMENT

KEY TERMS

business process reengineering (BPR) management practice seeking to make revolutionary changes in business processes.

continuous improvement (CI) endless pursuit of improvement of machinery, materials, labor utilization, and production methods through application of suggestions and ideas of team members.

fishbone diagrams often called *cause-and-effect diagrams;* way of determining likely root causes of a problem.

operations set of all activities associated with the production of goods and services.

production and operations management management of all activities directly related to the production of goods and services.

production system collection of inputs, conversion, transformation processes, outputs, control mechanisms, and managers involved in production and operations.

productivity ratio of outputs to inputs.

quality measure of conformance of a product or service to certain specifications or standards.

supply chain management management of the integration of the functions, information, and materials that flow across multiple firms in a supply chain (i.e., buying materials, transforming materials, and shipping to customers).

Taguchi method of quality control method of controlling quality that stresses robust product design and the quality loss function.

total quality management (TQM) concept of using quality
methods and techniques to strategic advantage within firms.

To many people, the term *production* means factories, machinery, and
equipment. The field of what has been known as *production management*
has expanded in scope to cover management of nonmanufacturing or service activities such as banking, hotel management, transportation, and education. Because of this broad scope, the field has taken a new name,
production and operations management or simply *operations management*
(OM).

Production and operations is the process by which goods and services
are created. We find productive processes in all kinds of organized activities such as factories, offices, supermarkets, and hospitals. Production and
operations management deals with decision making related to productive
processes to ensure that the resulting goods or services are produced according to specifications, in the amounts and by the schedule required, and
at minimum cost. Inputs of materials, labor, and resources are used to obtain goods or services using one or more conversion/transformation
processes, thereby adding value. Figure 1.1 depicts this process.

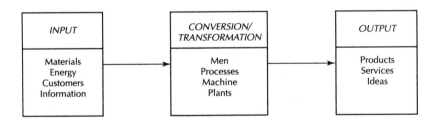

Figure 1.1. Conversion of Inputs to Outputs

Operations management begins with high-level business plans and strategies, over both the long and short run. These plans and strategies are based
on careful and sound projection of demand for the product or service.
Operating plans are derived from the long-term or short-term strategy and
are translated into master schedules, which, in turn, form production and
purchasing plans. Production planning and material control interact continuously with manufacturing in the execution of the plan. Finished goods are
distributed geographically as required by the markets served by the business.

OM is divided into the following five broad sections (the chapter numbers refer to chapters in this book):

1. Decision Making Tools and Methods (Chapter 2)

2. Demand Forecasting (Chapter 3)

3. Planning Systems

   Capacity Planning (Chapters 4 and 11)

   Locational Planning (Chapter 5)

   Aggregate Production Planning and Master Scheduling (Chapter 8)

4. Designing Systems

   Product/Service Design and Process Selection (Chapter 4)

   Facilities Layout (Chapter 7)

   Design of Work Systems (Chapter 6)

5. Operating and Controlling the System

   Inventory Management, Material Requirement Planning, and Just-in-Time (Chapters 9 and 10)

   Project Management and Control (Chapter 12)

   Operational Scheduling (Chapter 8)

   Queuing (Chapter 13)

   Quality Assurance (Chapter 14)

GENERAL DESCRIPTION OF PRODUCTION AND OPERATIONS SYSTEMS

Production and operations systems have inputs, which include the material, parts, paperwork forms, customers, and patients, as the case may be. These inputs are processed in some way by a series of operations whose sequence and number are specified for each input. The number of operations required may vary from one to any number and may take on any desired characteristics; that is, they may be mechanical, chemical, assembly, inspection and control, dispatching, receiving, shipping, personal contact (e.g., an interview), and paperwork operations.

The outputs of a production system include completed parts, products, chemicals, service to customers or patients, and completed paperwork. There is normally a provision for storage after the receipt of the input and between each operation in the system. The storage time may vary from zero to any finite value. Inputs are transported between all operations in the system, and any means of transportation may be used, including self-transportation in the case of clients and customers. An information system and decision maker interconnect the physical activities providing a basis for management decisions. These functions provide the equivalent of a "nervous system." Such production systems may occur in series or in parallel.

CONTINUOUS VERSUS INTERMITTENT SYSTEMS

Continuous flow production systems are those systems in which the facilities are standardized with respect to routings and flow because the inputs are standardized. Therefore, a standard set of processes and sequences of processes can be adopted. Continuous systems are represented in practice by production and assembly lines, large-scale office operations processing forms by some standard procedure, and continuous flow chemical operations.

Intermittent production systems are those systems in which the facilities must be flexible enough to handle a wide variety of products and sizes or the basic nature of the activity imposes change of important characteristics of the input (change in product design). In such instances, no single sequence pattern of operations is appropriate, so the relative location of the process centers or departments must be a compromise that is satisfactory for all inputs. Transportation facilities between operations must also be flexible to accommodate a wide variety of input characteristics as well as a wide variety of routes through the system. Intermittent systems are called such because the flow is intermittent.

PRODUCTION SYSTEMS

The problems that occur in production systems require two major types of decisions: those that relate to the design of the systems and those that relate to the operation and control of the systems (long-run and short-run decisions).

1. Long-run decisions related to system design

Selection and design of inputs (products)

Selection of equipment and processes

Production design of items processed (Production cost interacts strongly with the design of the item being processed.)

Job design

System location

Facility layout

2. Short-run decisions related to operation and control

Inventory and production control

Maintenance and reliability of the system

Quality control

Labor control

Cost control and improvement

The relative importance of these problems of production management varies considerably, depending on the nature of individual production systems. Nonetheless, each system has these problems to some degree. Part of the art of production management involves sensing the relative importance of the various problems in a given situation.

MANUFACTURING OPERATIONS VERSUS SERVICE OPERATIONS

Distinction between manufacturing and service operations is based on the following features:

- The nature and consumption of output
- Nature of work (jobs)
- Degree of consumer contact
- Uniformity of output
- Quality assurance
- Measurement of performance

Table 1.1 provides an overview of the different manufacturing and service operations.

Table 1.1 Differences Between Manufacturing and Service Operations

Characteristic	Manufacturing	Service
Output	Tangible	Intangible
Consumer contact	Low	High
Nature of work	Capital intensive	Labor intensive
Uniformity of output	High	Low
Difficulty of quality assurance	Low	High
Measurement of performance	Easy	Difficult

OPERATIONS STRATEGY

Operations strategy is concerned with setting broad policies and plans for using the production resources of the firm to best support the firm's long-term competitive strategy. Typical operations strategy issues include

- *Capacity requirements:* amount, timing, and type
- *Facilities:* size, location, and specialization
- *Technology:* equipment, automation, and linkages
- *Vertical integration:* extent of use of outside suppliers and distributors
- *Work force:* skill level, wage policies, employment security
- *Quality:* defect prevention, monitoring, and intervention
- *Production planning/materials control:* sourcing policies, centralization, decision rules
- *Organization:* structure, control/reward systems, role of staff groups

Each of these issues is discussed in detail in later chapters.

Four basic operations strategies were identified: cost, quality, speed of delivery, and flexibility. These four strategies translate directly into characteristics used to direct and measure manufacturing performance.

COST

Within every industry, there is usually a segment of the market that buys strictly on the basis of low cost. To compete in this niche successfully, a firm must be the low-cost producer. But even doing this does not always guarantee profitability and success. Products sold strictly on the basis of cost are typically commodity-like in nature. In other words, customers cannot distinguish the products of one firm from those of another. As a result, customers use cost as the primary determinant for making a purchase. However, this segment of the market is frequently very large and many companies are lured by the potential for significant profits, which they associate with the large unit volumes of product. As a consequence, competition in this segment is fierce—and so is the failure rate. After all, there can only be one low-cost producer, which usually establishes the selling price in the market.

QUALITY

Quality can be divided into two categories: product quality and process quality. The level of quality in a product's design will vary depending on the targeted market segment. Obviously, the quality of a child's first two-wheel bicycle is significantly different from that of the bicycle of a world-class cyclist. One advantage of offering higher-quality products is that they command higher prices in the marketplace. The goal in establishing the proper level of product quality is to focus on the requirements of the customer. Overdesigned products with too much quality will be viewed as being prohibitively expensive. Underdesigned products, on the other hand, will lose customers to products that cost a little more but that are perceived by the customers as offering much greater benefits. Process quality is critical in every market segment. In general, customers want products without defects. Thus, the goal of process quality is to produce error-free products through *total quality management (TQM)*.

SPEED OF DELIVERY

Another market niche considers speed of delivery to be an important determinant in its purchasing decision. Delivery time is the elapsed time between receiving a customer's order and filling it. Many companies seek to maintain or increase their customer base by focusing on the competitive priorities of fast delivery time. Often, the ability of a firm to provide dependable and fast delivery allows it to charge a premium price for its products.

FLEXIBILITY

Flexibility, from a strategic perspective, refers to the ability of a company to offer a wide variety of products to its customers. Flexibility is also a measure of how fast a company can convert its process(es) from making an old line of products to producing a new product line. Product variety is often perceived by the customer to be a dimension of speed of delivery.

PRODUCTIVITY

Productivity is the ratio of outputs to inputs. Productivity can be expressed on a partial factor basis or a total factor basis. Total factor productivity is the ratio of outputs to all inputs.

$$\text{Productivity} = \frac{\text{Outputs}}{\text{Labor} + \text{Capital} + \text{Materials} + \text{Energy}}$$

Outputs relative to one, two, or three of these inputs—labor, capital, materials, or energy—are partial measures of productivity. Output per labor hour, often called labor productivity or labor efficiency, is probably the most common partial measure of productivity. Productivity measures are relative measures. To be meaningful, productivity should be compared with something else such as similar operations within its industry or over time within the same operation.

EXAMPLE 1

Given output in finished units = $10,000 and inputs = $9,000, which is broken down into labor = $3,000, materials = $200, capital = $5,000, and energy = $800, then total measure:

Outputs/Inputs = $10,000/$9,000 = 1.11

Multifactor measures:

Output/(Labor + Material) = $10,000/($3,000 + $200) = 3.13

Output/(Labor + Material + Capital) = $10,000/($3,000 + $200 + $5,000)

$$= 1.22$$

Partial measures:

Output/Labor = $10,000/$3,000 = 3.33

Output/Energy = $10,000/$800 = 12.5

YOU SHOULD REMEMBER

The terms *productivity* and *efficiency* (normally stated as a percentage) are used interchangeably. These terms are *performance* measures.

Table 1.2 presents some examples of partial productivity measures.

Table 1.2 Some Examples of Partial Productivity Measures

Business	Productivity Measure
Retail business	Sales per square foot
Utilities	Kilowatts per ton of coal
Lumber mill	Board feet per cord of wood
Restaurant	Customers per labor hour

SUPPLY CHAIN MANAGEMENT

To remain competitive, companies are continually faced with challenges to reduce product development time, improve product quality, speed delivery time to customers, and reduce production costs and lead times. Increasingly, these challenges cannot be effectively met by isolated changes to specific organizational units, but instead they depend critically on the relationships and interdependencies among different firms (or subunits). With the movement toward a global market economy, companies are increasingly inclined toward specific, high-value-adding manufacturing niches. This, in turn, increasingly transforms these challenges into problems of establishing and maintaining efficient material flows along product supply chains. The ongoing competitiveness of a company is tied to the dynamics of the supply chain(s) in which it participates, and recognition of this fact is leading to many changes in the way organizations interact with their supply chain partners. Currently, research is concerned broadly with (1) the development of techniques and tools that enable modeling and analysis of emerging supply chain management strategies and practices and (2) the application of these tools to understand critical tradeoffs and alternatives in practical decision making contexts.

TOTAL QUALITY MANAGEMENT AND QUALITY COSTS

In order to be globally competitive in today's world-class manufacturing environment, firms are placing an increased emphasis on quality and productivity. Total quality management is an effort in this direction. Simply put, TQM is a system for creating competitive advantage by focusing the organization on what is important to the customer. Total quality management can be broken down as follows:

Total: the whole organization is involved and understands that customer satisfaction is everyone's job.

Quality: the extent to which products and services satisfy the requirements of internal and external customers.

Management: the leadership, infrastructure, and resources that support employees as they meet the needs of those customers.

QUALITY DEFINED

A quality product or service is one that conforms to customer satisfaction. Generally, there are two types of product quality—quality of design and quality of conformance. Quality of design measures the functionality of a product or service. It is the decision of a designer to include or exclude certain product features. The customer really measures quality through appearance, operation, and reliability. Quality of performance measures how closely products and services match the intent of the design. This characteristic traditionally has been the focus of a quality management program. In this regard, quality refers to doing it right the first time.

TOTAL QUALITY MANAGEMENT

TQM is supported by two key beliefs: that quality is what the customer says it is and that it must be thoroughly integrated into the very fabric of the organization, including its basic strategies, culture, and management systems. It is essentially an endless quest for perfect quality. It is a zero-defects approach. It views the optimal level of quality costs as the level where zero defects are produced. This approach to quality is opposed to the traditional belief, called *acceptable quality level (AQL),* which allows a predetermined level of defective units to be produced and sold. AQL is the level where the number of defects allows for the minimization of total quality costs. The rationale behind the traditional view is that there is a tradeoff between prevention and appraisal costs and failure costs. As prevention and appraisal costs are increased, failure costs should decrease.

Studies indicate that the total cost of poor quality, or the cost of not doing the right things right the first time, is 20 percent of gross sales for manufacturing companies and 30 percent for service industries. If U.S. production of goods and services is estimated at $5 trillion (as it was in 1998), then the potential for savings from improved quality is over a staggering $1 trillion, which can be saved or redirected for better use. Quality experts maintain that the optimal quality level should be about 2.5 percent of sales. The accounting department should be a major force in the firm that keeps track of and reports on quality costs.

• *PRINCIPLES OF TQM*

Making a product right the first time is one of the principal objectives of TQM. Implementing a successful TQM program will, in fact, reduce costs rather than increase them. There is no question that better quality will result in better productivity. This rule is based on the principle that when less time is spent on rework or repair, more time is available for manufacturing, which will increase productivity.

When an organization maintains accurate records of its cost of quality, TQM will demonstrate that effective quality assurance geared toward prevention rather than correction will pay for itself. Consider, for example, the situation where it is possible to eliminate 100 percent inspection with a good statistical process control (SPC) program. Elimination of high reject rates results in fewer products being repaired, reworked, or scrapped with the obvious reductions in cost.

Tying the cost of quality to TQM is necessary in order to motivate management who is cost motivated in both industry and government. In a TQM environment, management will use the cost data to measure the success of the program. The corporate financial planner can determine that overall product costs are being reduced by the TQM program. Given this success in the prevention of defects, the following failure costs will be reduced or eliminated:

Rework or repair

Inspection of rework

Testing of rework

Warranty costs

Returned material

Discounts, adjustments, and allowances

Obviously, the cost of prevention in TQM is minor when compared to these failure costs.

A checklist of TQM features follows:

- A systematic way to improve products and services
- A structured approach in identifying and solving problems
- A long-term method of quality control
- A process supported by management's actions
- A process that is supported by statistical quality control
- A technique that is practiced by everyone

• *ELEMENTS OF TQM*

The principle elements of TQM are straightforward and embrace a common-sense approach to management. However, each of the individual elements must be integrated into a structured whole to succeed. A description of the elements follows:

1. **A Focus on the Customer.** Every functional unit has a customer, whether it be an external consumer or an internal unit. TQM advocates that managers and employees become so customer focused that they continually find new ways to meet or exceed customers' expectations. We must accept the concept that quality gets customer orders and meets the customers' needs and expectations. This is the strategic goal of TQM.

2. **A Long-Term Commitment.** Experience in the United States and abroad shows that substantial gains come only after management makes a long-term commitment, usually five years or more, to improving quality. Customer focus must be constantly renewed to keep that goal foremost.

3. **Top Management Support and Direction.** Top management must be the driving force behind TQM. Senior managers must exhibit personal support by using quality improvement concepts in their management style, incorporating quality in their strategic planning process, and providing financial and staff support.

4. **Employee Involvement.** Full employee participation is also an integral part of the process. Each employee must be a partner in achieving quality goals. Teamwork involves managers, supervisors, and employees in improving service delivery, solving systemic problems, and correcting errors in all parts of work processes.

5. **Effective and Renewed Communications.** The power of internal communication, both vertical and horizontal, is central to employee involvement. Regular and meaningful communication from all levels must occur. This will allow an agency to adjust its ways of operating and reinforce the commitment of TQM at the same time.

6. **Reliance on Standards and Measures.** Measurement is the springboard to involvement, allowing the organization to initiate corrective action, set priorities, and evaluate progress. Standards and measures should reflect customers' requirements and changes that need to be introduced in the internal business of providing those requirements. The emphasis is on "doing the right thing right the first time."

7. **Commitment to Training.** Training is absolutely vital to the success of TQM. The process usually begins with awareness training for teams

of top-level managers. This is followed by courses for teams of mid-level managers, and finally by courses for nonmanagers. Awareness training is followed by an identification of areas of concentration, or of functional areas where TQM will first be introduced. Implementing TQM requires additional skills training, which is also conducted in teams.

8. **Importance of Rewards and Recognition.** Most companies practicing TQM have given wide latitude to managers in issuing rewards and recognition. Here, a common theme is that individual financial rewards are not as appropriate as awards to groups or team members because most successes are group achievements.

COSTS OF QUALITY

Market shares of many U.S. firms have eroded because foreign firms have been able to sell higher-quality products at lower prices. In order to be competitive, U.S. firms have placed an increased emphasis on quality and productivity in order to

- produce savings such as reducing rework costs and

- improve product quality.

Costs of quality are costs that occur because poor quality may exist or actually does exist. More specifically, quality costs are the total of the costs incurred by (1) investing in the prevention of nonconformance to requirements; (2) appraising a product or service for conformance to requirements; and (3) failing to meet requirements.

Quality costs are classified into three broad categories: prevention, appraisal, and failure costs. *Prevention costs* are those costs incurred to prevent defects. Amounts spent on quality training programs, research to determine customer needs, quality circles, and improved production equipment are considered in prevention costs. Expenditures made to prevent nonconformance will minimize the costs that will be incurred for appraisal and failure. *Appraisal costs* are costs incurred for monitoring or inspection; these costs compensate for mistakes not eliminated through prevention. *Failure costs* may be internal (such as scrap and rework costs and reinspection) or external (such as product returns due to quality problems, warranty costs, lost sales due to poor product performance, and complaint department costs).

• *QUALITY COST COMPONENTS*

Prevention Costs are the costs of all activities specifically designed to prevent poor quality in products or services. Examples are the costs of new product review, quality planning, supplier capability surveys, process capability evaluations, quality improvement team meetings, quality improvement projects, and quality education and training.

Appraisal Costs are the costs associated with measuring, evaluating or auditing products or services to assure conformance to quality standards and performance requirements. These include the costs of incoming and source inspection/test of purchased material, in process and final inspection/test, product, process, or service audits, calibration of measuring and test equipment, and the costs of associated supplies and materials.

Failure Costs are the costs resulting from products or services not conforming to requirements or customer/user needs. Failure costs can be either internal or external.

Internal Failure Costs are failure costs occurring prior to delivery or shipment of the product, or the furnishing of a service, to the customer. Examples are the costs of scrap, rework, reinspection, retesting, material review, and downgrading.

External Failure Costs are failure costs occurring after delivery or shipment of the product, and during or after furnishing of a service, to the customer. Examples are the costs of processing customer complaints, customer returns, warranty claims, and product recalls.

Total Quality Costs are the sum of all the preceding costs. It represents the difference between the actual cost of a product or service, and what the reduced cost would be if there was no possibility of substandard service, failure of products, or defects in their manufacture.

• *OPTIMAL QUALITY COSTS*

There are two views concerning optimal quality costs:

- The traditional view that uses an acceptable quality level
- The world-class view that uses total quality management

The traditional approach uses an acceptable quality level that permits a predetermined level of defective units to be produced and sold. The AQL is the level where the number of defects allowed minimizes total quality costs. The reasoning of the traditional approach is that there is a tradeoff between failure costs and prevention and appraisal costs. As prevention and appraisal costs increase, internal and external failure costs are expected to decrease. As long as the decrease in failure costs is greater than the corresponding increase in prevention and appraisal costs, a company should continue increasing its efforts to prevent or detect defective units.

The world-class view uses total quality control and views the optimal level of quality costs as the level where zero defects are produced. For firms operating in the advanced manufacturing environment, quality is a critical dimension. Quality costs can be managed differently than what is implied by the traditional AQL model. In reality, defects can be reduced below the AQL level, and quality costs can be reduced simultaneously. Thus, the optimal level of quality is defined as where zero defects are produced.

EXAMPLE 2

Consider how a supplier selection program can be used to reduce total quality costs. Initially, a supplier selection program will entail additional prevention and appraisal costs and a reduction in failure costs. However, once the desired quality level is achieved and the supplier relationships are on a sound footing, many of the prevention and appraisal activities can be eliminated. The result is a movement downward on the zero-defect cost graph.

Figure 1.2 graphically illustrates the relationship between these two cost components under two different views.

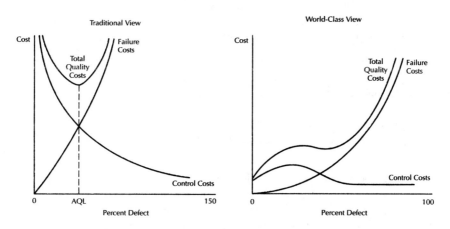

Figure 1.2. Traditional View Versus World-Class View

YOU SHOULD REMEMBER

Quality refers to doing it right the first time. TQM is a system for creating competitive advantage by focusing the organization on what is important to the customer. It can be broken down as follows: *Total:* the whole organization is involved and understands that customer satisfaction is everyone's job. *Quality:* the extent to which products and services satisfy the requirements of internal and external customers. *Management:* the leadership, infrastructure, and resources that support employees as they meet the needs of those customers.

Quality cost reports can be used to point out the strengths and weaknesses of a quality system. Improvement teams can use them to describe the monetary benefits and ramifications of proposed changes. Return-on-investment (ROI) models and other financial analyses can be constructed directly from quality cost data to justify proposals to management. In practice, quality costs can define activities of quality program and quality improvement efforts in a language that management can understand and act on—dollars.

The negative effect on profits, resulting from product or service of less than acceptable quality or from ineffective quality management, is almost always dynamic. Once started, it continues to mushroom until ultimately the company finds itself in serious financial difficulties because of the two-pronged impact of an unheeded increase in quality costs coupled with a declining performance image. To comprehend the economics of quality, management must clearly understand the interrelationship of these two factors.

YOU SHOULD REMEMBER

In addition to such quality gurus as Deming, Ishikawa, and Taguchi, the following scholars have made contributions to quality heritage:

Joseph M. Juran, *A Quality Trilogy.* Juran believes that over 80 percent of all quality problems are caused by factors over which management has control. Consequently, management continually needs to seek improvements through sound quality management, which Juran defines as a trilogy of quality planning, control, and improvement. He defined quality as fitness for use, including reliability, productibility, maintainability, and conformance.

Phillip B. Crosby, *Quality Is Free.* Crosby argued in his book, *Quality Is Free*, that producing quality is not costly but that producing poor quality is. He advocates that zero defects is the only acceptable quality level. Continuous improvement should be the means that management uses to achieve zero defects.

CONTINUOUS IMPROVEMENT

Continuous improvement (CI), based on a Japanese concept called *Kaizen*, is a management philosophy that endlessly pursues improvement of machinery, materials, labor use, and production methods by applying suggestions and ideas of team members. CI uses many different approaches, including:

- *5W2H Approach.* Asking various questions about the current process and how it can be improved. 5W2H refers to why, when, who, where, what, how to do, and how not to do.

- *Statistical Process Control.* Using traditional statistical control charts, which is covered in depth in Chapter 14.

- *Pareto Analysis.* Focusing attention on the most important problem areas. It is based on the concept that about 80 percent of the problems come from 20 percent of the items.

- *PDCA Cycle.* Providing a framework for improvement activities. PDCA refers to plan, do, check, and act.

- *Quality Circles.* Tapping employees for ideas concerning quality and productivity improvement. A circle is a voluntary group of workers who meet regularly to identify and solve problems of quality and productivity.

- *Fishbone (or Ishikawa) Diagrams.* Identifying potential causative factors for the problem areas. The diagrams use a chart resembling the skeleton of a fish in which the spine bone represents the major cause of quality problems and the connecting bones, contributing causes, revealing cause–effect linkages.

- *Benchmarking.* Examining excellent performers outside the industry and seeing how you can use their best practices. Benchmarking typically involves the following steps:

1. Identify those practices that need to be improved.

2. Identify a company that is the world leader in performing the process.

3. Interview the managers of the company and analyze data obtained.

QUALITY CERTIFICATIONS, REGISTRATIONS, AND AWARDS

In order to recognize a variety of achievements in quality assurance, there are different types of certifications, registrations, and awards.

• *SUPPLIER CERTIFICATION*

Your suppliers are an important part of your process. Firms using TQM soon learn that they need much better suppliers. They wish to use fewer suppliers that are "certified" by setting very rigorous certification standards and to provide help and training in how to achieve those standards. The supplier's reward is a much larger and more stable volume of business with the customer. A secondary reward is that it becomes a better supplier to its other customers.

• *ISO-9000 SERIES STANDARDS*

ISO-9000 is a series of quality standards, which the European Union (EU) has adopted for producers worldwide.

• *QUALITY AWARDS*

Beyond supplier certification and ISO-9000, prestigious awards have been developed for outstanding achievement in TQM:

- Deming Prize—Japan (named after W. Edwards Deming)
- Malcolm Baldrige National Quality Award—United States
- Canada Awards for Business Excellence—Canada

TAGUCHI METHOD OF QUALITY CONTROL

The Taguchi method of quality control is a method of controlling quality, developed by Genichi Taguchi, a past winner of the Deming Award, that emphasizes robust quality design and the quality loss function (QLF). Taguchi claims that quality is greatly determined at the design level. In addition to quality control in production, he emphasizes quality control in four other functions: (1) product planning, (2) product design, (3) process design, and (4) production service after purchase. Additionally, Taguchi's QLF quantitatively measures the success or failure of quality control. The traditional view is that any product that measures within the upper and lower specification limits is "good," and a product outside the limits is "bad." In contrast, the QLF presumes that *any* deviation from the target specification is important because it means economic losses for the customer. Furthermore, the economic losses increase quadratically as the actual value deviates from the target value. The QLF can be described by the following equation:

$$L(y) = k(y - T)^2$$

where L = quality loss
y = actual value of quality characteristic
k = a proportionality constant dependent upon the firm's external failure cost structure
T = target value of quality characteristic

EXAMPLE 3

Davidson Company has decided to estimate its quality loss using the Taguchi loss function. After some study, it was determined that k = $400 and T = 10 inches in diameter. The following table illustrates the computations of the quality loss for a sample of 4 units.

Table 1.3 Quality-Loss Computation

Unit	Actual Diameter (y)	$y - T$	$(y - T)^2$	$k(y - T)^2$
1	9.9	–0.10	0.010	$4.00
2	10.1	0.10	0.010	4.00
3	10.2	0.20	0.040	16.00
4	9.8	–0.20	0.040	16.00
Total			0.100	$40.00
Average			0.025	$10.00

Note that the average loss per unit is $10. The total expected loss for, say, 1,000 units would be $10,000 ($10 × 1,000 units).

BUSINESS PROCESS REENGINEERING

TQM seeks evolutionary changes in the processes, whereas the practice called business process reengineering (BPR) seeks to make revolutionary changes. BPR does this by taking a fresh look at what the firm is trying to do in all its processes and then eliminating non-value-added steps and streamlining the remaining ones to achieve the desired outcome.

KNOW THE CONCEPTS

DO YOU KNOW THE BASICS?

1. What is production/operations?
2. What factors distinguish between production and service operations?
3. What are the major decision areas in production/operations management?
4. What are the major components of a production system? Give two examples.
5. List four basic operations strategies.
6. Explain the difference between total and partial productivity.
7. What is continuous improvement? What are the major tools for this philosophy?
8. How does productivity measurement differ between manufacturing and service operations?
9. Contrast the world-class view with the traditional view in quality control.
10. List the types of quality costs.
11. Describe total quality management.
12. What is ISO-9000 Series Standards? List the key quality awards.
13. What is the logic of the Taguchi method?
14. What is supply chain management? Why is it so important in operations management?

TERMS FOR STUDY

5W2H approach
benchmarking
business process reengineering
(BPR)
continuous improvement (CI)
Deming Prize
fishbone diagrams
ISO-9000 Series Standards
operations
operation strategy

production and operations
management
production system
productivity
quality
quality circle
quality costs
supply chain management
Taguchi quality loss function
total quality management

PRACTICAL APPLICATION

1. Donovan Furniture Company provided the following data. Compare the labor, materials, and total productivity of 20X1 and 20X2.

		20X1	20X2
Output:	Sales	$22,000	$35,000
Inputs:	Labor	$10,000	$15,000
	Materials	8,000	12,500
	Capital equipment	700	1,200
	Energy	2,200	4,800
	Total inputs	$20,900	$33,500

2. Identify specific productivity and quality measures that would be useful in each of the following operations:

   a. bus system

   b. department store

   c. post office

   d. hotel

3. You go to a store to purchase three pairs of pants. Your waist is 28 inches (the most comfortable), but you can wear pants whose waist is anywhere between 27 to 29 inches. You select three different colors. The saleslady brings you the following three sizes: 28 inch, 27.5 inch, and 29 inch (she cannot find three pairs of pants, all size 28). Note that the "28 inches" is mentioned as the target value, "27 inches" is the lower specification limit (LSL), and "29 inches" is the upper specification limit (USL). Describe the loss arising from quality failure on each pair of pants if:

   a. The traditional loss function is used?

   b. The Taguchi QLF is used?

4. Major Metal Works manufactures a product that has a target value of 15 inches. k was estimated to be $200. During April, 5,000 units were produced. A sample of four units produced the following values:

Unit	Actual Diameter (y)
1	14.9
2	15.1
3	15.2
4	14.8

   a. Calculate the average loss per unit.

   b. Using the average loss, calculate the total expected loss for April.

ANSWERS

DO YOU KNOW THE BASICS?

1. Production/operations is the process by which goods and services are created.

2. Distinction between production and service operations is based on the following features: nature and consumption of output; nature of work (jobs); degree of consumer contact; uniformity of output; quality assurance; and measurement of performance.

3. Major decision areas in production/operations management include capacity planning, aggregate production planning and master scheduling, locational planning, material requirement planning and inventory management, project management and control, scheduling, queuing, quality assurance, product and service design, facilities layout, and design of work systems.

4. The major components of the production system are inputs, a conversion or creation process, and outputs. Examples follow:

System	Inputs	Conversion Process	Outputs
Auto assembly plant	Labor Energy Robots Parts	Welding Manual assembly Painting	Automobiles
Hospital	Patients Staff Beds Drugs Medical equipment Doctors	Operations Drug administration Health-status monitoring	Healthy individuals Lab results

5. Four basic operations strategies are cost, quality, speed of delivery, and flexibility.

6. Total productivity is the ratio of total output to all resources used in production—labor, capital, material, management, and energy—whereas partial productivity centers on only a single or a subset of these input variables.

7. CI is a management philosophy that seeks endless pursuit of improvement of machinery, materials, labor utilization, and production methods through application of suggestions and ideas of team members. CI uses two major approaches: Internal tools, wherein structured programs such as SPC are used and benchmarking, wherein excellent performers outside the industry are examined to determine how to use their best practices.

8. In manufacturing, physical input and outputs are easy to identify and quantify. For services, intangibles such as health, social benefits, and customer satisfaction are more difficult to define and measure. Quality measures such as waiting time per patient and response to treatment are often used as surrogates.

9. The traditional approach uses an AQL that permits a predetermined level of defective units to be produced and sold, whereas the world-class view uses total quality control and views the optimal level of quality costs as the level where zero defects are produced.

10. Quality costs are classified into three broad categories: prevention, appraisal, and failure.

11. TQM is a system for creating competitive advantage by focusing the organization on what is important to the customer. Total quality management can be broken down as follows: *Total:* the whole organization is involved and understands that customer satisfaction is everyone's job; *Quality:* the extent to which products and services satisfy the requirements of internal and external customers; and *Management:* the leadership, infrastructure, and resources that support employees as they meet the needs of those customers.

12. ISO-9000 Series Standards are a series of quality standards adopted by the European Community for manufacturers worldwide. Key quality awards are the Deming Prize in Japan (named after W. Edwards Deming); the Malcolm Baldrige National Quality Award in the United States; and the Canada Awards for Business Excellence in Canada.

13. The Taguchi method focuses on assuring quality through proper process and product design. Taguchi views any deviation from the "ideal quality" as a loss to society. Taguchi emphasizes minimization of variability in processes and robust design.

14. Supply chain management is concerned with managing the integration of the functions, information, and materials that flow across multiple firms in a supply chain (i.e., buying materials, transforming materials, and shipping to customers). It focuses on the best practices for integrating the information flow and more efficiently moving the product throughout the pipeline. To remain globally competitive, strategic goals pursued are to reduce product development time, improve product quality, speed delivery time to customers, and reduce production costs and lead times. These goals cannot be effectively met by isolated change to specific organizational units but instead depend critically on the relationships and interdependencies among supply chain partners.

PRACTICAL APPLICATION

1.

	20X1	20X2
Partial productivities:		
Labor	2.20	2.33
Materials	2.75	2.80
Total productivity	1.05	1.04

2.

   a. bus system: passengers per route, percent on schedule
   b. department store: sales per week, mistagged merchandise
   c. post office: delivery days per letter, percent lost items
   d. hotel: rooms cleaned, complaints per guest

3.

   a. There is no economic loss because the waist measurements (27.5, 28, and 29 inches) all fall within the limits of your requirements (27 inches to 29 inches).

   b. There is loss from the size 27.5 (0.5 inch deviation from the target) and a larger loss from the size 29 (1 inch deviation from target). There is no loss from the size 28 because it is exactly on target.

4.

   a.

Unit	Actual Diameter (y)	$y - T$	$(y - T)^2$	$k(y - T)^2$
1	14.9	−0.10	0.010	$4.00
2	15.1	0.10	0.010	4.00
3	15.2	0.20	0.040	16.00
4	14.8	−0.20	0.040	16.00
Total			0.100	$40.00
Average			0.025	$10.00

The average loss per unit is $10.

   b. The total expected loss for April is $50,000 ($10 × 5,000 units).

2
DECISION MAKING: CONCEPTS AND TOOLS

KEY TERMS

decision making under risk making a decision when the probability of occurrence of the different states of nature is known.

decision matrix also called payoff table, matrix consisting of the decision alternatives, the states of nature, and the decision outcomes.

decision theory systematic approach to making decisions especially under uncertainty.

decision tree graphical method of showing the sequence of possible decision alternatives.

graphical method graphical approach to solving an LP problem. It is easier to use but limited to the LP problems involving two (or at most three) decision variables.

linear programming (LP) mathematical technique designed to determine an optimal decision (or an optimal plan) chosen from a large number of possible decisions.

mathematical models quantitative representations of reality.

model representation of a real-life system.

optimization models prescriptive techniques for finding the best solutions to the problem at hand. Linear programming is an example.

shadow price profit that would be lost by not adding an additional hour of capacity.

simplex method linear programming algorithm, which is an iteration method of computation, to move from one corner-point solution to another until it reaches the best solution.

simulation descriptive models that can produce large quantities of detailed output because they work by mimicking many parts of the realworld system.

Operations managers are decision makers. They make many choices among alternatives as they deal with the various decision areas listed in Chapter 1. This chapter focuses on basic concepts of decision making:

- The types of decision making

- The decision making process

- The use of information systems for decision making

- Decision tools or models available to operations managers

DECISION MAKING UNDER UNCERTAINTY

The common basis for classifying a decision in decision theory is the amount of information available concerning the probability of occurrence of basic alternatives. There are two major classes of decision problems in this structure: decision making under certainty and decision making under risk or uncertainty. Decision making under certainty means that for each decision there is only one event and, therefore, only one outcome for each action. Decision making under risk or uncertainty, which is more common in reality, involves several events for each action with its probability of occurrence. The decision problem can best be approached using what is called *decision theory*. Decision theory is a systematic approach to making decisions especially under uncertainty. The seven basic steps taken in any decision process follow:

1. **Define the problem.** When management concludes that a problem exists, it should prepare a specific definition or exact statement of the problem.

2. **Select a goal.** The identification of problems as a gap between a desired result and a present or anticipated result indicates the impor-

tance of objectives or goals. Increased profits is an example of an operational goal.

3. **Identify any constraints.** Management's choice is always limited to some extent by law, regulatory action, moral values, resources available, or management preferences. Any constraints that might exist must be identified.

4. **Identify alternative courses of action.** Once a problem has been defined, the alternative actions should be identified.

5. **Forecast the environmental conditions.** The environmental conditions or states of nature should be estimated for each alternative course of action. The states of nature are the uncontrollable variables affecting the decision.

6. **Determine the potential outcomes or payoffs.** The alternative courses of actions and the states of nature should be considered along with the relevant revenues and costs to determine the financial consequences of each alternative course of action (i.e., a decision matrix). The decision matrix (or *payoff table*) is discussed in the next section.

7. **Select and apply decision rules.** Once a payoff table has been constructed, the management accountant must apply a decision rule. A decision rule is a set of instructions for analyzing the data to choose a course of action that will meet the company's objectives. The decision rule is to select the course of action that maximizes the expected monetary profit.

DECISION MATRIX

Decision theory uses an organized approach such as a decision matrix (or payoff table). It is characterized by

the *row* representing a set of alternative courses of action available to the decision maker;

the *column* representing the state of nature or conditions that are likely to occur and that the decision maker has no control over; and

the *entries* in the body of the table representing the outcome of the decision, known as payoffs, which may be in the form of costs, revenues, profits, or cash flows. By computing the expected value of each action, we will be able to pick the best one.

EXAMPLE 1

Assume the following probability distribution of daily demand for a product:

Daily Demand	0	1	2	3
Probability	0.2	0.3	0.3	0.2

Also assume that unit cost = $3, selling price = $5 (i.e., profit on sold unit = $2), and salvage value on unsold units = $2 (i.e., loss on unsold unit = $1). We can stock either 0, 1, 2, or 3 units. The question is how many units should be stocked each day? Assume that units from one day cannot be sold the next day. Then the payoff table can be constructed as follows:

State of Nature

Demand		0	1	2	3	Expected Value
Stock (probability)		(0.2)	(0.3)	(0.3)	(0.2)	
	0	$0	0	0	0	$0
Actions	1	−1	2	2	2	1.40
	2	−2	1[a]	4	4	1.90[b]
	3	−3	0	3	6	1.50

[a] Profit for (stock 2, demand 1) equals (No. of units sold)(Profit per unit) − (No. of units unsold)(Loss per unit) = (1)($5 − 3) − (1)($3 − 2)= $1.

[b] Expected value for (stock 2) is −2(0.2) + 1(0.3) + 4(0.3) + 4(0.2) = $1.90.

The optimal stock action is the one with the highest expected monetary value (i.e., stock 2 units).

EXPECTED VALUE OF PERFECT INFORMATION

Suppose that the decision maker can obtain a perfect prediction of which event (state of nature) will occur. The expected value with perfect information would be the total expected value of actions selected on the assumption of a perfect forecast. The expected value of perfect information can then be computed as the expected value with perfect information *minus* the expected value with existing information.

YOU SHOULD REMEMBER

Decision making under uncertainty is making a decision when the state of nature is unknown and the probability of occurrence of the different states of nature is *unknown*. Common decision selection guides follow:

- the *maxmax* criterion selects the alternative with the maximum possible monetary payoff. This is a criterion of extreme optimism.

- the *maxmin* is a more pessimistic criterion, under which you examine only the worst possible outcome of each act and select the alternative that will give the largest payoff if the worst circumstance occurs.

EXAMPLE 2

From the payoff table in Example 1, the following analysis yields the expected value with perfect information:

State of Nature

Demand	0	1	2	3	Expected Value
Stock (probability)	(0.2)	(0.3)	(0.3)	(0.2)	
Actions 0	$0				$0
1		2			0.6
2			4		1.2
3				6	1.2
					$3.00

Alternatively,

$$\$0(0.2) + 2(0.3) + 4(0.3) + 6(0.2) = \$3.00$$

With existing information, the best that the decision maker could obtain was select (stock 2) and obtain $1.90. With perfect information (forecast), the decision maker could make as much as $3. Therefore, the expected value of perfect information is $3.00 − $1.90 = $1.10. This is the maximum price the decision maker is willing to pay for additional information.

DECISION TREES

A decision tree is another approach used in discussions of decision making under uncertainty. It is a pictorial representation of a decision situation. A decision tree is a general approach to a wide range of OM decisions such as capacity expansion, product planning, process management, and location.

A decision tree is particularly valuable for evaluating different capacity expansion alternatives when demand is uncertain and sequential decisions are involved. For example, a company may expand a facility in 2001 only to discover in 2003 that demand is much higher than forecasted. In that case, a second decision may be necessary to determine whether to expand once again or to build a second facility.

As in the case of the decision matrix approach, the decision tree consists of decision alternatives, states of nature, probabilities attached to the states of nature, and conditional payoffs. Pictorially, it displays:

- *Nodes.* Square nodes, representing decision points, that are left by branches (which should be read from left to right), representing the *alternatives*. Branches leaving circular, or chance, nodes represent the *states of nature* (or *events*).

- *The probability of each state of nature.* The probability *p* is shown above each branch. The probabilities for all branches leaving a chance node must sum to 1.0.

- *The decision outcome.* The decision outcome is the payoff for each possible alternative-event combination shown at the end of each combination. Payoffs are given only at the start, before the analysis begins, for the end points of each alternative-event combination.

In Figure 2.1, for example, Payoff 1 is the financial outcome the manager expects if Alternative 1 is chosen and then State of Nature 1 occurs. No payoff can be associated yet with any branches farther to the left, such as

Alternative 1 as a whole because it is followed by a chance event and is not an end point. Payoffs often are expressed as the present value (PV) of monetary benefits.

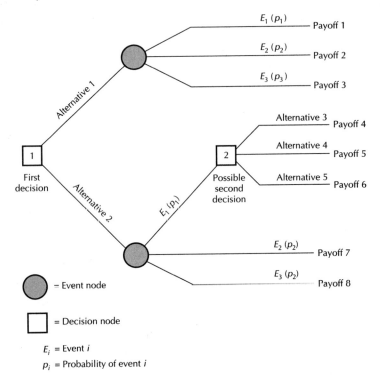

Figure 2.1. A Decision Tree Model

Decision trees are analyzed, step by step, as follows:

1. **Calculate expected payoffs** at the right side of the diagram, at the last stage of the problem, and then work backward.

   - For an event node, multiply the payoff by its respective probability. Add these products to get the event node's expected payoff.

   - For a decision node, pick the alternative that has the best expected payoff. If an alternative leads to an event node, its payoff is equal to that node's expected payoff (already calculated).

2. **Cross out (or "prune") the other branches not chosen** by marking two short lines through them. The decision node's expected payoff is the one associated with the single remaining unpruned branch.

3. Continue this process until the leftmost decision node is reached.
The unpruned branch extending from it is the best alternative to pursue.

If multistage decisions are involved, the manager must await subsequent events before deciding what to do next. If new probability or payoff estimates are obtained, the manager should repeat the process.

EXAMPLE 3

A local distributor must decide whether to build a small or a large facility at a new location. Demand at the location can be either small or large, with probabilities estimated to be 0.4 and 0.6, respectively. If a small facility is built and demand proves to be high, the distributor may choose not to expand (payoff = $223,000) or to expand (payoff = $270,000). If a small facility is built and demand is low, there is no reason to expand and the payoff is $200,000. If a large facility is built and demand proves to be low, the choice is to do nothing ($60,000) or to stimulate demand through local advertising. The response to advertising may be either moderate or substantial, with their probabilities estimated to be 0.3 and 0.7, respectively. If it is moderate, the payoff is estimated to be only $20,000; the payoff grows to $220,000 if the response is substantial. Finally, if a large facility is built and demand turns out to be high, the payoff is $800,000.

Figure 2.2 shows the probability of each state of nature (or event) and the payoff for each of the seven alternative-event combinations. The first decision is whether to build a small or a large facility. Its node is shown first, to the left, because it is the decision the distributor must make now. The second decision node—whether to expand at a later date—is reached only if a small facility is built and demand turns out to be high. Finally, the third decision point—whether to advertise—is reached only if the distributor builds a large facility and demand turns out to be low.

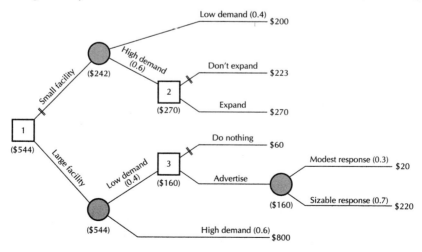

Figure 2.2. Decision Tree for Distributor

Now we can begin to analyze the decision tree, calculating the expected payoffs from right to left below the appropriate states of nature and decision nodes.

- For the event node dealing with advertising, the expected payoff is $160, or the sum of each event's payoff weighted by its probability [0.3($20) + 0.7($220)].

- The expected payoff for decision node 3 is $160 because *Advertise* ($160) is better than *Do nothing* ($60). Cross out the *Do nothing* alternative.

- The payoff for decision node 2 is $270 because *Expand* ($270) is better than *Don't expand* ($223). Eliminate *Don't expand.*

- The expected payoff for the event node dealing with demand, assuming that a small facility is built, is $242 [0.4($200) + 0.6($270)].

- The expected payoff for the event node dealing with demand, assuming that a large facility is built, is $544 [0.4($160) + 0.6($800)].

- The expected payoff for decision node 1 is $544 because the large facility's expected payoff is largest. Cross out *Small facility.*

The best alternative is to build the large facility. This foremost decision is the only one the distributor makes now. Ensuing decisions are made after learning whether demand actually is low or high.

YOU SHOULD REMEMBER

Decision trees are a kind of road map of a decision problem that lays out, in schematic form, the alternative decisions, events, and outcomes that face the decision maker. The decision tree approach enjoys the following advantages:

- It structures the decision process, making use of decision making in an orderly, sequential fashion.

- It forces us to examine all possible outcomes.

- It communicates the decision making process to others.

- It allows a group to discuss alternatives one at a time.

- It can be used with a computer.

MODELING A REAL-LIFE SYSTEM

Many decision making systems are model based. The real world is complex, dynamic, and expensive to deal with. For this reason, we use models instead of real-life systems. A *model* is an abstraction of a real-life system and is used to simulate reality. Especially in a computing environment, operations managers find that using models is an easy and less expensive way to understand what is happening and to make better decisions.

There are many different types of models. Common model types are briefly described next.

NARRATIVE MODELS

A narrative model is either written or oral. The narrative represents a topic or subject. In an organization, reports, documents, and conversations concerning a system are all important narratives. Examples include a salesperson verbally describing a product's competition to a sales manager and a written report describing the function of a new piece of manufacturing equipment.

PHYSICAL MODELS

The fashion model is an example of a physical model, as are dolls and model airplanes. Many physical models are computer designed or constructed. An aerospace engineer may develop a physical model of a shuttle to gain important information about how a large-scale shuttle might perform in space. A marketing department may develop a prototype of a new product.

MATHEMATICAL MODELS

A mathematical model is a quantitative representation of reality. These models are most popular for decision making in all areas of business. Any mathematical formula or equation is a model that can be used for simulation or "what-if" analysis. Once properly constructed, management can experiment with them just as a physical scientist does controlled experiments in the laboratory. In a sense, a mathematical model is a manager's laboratory. For example, the break-even formula used to compute the break-even point is simply

$$X_{be} = \frac{FC}{(P - V)}$$

where X_{be} = break-even point, P = price or average revenue per unit, V = unit variable cost, and FC = total fixed costs.

Break-even analysis can be used to solve many OM decision problems, such as

- Determining the volume at which the cost of "make" breaks even with the cost of "buy."

- Evaluating capacity alternatives by studying the relationship of costs, sales, and profit.

- Comparing production methods by finding the volume at which two different processes have equal total costs.

- Choosing location alternatives on the basis of quantitative factors that can be expressed in terms of total cost.

- Comparing facilities layouts (e.g., fixed-position layouts, process layouts, and product layouts) in terms of fixed costs and variable costs.

EXAMPLE 4

The Los Altos Community Hospital is considering a new procedure to be offered at $250 per patient. Variable costs are $50 per patient. Total fixed costs per year are $650,000. What is the break-even number of patients for this service? Using the formula,

$$X_{be} = \frac{FC}{(P - V)} = \frac{650,000}{250 - 50} = 3,250 \text{ patients}$$

GRAPHICAL MODELS

A *graphical model* is a pictorial representation of reality. Lines, charts, figures, diagrams, illustrations, and pictures are all types of graphical models. Graphical models assist decision makers in designing, developing, and using graphic displays of data and information. In addition, sophisticated graphical design and analysis such as computer-assisted design (CAD) is widely available. A graph that shows budget and financial projections and a break-even chart are good examples of graphical models. The break-even chart depicts the point at which sales revenues and costs are equal. Figure 2.3 presents the break-even chart for Example 4.

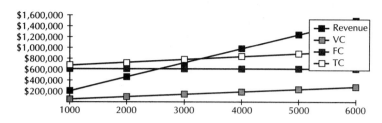

Figure 2.3. Break-Even Chart

STATISTICAL MODELS

Statistical models can be used to develop demand forecasts for capacity and production planning. Regression analysis is an example of statistical models. Other uses of statistical models in production and operations management are the techniques of work sampling and statistical quality control.

OPTIMIZATION MODELS

Optimization models refer to techniques for establishing complex sets of mathematical equations and inequalities that represent objectives and constraints. These models are *prescriptive* in that they try to provide the best possible solution to the problem at hand. They include mathematical programming such as linear programming (LP).

PROJECT PLANNING AND MANAGEMENT MODELS

Project planning and management models are used to navigate and coordinate large projects and to discover critical paths that could delay or jeopardize an entire project if they are not completed in a timely and cost-effective fashion. Program Evaluation and Review Technique (PERT) is widely used for this purpose.

SIMULATION MODELS

The primary use of a *simulation model* is to respond to "what if . . . " questions. These descriptive models can produce large quantities of detailed output because they work by mimicking many parts of the real-world system. One major weakness is that no automatic searching or optimizing is done by the model. (Any such features must be built on top of the simulation model and must be used as a submodel.) In such cases, the simulation may have to be performed many, many times while a search for the best decision parameters is underway. This can be quite expensive if the simulation is complex.

YOU SHOULD REMEMBER

Simulation is descriptive whereas optimization models such as LP are prescriptive.

LINEAR PROGRAMMING

In many business situations, resources are limited, and demand for them is great. The resources may be time, money, or materials, and the limitations are known as constraints. Linear programming is a technique that is useful for allocating scarce resources among competing demands.

LP is a mathematical technique designed to help managers find an optimal decision (or an optimal plan) chosen from a large number of possible decisions. The optimal decision is the one that meets the specified objective of the company, subject to various restrictions or constraints. The optimal decision yields the highest profit, contribution margin (CM), or revenue, or the lowest cost. A linear programming model consists of two important ingredients:

- *Objective function.* The company must define the specific objective to be achieved.

- *Constraints.* Constraints are in the form of restrictions on the availability of resources or meeting minimum requirements.

As the name linear programming indicates, both the objective function and constraints must be in *linear* form.

EXAMPLE 5

A firm wishes to find an optimal product mix. The optimal mix would be the one that maximizes its total profit or contribution margin within the allowed budget and production capacity. Or the firm may want to determine a least-cost combination of input materials while meeting production requirements, employing production capacities, and using available employees.

APPLICATIONS OF LP

Many problems in operations management have been modeled as LP problems. The following list identifies some problems that can be solved with LP:

- *Aggregate planning*

  Production or operations—finding the least-cost production schedule, taking into account inventory, hiring and layoff, overtime, and outsourcing costs, subject to various capacity and policy constraints; scheduling flights.

  Blending—selecting the least-cost mix of ingredients for manufactured products; blending gasoline.

  Staffing—finding the optimal manpower allocation.

- *Distribution*

  Shipping—determining a least-cost shipping pattern from plants to distribution centers or from warehouses to distributors.

- *Location*

  Warehouses or plants—selecting the best warehouse location to minimize shipping costs.

- *Scheduling*

  Shifts—finding the least-cost assignment of workers to shifts, subject to varying demand.

  Jobs—scheduling jobs to machines.

FORMULATION OF LP

1. **Decide what your variables should be.** Units of some output commodity like widgets is a good example.

2. **Decide whether you wish to maximize (e.g., profit) or minimize (e.g., cost).** If information is given on both cost and revenue, you will generally wish to work with profit figures.

3. **Construct an objective function as a sum of the variables times their respective unit profit or cost.** Be sure to include all variables.

4. **Express the constraints as functions of the variables you choose.** In how many ways can each particular type of capacity be

used up? That is the number of variables that should appear in each constraint equation.

5. **Beware of inequalities.** If your constraint is not to exceed some amount of productive capacity or warehouse space, the appropriate constraint inequality is ≤. If you must satisfy some level of demand, the appropriate constraint inequality is ≥.

6. **Always include a statement that you cannot have negative production or shipments.** For example, all variables take on nonnegative values (≥ 0).

In the following example, we will use this technique to find the optimal product mix.

EXAMPLE 6

The Omni Furniture Manufacturing Company produces two products: desk and table. Both products require time in two processing departments, Assembly Department and Finishing Department. Data on the two products are as follows:

Products

Processing	Desk	Table	Available Hours
Assembly	2	4	100
Finishing	3	2	90
Profit per unit	$25	$40	

The company wants to find the most profitable mix of these two products. Define the decision variables as follows:

x_1 = Number of units of desk to be produced
x_2 = Number of units of table to be produced

The objective function to maximize total profit (Z) is expressed as

$$Z = 25x_1 + 40x_2$$

Then, formulate the constraints as inequalities:

$$2x_1 + 4x_2 \leq 100 \text{ (Assembly constraint)}$$
$$3x_1 + 2x_2 \leq 90 \text{ (Finishing constraint)}$$

In addition, implicit in any LP formulation are the constraints that restrict x_1 and x_2 to be nonnegative, i.e.,

$$x_1, x_2 \geq 0$$

Our LP model is:

Maximize: $Z = 25x_1 + 40x_2$

Subject to: $2x_1 + 4x_2 \leq 100$

$3x_1 + 2x_2 \leq 90$

$x_1, x_2 \geq 0$

COMPUTATION METHODS OF LP

Solution methods available to solve LP problems include

- The graphical method and
- The simplex method.

The *graphical method* is easier to use but is limited to the LP problems involving two (or at most three) decision variables. To use the graphical method, follow these steps.

1. **Change inequalities to equalities.**

2. **Graph the equalities.** To graph the equality, (1) set one variable equal to zero and find the value of the other and connect those two points on the graph and (2) mark these intersections on the axes and connect them with a straight line.

3. **Identify the correct side for the original inequalities by shading.** Repeat steps 1–3 for each constraint.

4. **Identify the feasible region, the area of feasible solutions.**

5. **Solve the constraints** (expressed as equalities) simultaneously for the various corner points of the feasible region.

6. **Determine the profit or contribution margin at all corners in the feasible region.**

YOU SHOULD REMEMBER

Feasible solutions are values of decision variables that satisfy all the constraints simultaneously. They are found on and within the boundary of the feasible region. The graphical approach is based on two important LP properties:

- The optimal solution lies on the boundary of the feasible region, which implies that we can ignore the (infinitely numerous) interior points of the feasible region when searching for an optimal solution.

- The optimal solution occurs at one of the corner points (basic feasible solutions) of the feasible region.

EXAMPLE 7

Using the data and the LP model from Example 6, follow steps 1–6. We obtain the following feasible region (shaded area).

1. Change inequalities to equalities.

$$2x_1 + 4x_2 = 100$$
$$3x_1 + 2x_2 = 90$$

2. Graph the equalities. To graph the equality, set one variable equal to zero, find the value of the other, mark the points on the axes, and connect those two points with a straight line.

For equation 1:
If $x_1 = 0$, $x_2 = 25$; if $x_2 = 0$, then $x_1 = 50$; connect $x_2 = 25$ and $x_1 = 50$.

For equation 2:
If $x_1 = 0$, $x_2 = 30$; if $x_2 = 0$, then $x_1 = 45$; connect $x_2 = 30$ and $x_1 = 45$.

3. Identify the correct side for the original inequalities. The correct side is the line and the area below it for less-than or equal-to constraints.

4. Identify the area of feasible solutions. The area of feasible solutions is the duplicated area as indicated by the shaded area in Figure 2.4.

5. Solve the constraints (expressed as equalities) simultaneously for the various corner points of the feasible region.

6. Determine the profit or contribution margin at all corners in the feasible region.

We evaluate all the corner points as follows:

Corner Points	x_1	x_2	Profit $\$25\,x_1 + \$40\,x_2$			
a	30	0	$25(30) + \$40(0)$	=	$750	
b	20	15	$25(20) + 40(15)$	=	1,100	
c	0	25	$25(0) + 40(25)$	=	1,000	
d	0	0	$25(0) + 40(0)$	=	0	

The corner point b ($x_1 = 20$, $x_2 = 15$) produces the most profitable solution ($Z^* = \$1,100$). This point can be found by solving two equations that created it simultaneously:

$$2x_1 + 4x_2 = 100 \qquad (1)$$
$$3x_1 + 2x_2 = 90 \qquad (2)$$

Multiplying equation 2 through by 2 and subtracting from equation 1, we obtain

$$2x_1 + 4x_2 = 100 \qquad (1)$$
$$\underline{6x_1 + 4x_2 = 180} \qquad (2)$$
$$-4x_1 = -80$$
$$x_1 = 20$$

Substituting $x_1 = 20$ into equation 1 or 2 yields $x_2 = 15$.

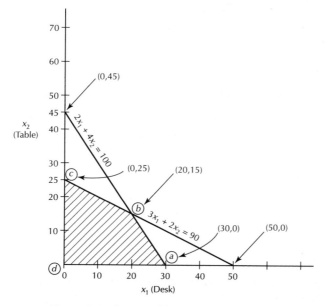

Figure 2.4. The Feasible Region and Corner Points

THE SIMPLEX METHOD

The *simplex method* is the technique most commonly used to solve LP problems. It is an algorithm, which is an iteration method of computation, to move from one solution to another until it reaches the best solution. Steps in the simplex maximization procedure can be summarized as follows:

1. **Convert constraint inequalities to equalities by adding a slack variable** (+S with an appropriate subscript) to every equation with a $\leq$ sign. Set up the initial *simplex tableau.*

2. **Copy the coefficients of your objective function into a simplex tableau.** Be sure to have a separate column for every real or slack variable as well as for the amount on the right-hand side of the constraint equations.

3. **Compute values for the Z row.** Multiply the values in each constraint row by the row's C. Add the results within each column. Compute the $(C_j - Z_j)$ row and evaluate the net profit contribution of each column.

4. **Elect the column (or variable) with the most positive net contribution** $(C_j - Z_j)$. The column so selected is called the *pivot column.*

YOU SHOULD REMEMBER

Before introducing a new variable, we need a procedure for evaluating the economic effects of each variable that could be introduced. This is the purpose of the Z_j and $(C_j - Z_j)$ rows of the tableau.

C_j represents the amount of increase in the objective function if variable j is added into the solution.

Z_j represents the amount of decrease in the objective function if variable j is introduced.

$(C_j - Z_j)$ is the net increase.

---

5. **Determine which variable will be replaced.** This is done in the following manner:

   - Divide the right-hand-side values by their corresponding numbers in the pivot column.

- Select the row with the *smaller nonnegative ratio* as the row to be replaced. The row so selected is called the *pivot row.*

6. **Circle the pivot element,** which is the element in the pivot column and the pivot row. Develop the new tableau by calculating the new rows using the formula:

   - For the new row of the old pivot row, divide each number in the old pivot row by the pivot element.

   - For all other rows,

$$\text{New row} = \begin{pmatrix} \text{Element in} \\ \text{old row} \end{pmatrix} - \left(\begin{pmatrix} \text{Intersectional} \\ \text{element of} \\ \text{old row} \end{pmatrix} \times \begin{pmatrix} \text{Corresponding} \\ \text{elements in the} \\ \text{new row of the} \\ \text{old pivot row} \end{pmatrix} \right)$$

7. **See if there are positive values in the $(C_j - Z_j)$ row of the new tableau.** If no columns have positive values, you have already found the optimal solution. Otherwise, return to step 4.

YOU SHOULD REMEMBER

If the left-hand side is greater (>) than the right-hand side, which is usually the case in a *minimization* problem, we say that there is a *surplus.* Then, we need $-s_1$ and $-s_2$ for a conversion to equalities, instead.

EXAMPLE 8

To illustrate the simplex method, refer to Example 6.

First, we introduce *slack variables* to convert *inequalities* to *equalities*, as follows:

$$2x_1 + 4x_2 \leq 100 \longrightarrow 2x_1 + 4x_2 + s_1 = 100$$

$$3x_1 + 2x_2 \leq 90 \longrightarrow 3x_1 + 2x_2 + s_2 = 90$$

pivot row

C_j		8	6	0	0	
	In Solution	x_1	x_2	s_1	s_2	Solution Quantity
0	s_1	④	2	1	0	60 ←
0	s_2	2	4	0	1	48
	Z_j	0	0	0	0	0
	$C_j - Z_j$	8	6	0	0	

pivot column

The initial tableau indicates the starting solution: $x_1 = x_2 = 0$, $s_1 = 60$, $s_2 = 48$, and $Z = 0$.

Note that the pivot column is the x_1 column, because it has the highest positive number in the $C_j - Z_j$ column. The pivot row is the s_1 row, since it has the lowest ratio, among $60/4 = 15$ and $48/2 = 24$. So the pivot element is 4 (see circled number).

For the new row of the old pivot row, divide each number in the old pivot row by the pivot element.

x_1	x_2	s_1	s_2	Solution Quantity
4/4 = 1	2/4 = 1/2	1/4	4/4 = 0	60/4 = 15

For other rows:

	x_1	x_2	s_1	s_2	Solution Quantity
	2	4	0	1	48
$- 2 \times$ (new row)	$- 2(1)$	$- 2(1/2)$	$- 2(1/4)$	$- 2(0)$	$- 2(15)$
	0	3	$- 1/2$	1	18

The new Z row can now be computed. Multiply the row unit profits and the coefficients in each column for each row. Sum the results within each column.

Row	Profit	x_1	x_2	s_1	s_2	Solution Quantity
x_1	8	8(1)	8(1/2)	8(1/4)	8(0)	8(15)
s_1	0	0(0)	0(3)	0(-1/2)	0(1)	0(18)
(new Z row)		8	4	2	0	120

Next, we can compute the $C - Z$ row:

Column	x_1	x_2	s_1	s_2
C	8	6	0	0
Z	8	4	2	0
C - Z	0	2	-2	0

pivot row

C_j		8	6	0	0	
	In Solution	x_1	x_2	s_1	s_2	Solution Quantity
8	x_1	1	1/2	1/4	0	15
0	s_2	0	③	-1/2	1	18
	Z_j	8	4	2	0	120
	$C_j - Z_j$	0	2	-2	0	

pivot column

The pivot column is the x_2 column, because it has the highest positive number in the $C_j - Z_j$ column. The pivot row is the s_2 row, because it has the lowest ratio, among $15/(1/2) = 30$ and $18/3 = 6$. So the pivot element is 3.

For the new row of the old pivot row, divide each number in the old pivot row by the pivot element.

x_1	x_2	s_1	s_2	Solution Quantity
0/3 = 0	3/3 = 1	(-1/2)/3 = -1/6	1/3	18/3 = 6

For other rows:

	x_1	x_2	s_1	s_2	Solution Quantity
	1	1/2	1/4	0	15
-1/2 × (new row)	1/2(0)	1/2(1)	1/2(-1/6)	1/2(1/3)	1/2(6)
	1	0	1/3	-1/6	12

The new Z row can now be computed. Multiply the row unit profits and the coefficients in each column for each row. Sum the results within each column.

Row	Profit	x_1	x_2	s_1	s_2	Solution Quantity
x_1	8	8(1)	8(0)	8(1/3)	8(-1/6)	8(12)
s_1	6	6(0)	6(1)	6(-1/6)	6(1/3)	6(6)
(new Z row)		8	6	5/3	2/3	132

Next, we can compute the $C - Z$ row:

Column	x_1	x_2	s_1	s_2
C	8	6	0	0
Z	8	6	5/3	2/3
C – Z	0	0	–5/3	–2/3

C_i		8	6	0	0	
	In Solution	x_1	x_2	s_1	s_2	Solution Quantity
8	x_1	1	0	1/3	–1/6	12
6	s_2	0	1	–1/6	1/3	6
	Z_i	8	6	–5/3	2/3	132
	$C_i - Z_i$	0	0	–5/3	–2/3	

This is an optimal tableau since there are *no* positive numbers in the $C_j - Z_j$ row.

The optimal solution is $x_1 = 12$, $x_2 = 6$, and $Z^* = 132$.

ASSUMPTIONS

Four basic assumptions are fundamental to the general linear programming problem:

- *Linearity.* The objective function and the constraint equations are assumed to be linear (straight lines).

- *Certainty.* The method does not have provisions for probability. The stated conditions are assumed to follow precisely the given mathematical expressions.

- *Divisibility.* The values of the decision variable may take on fractional or integer values (e.g., it is possible to produce $58.6i$ gallons of a product).

- *Nonnegativity.* The values of the variables that the method selects (decision variables) must be greater than or equal to zero.

CAN THE COMPUTER HELP?

We can use a computer LP software package such as *LINDO (Linear Interactive and Discrete Optimization)* and *What's Best!* to quickly solve an LP problem.

The following shows LINDO output for Example 6.

Computer Printout for LP

VARIABLE	VARIABLE VALUE	ORIGINAL COEFF	COEFF. SENS.	
X 1	20	25	0	Note: $X_1 = 20$
X 2	15	40	0	$X_2 = 15$

CONSTRAINT NUMBER	ORIGINAL RHS	SLACK OR SURPLUS	SHADOW PRICE
1	100	0	8.75
1	90	0	2.50

OBJECTIVE FUNCTION VALUE: <u>1100</u>   Note: $Z = \$1,100$

SENSITIVITY ANALYSIS

OBJECTIVE FUNCTION COEFFICIENTS

VARIABLE	LOWER LIMIT	ORIGINAL COEFFICIENT	UPPER LIMIT
X 1	20	25	60
X 2	16.67	40	50

RIGHT HAND SIDE

CONSTRAINT NUMBER	LOWER LIMIT	ORIGINAL VALUE	UPPER LIMIT
1	60	100	180
2	50		

SHADOW PRICES (OPPORTUNITY COSTS)

An operations manager who has solved an LP problem might wish to know whether it pays to add capacity in hours in a particular department. The manager might be interested in the monetary value to the firm of adding, say, an hour per week of assembly time. This monetary value is usually the additional profit that could be earned. This amount is the *shadow price* (also known as the *opportunity cost*), the profit that would be lost by not adding an additional hour of capacity. To justify a decision in favor of a short-term capacity decision, the manager must be sure that the shadow price exceeds the actual price of that expansion. For example, suppose that the shadow price of an hour of assembly capacity is $6.50, whereas the actual market price is $8.00. This means that it does not pay to obtain an additional hour of the assembly capacity.

Shadow prices are computed, step by step, as follows:

1. **Add one hour to the constraint of a given LP problem under consideration.** It is preferable to add more than one hour to make it easier to show graphically.

2. **Resolve the problem and find the maximum profit Z.**

3. **Compute the difference** between the profit of the original LP problem and the profit determined in step 2, which is the shadow price.

There is no need to go through these tedious computational steps. The LINDO output provides the shadow prices:

Assembly capacity = $8.75
Finishing capacity = $2.50

The firm would be willing to pay up to $70 to obtain an additional 8 hours of the assembly capacity per week, or $8.75 per hour per week. In other words, the firm's opportunity cost of not adding an additional hour is $8.75.

KNOW THE CONCEPTS

DO YOU KNOW THE BASICS?

1. What is the decision making process?
2. Differentiate among decision making under certainty, risk, and uncertainty.
3. List the types of models that are useful to operations managers.
4. What is a decision matrix? What are the major components of this matrix?
5. What is the expected value of perfect information? How is it computed?

6. What are project planning and management models used for? Give a popular technique for this.

7. What is a popular statistical model used by operations managers?

8. What is linear programming? Why is it called linear?

9. List four popular applications of LP for operations decisions.

10. What are the two ingredients of LP?

11. What are two major computational methods of LP? Briefly describe the pro and con of each.

12. What is meant by shadow prices in LP? How can it be used in a short-term capacity decision?

TERMS FOR STUDY

basic feasible solution	mathematical models
constraints	model
decision making process	nonnegativity constraints
decision making under uncer- tainty	objective function optimal solution
decision matrix	optimization models
decision tree	payoff table
feasible solution	shadow price
linear	simulation models
linear programming	statistical models

PRACTICAL APPLICATION

1. The manager of a restaurant must place his order for hot dogs weekly. A review of his sales records for the past 50 weeks reveals the following frequency of hot dogs sold:

Hot Dogs	Number of Weeks
2000	15
3000	20
4000	15
	50 weeks

Hot dogs sell for $1.00 each and cost $0.60 each. Unsold hot dogs are donated to a nearby orphanage.

a. Construct the payoff table and determine the optimal number of hot dogs to order each week.

b. Compute the expected value of perfect information.

2. A retailer stocks bunches of fresh-cut flowers. He has an uncertain demand; the best estimates available follow:

Demand (bunches)	Probability
20	0.10
25	0.30
40	0.50
60	0.10
	1.00

The retailer buys these for $6 a bunch and sells them for $10.

a. Set up the payoff table (or decision matrix).

b. If he stocks 40 every day, what will his expected profit per day be?

c. What would the expected profit per day be with a 60-unit stock?

d. What quantity should he buy every day to maximize expected profits?

e. What is the expected value of perfect information for him?

3. Vendo Company operates the concession stands at the university football stadium. Records of past sales indicate that there are basically four kinds of football weather, that sales of hot dogs depend on the weather, and that the percentage of football games played in each kind of weather is as follows:

Weather	Game Days (%)	Number of Hot Dogs Sold
Snow	10	10,000
Rain	20	20,000
Clear/Warm	40	30,000
Clear/Cold	30	40,000

Hot dogs cost Vendo Company $0.30 each and are sold for $0.50. Hot dogs unsold at the end of each game are worthless. Ignore income taxes.

a. Prepare a table with four rows and four columns showing the contribution margin from each of the four purchasing strategies of buying

10,000, 20,000, 30,000, or 40,000 hot dogs and the four weather conditions (snow, rain, clear/warm, and clear/cold).

b. Assuming that the chances of snow, rain, clear/warm, and clear/cold are 10%, 20%, 40%, and 30%, respectively, compute the expected contribution margin from each of the following purchasing strategies:

    i.   Buy 10,000 hot dogs.

    ii.   Buy 20,000 hot dogs.

    iii. Buy 30,000 hot dogs.

    iv. Buy 40,000 hot dogs.

c. What is the optimal purchasing strategy in the absence of a weather forecast, and what is the expected contribution margin from following this strategy? (This answer will be the largest of the four expected payoffs computed in b.)

d. If Vendo had a perfect weather forecast for each game, it would buy 10,000 hot dogs when snow is predicted, 20,000 when rain is predicted, 30,000 when clear/warm is predicted, and 40,000 when clear/cold is predicted. What is the expected average contribution margin per football game assuming the availability of a perfect weather forecast per football game?

e. What is the expected dollar value of the information from a perfect weather forecast?

4. Assume XYZ Corporation wishes to introduce one of two products to the market this year. The probabilities and present values (PV) of projected cash inflows follow:

Product	Initial Investment (I)	PV of Cash Inflows	Probabilities
A	$225,000		1.00
		$450,000	0.40
		$200,000	0.50
		–$100,000	0.10
B	$ 80,000		1.00
		$320,000	0.20
		$100,000	0.60
		–$150,000	0.20

Which product should be chosen?

Use the net present value (NPV) as the selection criterion. The NPV is PV – I.

5. Based on the industry supply and demand analysis, Madden Corporation wishes to build a full-scale manufacturing facility. It is considering:

Action A. Build a large plant, costing $6 million.
Action B. Build a small plant, costing $2 million.

The probabilities of various demands and present values of projected cash inflows for these demand situations follow:

Action	Demand Conditions	PV of Cash Inflows	Probabilities
A	High	$8 million	0.5
	Medium	$4 million	0.3
	Low	$1.5 million	0.2
B	High	$2.5 million	0.5
	Medium	$2 million	0.3
	Low	$1.5 million	0.2

a. Construct a decision tree to analyze the two options.

b. Which option would you choose? Comment on your decision.

6. The Carson Company makes two products, X and Y. Their contribution margins are $50 and $90, respectively. Each product goes through three processes: cutting, finishing, and painting. The number of hours required by each process for each product and capacities available follow:

Hours Required in Each Process

Product	Cutting	Finishing	Painting
X	2	4	3
Y	1	6	2
Capacities in Hours	300	500	250

Formulate the objective function and constraints to determine the optimal product mix.

7. A company fabricates and assembles two products, A and B. It takes three minutes to fabricate each unit of A, and six minutes to fabricate each unit of B. Assembly time per unit for product A is one minute, and for product B, nine minutes. There are 600 minutes of fabrication time and 1,800 minutes of assembly time available. The company makes a contribution margin of $2 on each unit of A it sells, and $1 on each unit of B.

a. Express the problem as an LP model.

b. Solve this problem by the graphical method. What quantities of A and B should be produced in order to maximize profits? What will be the profits earned at these production levels?

8. John Shops manufactures two products: tables and desks. The LP model is

$$\text{Maximize: } Z = 80x_1 + 40x_2$$

$$\text{Subject to: } 6x_1 + 4x_2 \leq 2{,}400 \text{ (matching time capacity)}$$

$$2x_1 + 3x_2 \leq 1{,}500 \text{ (assembly time capacity)}$$

$$9x_1 + 3x_2 \leq 2{,}700 \text{ (finishing time capacity)}$$

$$x_1, x_2 \geq 0$$

Solve this problem by the simplex method.

9. After a number of pivot steps, the tableau of a given LP problem assumes the following form:

C_j	4	3	0	0	
	x_1	x_2	s_1	s_2	Solution Quantity
	0	1	2	−1	2
	1	0	−1	1	2
$C_j - Z_j$	0	0	2	1	

a. Is this an optimal tableau? Why?

b. What are the values of x_1, x_2, and Z^*?

10. The following simplex tableau shows an intermediate solution to a maximization problem.

C_j		40	30	0	0	0	
	In Solution	x_1	x_2	s_1	s_2	s_3	Solution Quantity
40	x_1	1	0	1	0	0	16
0	s_2	0	1	0	1	0	8
0	s_3	0	2	−1	0	1	8

a. Compute the new $C_j - Z_j$ row.

b. Obtain the optimal solution and the optimal objective function values.

ANSWERS

DO YOU KNOW THE BASICS?

1. The decision making process is the process of defining a problem and its environment, identifying alternatives, evaluating alternatives, selecting an alternative, and implementing the decision.

2. Decision making under certainty means that for each decision there is only one event and therefore only one outcome for each action. Decision making under risk or uncertainty, which is more common in reality, involves several events for each action with its probability of occurrence. Decision making under uncertainty is a decision made when the probability of occurrence of the different states of nature is *unknown*.

3. Models can be narrative, graphical, statistical, mathematical, optimization, physical, project planning and management, and simulation.

4. A decision matrix is an organized approach to decision making under risk. It is characterized by

   (1) the *row* representing a set of alternative courses of action available to the decision maker; (2) the *column* representing the state of nature or conditions that are likely to occur and the decision maker has no control over; and (3) the *entries* in the body of the table representing the outcome of the decision, known as payoffs, which may be in the form of costs, revenues, profits, or cash flows. By computing expected value of each action, we will be able to pick the best one.

5. It is the value of a perfect forecast. The expected value of perfect information can be computed by subtracting the expected value with existing information from the expected value with perfect information.

6. Project planning and management models are used to navigate and coordinate large projects and to discover critical paths that could delay or jeopardize an entire project if they are not completed in a timely and cost-effective fashion. Program Evaluation and Review Technique (PERT) is widely used for this purpose.

7. Regression analysis is an example. It can be used to develop demand forecasts for capacity and production planning.

8. Linear programming is a mathematical technique designed to determine an optimal decision (or an optimal plan) chosen from a large number of possible decisions. The optimal decision is the one that meets the specified objective of the company, subject to various restrictions or constraints. It is linear because we assume both the objective function and constraints are linear.

9. Four popular applications of LP are selecting the least-cost mix of ingredients for manufactured products; determining the most profitable mix of products, scheduling jobs to machines, and determining a least-cost shipping pattern.

10. Two ingredients of LP are the objective function and inequality constraints (including nonnegativity constraints).

11. Two major computational methods of LP are (1) the simplex method and (2) the graphical method. The simplex method is the technique most commonly used to solve LP problems. It is an algorithm, which is an iterative method of computation, to move from one solution to another until it reaches the best solution. The graphical approach is easier to use but limited to the LP problems involving two (or at most three) decision variables.

12. Shadow price, also known as opportunity cost, is the profit that would be lost by not adding an additional hour of capacity. To justify a decision in favor of a short-term capacity decision, the manager must be sure that the shadow price exceeds the actual price of that expansion.

PRACTICAL APPLICATION

1.

a. The payoff table follows:

		State of Nature			
	Demand	2,000	3,000	4,000	
Stock (Probability)		(0.3)	(0.4)	(0.3)	Expected Profit
2,000		$800	$800	$800	$800
Action 3,000		$200[a]	$1,200	$1,200	900[b]
4,000		($400)	$800	$1,600	680[c]

[a] 2,000 units sold, Profit: 2,000 × $0.40 = $800
1,000 units unsold, Cost: 1,000 × $0.60 = $600
$200

[b] Expected profit for 3,000 hot dogs:

($200)(0.3) + ($1,200)(0.4) + ($1,200)(0.3) = $60 + $480 + $360 = $900

^{c} Expected profit for 4,000 hot dogs:

$$(-\$400)(0.3) + (\$800)(0.4) + (\$1,600)(0.3) = -\$120 + \$320 + \$480 = \$680$$

Therefore, the manager should order 3,000 hot dogs weekly, which will maximize the expected profit (i.e., $900).

b. The expected value with perfect information is

$$(\$800)(0.3) + (\$1,200)(0.4) + (\$1,600)(0.3) = \$240 + \$480 + \$480 = \$1,200$$

Thus, the expected value of perfect information is

$$\$1,200 - \$900 = \$300$$

which is the maximized amount of money the manager would be willing to pay for perfect information.

2.

a. The payoff table follows:

Stock (Probability)	Demand 20 (0.1)	25 (0.3)	40 (0.5)	60 (0.10)	Expected Profit
20	$80	$80	$80	$80	$80
25	50	100	100	100	95
40	(40)	10	160	160	95
60	(160)	(110)	40	240	(5)

b. From the payoff table, $95.

c. From a, ($5).

d. From a, either 25 units or 40 units.

e. Expected value with perfect information

$$(\$80)(0.1) + (\$100)(0.3) + (\$160)(0.5) + (\$240)(0.1) = \$142$$

Therefore, expected value of perfect information is

$$\$142 - \$95 = \$47$$

3.

a. Payoff in Income (Loss) due to the combination of purchase strategy and weather outcome.

Purchase Strategy	Snow 10,000	Rain 20,000	Clear/Warm 30,000	Clear/Cold 40,000
10,000	$2,000	$2,000	$2,000	$2,000
20,000	($1,000)	$4,000	$4,000	$4,000
30,000	($4,000)	$1,000	$6,000	$6,000
40,000	($7,000)	($2,000)	$3,000	$8,000

b.

i. Buy 10,000: $0.10 \times \$2,000 + 0.20 \times \$2,000 + 0.40 \times \$2,000 + 0.30 \times \$2,000 = \$2,000$

ii. Buy 20,000: $0.10 \times (\$1,000) + 0.20 \times \$4,000 + 0.40 \times \$4,000 + 0.30 \times \$4,000 = \$3,500$

iii. Buy 30,000: $0.10 \times (\$4,000) + 0.20 \times \$1,000 + 0.40 \times \$6,000 + 0.30 \times \$6,000 = \$4,000$

iv. Buy 40,000: $0.10 \times (\$7,000) + 0.20 \times (\$2,000) + 0.40 \times \$3,000 + 0.30 \times \$8,000 = \$2,500$

c. Buy 30,000 hot dogs and expect to earn $4,000 on average per game.

d. $0.10 \times \$2,000 + 0.20 \times \$4,000 + 0.40 \times \$6,000 + 0.30 \times \$8,000 = \$5,800$

Buying the correct amount for each weather possibility implies an expected average income of $5,800 per game.

e. $5,800 – $4,000 = $1,800.

4. A decision tree analyzing the two products is given in Figure 2.5.

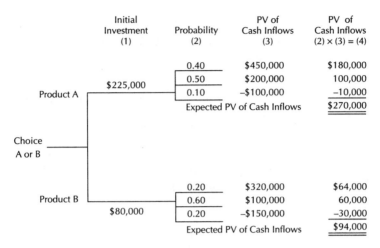

	Initial Investment (1)	Probability (2)	PV of Cash Inflows (3)	PV of Cash Inflows (2) × (3) = (4)
		0.40	$450,000	$180,000
	$225,000	0.50	$200,000	100,000
Product A		0.10	–$100,000	–10,000
		Expected PV of Cash Inflows		$270,000
		0.20	$320,000	$64,000
Product B		0.60	$100,000	60,000
	$80,000	0.20	–$150,000	–30,000
		Expected PV of Cash Inflows		$94,000

For product A:

Expected NPV (Net Present Value) = Expected PV – I = $270,000 – $225,000 = $45,000

For product B:

Expected NPV = $94,000 – $80,000 = $14,000

Figure 2.5. A Decision Tree

5.

  a. Expected NPVs for A and B follow:

Action	Demand Conditions	PV of Cash Inflows ($) (1)	Probabilities (2)	(1) × (2)
A	High	8 million	0.5	$4 million
	Medium	4 million	0.3	1.2 million
	Low	1.5 million	0.2	3 million
			PV	$8.2 million
			I	6 million
			Expected *NPV* =	2.2 million
B	High	3 million	0.5	$1.5 million
	Medium	2 million	0.3	0.6 million
	Low	1.5 million	0.2	0.3 million
			PV	$2.4 million
			I	2 million
			Expected *NPV* =	0.4 million

b. Choose action A because its expected NPV is greater than action B's. This approach does not tell us how risky each option is.

6.

Let X = number of units of product X to be produced

Y = number of units of product Y to be produced

Then, the LP formulation is as follows:

Maximize: $Z = \$50X + \$90Y$

Subject to: $2X + 1Y \le 300$

$4X + 6Y \le 500$

$3X + 2Y \le 250$

$X, Y \ge 0$

7.

a. Let A = number of units of product A to produce

Let B = number of units of product B to produce

Maximize: $Z = \$2A + \$1B$

Subject to: $3A + 6B \le 600$ (fabrication)

$1A + 9B \le 1,800$ (assembly)

$A, B \ge 0$

b.

1.	$A = 0$, $B = 100$	$Z = \$100$
2.	$A = 200$, $B = 0$	$Z = \$400$

Thus, 200 units of A should be produced and no units of B. Profit will be $400 at this level. See Figure 2.6.

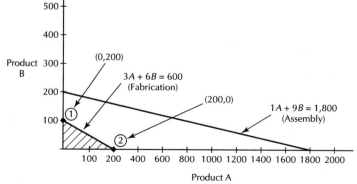

Figure 2.6.

8.

The initial tableau can be set up as follows:

C_i		80	40	0	0	0	
	In Solution	x_1	x_2	s_1	s_2	s_3	Solution Quantity
0	s_1	6	4	1	0	0	2,400
0	s_2	2	3	0	1	0	1,500
0	s_3	⑨	3	0	0	1	2,700
	Z_i	0	0	0	0	0	0
	$C_i - Z_i$	80	40	0	0	0	

pivot column *pivot row*

The pivot column is the x_1 column, because it has the highest positive number. The pivot row is the s_3 row because it has the lowest ratio among $2400/6 = 400$, $1500/2 = 750$, and $2700/9 = 300$.

So the pivot element is 9 (the one circled).

Tableau 1

C_i		80	40	0	0	0	
	In Solution	x_1	x_2	s_1	s_2	s_3	Solution Quantity
0	s_1	0	②	1	0	-2/3	600
0	s_2	0	7/3	0	1	-2/9	900
80	s_3	1	1/3	0	0	1/9	300
	Z_i	80	80/3	0	0	80/9	24,000
	$C_i - Z_i$	0	40/3	0	0	-80/9	

pivot column *pivot row*

The pivot column is the x_2 column, because it has the highest positive number. The pivot row is the s_1 row, because it has the lowest ratio among $600/2 = 300$, $900/(7/3) = 385\ 7/8750$, and $300/(1/3) = 900$. So the pivot element is 2.

Final Tableau

C_j		80	40	0	0	0	
	In Solution	x_1	x_2	s_1	s_2	s_3	Solution Quantity
40	x_2	0	1	1/2	0	-1/3	300
0	s_2	0	0	-7/6	1	5/9	200
80	x_1	1	0	-1/6	0	2/9	200
	Z_j	80	40	20/3	0	40/9	28,000
	$C_j - Z_j$	0	0	-20/3	0	-40/9	

This is an optimal simplex tableau, because there are no positive numbers in the $Cj - Zj$ row. The optimal solution is $x_1 = 200$, $x_2 = 300$, and $Z^* = \$28,000$.

9.

a. Yes, because there are no positive values in the $C_j - Z_j$ row.

b. The optimal solution is $x_1 = 2$, $x_2 = 2$, and $Z^* = \$4(2) + \$3(2) = \$14$.

10.

a. The new Z row can now be computed. Multiply the row unit profits and the coefficients in each column for each row. Sum the results within each column.

Row	Profit	x_1	x_2	s_1	s_2	s_3	Solution Quantity
x_1	40	40(1)	40(0)	40(1)	40(0)	40(0)	40(16)
s_2	0	0(0)	0(1)	0(0)	0(1)	0(0)	0(8)
s_3	0	0(0)	0(2)	0(-1)	0(0)	0(1)	0(8)
New Z row		40	0	40	0	0	640

Next, we can compute the $C - Z$ row:

Column	x_1	x_2	s_1	s_2	s_3
C	40	30	0	0	0
Z	40	0	40	0	0
C - Z	0	30	-40	0	0

C_i	In Solution	40 x_1	30 x_2	0 s_1	0 s_2	0 s_3	Solution Quantity
40	x_1	1	0	1	0	0	16
0	s_2	0	1	0	1	0	8
0	s_3	0	(2)	-1	0	1	8
	Z_j	40	0	40	0	0	640
	$C_j - Z_j$	0	30	-40	0	0	

b. The pivot column is the x_2 column, because it has the highest positive number. The pivot row is the s_3 row, because it has the lowest ratio among $16/0 = \infty$, $8/1 = 8$, and $8/2 = 4$. So the pivot element is 2.

One more iteration will generate the following optimal tableau.

C_i	In Solution	40 x_1	30 x_2	0 s_1	0 s_2	0 s_3	Solution Quantity
40	x_1	1	0	1	0	0	16
0	s_2	0	0	1/2	1	-1/2	4
30	x_2	0	1	-1/2	0	1/2	4
	Z_j	40	30	25	0	15	760
	$C_j - Z_j$	0	0	-25	0	-15	

This is an optimal simplex tableau because there are no positive numbers in the $C_j - Z_j$ row. The optimal solution is $x_1 = 16$, $x_2 = 4$, and $Z^* = \$760$.

3
FORECASTING

KEY TERMS

classical decomposition approach to forecasting that seeks to decompose the underlying pattern of a time series into cyclical, seasonal, trend, and random subpatterns.

correlation coefficient measure of the degree of correlation between two variables. The range of values it takes is between −1 and +1.

Delphi method qualitative forecasting technique for arriving at group consensus in an anonymous fashion.

deseasonalized data removal of the seasonal pattern in a data series. Deseasonalizing facilitates the comparison of month-to-month changes.

exponential smoothing forecasting technique that uses a weighted moving average of past data as the basis for a forecast.

least-squares method statistical technique for fitting a straight line through a set of points in such a way that the sum of the squared distances from the data points to the line is minimized.

mean absolute deviation (MAD) mean or average of the sum of all the forecast errors with regard to sign.

moving average average that is updated as new information is received.

regression analysis statistical procedure for estimating mathematically the average relationship between the dependent variable (e.g., sales) and one or more independent variables (e.g., price and advertising).

simple regression regression analysis that involves one independent variable. For example, the demand for automobiles is a function of its price only.

trend analysis special form of simple regression in which time is the independent variable.

The most important function of business is probably forecasting. A forecast is a starting point for planning. The objective of forecasting is to reduce risk in decision making. In business, forecasts are the basis for capacity planning, production and inventory planning, manpower planning, planning for sales and market share, financial planning and budgeting, planning for research and development, and top management's strategic planning. In this chapter, we examine several aspects of forecasting, and we present some popular forecasting models. Demand is a key determinant in two major categories of decisions that are discussed throughout the book: decisions about the design of the production system and decisions about how to operate the production system.

WHO USES FORECASTS?

Forecasts are needed for marketing, production, purchasing, manpower, and financial planning. Furthermore, top management needs forecasts for planning and implementing long-term strategic objectives and planning for capital expenditures. More specifically, production planners need forecasts in order to (1) schedule production activities, (2) order materials, (3) establish inventory levels, and (4) plan shipments. Some other areas that need forecasts include material requirements (purchasing and procurement), labor scheduling, equipment purchases, maintenance requirements, and plant capacity planning.

As soon as the company makes sure that it has enough capacity, the production plan is developed. If the company does not have enough capacity, it will require planning and budgeting decisions for capital spending for capacity expansion. Figure 3.1 displays the relationship between demand forecasting and production/operations systems.

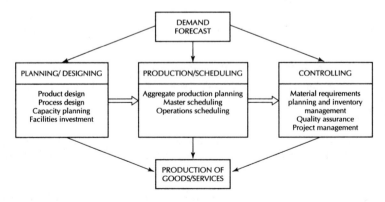

Figure 3.1. Relationship Between Demand Forecasting and Production/Operations Systems

FORECASTING METHODS

The company may choose from a wide range of forecasting techniques. There are basically two approaches to forecasting: qualitative and quantitative. They are as follows:

- *Qualitative approach*—forecasts based on judgment and opinion

  Expert opinions

  Delphi technique

  Sales-force polling

  Consumer surveys

- *Quantitative approach*

  Moving averages and weighted moving averages

  Exponential smoothing and trend effects

  Simple regression

  Multiple regression

  Trend analysis and classical decomposition

Quantitative models work superbly as long as little or no systematic change in the environment takes place. When patterns or relationships do change, by themselves, the objective models are of little use. It is here where the qualitative approach based on human judgment is indispensable. Because judgmental forecasting also bases forecasts on observation of existing trends, they too are subject to a number of shortcomings. The advantage, however, is that they can identify systematic change more quickly and interpret better the effect of such change on the future.

SELECTION OF FORECASTING METHOD

The choice of a forecasting technique is significantly influenced by the stage of the product life cycle and sometimes by the firm or industry for which a decision is being made.

In the beginning of the product life cycle, relatively small expenditures are made for research and market investigation. During the first phase of product introduction, these expenditures start to increase. In the rapid growth stage, considerable amounts of money are involved in the decisions; therefore, a high level of accuracy is desirable. After the product has entered the maturity stage, the decisions are more routine, involving marketing and manufacturing. These are important considerations when determining the appropriate sales forecast technique.

After evaluating the particular stages of the product and determining firm and industry life cycles, a further probe is necessary. Instead of selecting a forecasting technique by using whatever seems applicable, decision makers should determine what is appropriate. Some of the techniques are quite simple and rather inexpensive to develop and use, whereas others are extremely complex, require significant amounts of time to develop, and may be quite expensive. Some are best suited for short-term projections, whereas others are better prepared for intermediate or long-term forecasts.

What technique or techniques to select depends on the following criteria:

- What is the cost associated with developing the forecasting model compared with potential gains resulting from its use? The choice is one of benefit–cost tradeoff.

- How complicated are the relationships that are being forecasted?

- Is it for short- or long-term purposes?

- How much accuracy is desired?

- Is there a minimum tolerance level of errors?

- How much data are available? Techniques vary in the amount of data they require.

THE QUALITATIVE APPROACH

The qualitative (or judgmental) approach can be useful in formulating short-term forecasts and also can supplement the projections based on the use of any of the qualitative methods. Four of the better known qualitative forecasting methods are expert opinions, Delphi method, sales-force polling, and consumer surveys.

EXPERT OPINIONS

The subjective views of executives or experts from sales, production, finance, purchasing, and administration are averaged to generate a forecast about future sales. Usually the expert opinions method is used in conjunction with some quantitative method such as trend extrapolation. The management team modifies the resulting forecast based on their expectations.

THE DELPHI METHOD

The Delphi method is a group technique in which a panel of experts are individually questioned about their perceptions of future events. The experts do not meet as a group in order to reduce the possibility that consensus is reached because of dominant personality factors. Instead, the forecasts and accompanying arguments are summarized by an outside party and returned to the experts along with further questions. This process continues until a consensus is reached by the group, especially after only a few rounds. The experts are not influenced by peer pressure to forecast a certain way because the answer is not intended to be reached by consensus or unanimity.

SALES-FORCE POLLING

Some companies use as a forecast source salespeople who have continual contacts with customers. They believe that their sales force, which is closest to the ultimate customers, may have significant insights regarding the state of the future market. Forecasts based on sales-force polling may be averaged to develop a future forecast. Or they may be used to modify other quantitative and/or qualitative forecasts that have been generated within the company.

CONSUMER SURVEYS

Some companies conduct their own market surveys regarding specific consumer purchases. Surveys may consist of telephone contacts, personal interviews, or questionnaires as a means of obtaining data. Extensive statistical analysis is usually applied to survey results in order to test hypotheses regarding consumer behavior.

STEPS IN THE FORECASTING PROCESS

There are six basic steps in the forecasting process.

1. Determine the what and why of the forecast and what will be needed. This will indicate the level of detail required in the forecast (e.g., forecast by region, forecast by product), the amount of resources (e.g., computer hardware and software, manpower) that can be justified, and the level of accuracy desired.

2. Establish a time horizon, short-term or long-term. More specifically, project for the next year or next 5 years, etc.

3. Select a forecasting method.

4. Gather the data and develop a forecast.

5. Identify any assumptions that had to be made in preparing the forecast and using it.

6. Monitor the forecast to see if it is performing in a manner desired. Develop an evaluation system for this purpose. If not, return to step 1.

MOVING AVERAGES AND SMOOTHING METHODS

This section discusses several forecasting methods that fall in the quantitative approach category. The discussion includes the naive approach, moving averages, exponential smoothing, and regression analysis.

THE NAIVE APPROACH

The naive forecasting approach is based exclusively on historical observation of data. It does not attempt to explain the underlying causal relationships that produce the variable being forecast. A simplest example of a naive model type would be the use of the actual sales of the current period as the forecast for the next period. Let us use the symbol Y'_{t+1} as the forecast value and the symbol Y_t as the actual value. Then

$$Y'_{t+1} = Y_t$$

MOVING AVERAGES

Moving averages are averages that are updated as new information is received. With the moving average, a manager simply employs the most recent observations to calculate an average, which is used as the forecast for the next period.

EXAMPLE 1

Assume that the marketing manager has the following sales data.

Date		Actual Sales, Y_t
Jan.	1	46
	2	54
	3	53
	4	46
	5	58
	6	49
	7	54

In order to predict the sales for the seventh and eighth days of January, the manager has to pick the number of observations for averaging purposes. Let us consider two cases: a six-day moving average and a three-day average.

Case 1

$$Y'_7 = \frac{46 + 54 + 53 + 46 + 58 + 49}{6} = 51$$

$$Y'_8 = \frac{54 + 53 + 46 + 58 + 49 + 54}{6} = 52.3$$

where Y' = predicted

Case 2

$$Y'_7 = \frac{46 + 58 + 49}{3} = 51$$

$$Y'_8 = \frac{58 + 49 + 54}{3} = 53.7$$

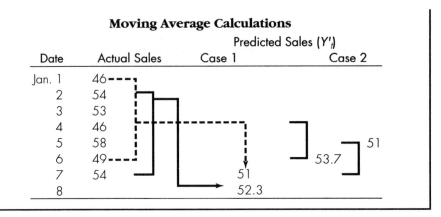

Moving Average Calculations

Date	Actual Sales	Predicted Sales (Y'_t) Case 1	Case 2
Jan. 1	46		
2	54		
3	53		
4	46		
5	58		51
6	49		53.7
7	54	51	
8		52.3	

In terms of weights given to observations, in case 1, the old data received a weight of 5/6, and the current observation got a weight of 1/6. In case 2, the old data received a weight of only 2/3 whereas the current observation received a weight of 1/3. Thus, the marketing manager's choice of the number of periods to use in a moving average is a measure of the relative importance attached to old versus current data.

• ADVANTAGES AND DISADVANTAGES

The moving average is simple to use and easy to understand. However, there are two shortcomings.

- You must retain a great deal of data and carry it along with you from forecast period to forecast period.

- All data in the sample are weighted equally. If more recent data are more valid than older data, why not give it greater weight?

The forecasting method known as exponential smoothing gets around these disadvantages.

• WEIGHTED MOVING AVERAGE

A weighted moving average allows any weights to be placed on each sales figure, providing the sum of all weights equals 1.

EXAMPLE 2

In Example 1, the best forecast is derived by using 50 percent of the actual sales for the most recent day, 40 percent of the sales for two days ago, 30 percent of the sales for three days ago. Then the forecast for day 8 would be

$$Y'_8 = 0.50(54) + 0.40(49) + 0.30(58) = 27 + 19.6 + 17.4 = 64$$

YOU SHOULD REMEMBER

Experience and trial and error are the simplest ways to choose weights. If the most recent past is believed to be the most reliable indicator of what to expect in the future, it should get greater weighting.

EXPONENTIAL SMOOTHING

Exponential smoothing is a popular technique for short-run forecasting by operations managers. It uses a weighted average of past data as the basis for a forecast. The procedure gives the greatest heaviest weight to more recent information and lesser weights to observations in the more distant past. The reason for this is that the future depends upon the recent past more than on the distant past. One disadvantage of the method, however, is that it does not include industrial or economic factors such as market conditions, prices, or the effects of competitors' actions.

YOU SHOULD REMEMBER

Exponential smoothing is known to be effective when there is randomness and no seasonal fluctuations in the data.

• *THE MODEL*

The formula for exponential smoothing is

$$F_t = F_{t-1} + \alpha(A_{t-1} - F_{t-1}) \ \text{ or } \ \alpha A_{t-1} + (1 - \alpha) F_{t-1}$$

or in words,

$$F_{\text{new}} = F_{\text{old}} + \alpha(A_{\text{old}} - F_{\text{old}})$$

where F_{new} = exponentially smoothed average to be used as the forecast

A_{old} = most recent actual data

F_{old} = most recent smoothed forecast

$$\alpha = \text{smoothing constant}$$

The higher the α, the higher the weight given to the more recent information.

EXAMPLE 3

Consider the following sales data.

Time Period, t	Actual Sales, A_t ($000)
1	60.0
2	64.0
3	58.0
4	66.0
5	70.0
6	60.0
7	70.0
8	74.0
9	62.0
10	74.0
11	68.0
12	66.0
13	60.0
14	66.0
15	62.0

To initialize the exponential smoothing process, we must have the initial forecast. The first smoothed forecast to be used can be

- First actual observations.

- An average of the actual data for a few periods.

For illustrative purposes, let us use a six-period average as the initial forecast F_7 with a smoothing constant of $\alpha = 0.40$. Then

$$F_7 = (A_1 + A_2 + A_3 + A_4 + A_5 + A_6)/6$$

$$= (60 + 64 + 58 + 66 + 70 + 60)/6 = 63$$

Note that $A_7 = 70$. Then F_8 is computed as follows:

$$F_8 = F_7 + \alpha(A_7 - F_7)$$

$$= 63 + (0.40)(70 - 63)$$

$$= 63 + 2.80 = 65.80$$

Similarly,

$$F_9 = F_8 + \alpha(A_8 - F_8)$$

$$= 65.8 + (0.40)(74 - 65.80)$$

$$= 65.8 + 3.28 = 69.08$$

and

$$F_{10} = F_9 + \alpha(A_9 - F_9)$$

$$= 69.08 + (0.40)(62 - 69.08)$$

$$= 69.08 - 2.83 = 66.25$$

By using the same procedure, the values of F_{11}, F_{12}, F_{13}, F_{14}, and F_{15} can be calculated. Table 3.1 shows a comparison between the actual sales and predicted sales by the exponential smoothing method.

Because of the negative and positive differences between actual sales and predicted sales, the forecaster can use a higher or lower smoothing constant (α) in order to adjust his/her prediction as quickly as possible to large fluctuations in the data series. For example, if the forecast is slow in reacting to increased sales, (that is to say, if the difference is negative), he/she might want to try a higher value. For practical purposes, the optimal α may be picked by minimizing what is known as the *mean squared error (MSE)*, which is a popular measure of forecasting performance.

$$\text{MSE} = (A_t - F_t)^2/(n - i)$$

where i = the number of observations used to determine the initial forecast (in our example, $i = 6$).

Table 3.1. Comparison of Actual Sales and Predicted Sales

Time Period, t	Actual Sales, A_t ($000)	Predicted Sales, F_t ($000)	Difference $(A_t - F_t)$ ($000)	Difference^2 $(A_t - F_t)^2$ ($000)
1	60.0			
2	64.0			
3	58.0			
4	66.0			
5	70.0			
6	60.0			
7	70.0	63.00	7.00	49.00
8	74.0	65.80	8.20	67.24
9	62.0	69.08	−7.08	50.13
10	74.0	66.25	7.75	60.06
11	68.0	69.35	−1.35	1.82
12	66.0	68.81	−2.81	7.90
13	60.0	67.69	−7.69	59.14
14	66.0	64.61	1.39	1.93
15	62.0	65.17	−3.17	10.05
				307.27

In our example,

$$MSE = 307.27 / (15 - 6) = 307.27 / 9 = 34.14$$

The idea is to select the α that minimizes MSE, which is the average sum of the variations between the historical sales data and the forecast values for the corresponding periods. An α value that yields an approximately equivalent degree of smoothing as a moving average of n periods is

$$\alpha = \frac{2}{n + 1}$$

• *EXPONENTIAL SMOOTHING WITH TREND EFFECTS*

An upward or downward trend in a time series data causes the exponential smoothing forecast to always lag behind (be above or below) the actual occurrence. A technique frequently used to correct this situation is called *Holt's two-parameter method,* or simply *Holt's method.* Exponentially smoothed forecasts can be corrected by adding in a trend adjustment. To adjust for the trend, two smoothing constants are incorporated in the model. Besides α, the trend equation also uses a smoothing constant β. The β reduces the impact of the error that occurs between the actual and the forecast.

The model to compute the forecast including trend (*FT*) involves three equations:

- *The exponentially smooth series*

$$F_t = \alpha A_t + (1 - \alpha)(F_{t-1} + T_{t-1})$$

- *The trend estimate*

$$T_t = \beta(F_t - F_{t-1}) + (1 - \beta) T_{t-1}$$

- *The forecast for the next period*

$$FT_{t+1} = F_t + T_t$$

As can be seen, the trend equation uses a smoothing constant β in the same way as the exponential equation. A high β will emphasize the latest trend and be more responsive to recent changes in trend. The initial trend adjustment T_{t-1} is sometimes assumed to be zero.

EXAMPLE 4

The following illustrates Holt's method. To begin with we assume two estimated initial values and two smoothing constant values: $F_1 = 500$, $T_1 = 0$, $\alpha = 0.3$, and $\beta = 0.1$.

Time Period, t	Actual Sales, $A_t(\$000)$	F_t	Trend, T_t	Predicted Sales, FT_{t+1} ($000)
1	500.0	500.0	0.0	—
2	350.0	455.0	−4.5	500.0
3	250.0	390.4	−10.5	450.5
4	400.0	385.9	−9.9	379.8
5	450.0	398.2	−7.7	376.0
6	350.0	378.3	−8.9	390.5

The computations leading to the forecast for period 3 follow.

1. Update the exponentially smoothed series.

$$F_t = \alpha A_t + (1 - \alpha)(F_{t-1} + T_{t-1})$$

$$F_2 = \alpha A_2 + (1 - \alpha)(F_1 + T_1) = 0.3(350) + 0.7(500 + 0) = 455$$

2. Update the trend estimate.

$$T_t = \beta(F_t - F_{t-1}) + (1 - \beta)\, T_{t-1}$$

$$T_2 = \beta(F_2 - F_1) + (1 - \beta)\, T_1 = 0.1(455 - 500) + 0.9(0) = -4.5$$

3. Forecast one period into the future.

$$FT_{t+1} = F_t + T_t$$

$$FT_3 = F_2 + T_2 = 455 + (-4.5) = 450.5$$

REGRESSION ANALYSIS

Regression analysis is a statistical procedure for estimating mathematically the average relationship between the dependent variable and the independent variable(s). *Simple regression* involves one independent variable (e.g., price or advertising in a demand function), whereas *multiple regression* involves two or more variables, (e.g., price and advertising together).

In this chapter, we will discuss only *simple (linear) regression* to illustrate the *least-squares method*, which means that we will assume the $Y = a + bX$ relationship.

THE LEAST-SQUARES METHOD

The least-squares method is widely used in regression analysis for estimating the parameter values in a regression equation. The regression method includes all the observed data and attempts to find a line of best fit. To find this line, a technique called the least-squares method is used.

To explain the least-squares method, we define the error as the difference between the observed value and the estimated one and denote it with *u*. Symbolically,

$$u = Y - Y'$$

where Y = observed value of the dependent variable

Y' = estimated value based on $Y' = a + bX$

The least-squares criterion requires that the line of best fit be such that the sum of the squares of the errors (or the vertical distance in Figure 3.2 from the observed data points to the line) is a minimum. In other words,

$$\text{Minimum: } \Sigma u^2 = \Sigma(Y - a - bX)^2$$

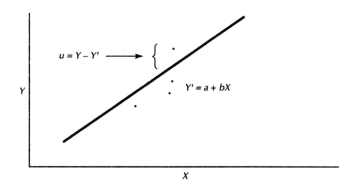

Figure 3.2. Y and Y'

Using differential calculus, we obtain the following equations, called normal equations:

$$\Sigma Y = na + b\Sigma X$$

$$\Sigma XY = a\Sigma X + b\Sigma X^2$$

Solving the equations for b and a yields

$$b = \frac{n\Sigma XY - (\Sigma X)(\Sigma Y)}{n\Sigma X^2 - (\Sigma X)^2}$$

$$a = \bar{Y} - b\bar{X}$$

where $\bar{Y} = \Sigma Y/n$ and $\bar{X} = \Sigma X/n$

EXAMPLE 5

To illustrate the computations of b and a, we will refer to the following data. All the sums required are computed and shown.

Computed Sums

Advertising, X ($000)	Sales, Y ($000,000)	XY	X²	Y²
77	5.5	423.5	5,929	30.25
75	5.1	382.5	5,625	26.01
72	4.7	338.4	5,184	22.09
73	4.8	350.4	5,329	23.04
71	4.6	326.6	5,041	21.16
368	24.7	1,821.4	27,108	122.55

From this table,

$$\Sigma X = 368 \quad \Sigma Y = 24.7 \quad \Sigma XY = 1,821.4 \quad \Sigma X^2 = 27,108$$

$$\bar{X} = \Sigma X/n = 368/5 = 73.6 \quad \bar{Y} = \Sigma Y/n = 24.7/5 = 4.94$$

Substituting these values into the formula for b first:

$$b = \frac{n\Sigma XY - (\Sigma X)(\Sigma Y)}{n\Sigma X^2 - (\Sigma X)^2} = \frac{(5)(1,821.4) - (368)(24.7)}{(5)(27,108) - (368)^2} = \frac{17.4}{116} = 0.15$$

$$a = \bar{Y} - b\bar{X} = 4.94 - (0.15)(73.6) = -6.10$$

Thus, $\qquad Y' = -6.10 + 0.15X$

Note that ΣY^2 is not used here but rather is computed for r and (r^2).

YOU SHOULD REMEMBER

Before attempting a least-squares regression approach, it is extremely important to plot the observed data on a diagram, called the scatter graph (see Figure 3.2). The reason is that you might want to make sure that a linear (straight-line) relationship existed between Y and X in the past sample. If for any reason there was a nonlinear relationship detected in the sample, the linear relationship we assumed ($Y = a + bX$) would not give us a good fit.

REGRESSION STATISTICS

Regression analysis is a statistical method. Hence, it uses a variety of statistics to tell about the accuracy and reliability of the regression results. They include

- Correlation coefficient (r) and coefficient of determination (r^2)

- Standard error of the estimate (S_e) and prediction confidence interval

CORRELATION COEFFICIENT AND COEFFICIENT OF DETERMINATION

In order to obtain a good fit and achieve a high degree of accuracy, you should be familiar with a statistic known as the correlation coefficient. The correlation coefficient r measures the degree of correlation between Y and X. The range of values it takes on is between –1 and +1. More widely used, however, is the coefficient of determination, designated r^2 (read as r-squared). Simply put, r^2 tells us how good the estimated regression equation is. In other words, it is a measure of "goodness of fit" in the regression. Therefore, the higher the r^2, the more confidence we have in our estimated equation. More specifically, the coefficient of determination represents the proportion of the total variation in Y that is explained by the regression equation. It has the range of values between 0 and 1.

EXAMPLE 6

The statement "Sales is a function of advertising expenditure with $r^2 =$ 75%," can be interpreted as "75% of the total variation of sales is explained by the regression equation or the change in advertising, and the remaining 25% is accounted for by something other than advertising, such as price and income."

The coefficient of determination is computed as

$$r^2 = 1 - \frac{\Sigma(Y - Y')^2}{\Sigma(Y - \bar{Y})^2}$$

In a simple regression situation, however, there is a short-cut method available:

$$r^2 = \frac{[n\Sigma XY - (\Sigma X)(\Sigma Y)]^2}{[n\Sigma X^2 - (\Sigma X)^2][n\Sigma Y^2 - (\Sigma Y)^2]}$$

The coefficient of correlation r is the *square root* of the coefficient of determination:

$$r = \frac{[n\Sigma XY - (\Sigma X)(\Sigma Y)]}{\sqrt{[n\Sigma X^2 - (\Sigma X)^2][n\Sigma Y^2 - (\Sigma Y)^2]}}$$

YOU SHOULD REMEMBER

- Comparing this formula with the one for b, we see that the only additional information we need to compute r^2 or r is ΣY^2.

- $r^2 = (r)^2$ or $r =$ the square root of $r^2 = \sqrt{r}$.

EXAMPLE 7

To illustrate the computations of various regression statistics, we will refer to the data in Example 5. Using the shortcut method for r^2,

$$r^2 = \frac{(17.4)^2}{[(5)(27,108) - (368)^2][(5)(122.55) - (24.7)^2]} = \frac{302.76}{(116)(612.75 - 610.09)}$$

$$= \frac{302.76}{308.56} = 0.9812 = 98.12\%$$

This means that about 98.12% of the total variation in sales is explained by advertising and the remaining 1.88% is still unexplained. A high r^2 indicates an excellent fit in our estimated forecasting model. Advertising turns out to be an important factor.

$$r = \frac{\sqrt{302.76}}{\sqrt{308.56}} = \sqrt{0.9812} \; 0.9905$$

or $\qquad r^2 = (0.9905)^2 = 0.9812 = 98.12\%.$

STANDARD ERROR OF THE ESTIMATE AND PREDICTION CONFIDENCE INTERVAL

The standard error of the estimate, designated S_e, is defined as the standard deviation of the regression. It is computed as

$$S_e = \sqrt{\frac{\Sigma(Y-Y')^2}{n-2}} = \sqrt{\frac{\Sigma Y^2 - a\Sigma Y - b\Sigma XY}{n-2}}$$

This statistic can be used to gain some idea of the accuracy of our predictions.

EXAMPLE 8

Going back to our example data, S_e is calculated as

$$S_e = \sqrt{\frac{(122.55) - (-6.10)(24.7) - (0.15)(1821.4)}{6-2}}$$

$$= \sqrt{\frac{122.55 + 150.67 - 273.21}{4}} = 0.05$$

Suppose you wish to make a prediction regarding an individual Y value such as a prediction about the sales when advertising is $70. Usually, we would like to have some objective measure of the confidence we can place in our prediction, and one such measure is a *confidence (or prediction) interval* constructed for Y.

A confidence interval for a predicted Y can be constructed in the following manner.

$$Y' \pm t\, S_e$$

where $Y' =$ the predicted value of Y given a value for X.

Note: t is the critical value for the level of significance employed. For example, for a significance level of 0.025 (which is equivalent to a 95% confidence level in a two-tailed test), the critical value of t for 4 degrees of freedom is 2.776 (see Table 5 in the Appendix).

EXAMPLE 9

If you want to have a 95% confidence interval of your prediction, the range for the prediction, given an advertising expense of $70 (in thousands) would be between $3.01 and $5.79 (in millions).

Note that $Y' = -6.10 + 0.15X = -6.10 + 0.15\,(\$70) = \$4.40$. The confidence interval is therefore established as follows:

$$\$4.40 \pm (2.776)(0.5) = \$4.40 \pm 1.39$$

which means, the range for the prediction, given an advertising expense of $70, would be between $3.01 ($4.40 − 1.39) and $5.79 ($4.40 + 1.39).

USE OF COMPUTER SOFTWARE FOR REGRESSION

Spreadsheet programs such as Microsoft's Excel, Lotus 1-2-3, and Quattro Pro have a regression routine that you can use without any difficulty. As a matter of fact, in reality, you do not compute the values a, b, r, and r^2 manually. The following summary is a portion of the Excel regression output for Example 9.

Summary Output

	Regression Statistics
Multiple *r*	0.990557
r-squared	0.981203
Adjusted *r*-squared	0.974937
Standard error	0.057735
Observations	5

	Coefficients	Standard Error	*t* Statistic
Intercept	–6.1	0.88259	–6.911475
X variable	0.15	0.011987	12.513992

MULTIPLE REGRESSION

Multiple regression analysis is a powerful statistical technique that is perhaps the one most widely used by forecasters. Multiple regression attempts to estimate statistically the average relationship between the dependent variable (e.g., sales) and two or more independent variables (e.g., price, advertising, income).

YOU SHOULD REMEMBER

In reality, forecasters will face more multiple regression situations than simple regression. Multiple regression is beyond the scope of this book.

TIME SERIES ANALYSIS AND CLASSICAL DECOMPOSITION

A time series is a sequence of data points at constant time intervals such as a week, month, quarter, and year. *Time series analysis* breaks data into components and projects them into the future. The four commonly recognized components are trend, seasonal, cyclical, and irregular variation.

- The *trend component* (*T*) is the general upward or downward movement of the average over time. These movements may require many years of data to determine or describe them. The basic forces underlying the trend include technological advances, productivity changes, inflation, and population change.

- The *seasonal component* (*S*) is a recurring fluctuation of data points above or below the trend value that repeats with a usual frequency of one year. (e.g., Christmas sales).

- *Cyclical components* (*C*) are recurrent upward and downward movements that repeat with a frequency that is longer than a year. This movement is attributed to business cycles (such as recession, inflation, unemployment, and prosperity), so the periodicity (recurrent rate) of such cycles does not have to be constant.

- The *irregular* (or *random*) *component* is a series of short, erratic movements that follow no discernible pattern. It is caused by unpredictable or nonrecurring events such as floods, wars, strikes, elections, environmental changes, and the passage of legislation.

TREND ANALYSIS

Trends are the general upward or downward movements of the average over time. These movements may require many years of data to determine or describe them. They can be described by a straight line or a curve. The basic forces underlying the trend include technological advances, productivity changes, inflation, and population change. Trend analysis is a special type of simple regression. This method involves a regression whereby a trend line is fitted to a time series of data. In practice, however, one typically finds linear and nonlinear curves used for business forecasting.

The *linear* trend line equation can be shown as

$$Y = a + bt$$

where *t* = time.

The formula for the coefficients *a* and *b* are essentially the same as those for simple regression.

$$b = \frac{n\Sigma tY - \Sigma t\Sigma Y}{n\Sigma t^2 - (\Sigma t)^2}$$

$$a = \overline{Y} - b\overline{t}$$

DECOMPOSITION OF TIME SERIES

When sales exhibit seasonal or cyclical fluctuations, we use a forecasting method called *classical decomposition* for dealing with seasonal, trend, and cyclical components together. The classical decomposition model is a time-series model used for forecasting. This means that the method can be used to fit the time-series data only, whether it is monthly, quarterly, or annually. The types of time-series data the company deals with include sales, earnings, cash flows, market share, and costs. As long as the time series displays the patterns of seasonality and cyclicality, the model constructed would be very effective in projecting the future variable.

We assume that a time series is combined into a model that consists of the four components—trend *(T)*, cyclical *(C)*, seasonal *(S)*, and random *(R)*.

The model we assume is of a multiplicative type, i.e.,

$$Y_t = T \times C \times S \times R$$

We illustrate, step by step, the classical decomposition method by working with the quarterly sales data. The approach basically involves the following four steps:

1. **Determine seasonal indices, using a four-quarter moving average.**

2. **Deseasonalize the data.**

3. **Develop the linear least-squares equation in order to identify the trend component of the forecast.**

4. **Forecast the sales for each of the four quarters of the coming year.**

EXAMPLE 10

We will illustrate the classical decomposition approach by working with the quarterly sales data presented in Table 3.2 and Figure 3.3. These data show the VCR set sales (in thousands of units) for a particular manufacturer over the past four years.

Table 3.2. Quarterly Sales Data for VCRs over the Past 4 Years

Year	Quarter	Sales, ($000)
1	1	5.8
	2	5.1
	3	7.0
	4	7.5
2	1	6.8
	2	6.2
	3	7.8
	4	8.4
3	1	7.0
	2	6.6
	3	8.5
	4	8.8
4	1	7.3
	2	6.9
	3	9.0
	4	9.4

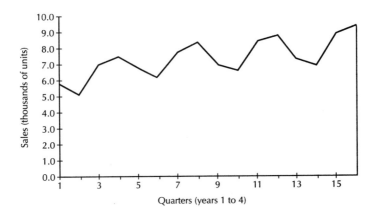

Figure 3.3. Quarterly VCR Sales

We begin our analysis by showing how to identify the seasonal component of the time series. Looking at Figure 3.3, we can easily see a seasonal pattern for the VCR sales. Specifically, we observe that sales are lowest in the second quarter of each year, followed by higher sales in quarters 3 and 4. The step-by-step computational procedure used to eliminate the seasonal component follows.

1. **Use *moving average* to measure the combined trend-cyclical (TC) components of the time series.** This way we eliminate the seasonal and random components, S and R.

    More specifically, step 1 involves the following sequences of steps:

    a. **Calculate the four-quarter moving average for the time series.** Note, however, that the moving average values computed do not correspond directly to the original quarters of the time series.

    b. **Use the midpoints between successive moving-average values to resolve this difficulty.** For example, because 6.35 corresponds to the first half of quarter 3 and 6.6 corresponds to the last half of quarter 3, we use (6.35 + 6.6)/2 = 6.475 as the moving-average value for quarter 3. Similarly, we associate (6.6 + 6.875)/2 = 6.7375 with quarter 4. A complete summary of the moving-average calculation is shown in Table 3.3.

Table 3.3. Moving Average Calculations for the VCRs Sales Time Series

Year	Quarter	Sales (Thousands of Units)	Four-Quarter Moving Average	Centered Moving Average
1	1	5.8		
	2	5.1		
			6.35	
	3	7.0		6.475
			6.6	
	4	7.5		6.7375
			6.875	
2	1	6.8		6.975
			7.075	
	2	6.2		7.1875
			7.3	
	3	7.8		7.325
			7.35	
	4	8.4		7.4
			7.45	
3	1	7.0		7.5375
			7.625	
	2	6.6		7.675
			7.725	
	3	8.5		7.7625
			7.8	
	4	8.8		7.8375
			7.875	
4	1	7.3		7.9375
			8	
	2	6.9		8.075
			8.15	
	3	9.0		
	4	9.4		

   c. **Calculate the ratio of the actual value to the moving-average value for each quarter in the time series having a four-quarter moving average entry.** This ratio in effect represents the seasonal-random component, $SR = Y/TC$. The ratios calculated this way appear in Table 3.4.

Table 3.4. Seasonal Random Factors for the Series

Year	Quarter	Sales (Thousands of Units)	Four-Quarter Moving Average	Centered Moving Average, TC	Seasonal Random Component $SR = Y/TC$
1	1	5.8			
	2	5.1			
			6.35		
	3	7.0		6.475	1.081
			6.6		
	4	7.5		6.738	1.113
			6.875		
2	1	6.8		6.975	0.975
			7.075		
	2	6.2		7.188	0.863
			7.3		
	3	7.8		7.325	1.065
			7.35		
	4	8.4		7.400	1.135
			7.45		
3	1	7.0		7.538	0.929
			7.625		
	2	6.6		7.675	0.860
			7.725		
	3	8.5		7.763	1.095
			7.8		
	4	8.8		7.838	1.123
			7.875		
4	1	7.3		7.938	0.920
			8		
	2	6.9		8.075	0.854
			8.15		
	3	9.0			
	4	9.4			

d. Arrange the ratios by quarter and then calculate the average ratio by quarter in order to eliminate the random influence. For example, for quarter 1

$$(0.975 + 0.929 + 0.920)/3 = 0.941$$

e. Determine the seasonal index, as shown in Table 3.5. This final step adjusts the average ratio slightly (e.g., for quarter 1, 0.941 becomes 0.940).

Table 3.5. Seasonal Component Calculations

Quarter	Seasonal/Random, SR	Seasonal Factor, S	Adjusted S
1	0.975		
	0.929		
	0.920	0.941	0.940
2	0.863		
	0.860		
	0.854	0.859	0.858
3	1.081		
	1.065		
	1.095	1.080	1.079
4	1.113		
	1.135		
	1.123	1.124	1.123
		4.004	4.000

2. **After obtaining the seasonal index, remove the effect of season from the original time series.** This process is referred to as deseasonalizing the time series. For this, we must divide the original series by the seasonal index for that quarter. This is shown in Table 3.6 and graphed in Figure 3.4.

3. **Develop the least-squares trend equation.** Looking at the graph, we see that the time series seems to have an upward linear trend. This procedure is also shown in Table 3.6.

Table 3.6. Deseasonalized Data

Year	Quarter	Sales (Thousands of Units)	Seasonal, S	Deseasonalized Data	t
1	1	5.8	0.940	6.17	1
	2	5.1	0.858	5.94	2
	3	7.0	1.079	6.49	3
	4	7.5	1.123	6.68	4
2	1	6.8	0.940	7.23	5
	2	6.2	0.858	7.23	6
	3	7.8	1.079	7.23	7
	4	8.4	1.123	7.48	8
3	1	7.0	0.940	7.45	9
	2	6.6	0.858	7.69	10
	3	8.5	1.079	7.88	11

Year	Quarter	Sales (Thousands of Units)	Seasonal, S	Deseasonalized Data	t
	4	8.8	1.123	7.84	12
4	1	7.3	0.940	7.76	13
	2	6.9	0.858	8.04	14
	3	9.0	1.079	8.34	15
	4	9.4	1.123	8.37	16
				117.82	136

$$\overline{t}\,(t\text{-bar}) = 8.5 \quad \overline{y}\,(y\text{-bar}) = 7.3638$$

$$b = 0.1469$$

$$a = 6.1147$$

which means $y = 6.1147 + 0.1469\ t$ for the forecast periods:

$$t = 17$$
$$18$$
$$19$$
$$20$$

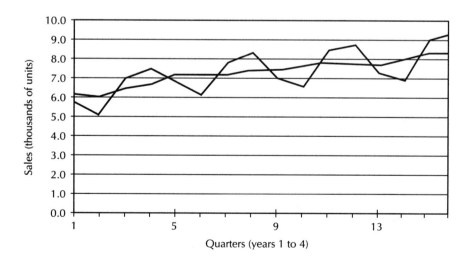

Figure 3.4. Quarterly VCR Sales: Original versus Deseasonalized

4. **Develop the forecast using the trend equation and adjust these forecasts to account for the effect of season.** The quarterly forecast, as shown in Table 3.7, can be obtained by multiplying the forecast based on trend by the seasonal factor.

Table 3.7. Quarter-to-Quarter Sales Forecasts for Year 5

Year	Quarter	Trend Forecast	Seasonal Factor	Quarterly Forecast
5	1	8.6128[a]	0.940	8.0971
	2	8.7598	0.858	7.5170
	3	8.9067	1.079	9.6121
	4	9.0537	1.123	10.1632

[a] $y = 6.1147 + 0.1469t = 6.1147 + 0.1469 (17) = 8.6128$.

COMPUTER SOFTWARE FOR FORECASTING

Forecasters in the real world of business use computers to do their calculations. Besides the spreadsheet software illustrated earlier, there are numerous user-friendly software available for use in forecasting. Some are briefly explained here.

- Statistical packages such as SPSS, SAS, and MINITAB.

- American Software Inc.'s ForeThought.

- General Electric's Time Series Forecasting program FCST1, a linear regression trend-analysis, seasonalized forecasting model. Its FCST2 program creates several forecasts with four different methods of exponential smoothing.

- IBM's Consumer Goods System (COGS), a forecasting and inventory control information system specifically oriented to the manufacturing process and distribution industries.

- IBM's Inventory Management Program and Control Technique (IMPACT), an information system for wholesale and other users in distribution systems.

EVALUATION OF FORECASTS

The cost of a prediction error can be substantial. The forecaster must always find the ways to improve his forecasts. That means that he might want to examine some objective evaluations of alternative forecasting techniques. The performance of a forecast should be checked against its own record or against that of other forecasts. Various statistical measures can be used to measure performance of the model. Of course, the performance is measured in terms of forecasting error, where error is defined as the difference between a predicted value and the actual result:

$$\text{Error } (e) = \text{Actual } (A) - \text{Forecast } (F)$$

MAD AND MSE

The commonly used measures for summarizing historical errors include the *mean absolute deviation* (MAD) and the *mean squared error* (MSE). The formulas used to calculate these are

$$\text{MAD} = \Sigma |e| / n$$

$$\text{MSE} = \Sigma\, e^2 / (n - 1)$$

The following example illustrates the computation of MAD and MSE.

EXAMPLE 11

Sales data of a microwave oven manufacturer follow:

Period	Actual, A	Forecast, F	$e = (A - F)$	$|e|$	e^2
1	217	215	2	2	4
2	213	216	–3	3	9
3	216	215	1	1	1
4	210	214	–4	4	16
5	213	211	2	2	4
6	219	214	5	5	25
7	216	217	–1	1	1
8	212	216	–4	4	16
			–2	22	76

Using the figures,

$$\text{MAD} = \Sigma |e| / n = 22/8 = 2.75$$

$$\text{MSE} = \Sigma e^2 / (n - 1) = 76/7 = 10.86$$

One way these measures are used is to evaluate forecasting ability of alternative forecasting methods. For example, using either MAD or MSE, a forecaster could compare the results of exponential smoothing with alphas and elect the one that performed best in terms of the lowest MAD or MSE for a given set of data. Also, it can help select the best initial forecast value for exponential smoothing.

CONTROL OF FORECASTS

It is important to monitor forecast errors to ensure that the forecast performs well. If the model performs poorly based on some criteria, the forecaster might reconsider the use of the existing model or switch to another forecasting model or technique. The forecasting control can be accomplished by comparing forecasting errors to predetermined values, or limits. Errors that fall within the limits would be judged acceptable, whereas errors outside of the limits would signal that corrective action is desirable.

Forecasts can be monitored using either tracking signals or control charts.

TRACKING SIGNALS

A tracking signal is based on the ratio of cumulative forecast error to the corresponding value of MAD.

$$\text{Tracking signal} = \Sigma(A - F) \, / \, \text{MAD}$$

The resulting tracking signal values are compared to predetermined limits. These are based on experience and judgment and often range from ± 3 to ± 8. Values within the limits suggest that the forecast is performing adequately. By the same token, when the signal goes beyond this range, corrective action is appropriate.

EXAMPLE 12

Going back to Example 11, the deviation and cumulative deviation have already been computed:

$$\text{MAD} = \Sigma |A - F| \, / \, n = 22 \, / \, 8 = 2.75$$

$$\text{Tracking signal} = \Sigma(A - F) \, / \, \text{MAD} = -2 \, / \, 2.75 = -0.73$$

A tracking signal is as low as –0.73, which is substantially below the limit (–3 to –8). It would not suggest any action at this time.

Note: After an initial value of MAD has been computed, the estimate of the MAD can be continually updated using exponential smoothing:

$$\text{MAD}_t = \alpha(A - F) + (1 - \alpha)\,\text{MAD}_{t-1}$$

CONTROL CHARTS

The control chart approach involves setting upper and lower limits for individual forecasting errors instead of cumulative errors. The limits are multiples of the estimated standard deviation of forecast S_f, which is the square root of MSE. Frequently, control limits are set at 2 or 3 standard deviations:

$$\pm 2 (\text{or } 3)\ S_f$$

Note: Plot the errors and see if all errors are within the limits, so that the forecaster can visualize the process and determine if the method being used is in control.

EXAMPLE 13

For the following sales data, using the naive forecast, we will determine if the forecast is in control. For illustrative purposes, we will use 2 sigma control limits.

Year	Sales	Forecasts	Error	Error²
1	320			
2	326	320	6	36
3	310	326	−16	256
4	317	310	7	49
5	315	317	−2	4
6	318	315	3	9
7	310	318	−8	64
8	316	310	6	36
9	314	316	−2	4
10	317	314	3	9
			−3	467

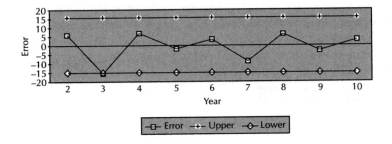

Figure 3.5. Control Chart for Forecasting Errors

First, compute the standard deviation of forecast errors

$$S_f = \sqrt{e^2 / (n-1)} = \sqrt{467/(9-1)} = 7.64$$

Two sigma limits are then plus or minus $2(7.64) = -15.28$ to $+15.28$

Note that the forecast error for year 3 is below the lower bound, so the forecast is not in control (See Figure 3.5). The use of other methods such as moving average, exponential smoothing, or regression would possibly achieve a better forecast.

YOU SHOULD REMEMBER

A system of monitoring forecasts needs to be developed. The computer may be programmed to print a report showing the past history when the tracking signal "trips" a limit.

KNOW THE CONCEPTS

DO YOU KNOW THE BASICS?

1. Discuss the difference between quantitative and qualitative (judgmental) forecasting methods. What circumstances would warrant one over the other?
2. Discuss the role of forecasting in production/operations management.
3. Illustrate, by examples of typical applications, the various types of qualitative forecasting techniques often used.

4. What are the basic steps in forecasting? Discuss each.
5. Define a time series.
6. How are moving averages calculated?
7. What is exponential smoothing and when it is most effective?
8. List the basic approaches involved in the classical decomposition of time series.
9. Explain the two popular measures of forecast accuracy.
10. How are quantitative and judgmental forecasts used together in practice?
11. What is a tracking signal and how it is used?

TERMS FOR STUDY

classical decomposition	mean squared error (MSE)
correlation coefficient	moving average
Delphi method	simple regression
exponential smoothing	standard error of the estimate
exponential smoothing with trend effects	time series
	tracking signal
least-squares method	trend analysis
mean absolute deviation (MAD)	weighted moving average

PRACTICAL APPLICATION

1. The AZ Ice Cream Shoppe has recorded the demand for a particular flavor during the first seven days of August.

Date		Actual Sales, Y_t
Aug.	1	56
	2	64
	3	63
	4	56
	5	68
	6	59
	7	64

Predict the sales for the eighth day of August, using (a) a five-day moving average, (b) a three-day average, and (c) a weighted three-day moving average with weights of 0.5, 0.4, and 0.1.

2. Develop a forecast for period 6 using an α of 0.4 and period 1 value as the initial forecast.

Period	Number of Customer Complaints
1	45
2	34
3	35
4	42
5	48

3. The following time series shows the sales of a particular product over the past 12 months:

Month	Sales
1	105
2	135
3	120
4	105
5	90
6	120
7	145
8	140
9	100
10	80
11	100
12	110

Compute the exponential-smoothing values for the time series and MSE (Assume α = 0.5).

4. Develop an exponential smoothed forecast with trend effects for a firm with the following demand. Assume that α = 0.3, β = 0.4, F_0 = 650, and T_0 = 0.

Period	1	2	3	4	5	6
Demand	700	685	648	717	713	728

5. The following are the advertising and sales data of Jupiter Corporation over an 8-month period.

Advertising ($000)	Sales ($000)
320	2,600
200	1,500
230	2,150
240	2,250
720	4,700
560	3,700
470	3,300
750	4,750

  a. Develop the sales forecasting equation by using the method of least squares.

  b. Compute the coefficient of correlation and the coefficient of determination.

  c. Comment on the choice of advertising in predicting sales.

6. Data for total power costs and machine hours follow.

Power Costs ($000)	Machine Hours (thousands of hours)
4	6
8	7
8	9
6	5
7	8
5	6

  a. Fit a linear regression line using the method of least squares. Estimate the power costs when 8 machine hours are used.

  b. Compute the coefficient of determination.

  c. Does the regression equation need to be improved?

7. The Viacam Manufacturing Company makes a product called Zone. Some of the manufacturing expenses are easily identified as fixed or directly variable with production. Management is confronted with the problem of preparing a budget for the indirect manufacturing costs. The following details are provided for the first 5 months of the past year:

Month	Number of Units Produced, X	Indirect Manufacturing Costs, Y ($)
1	100	$1,000
2	200	1,250
3	300	2,250
4	400	2,500
5	500	3,750

Determine the cost function using the method of least squares.

8. JON Engineering, Inc., has developed the following sales forecasting model:

$$Y' = 123.5 + 2.3\ X \text{ where } X = \text{advertising}$$
$$r^2 = 0.99$$

Standard error of the estimate $(S_e) = 31.2$

a. Make a forecast when advertising is $200.

b. What will be the range (prediction interval) of this forecast using two standard errors of estimate?

9. An ice cream parlor experienced the following weekly actual and forecasted data for sales last month:

Week	Actual Demand (gallons)	Forecast Demand (gallons)
1	200	210
2	225	235
3	200	225
4	260	270

Compute MAD.

10. Given the following sales data, prepare a naive forecast, which is actual sales of the previous year, for each of the 10 years and determine if the forecast is in control. Use 2 sigma control.

Year	Sales
1	220
2	226
3	210
4	217
5	215

11. Sara-Lee Auto has the following sales record (in millions of dollars) for the last four years.

Year	Quarter 1	2	3	4
20X1	4.8	4.1	6.0	6.5
20X2	5.8	5.2	6.8	7.4
20X3	6.0	5.6	7.5	7.8
20X4	6.3	5.9	8.0	8.4

a. Determine a centered four-period moving average initially, and then a centered two-period moving average of the four-period moving average.

b. Deseasonalize auto sales.

c. Compute a linear trend equation for the deseasonalized data.

d. Predict car sales the first quarter for year 20X5.

ANSWERS

DO YOU KNOW THE BASICS?

1. Quantitative methods are based on the analysis of historical data whereas qualitative (judgmental) methods depend on expert opinion. Obviously, if historical data are unavailable, quantitative methods cannot be used. Such would be the case with technology forecasts. For such data as sales and costs, quantitative approaches are useful. Quite frequently a combination of the two is used.

2. Forecasts are needed (a) to plan resource requirements such as production facilities, (b) to plan work force levels and purchases of materials, and (c) for financial planning and capacity planning.

3. (a) Preliminary data analysis of scatter diagram; (b) determination of forecasts choice of method—quantitative and/or judgmental; (c) evaluation and determination of a final forecast—consideration of accuracy and implications of errors, data collection, and processing; and (d) control and feedback—comparison of actual observations with forecasts.

4. Expert opinion—new technologies or new products unlike any currently on the market; Delphi method—space travel, long-range economic conditions; and sales polling or consumer surveys—new products, restaurants, fast food, consumer appliances.

5. A time series is a set of observations measured at successive points in time or over successive periods of time.

6. A moving average is an average of the most recent n data values for any point in time.

7. Exponential smoothing is a weighting of the current actual value and the previous forecast. As such, it is essentially a weighted average of the previous time-series values with more emphasis placed on the most recent observations. It is known to be effective when there is randomness and no seasonal fluctuations in the data.

8. The approach basically involves the following four steps: (a) determine seasonal indices, using a four-quarter moving average, (b) deseasonalize the data, (c) develop the linear least-squares equation to identify the trend component of the forecast, and (d) forecast the sales for each of the four quarters of the coming year.

9. Forecast errors are measured by mean absolute deviation (MAD) and mean squared error (MSE). These enable one to measure forecast errors quantitatively.

10. Because quantitative methods are slow to adapt to unexpected changes in the environment, qualitative (judgmental) forecasts are often also used. Quantitative forecasts are frequently modified by judgmental forecasts.

11. It is a moving sum of forecast errors divided by MAD. It is computed to measure the adequacy of a forecasting technique.

PRACTICAL APPLICATION

1.

   a. Using a five-day moving average

$$Y'_8 = \frac{63 + 56 + 68 + 59 + 64}{5} = 62$$

   where Y' = predicted.

   b. Using a three-day average,

$$Y'_8 = \frac{68 + 59 + 64}{3} = 63.7$$

c.　　$Y'_8 = 0.5(64) + 0.4(59) + 0.1(68) = 32 + 23.6 + .68 = 56.28$

2.

Period	Number of Customer Complaints	Forecast = $Y'_{t+1} = \alpha Y_t + (1 - \alpha) Y'_t$
1	45	
2	34	45
3	35	0.4(34) + 0.6(45) = 40.6
4	42	0.4(35) + 0.6(40.6) = 38.4
5	48	0.4(42) + 0.6(38.4) = 39.8

For period 6, 0.4(48) + 0.6(39.8) = 43.1.

3.

Month	Sales	Forecast	Error	Error Squared
1	105			
2	135	105	30	900
3	120	0.5(135) + 0.5(105) = 120	0	0
4	105	0.5(120) + 0.5(120) = 120	−15	225
5	90	0.5(105) + 0.5(120) = 112.50	−22.5	506.25
6	120	0.5(90) + 0.5(112.5) = 101.25	18.75	351.56
7	145	0.5(120) + 0.5(101.25) = 110.63	34.37	1,181.30
8	140	0.5(145) + 0.5(110.63) = 127.81	12.19	148.60
9	100	0.5(140) + 0.5(127.81) = 133.91	−33.91	1,149.89
10	80	0.5(100) + 0.5(133.91) = 116.95	−36.95	1,365.30
11	100	0.5(80) + 0.5(116.95) = 98.48	1.52	2.31
12	110	0.5(100) + 0.5(98.48) = 99.24	10.76	115.78
				5,945.99

$$\text{MSE} = \Sigma e^2 / (n - 1) = 5945.99/(12 - 1) = 540.54$$

4.

Time Period, t	Actual Sales, A_t ($)	F_t	Trend, T_t	Predicted Sales, FT_{t+1} ($)
1	700.00	665.00	6.00	$650.00
2	685.00	675.20	7.68	$671.00
3	648.00	672.42	3.49	$682.88
4	717.00	688.24	8.43	$675.91
5	713.00	701.56	10.39	$696.66
6	728.00	716.76	12.31	$711.95

To forecast for period 2:

Update the exponentially smoothed series:

$$F_1 = \alpha A_1 + (1 - \alpha)(F_0 + T_0) = 0.3(700) + 0.7(650 + 0) = 665$$

Update the trend estimate:

$$T_1 = \beta(F_1 - F_0) + (1 - \beta)T_0 = 0.4(665 - 650) + 0.6(0) = 6$$

Forecast one period into the future:

$$FT_2 = F_1 + T_1 = 665 + 6 = 671$$

5.

a. Based on the method of least squares, we obtain:

Advertising, X ($)	Sales, Y ($)	XY ($)	X^2 ($)	Y^2 ($)
320	2,600	832,000	102,400	6,760,000
200	1,500	300,000	40,000	2,250,000
230	2,150	494,500	52,900	4,622,500
240	2,250	540,000	57,600	5,062,500
720	4,700	3,384,000	518,400	22,090,000
560	3,700	2,072,000	313,600	13,690,000
470	3,300	1,551,000	220,900	10,890,000
750	4,750	3,562,500	562,500	22,562,500
3,490	24,950	12,736,000	1,868,300	87,927,500

From the table,

$$n = 8, \ \Sigma X = 3{,}490, \ \Sigma Y = 24{,}950, \ \Sigma XY = 12{,}736{,}000, \ \Sigma X^2 = 1{,}868{,}300$$

Substituting these values into the formula,

$$b = \frac{n \Sigma XY - (\Sigma X)(\Sigma Y)}{n \Sigma X^2 - (\Sigma X)^2} = \frac{(8)(12{,}736{,}000) - (3{,}490)(24{,}950)}{(8)(1{,}868{,}300) - (3{,}490)^2} = \$5.35$$

$$a = (\Sigma Y/n) - b(\Sigma X/n) = 24{,}950/8 - (1.22)(3{,}490/8) = 3{,}119 - 2{,}334 = \$785$$

Thus, the cost function formula is $785 + $5.35X.

b.

$$r = \frac{[n \Sigma XY - (\Sigma X)(\Sigma Y)]}{\sqrt{[n \Sigma X^2 - (\Sigma X)^2][n \Sigma Y^2 - (\Sigma Y)^2]}}$$

$$r = \frac{(8)(12{,}736{,}000) - (3{,}490)(24{,}950)}{\sqrt{[(8)(1{,}868{,}300) - (3{,}490)^2][(8)(87{,}927{,}500) - (24{,}950)^2]}}$$

$$= \ 14{,}812{,}500/14{,}961{,}453 \ = 0.99$$

Then, $r^2 = (0.99)^2 = 0.9801 = 98.01\%$.

c. Advertising was an excellent choice in explaining the behavior of sales as the high *r*-squared indicated: 98.01% of the total change in sales was explained by advertising alone. Only 1.99% was due to chance. The following is the regression output generated by MINITAB.

Predictor	Coefficient	Standard Deviation	t-Ratio	p
Constant	782.8	150.1	5.21	0.002
Adv.	5.3546	0.3107	17.23	0.000
s = 182.7	r^2 = 98.0%	r^2(adj) = 97.7%		

6.

a.

Power Costs, Y	Machine Hours, X	XY	X²	Y²
4	6	24	36	16
8	7	56	49	64
8	9	72	81	64
6	5	30	25	36
7	8	56	64	49
5	6	30	36	25
$38	41	268	291	254

$$b = \frac{(6)(268) - (41)(38)}{(6)(291) - (41)(41)} = \frac{50}{65} = 0.77$$

$$a = 38/6 - (0.77)(41/6) = 1.07$$

The estimated regression equation is

$$Y' = \$1.07 + \$0.77X$$

where Y' = estimated power costs and X = machine hours. The estimated power cost for 8 machine hours will be

$$Y' = \$1.07 + \$0.77(8 \text{ hours}) = \$7.23$$

b.
$$r^2 = \frac{(50)^2}{(65)[(6)(254) - (38)^2]} = \frac{2,500}{5,200} = 0.48$$

$$= 48\%$$

which means that the machine hours account for only 48% of the change in power costs.

c. Yes, a low r^2 (48%) indicates that the machine hour basis was not good enough to explain fully the behavior of power costs. Fifty-two percent is still unexplained by the estimated equation. Often factors like the weather may be responsible for part of the variation in such costs.

7.

X	Y	XY	X²
100	$ 1,000	$ 100,000	10,000
200	1,250	250,000	40,000
300	2,250	675,000	90,000
400	2,500	1,000,000	160,000
500	3,750	1,875,000	250,000
1,500	10,750	3,900,000	550,000

From the table,

$$n = 5, \quad \Sigma X = 1,500, \quad \Sigma Y = 10,750, \quad \Sigma XY = 3,900,000, \quad \Sigma X^2 = 550,000$$

Substituting these values into the formula,

$$b = \frac{n\Sigma XY - (\Sigma X)(\Sigma Y)}{n\Sigma X^2 - (\Sigma X)^2} = \frac{(5)(3,900,000) - (1,500)(10,750)}{(5)(550,000) - (1,500)^2} = \frac{3,375,000}{500,000}$$

$$= 6.75$$

$$a = (\Sigma Y/n) - b(\Sigma X/n) = 10,750/5 - (6.75)(1,500/5) = \$125$$

Thus, the formula is $\$125 + \$6.75X$.

8.

    a. $Y' = 123.5 + 2.3 (\$200) = 583.5$.

    b. The range (prediction interval) of this forecast using two standard errors of estimate will be

$$\$583.5 \pm 2 (31.2) = 62.4 \text{ or } \$521.1 \text{ to } \$645.9.$$

9.

Week	Actual, A (gallons)	Forecast, F (gallons)	e = (A − F)	|e|
1	200	210	−10	10
2	225	235	−10	10
3	200	225	−25	25
4	260	270	−10	10
				55

Using the figures,

$$MAD = \Sigma |e|/n = 55/4 = 13.75$$

10. The computation follows.

Year	Sales	Forecasts	Error	Error^2
1	220			
2	226	220	6	36
3	210	226	-16	256
4	217	210	7	49
5	215	217	-2	4
			-5	345

First, compute the standard deviation of forecast errors:

$$S_f = \sqrt{e^2/(n-1)} = \sqrt{345/(5-1)} = 9.29$$

Two sigma limits are then ± 2(9.29) = −18.58 to +18.58. The forecast errors appear to be within the limits, so the forecast is in control, although more observations are desired.

11.

    a.

Year	Quarter	Sales ($000,000)	Four-Quarter Moving Average	Centered Moving Average
1	1	4.8		
	2	4.1		
			5.35	
	3	6.0		5.475
			5.6	
	4	6.5		5.7375
			5.875	
2	1	5.8		5.975
			6.075	
	2	5.2		6.1875
			6.3	
	3	6.8		6.325
			6.35	
	4	7.4		6.4
			6.45	
3	1	6.0		6.5375
			6.625	
	2	5.6		6.675

Year	Quarter	Sales ($000,000)	Four-Quarter Moving Average	Centered Moving Average
			6.725	
	3	7.5		6.7625
			6.8	
	4	7.8		6.8375
			6.875	
4	1	6.3		6.9375
			7	
	2	5.9		7.075
			7.15	
	3	8.0		
	4	8.4		

b. Seasonal random factors for the series are computed as follows:

Year	Quarter	Sales ($000,000)	Four-Quarter Moving Average	Centered Moving Average, TC	Seasonal Random, SR = Y/TC
1	1	4.8			
	2	4.1			
			5.35		
	3	6.0		5.475	1.096
			5.6		
	4	6.5		5.738	1.133
			5.875		
2	1	5.8		5.975	0.971
			6.075		
	2	5.2		6.188	0.840
			6.3		
	3	6.8		6.325	1.075
			6.35		
	4	7.4		6.400	1.156
			6.45		
3	1	6.0		6.538	0.918
			6.625		
	2	5.6		6.675	0.839
			6.725		
	3	7.5		6.763	1.109
			6.8		
	4	7.8		6.838	1.141
			6.875		

Year	Quarter	Sales ($000,000)	Four-Quarter Moving Average	Centered Moving Average, TC	Seasonal Random Component SR = Y/TC
4	1	6.3		6.938	0.908
			7		
	2	5.9		7.075	0.834
			7.15		
	3	8.0			
	4	8.4			

c. The following shows seasonal component calculations:

Quarter	Seasonal-Random, SR	Seasonal Factor, S	Adjusted S
1	0.971		
	0.918		
	0.908	0.932	0.931
2	0.840		
	0.839		
	0.834	0.838	0.836
3	1.096		
	1.075		
	1.109	1.093	1.092
4	1.133		
	1.156		
	1.141	1.143	1.141
		4.006	4.000

Year	Quarter	Sales ($000,000)	Seasonal Factor, S	Des. Data	t	tY	t²
1	1	4.8	0.931	5.16	1	5.16	1
	2	4.1	0.836	4.90	2	9.80	4
	3	6.0	1.092	5.50	3	16.49	9
	4	6.5	1.141	5.69	4	22.78	16
2	1	5.8	0.931	6.23	5	31.16	25
	2	5.2	0.836	6.22	6	37.30	36
	3	6.8	1.092	6.23	7	43.61	49
	4	7.4	1.141	6.48	8	51.87	64
3	1	6.0	0.931	6.45	9	58.02	81
	2	5.6	0.836	6.70	10	66.96	100
	3	7.5	1.092	6.87	11	75.58	121
	4	7.8	1.141	6.83	12	82.00	144
4	1	6.3	0.931	6.77	13	88.00	169
	2	5.9	0.836	7.05	14	98.76	196
	3	8.0	1.092	7.33	15	109.94	225
	4	8.4	1.141	7.36	16	117.75	256
				101.77	136	915.18	1496

$$b = \frac{n\Sigma tY - \Sigma t\Sigma Y}{n\Sigma t^2 - (\Sigma t)^2} = \frac{(16)(915.18) - (136)(101.77)}{(16)(1496) - (136)^2} = 0.147$$

$$a = \overline{Y} - b\overline{t} = (101.77/16) - (0.147)(136/16) = 5.11$$

which means that $y = 5.11 + 0.147t$ for the forecast periods.

d. The trend forecast for the first quarter of year 20X5 is $Y = 5.11 + 0.147t = 5.11 + 0.147(17) = 7.61$. Adjusting for seasonality yields the forecast $7.61 \times 0.931 = \$7.08$.

4

PRODUCT PLANNING, PROCESS SELECTION, AND CAPACITY PLANNING

KEY TERMS

assembly chart graphical method for visualizing how the various parts and subassemblies flow into the assembly process.

capacity rate at which work is capable of being produced.

computer-aided design (CAD) use of a computer to interact with a designer in developing and testing product ideas without actually building prototypes.

computer-aided manufacturing (CAM) manufacturing system using computer software that controls the actual machine on the shop floor.

computer-integrated manufacturing (CIM) computer information systems using a shared manufacturing database for engineering design, factory production, and information management.

flexible manufacturing system (FMS) computer-controlled process technology suitable for producing a moderate variety of products in moderate, flexible volumes.

flow process chart description of the sequence of operations in a production process. These generally are operation, inspection, movement, storage, and delay.

make–buy decision decision as to whether a given item should be manufactured internally or purchased outside.

modular design design of components that can be assembled in a variety of ways to meet individual consumer needs.

process planning planning involving a total analysis of the product and its processing requirements, decisions concerning the purchase of items outside versus their internal manufacture, and techniques for selecting among competing processes.

process selection an economic analysis to determine which process should be chosen when operations can be performed by more than one process.

product analysis analysis of product assembly. The early phases of product analysis may produce diagrams that "explode" the product into its various subassemblies and parts. These diagrams may be pictorial or schematic.

production design the conscious effort to design for low manufacturing cost.

reliability probability that a product or process will perform satisfactorily over a period of time under specified operating conditions.

theory of constraints (TOC) approach seeking to identify a company's constraints or bottlenecks and to exploit them so that throughput is maximized and inventories and operating costs are minimized.

value analysis process of trying to reduce product costs by substituting less-costly materials, redesigning nonessential parts, and the like.

The task of planning any system must be undertaken with considerable care. Planning is a function of management at all levels. The planning activities of the operations manager differ from planning by other functional area managers. Planning the operations system involves product design, the determination of processes required, the decision establishing the capacity of the system, and the design and measurement of the work system. Establishing a sequence for planning is difficult because a great deal of the planning function is correlated and executed simultaneously. The order in which operations planning activities are discussed does not necessarily represent the actual sequence in which it will occur. The planning function of the operations manager will be examined in this and succeeding chapters.

PRODUCT DESIGN

The basic limiting characteristics of the production system design are set during the product design phase. In designing the product, or the item to be processed in nonmanufacturing systems, the product designer specifies materials, tolerances, basic configurations, methods of joining parts, and the like, and through these specifications sets the minimum possible production cost. The conscious effort to design for low manufacturing cost is often referred to as *production design*. Given the product design, *process planning* for manufacture must be carried out to specify the process required and the sequence of the processes. We will cover the general topics of processes and process planning later; now we wish to focus our attention on the product design and its implications for the productive system that must be designed.

The two basic steps in designing a product are functional design and production design.

FUNCTIONAL DESIGN

In the functional design step the product is designed to be functional. Decisions are made on dimensions, materials to be used, type of final finish required for appearance, and so on. At this stage, the designer is more concerned with the product itself than the methods of production. The main concerns are functional considerations, customer appeal, cost, and ease of operation and maintenance.

PRODUCTION DESIGN

In the production design stage, the designer considers introduction of modifications and new concepts into the product to make it more suitable for production. Some of the concepts employed at this stage follow:

- *Standardization.* The designer can facilitate the production of the part by standardization of a part or the whole product. Standardization can also cut production costs by eliminating the need for planning for several different product varieties. It allows firms to work larger, and often economical, quantities of fewer items. However, standardization has limitations. It can forestall improvements and limits the options available to consumers.

- *Modular designs.* Modular designs facilitate production and maintenance. This type of design is used extensively in computers. Products are made of easily detachable subassemblies or sections.

- *Simplification.* Sometimes the designer may include some features in the design that, although not very critical to the function of the product, create severe problems in the production stage. To correct these situations, sometimes some part of the design must be simplified.

Once developed, many products also undergo *value analysis* (or *value engineering*). This is an attempt to see if any materials or parts can be substituted or redesigned in such a way as to continue to perform the desired or intended function, but at a lower cost.

INTERACTION BETWEEN PRODUCT DESIGN AND PRODUCTION COSTS

The nature of the product design can affect costs in a wide variety of cost categories, going far beyond the direct labor and material costs involved. Based on studies in the aerospace industry, a list of cost categories affected by product design follows:

- Raw material

- Equipment

- Direct labor

- Indirect labor

- Tooling

- Engineering

- Sales and administration

Many of the indirect costs tend to be hidden. For example, the number of individual parts in a design can drastically affect the indirect costs due to greater paperwork and the greater cost of ordering, storing, and controlling the larger number of parts. Thus, the selection of product design details must reflect consideration of all the foregoing factors.

BASIC PRODUCT DESIGN ALTERNATIVES

A great deal of the flexibility open to the product designer lies in the selection of materials, which in turn often specify basic kinds of processes. For example, if the designer selects a molded plastic material, then the entire mode of production and the basic sequence of activities are also set. Yet, there are usually alternatives that may extend through the entire range of die castings, forgings, stamped and formed parts, sand castings, and parts machined from solid metal. Each is appropriate under a certain combination of conditions of functional requirements and manufacturing costs. The volume to be produced should be an extremely important factor because, for a given functional requirement, some processes are well adapted to smaller volumes, whereas others are appropriate for larger volumes. The break-even volume between any two processes depends on the particular situation. Some of the ways in which contrasting designs can affect costs follow.

PROCESSES AND MATERIALS

As already noted, the particular material and related process often go together. There are wide variations in the associated costs. For example, the material cost for molded plastics is medium to high, as is the tool and die cost. However, direct labor costs, finishing costs, etc., are likely to be low, making the material and process appropriate for many applications of large volume.

• *JOINING OF PARTS*
Designs can specify many different methods for joining parts, including welding, spot welding, bolting, riveting, staking, and sometimes stapling. Not all of these alternatives are always open to designers. Usually more than one alternative is available, and costs of production can be significantly different.

• *TOLERANCES*
If tolerances are specified more tightly than is necessary for functional requirements, a more costly process may be required. On the other hand, in some situations, a closer tolerance specification can minimize assembly and adjustment costs. The overall implications need to be considered.

• *SIMPLIFIED DESIGNS*
As noted previously, the fewer the parts involved, the smaller will be certain indirect costs. When two or more parts are finally assembled rigidly together, the questions of whether a one-piece design is appropriate should be

raised. If a single material can meet service requirements, then not only will assembly costs be reduced, but the indirect costs of control will also be reduced.

• *REDUCED PROCESSING*

The selection of the initial state of the raw material can often reduce processing. A wide variety of intermediate shapes and cross sections of plastic and metal materials are produced, and designers can often select one of these materials to be the initial raw material, thereby reducing the amount of further processing.

QUALITY FUNCTION DEPLOYMENT

Quality function deployment (QFD) is a structured way to integrate product/service design and process design. It attempts to transform customer requirements and competitive capabilities into provider targets, extending from product and process research to operations, marketing, and distribution. The structure begins with developing a "house of quality," a matrix consisting of (1) customer needs (the "whats")—the "voice of the customer," (2) the company's and key competitors' abilities to satisfy those needs (the "hows"), and (3) the "roof" of the house showing any correlation between the operating requirements. This analysis allows a firm to compare the firm to its competitors and to set target values on each of the operating requirements.

The design team uses the basic house of quality in the product-planning stage. More detailed matrices may be devised for three remaining stages of design (i.e., product design, process planning, and process control), as shown in Figure 4.1.

PROCESSES AND PROCESS PLANNING

Some aspects of process planning take place jointly with the product design phase. Nevertheless, given the product design, someone must consider the processes required in order to design the production system to be used. We will first consider processes in the general sense and then the nature of process planning.

PROCESSES

Processes involve transformations of some kind. The transformation process may be chemical, physical (changes in shape or form), assembly, transportation, or clerical. Taking another dimension, transformation processes may also cover a spectrum extending from completing manual tasks through man–machine systems to automated processes. The special aspects of manual tasks and the man–machine relationship are covered separately in Chapter 6 on job design and man–machine systems.

• CHEMICAL PROCESSES

Chemical processes are particularly important in the petroleum, plastics, and metal industries. Chemical processes are often of the batch type; however, continuous flow chemical processes are also important in manufacturing such products as petroleum and soaps and detergents.

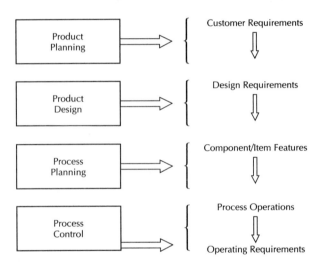

Figure 4.1. An Overview of Quality Function Deployment

• PROCESSES TO CHANGE SHAPE OR FORM

The mechanical industries best illustrate processes to change shape or form, the best-known example being the metals machine shop. Other examples are in woodworking and plastics molding. The metals industry commonly produces intermediate shapes such as bars, sheets, billets, and beams, which can be used as raw materials for further processing.

• ASSEMBLY PROCESSES

The modern assembly line and the kinds of activities associated with it are typical. These activities include welding, soldering, riveting, screw-fastening, stapling, and adhesive joining. Assembly processes are dominantly manual in character, with mechanical aids to reduce fatigue and increase productivity. Much of the analysis of these kinds of tasks depends on motion study and study of the relationship between the worker and his workplace and tools.

• *TRANSPORT PROCESSES*

Internal material handling represents one of the costly kinds of operations within a manufacturing system. The transformation involved is the transformation of place. Some of the basic layout types in manufacturing are designed to minimize transport processes and/or to take advantage of a particularly effective transport process.

• *CLERICAL AND INFORMATION PROCESSES*

Clerical activities focus on the transformation of information and are characterized both by manual activity and by the most sophisticated integrated information systems. Information systems processes are currently receiving a great deal of attention, partly because of the tremendous growth of clerical and information system costs.

YOU SHOULD REMEMBER

Major factors affecting choice of process designs include
- Degree of automation
- Production flexibility—product and volume flexibility
- Nature of product/service demand
- Level of quality

GENERAL- AND SPECIAL-PURPOSE EQUIPMENT

General-purpose equipment finds its field of application in operations characterized by relatively low volume and/or changing part of product design. General-purpose equipment meets the needs of flexibility. In a machine shop, the general-purpose machines are the lathes, drill presses, grinders, and the like. The large batch-type computing machines are general purpose in nature.

Special-purpose equipment has ordinarily been designed for, or adapted to, a specialized highly repetitive job. For example, in a machine shop, a special drill press might be designed to drill a series of holes to a specified depth in a specified material. Ordinarily, such machines have evolved from their general-purpose counterparts but have been redesigned for specialized needs because of high-volume use. Special-purpose machines are likely to be expensive and inflexible, resulting in low or no salvage value. On the other hand, they are ordinarily very productive for their special purpose.

AUTOMATION

Automation is a further step in the substitution of machine power for manpower. With automation, machines now perform many of the *control* functions formerly performed by human operators. The ultimate development of automation is a completely integrated automatic sequence of operations commonly termed the automated factory.

There are two main branches of automation, one requiring information feedback. The branch that does not involve information feedback is essentially the automatic handling of parts between operations in such a way that the part or product is indexed and laced in position for the subsequent operation. The entire sequence of operations is carefully coordinated with the result that we have essentially a single giant machine. Automation not involving information feedback may be characterized as progressive mechanization and is often called *open loop* automation. It is common in very high-volume mechanical industries such as the fabrication of automobile parts. There are basically three levels of automation: the stand-alone piece of equipment, the cell, and the completely integrated factory.

• *NUMERICAL CONTROL*

One very important branch of automation is the field of computerized numerically controlled processes. It is stand-alone machines controlled by a computer. In the mechanical industries, for example, numerically controlled machine tools are under the operation control of a digital computer that specifies the positions and paths of the cutter tools. In these systems, the information feedback loops continually compare actual tool position with programmed tool position, calling for correction when necessary.

For numerically controlled machine tools, there are two kinds of control. *Position control* can control the tool in two dimensions and is ideally suited for machine tools such as the drill press. Current systems use a punched tape for instructions, which are coded to indicate the beginning of a new block of data concerning the position reading for the x dimension and the y dimension. Drive motors respond to the instructions and position the tool in exactly the programmed location through the feedback control loops. The system then calls for the drill head to drill the holes and retract, finally signaling the tape unit to read in the next position. *Contour control* adds the third dimension, specifying not only position but the actual path that the cutter must take. Even though the programming problem is more complex with contour control, complex curves and surfaces can be specified.

Such systems have great inherent flexibility in terms of the operations and shapes that can be produced as well as in changeover from one order to the next. A major advantage is that the machine tool is not tied up during setup because almost all the preparation time is in programming, which can be done externally to the production process itself.

• *ROBOTRY*

It is usually possible to develop mechanical robots to do most highly repetitive manual jobs. Only their costs stands in the way of more of them.

• *THE CELL*

The cell goes one step farther and integrates computer-controlled machines and automated material handling equipment. A particular example of a cell is the *flexible manufacturing system* (FMS). The FMS is a system that produces a family of products from start to finish using robots and other automated equipment under the control of a computer system. This ability to produce a variety of products with the same set of equipment is clearly advantageous. There may be several cells within a factory. Figure 4.2 illustrates such a system.

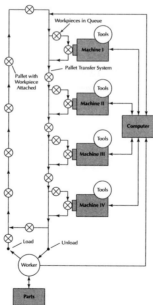

SOURCE: Adapted with permission from "Computer-Managed Parts Manufacture," by Nathan H. Cook, SCIENTIFIC AMERICAN, February 1975, 21–29. Copyright © 1975 by SCIENTIFIC AMERICAN Inc. All rights reserved.

Figure 4.2. A Flexible Manufacturing System

Although the initial cost of these systems is high, per-unit production costs are low, quality of products is high, and product flexibility is high.

• *COMPUTER-INTEGRATED MANUFACTURING*

If automation is justified, it may man installation of computer-integrated manufacturing (CIM). CIM implies the following capabilities: (1) the products are designed through the use of a *computer-aided design (CAD) system*; (2) a *computer-aided engineering (CAE) system* is used to test the design; (3) the product is manufactured using a *computer-aided manufacturing (CAM) system* (CAM systems use computer-controlled machines and robots); and (4) an information system connects the various automated components. In a CIM system, all automated components are linked by a centrally controlled information system.

• *FLEXIBLE MANUFACTURING SYSTEM*

The flexible manufacturing system is an approach that allows manufacturing facilities to change from making one product to another rapidly and efficiently. For example, a VCR factory can use FMS to produce different models using a similar facility, which can be rescheduled and rearranged to fit into different manufacturing patterns. For some firms, FMS is an extension of CIM. With older systems, an assembly line was set up to make one type of product, and it could take days or months to change the equipment to manufacture another model or other products. The changeover process was also costly. Today, facilities are designed to be flexible and adaptive. One major advantage of an FMS is the ability to react to market needs or competition. FMS is implemented using computer systems, robotics, and other manufacturing techniques. The trend is to let the computer make the necessary changes to the equipment, assembly lines, and other processes.

PROCESS PLANNING

In the functional sense, process planning begins during the engineering design of the product; however, in the organizational sense, the term *process planning* assumes that, given the product, we must design a system for processing. This involves a total analysis of the product and its processing requirements, decisions concerning the purchase of items outside versus their internal manufacture, and techniques for selecting among competing processes.

PRODUCT ANALYSIS

Given the product design, usually summarized on engineering drawings, the various parts are subjected to an analysis to determine the necessary manufacturing steps. Product analysis is most complex for assembled products that are made up of a large number of parts. Thus, the early phases of product analysis may produce diagrams that "explode" the product into its various subassemblies and parts. These diagrams may be pictorial or schematic.

ASSEMBLY CHARTS

Assembly charts, often called *gozinto* charts (from the words *goes into*), are used to provide an overall *microview* of how materials and subassemblies are united to form finished products. Figure 4.3 shows an assembly chart constructed for the manufacture of a wood telephone stand. In the assembly chart, the assembly and inspection operations are shown with symbols on the right, and the parts and materials that flow into each assembly operation are shown on the left. Thus, we have a schematic explosion of the product showing how the various parts and materials flow together to produce the assembled unit. Basic decisions concerning the advisability of subassembly units can be made at this time. Also, consideration can be given to the advisability of purchasing various items outside versus manufacturing them internally. For example, in the telephone stand, the shellac, lacquer, and wood screws are fairly obvious candidates for outside purchase. The economic analysis of make–buy policies will be considered later.

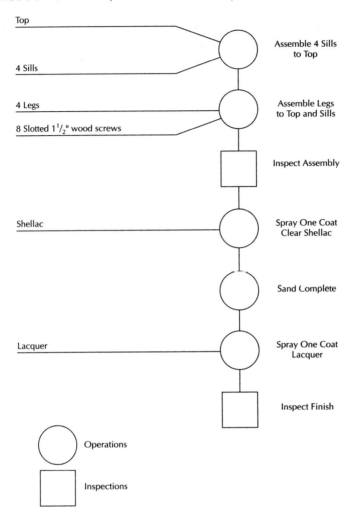

Figure 4.3. Assembly Chart for Telephone Stand

FLOW DIAGRAMS

A flow diagram traces the flow of information, customers, employees, equipment, or materials through a process. There is no precise format, and the diagram can be drawn simply with boxes, lines, and arrows. Figure 4.4 is a flow diagram of an automobile repair process. In this figure, the dotted line of visibility divides activities that are directly visible to the customers from those that are not. Such information is especially valuable for service operations involving considerable customer contact. Operations are essential to success. Areas of failure are identified.

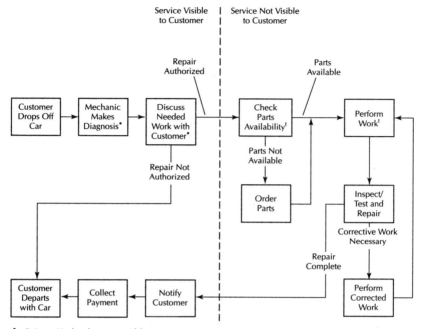

Service Visible to Customer | Service Not Visible to Customer

Figure 4.4. Flow Diagram for Automobile Repair

* = Points critical to the success of the service
† = Points at which failure is most often experienced

Source: Adapted with permission from "Note on Service Mapping," by J. L. Heskett and R. Anthony, HARVARD BUSINESS SCHOOL OF PUBLISHING, No. 693-065, Winter 1993/1994, 5.

OPERATION PROCESS CHARTS

Given the assembly diagram in Figure 4.3, the next step is to detail the operations and inspections required to fabricate each of the parts which will be manufactured internally. This is done by extending the detail for each part. Figure 4.3, as discussed earlier, is an operation process chart for the telephone stand and shows the operations and inspections required for the top, sills, and legs of the telephone stand. The summary shows that 20 fabrication and assembly operations and 5 inspections are required. The time requirements in minutes per unit are shown for each of the operations, the inspections being set up for daywork operations.

FLOW PROCESS CHARTS

While the operation process chart details the skeleton of activities which must be performed, it purposely leaves out the required nonproductive activities such as transport and storage. Figure 4.5 shows the individual steps required to process a given operation. This planning tool breaks down the operations into five classes—operation, inspect, transport, delay, and store. The frequency of occurrence of each class, distance traveled, and description and time for each step are recorded. A final step would be to draw the flow process chart on the physical layout in order to be able to visualize the physical flow of relationships and the distances traveled.

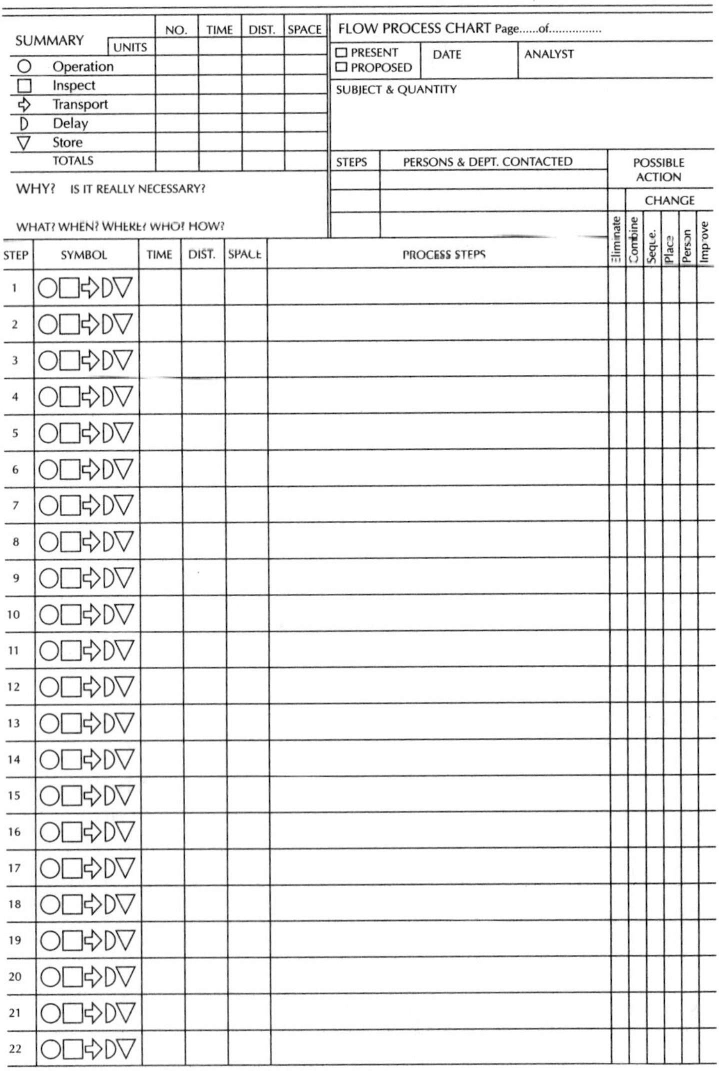

Figure 4.5. Flow Process Chart

ANALYSIS OF FLOW CHARTS

Flow charts can be used as planning aids both for new products and for the analysis and improvement of existing products. The analytical process may be summarized by the following questions:

- *Why* is the activity being done? This should establish the objective of the activity. If a valid objective cannot be established, perhaps the activity should be eliminated.

- *What* is being done? Establish the value of work being done in relation to the basic objective.

- *Where* is the activity being done? Establish that the location is the most efficient for the activity.

- *When* is the work being done? Is this the most efficient sequence of activities?

- *Who* does the work?

- *How* is the work being performed? Can the activity be made simpler and easier for employees and equipment?

MAKE–BUY ANALYSIS

In deciding whether a given item should be manufactured internally or purchased outside, important economic factors and some intangible and noneconomic factors influence the organization's make versus buy policies.

ECONOMIC ANALYSIS

In general, make–buy policies will reflect the economic analysis. If internal manufacture is less expensive, that course of action will be taken. If the reverse is true, the item will be purchased outside. As noted in the materials on cost analysis, every situation must be analyzed in terms of the *incremental costs*. It can also be handled by using a simple break-even problem: Where (at what quantity) does the cost of "make" break even with the cost of "buy"? There are often advantages to the internal manufacture because of existing capacity. In such situations, the internal costs of manufacture may be mainly the direct costs of labor and material, equipment and overhead items being already available. On the other hand, the reverse conditions might be true, favoring outside purchase, if it were necessary to acquire special equipment in order to manufacture an item internally.

EXAMPLE 1

David Davidson, purchasing agent for Donald Corporation, buys a part for $9.00 per unit. Engineers at the company estimate that they could make the part for $6.00 per unit but would incur additional fixed costs of $210,000 per year. Should they make the part?

David sets the cost of buy equal to the cost of make and solves for the break-even quantity. In other words,

$$\$9x = \$6x + \$210,000$$

$$\$3x = \$210,000$$

$$x = 70,000 \text{ units}$$

So, if annual quantity is less than 70,000 units, buy the part; otherwise, make it in-house.

INTANGIBLE FACTORS

Quality, reliability, availability of supply, control for trade secrets, existing patents, flexibility, and alternative sources of supply are all factors that may bear on a particular make–buy decision.

MAKE–BUY POLICIES

The policies followed by a given organization are usually based largely on the economic criterion, modified by the intangible factors. Many times, intangible factors will dominate, such as when reciprocal agreements are made with important customers or when customer goodwill is a dominating factor in the decision.

PROCESS SELECTION

When operations can be performed by more than one process, an economic analysis should normally be made to determine which process should be chosen. The analysis follows the general concepts of the break-even charts, which we discussed earlier. For each process, we must estimate costs of setup and tooling, representing the fixed costs, and the variable costs of labor and material. These may be related graphically, as shown in Figure 4.6, which indicates the break-even points for three lathe processes. For the particular operation in Figure 4.6, the engine lathe would be appropriate for quantities up to approximately 10 units, the turret lathe would be economical for quantities between 10 and 60 units, and the automatic screw machine would be economical for quantities above 60 units.

Other factors such as expediency, quality control, availability, and simply preference for a particular process often dominate in process selection. Also, there are often deviations from plans at the time of production, as when the desired machine is down because of maintenance.

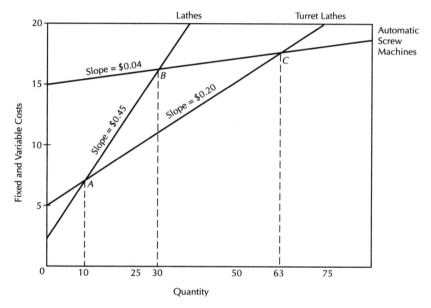

Figure 4.6. Break-Even Chart for Three Lathe Processes

RELIABILITY AND MAINTENANCE

Good quality in design, materials, and processes can eliminate many manufacturing problems and thus reduce cost and increase productivity. A good design should seek out possible causes of product failure and minimize their chances of occurrence. This is critical to the success of the product in the marketplace and prevention of product liability claims and excessive warranty costs.

Reliability is a term that is often confused with quality. Quality, as we defined it in Chapter 1, is conformance to specification. Reliability, on the other hand, includes the dimension of time. Specifically, *reliability* is defined as the *probability* that a product or process will perform satisfactorily over a period of time under specified operating conditions. For example, an auto part maker might state that the reliability of a 48-month auto battery is 0.94. This means that 94 out of 100 batteries should last 48 months under normal operating conditions (12,000 miles per year, for example).

High quality does not necessarily mean high reliability. A product may meet all the specifications, but may not last over a long period of time. However, reliability must be designed into products. This often presents a dilemma for product designers since increased reliability often means higher costs, more weight, and larger sizes of products. Thus, tradeoffs are typically made between these characteristics and reliability.

MEASURES OF RELIABILITY

There are several important measures of reliability. They are important for product design and for establishing maintenance policies. They include:

- *Mean time between failures (MTBF)*. Denoted by the Greek letter μ, MTBF is a measure of reliability for products that fail and can be repaired. For example, the MTBF for a particular type of automatic nozzle on gasoline pumps might be 18 months. This means that, on the average, a failure will occur every 18 months. The MTBF is useful in developing preventive maintenance policies.

- *Mean time to repair (MTTR)*. It is the average required to replace (or repair) a product.

- *Availability (A)*. It is the proportion of time the item is ready for use. The formula is

$$A = \frac{MTBF}{MTBF + MTTR}$$

- *Failure rate (λ)*. It is the average number of failures per time period, which is measured as the number of failures per unit per time. The failure rate is defined as

$$\frac{\text{Number of failures}}{\text{Number of units tested} \times \text{total length of time}}$$

For example, if 5,000 light bulbs are tested for 100 hours and 120 fail during this time period, the failure rate is

$$\frac{120 \text{ failures}}{(5{,}000 \text{ units tested})(100 \text{ hours})} = 0.00024 \text{ failures per unit per hour}$$

The failure rate can also be computed as:

$$\frac{1}{\text{MTBF}} \text{ or } \frac{1}{\mu}$$

- *Reliability (R)*. It is the probability an item will work for a given time period t and is computed as

$$R = e^{-\lambda t}$$

where e = the base of natural logarithm = 2.718
λ = constant failure rate
t = length of time period

EXAMPLE 2

Mike Constas, a newly appointed director of maintenance at Hoch Eclectic, is concerned with downtime of the 48 winding machines. Maintenance records show that the MTBF is about 80 days on each machine and that the MTTR is one day.

Availability: $A = 80/(80 + 1) = 0.988$ or 98.8% of the time

Failure rate: $\lambda = 1/80 = 0.0125$ failures per day for each machine

Reliability: $R = e^{-0.0125(80)} = e^{-1.0} = 0.368$

In general, the failure rate of a product is not constant but follows a pattern as shown in Figure 4.7.

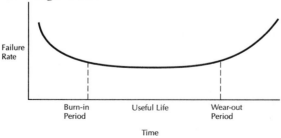

Figure 4.7. Failure Rate Curve

During the early period of operation, called the burn-in, debugging, or infant mortality period, the failure rate is high. This is often caused by poor materials or lack of quality. In the next phase, the failure rate is lower and somewhat stable. At the last stage, the product begins to wear out and the failure rate rises.

When the product enters the wear-out phase, the probability distribution of remaining life is sometimes depicted by the bell-shaped, normal distribution. If the mean and variance of product life are known, we are able to compute the probability that the remaining life will exceed a given life.

EXAMPLE 3

From actual road tests, a new steel-belted tire was estimated to have the mean tire mileage μ = 36,500 miles and the standard deviation, σ = 5,000 miles. Suppose that a 36,000-mile warranty is contemplated. What percentage of tires can be expected to last more than 40,000 miles? The situation can be seen as trying to find the area of the shaded region in Figure 4.8.

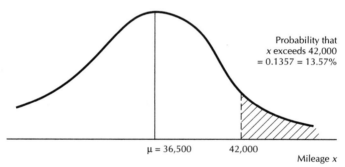

Figure 4.8. Tire Mileage

At x = 42,000 miles, we have

$$z = \frac{x - \mu}{\sigma} = (42{,}000 - 36{,}500)/5{,}000 = 1.1$$

From Table 3 in the Appendix, we find that this area is 0.5000 − 0.3643 = 0.1357, which means that about 13.57% of the tires will exceed 42,000 miles. In other words, if the warranty is set 42,000 miles, for example, then 86.43% of the tires will wear out before 42,000 miles.

PROCESS RELIABILITY

Many production systems are made up of several machines or operations in series. For example, individual parts are transferred from one operation to the next by a robot; thus if one machine or robot fails, the entire production process must stop. If we know the individual reliability of each machine, we can compute the total reliability of an n-machine series system R by taking the product of the individual reliabilities:

$$R = R_1 R_2 ... R_n$$

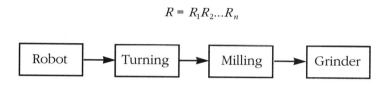

If we assume that the reliability of the robot, turning center, milling machine, and grinder are 0.99, 0.98, 0.99, and 0.96, respectively, then the total reliability is

$$R = (0.99)(0.98)(0.99)(0.96) = 0.92$$

Thus, there is a 92% chance that the system will be working over a specified period of time. This calculation assumes that each operation is independent of the others.

Suppose that the system is redesigned with two grinders. We say that the grinders are in *parallel,* as shown here, because even if one fails, the system can still operate.

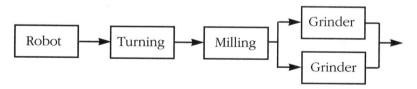

We compute the reliability of the parallel grinders by using the following formula:

$$R = 1 - (1 - p_1)(1 - p_2)...(1 - p_n)$$

p_j is the reliability of the jth component in parallel ($j = 1, 2,...n$). Thus if each grinder has a reliability of 0.96, the reliability of both grinders is

$$R_{\text{grinders}} = 1 - (1 - 0.96)(1 - 0.96) = 1 - 0.0016 = 0.9984$$

Notice that total grinder reliability has increased considerably by adding the extra machine.

To compute the total system reliability, use 0.9984 as the reliability of the grinders. Basically, we replace the parallel grinders with one grinder having a reliability of 0.9984, as follows:

$$R = (0.99)(0.98)(0.99)(0.9984) = 0.96$$

YOU SHOULD REMEMBER

If a series system has parallel components, we first compute the reliability of the parallel components using the formula for $R_{grinders}$ and then apply the original formula to compute total system reliability. Adding extra machines helps increase reliability. But good quality control and testing, improved production methods, better materials, and preventive maintenance are other ways.

MAINTENANCE

When production machines break down, we must absorb the costs of downtime and possible lost sales, idle direct and indirect labor, delays in dependent processes, and increased scrap, as well as the costs of maintenance and repair. In designing maintenance programs, our objective is to balance the costs of maintenance and repair against the costs that result from breakdown. The policies under managerial control that can be used to optimize the maintenance system are

- Determining the appropriate level of preventive maintenance.
- Determining the size of repair facilities and crews.
- Determining the appropriate level of slack in the system at critical stages.

A fundamental point to keep in mind about the reliability of systems in general and of machines in particular relates to series and parallel components. When a large number of components must function in series, if any one of the components fails, the system fails. For example, a machine made up of 50 components in series, each with an average reliability of 99.5%, has as a system a whole reliability of only 80%. Thus, even though the probability of component breakdown is very small, system reliability may not be very good. This is the basic reason why complex machines are likely to be prone to breakdown. The reliability of a system in which the components are in parallel is quite different. With parallel components, there are two or more elements which are in some way performing the same function. Thus, for the system to fail, all the components in parallel must fail, thereby increasing the reliability of the system. Slack or excess capacity in effect provides the equivalent of a component in parallel, so that if one machine fails, another takes over its function.

PREVENTIVE MAINTENANCE

The concept behind a preventive maintenance program is to find a cycle for preventive maintenance that anticipates some substantial fraction of breakdowns before they occur. Thus, while preventive maintenance would have to occur more often than the average breakdown, in some cases such servicing may prevent the occurrence of certain kinds of costs associated with machine downtime. This would be particularly true if the preventive maintenance could occur during off-hours. The nature of the breakdown time distribution may be a guide to the possible value of preventive maintenance. In general, breakdown time distributions that exhibit low-to-moderate variability will be excellent candidates for preventive maintenance. The obvious reason is that low variability in the breakdown time distribution in effect means that we can forecast reasonably well when breakdowns will occur. Being able to forecast breakdowns means that we can anticipate breakdowns by establishing a preventive maintenance cycle that is somewhat shorter than the expected average breakdown time. An equally important factor, however, is the relative costliness of a preventive servicing versus a repair that results from breakdown. It is often true that the preventive servicing is cheaper than the average repair.

Thus, we can make a general policy statement when these two conditions hold: when we have a breakdown time distribution that exhibits low variability and when the time for a preventive servicing is less than the time for an average repair servicing. Under these conditions, there will be an optimum preventive maintenance cycle that will maximize the percentage of time that the machine is in working order.

There is a second-level general policy statement that can be made if the preventive maintenance can take place outside normal operating times, such as during second or third shifts, vacations, and lunch hours, when the machine would normally be down anyway. Under such conditions, preventive maintenance will be less costly than repair, even when as much time is required for preventive maintenance as is required for repair. The reasoning is that the preventive maintenance cycle does not detract from machine running time. An optimal solution would be one that minimized the total of downtime costs, preventive maintenance costs, and repair costs. The effect of the downtime costs would be to justify shorter standard preventive maintenance cycles and to justify making the repairs more quickly (at higher cost) when they do occur.

ECONOMIC TRADEOFFS IN MAINTENANCE

The principal objective of maintenance is to maintain equipment in good condition. This results in improved efficiency of labor, reduction of downtime caused by unexpected breakdowns, and a general increase in productivity. An efficient maintenance program also keeps costs down in relation to the level of production. There are two types of maintenance activities: repair due to machine failure and preventive maintenance. Determining an appropriate maintenance policy for a piece of equipment should take into account the economic and operational tradeoffs involved. Figure 4.9 illustrates these economic tradeoffs that are typical of preventive maintenance problems.

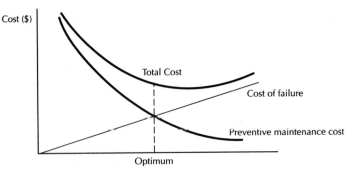

Figure 4.9. Economic Tradeoffs in Maintenance

The following example illustrates how reliability data can be used to determine an appropriate maintenance policy.

EXAMPLE 4

A part of a bathroom-tissue production system is a saw/wrapper machine, which cuts long rolls into smaller pieces and wraps them into packages prior to placing them into cartons. The MTBF is currently 34 hours. At present, the machine is repaired only when it fails, at an average cost of $50. The company is considering a preventive maintenance program that will cost $30 for each inspection and adjustment. The question is: should this be done, and if so, how often should preventive maintenance occur?

To find the best policy, we compute and compare average annual cost. Consider, for example, the current policy. Assuming 260 working days per year and 1 shift per day, there are 2,080 hours of available time. If the MTBF is 34 hours, then we expect 2,080/34 = 61.2 breakdowns per year. Hence, the annual cost will be (61.2)($50) = $3,060. Now suppose that the machine is inspected every 25 hours and adjusted. If we assume that the time until the next failure after adjustment follows the distribution in Figure 4.9, then the probability of a failure under this policy is zero. However, inspection every 25 hours will occur 2,080/25 = 83.2 times per year, resulting in a cost of (83.2)($30) =$2,496. Next, suppose we inspect every 30 hours. From Table 4.1, the probability of a failure occurring before the next inspection is 0.20. Thus the total expected annual cost will be the cost of inspection, ($30)(2,080/30) =$2,080, plus the expected cost of emergency repair, ($50)(2,080/30)(0.2) =$693. The total is $2,773. We may perform similar calculations for other maintenance intervals. The results are shown in Table 4.2. Thus we see that a maintenance interval of 25 hours results in a minimal cost policy.

Table 4.1. Probability Distribution of Time Between Failures

Time Between Failures	Probability
27.5	0.2
32.5	0.4
37.5	0.3
42.5	0.1

Table 4.2. Cost Computation for Preventive Maintenance

(1) Time Between Inspections	(2) Number of Inspections per Year	(3) Probability of Failure Before Next Inspection	(4) Inspection Costs ($)	(5) Failure Costs ($)	Total Costs ($)
25	83.2	0	2,496	0	2,496
30	69.3	0.2	2,080	693	2,773
35	59.4	0.6	1,782	1,782	3,564
40	52	0.9	1,560	2,340	3,900

YOU SHOULD REMEMBER

In this example, note that as the time between inspections increases, the inspection cost decreases, but the failure cost increases. These economic tradeoffs are typical of preventive maintenance problems and will generally follow a graph similar to that of Figure 4.9.

CAPACITY PLANNING

Capacity is the rate at which work is normally produced or the amount of output actually achieved. No single measure of capacity will be appropriate in every situation. Table 4.3 provides some examples of commonly used measures of capacity. Three definitions of capacity are useful:

- *Design capacity:* the maximum output that can possibly be achieved.
- *Effective capacity:* the maximum possible output given quality factors, product mix, machine maintenance, scheduling difficulties, and the like.
- *Actual output:* the rate of output actually attained. It is typically less than the effective output caused by machine breakdowns.

Production typically is planned sales (forecasted sales) plus desired ending inventory minus beginning inventory. It can be constrained, however, by

Machine breakdowns

Shortage of materials

Lack of skilled labor

Other related problems

These different measures of capacity are useful in defining two measures of system effectiveness: efficiency and utilization. *Efficiency* is the ratio of actual output to effective capacity, whereas *utilization* is the ratio of actual output to design capacity:

$$\text{Efficiency} = \frac{\text{Actual output}}{\text{Effective capacity}}$$

$$\text{Utilization} = \frac{\text{Actual output}}{\text{Design output}}$$

Efficiency may be misleading when effective capacity is low compared with design capacity. In this situation, high efficiency appears to indicate effective use of capacity when, in reality, this is not the case.

EXAMPLE 5

Given the following data on relevant capacity definitions:

Design capacity = 100 cars per week

Effective capacity = 80 cars per week

Actual output = 72 cars per week

$$\text{Efficiency} = \frac{\text{Actual output}}{\text{Effective capacity}} = 72/80 = 90\%$$

$$\text{Utilization} = \frac{\text{Actual output}}{\text{Design output}} = 72/100 = 72\%$$

Note here that 90% use of effective capacity is quite satisfactory, but compared with the design capacity of 100 units per week, 72% is much less impressive.

Decisions as to whether to expand capacity can be strategic or tactical. Strategic decisions involve the size of facilities, the amount of equipment available, and/or the amount of labor and materials available. Tactically, capacity can be increased by way of adding one more shift, going into overtime, and/or outsourcing. Strategic requires long-term capital expenditures (to be discussed in Chapter 11).

Table 4.3. Measures of Capacity

Type of Business	Input Measures	Output Measures
Oil refinery	Size of refinery	Barrels of fuel oil per day
Retail sales	Number of square feet	Units sold per day
Theater	Number of seats	Number of performances per week
Steel mill	Size of furnace	Tons of steel per week
Airline	Number of seats	Number of flights
Auto manufacturing	Machine hours/ labor hours per month	Number of cars per shift

EVALUATING ALTERNATIVE CAPACITIES

There are several ways to evaluate alternative capacities, including break-even analysis, capital budgeting (discussed in Chapter 11), and the decision tree approach to capacity decisions.

BREAK-EVEN ANALYSIS

Break-even analysis (discussed in Chapter 2) allows operations managers to perform many useful analyses. It deals with how profit and costs change with a change in volume. More specifically, it looks at the effects on profits of changes in such factors as variable costs, fixed costs, selling prices, volume, and mix of products sold. By studying the relationship of costs, sales, and profit, management is better able to evaluate capacity alternatives.

EXAMPLE 6

A firm is considering three capacity alternatives: A, B, and C. Alternative A would have an annual fixed cost of $100,000 and variable costs of $22 per unit. Alternative B would have an annual fixed cost of $120,000 and variable costs of $20 per unit. Alternative C would have an annual fixed cost of $80,000 and variable costs of $30 per unit. Revenue is expected to be $50 per unit.

Using the break-even formula

$$Q = \frac{FC}{(P-V)}$$

we obtain break-even quantities for A, B, and C:

$$Q_A = \$100,000/(\$50 - \$22) = \$3,571$$

$$Q_B = \$120,000/(\$50 - \$20) = \$4,000$$

$$Q_C = \$80,000/(\$50 - \$30) = \$4,000$$

Other things being equal, the lower the break-even point, the safer (or less risky) the option is. From that standpoint, A would be the best choice.

DECISION TREE APPROACH TO CAPACITY DECISIONS

A decision tree can be particularly valuable for evaluating different capacity expansion alternatives when demand is uncertain and sequential decisions are involved.

EXAMPLE 7

Based on the industry supply and demand analysis, Madden Corporation wishes to build a full-scale manufacturing facility. It is considering:

A: Build a large plant, costing $6 million

B: Build a small plant, costing $2 million

The probabilities of various demands and present values of projected cash inflows for these demand situations follow. (Present value analysis is fully discussed in Chapter 11.)

Action	Demand Conditions	PV of Cash Inflows ($)	Probabilities
A	High	8 million	0.5
	Medium	4 million	0.3
	Low	1.5 million	0.2
B	High	2.5 million	0.5
	Medium	2 million	0.3
	Low	1.5 million	0.2

We can construct a decision tree to analyze the two options, as follows:

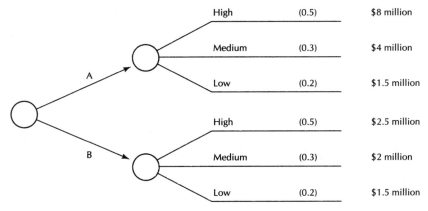

Expected NPVs for A and B are as follows:

Action	Demand Conditions	PV of Cash Inflows ($) (1)	Probabilities (2)	Expected PV ($) (1) × (2)
A	High	8 million	0.5	4 million
	Medium	4 million	0.3	1.2 million
	Low	1.5 million	0.2	0.3 million
			PV =	1.9 million
			I =	6 million
			Expected NPV =	–4.1 million
B	High	3 million	0.5	1.5 million
	Medium	2 million	0.3	0.6 million
	Low	1.5 million	0.2	0.3 million
			PV =	2.4 million
			I =	2 million
			Expected NPV =	0.4 million

You may choose option B because its expected NPV is greater than that for option A. In fact, option A has a negative NPV. This approach does not tell us how risky each option is.

THEORY OF CONSTRAINTS AND BOTTLENECKS MANAGEMENT

Bottlenecks occur whenever demand (at least temporarily) exceeds capacity. For example, although a legal secretary has enough total time to do all her word-processing, she may be given several jobs in quick succession, so that a queue (waiting line) builds up. This is a bottleneck, which delays the other activities waiting for the word-processing to be finished. The *theory of constraints (TOC)* seeks to maximize "throughput" by

- Larger lot sizes at bottleneck work stations, to avoid time lost on changeovers.

- Small transfer batches—forwarding a small batch of work to the next work station, so that the next operation can begin before the entire lot is finished at the preceding work station.

- Rules for inserting buffer stock before or after certain bottlenecks.

KNOW THE CONCEPTS

DO YOU KNOW THE BASICS?

1. What role do assembly drawings, parts lists, and assembly charts play in process design?
2. Discuss the principal differences between general-purpose and special-purpose equipment and the selection decision.
3. List some of the major types of material-handling equipment and their applications in manufacturing.
4. How does one classify the differences between continuous-flow, mass production, batch processing, job shop, and project systems?
5. What are the limitations of quality function deployment for designing a product or service?
6. Discuss the importance of reliability in production systems.
7. What types of maintenance activities are commonly performed? How does a manager determine preventive maintenance policies?
8. Define capacity.
9. What does capacity planning involve?
10. List three popular approaches to evaluation capacity alternatives.
11. Briefly describe the theory of constraints.

TERMS FOR STUDY

automation
capacity
capacity planning
computer-aided design (CAD)
computer-aided manufacturing
   (CAM)
computer-integrated manufacturing (CIM)
failure rate
flexible manufacturing system
   (FMS)

make–buy decision
mean time between failures
   (MTBF)
modular design
process planning
process selection
product analysis
production design
reliability
standardization
theory of constraints (TOC)

PRACTICAL APPLICATION

1. Given the bill of material for an automobile brake assembly (Figure 4.10), draw an assembly chart. The sequence of activities is shown in the assembly from left to right.

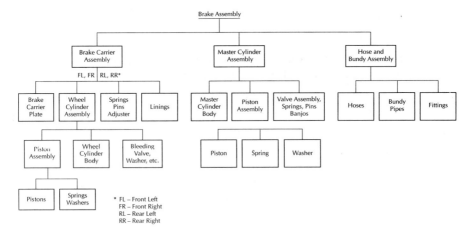

Figure 4.10. The Bill of Material for Brake Assembly

2. The maintenance records show the following historical time between failure and repair time for a certain punch press. The first breakdown happened on May 5.

Date	May 5	June 6	July 19	Sep. 7	Oct. 30
Number of hours of use before breakdown	221	335	190	250	284
Number of hours spent on repair	12	18	16	10	14

    a. Calculate the following:

        1. Mean time between failures

        2. Mean time to repair

        3. Availability of the machine

        4. Average number of failures per time period

        5. Reliability of the machine in 256 hours of use

    b. The machine is used 8 hours a day, 20 days per month, on the average. A contract requires 160 hours of the machine time and is due within one month. Calculate the probability that the machine will not break down during this period and will not cause a delay.

3. Given the following system (the probability of failure of each component is shown below each box), what is the overall reliability of the system?

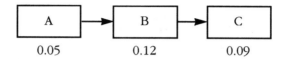

A	B	C
0.05	0.12	0.09

If the component B is backed up with another component with a probability of failure = 0.05, what is the overall reliability?

4. The lifetime of a new stereo is estimated to be 8 years with a standard deviation of 1.5 years.

   a. Determine the probability of the stereo failing after 4 years.
   b. If there is a full replacement guarantee of 3 years, what is the expected proportion of replacement?
   c. If the company is willing to replace up to 5%, what guarantee period should it specify?

5. The probability of breakdown of Machine A versus the number of hours elapsed after previous maintenance follows:

Number of Hours After Previous Maintenance	Probability
10	0.01
20	0.05
30	0.15
40	0.15
50	0.15
60	0.15
70	0.20
80	0.14

The number of working days in a year is 250 on a two-shift basis. A breakdown costs $350 to repair, and a preventive maintenance costs $150. Determine

   a. Mean time between failures
   b. Maintenance cost if no preventive maintenance is followed
   c. Cost of a preventive maintenance policy carried out once every 10 hours

    d. Best maintenance policy—decrease the frequency of preventive maintenance in increments of 10 hours and evaluate total costs.

6. A firm buys a stock item at a cost of $5 each. The company can make the item by incurring a one-time fixed cost of $10,000, and variable cost of $3 per unit. What is the break-even quantity? What does this quantity mean?

7. A solar panel maker is making a decision about whether to make or buy a part. If the firm invests $3,500 in a new die, it will be able to make this part in-house for an added cost of $1 per unit in variable costs. If, however, it buys the part, the vendor has quoted two prices, $1.55 each for quantities up to 10,000 units and $1.30 each for all orders of over 10,000. Calculate the two break-even crossover points.

8. Title Insurance Company processes all titles sequentially through four centers. The capacity and actual average output of each individual work station follows:

Work Station	A	B	C	D	Actual Average Output
Number of Titles	25	30	23	39	19 titles per day

Calculate (a) the effective capacity of the system, (b) efficiency, and (c) utilization, assuming design capacity of 39 titles.

9. Saint Motors is considering two plant sizes, large and small, to build for a new car it is developing. The cost of constructing a large plant is $25 million and the cost of building a small plant is $15 million. The automaker believes a 70% chance exists that the demand for this new car will be high and a 30% chance that it will be low. The following table summarizes the payoffs (in millions of dollars) the company expects to receive for each plant size and demand combination.

Plant Size	Demand	
	High	Low
Large	$175	$ 95
Small	$125	$105

    a. Construct a decision tree for this problem.

    b. What is the optimal decision?

ANSWERS

DO YOU KNOW THE BASICS?

1. In order to select appropriate processes and equipment, one must first understand what is being produced. Assembly drawings, parts lists, and assembly charts provide information about the individual components that must be made and assembled.

2. Special-purpose equipment may be limited to a few uses, whereas general-purpose equipment can handle a large variety of jobs. One should consider the variety of work available, output rate desired, and cost when selecting between these two types of equipment.

3. Industrial trucks—used to move large items between many locations; good for warehouse operations. Conveyors—used for uniform loads over fixed paths; good for production lines or in-process storage and inspection. Cranes—used when floor space utilization makes forklifts undesirable or when products are bulky and heavy and require frequent movement. Automated storage and retrieval systems—used primarily in warehouses for fast turnover of uniform loads. Tractor-trailer systems—used for large volumes of bulky or heavy material over long distances.

4. The differences can be classified by product volume, variety, degree of automation, and frequency of setup or change.

5. The QFD approach can be very time consuming; it is based on customer perceptions, and the results reflect a compromise on consumer wants. Nevertheless, meaningful results can be achieved if the approach is effectively applied to important dimensions of the product.

6. A process with low reliability will usually incur high costs, lower productivity, and lower quality of the product being made. It also will cause scheduling problems within the plant and lead to customer dissatisfaction.

7. Repair resulting from failure, preventive maintenance. A preventive maintenance policy is determined by analyzing the expected cost for various time intervals between inspections based on failure probabilities. In general, as the time interval increases, failure costs increase, while inspection costs decrease. The minimum cost time interval is sought.

8. Capacity refers to a system's potential for producing goods or delivering services over a specified time interval.

9. Capacity planning involves both long- and short-term considerations. Long-term consideration relates to the overall level of capacity, whereas short-term concerns relate to variations in capacity requirements caused by seasonal, random, irregular fluctuations in demand.

10. Three popular approaches to evaluation capacity alternatives are break-even analysis, capital budgeting, and decision tree approach to capacity decisions.

11. The TOC identifies a company's constraints or bottlenecks and exploits them so that throughput is maximized and inventories and operating costs are minimized. It then develops a specific approach to manage constraints to support the objective of continuous improvement.

PRACTICAL APPLICATION

1. See Figure 4.11.

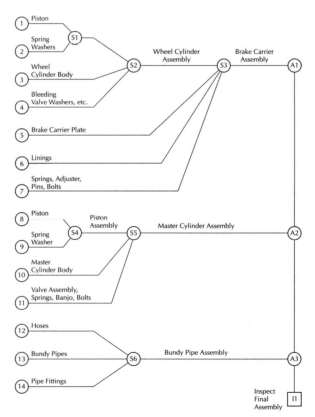

Figure 4.11. Assembly Chart for an Automobile Brake

2.

   a.

      1. MTBF = μ = (221 + 335 + 190 + 250 + 284)/5 = 256 hours

      2. MTTR = (12 + 18 + 16 + 10 + 14)/5 = 14 hours

      3. A = 256/(256 + 14) = 0.948

      4. λ = 1/μ = 1/256 = 0.0039 failure per hour

      5. $R = e^{-\lambda t}$ = 2.7183$^{(-0.0039 \times 256)}$ = 0.368

   b. $R = e^{-\lambda t}$ = 2.7183$^{(-0.0039 \times 160)}$ = 0.535

3. Reliability of the first system = (0.95)(0.88)(0.91) = 0.7608. For the following system:

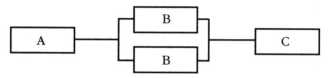

Reliability = $R_A \times R_B \times R_C$ = 0.95 × [1 − (0.12)(0.15)] × 0.91 = 0.95 × 0.982 × 0.91 = 0.85

Thus, the reliability in the second system is improved from 0.76 to 0.85.

4.

   a. For a useful life of 4 years,

$$z = \frac{x - \mu}{\sigma} = (4 - 8)/1.5 = -2.67$$

The probability that the product fails within 4 years is 0.0038 (1 − 0.9962).

   b. z = (3 − 8)/1.5 = −0.33. The probability is 0.0004 (1 − 0.9996).

   c. For replacement probability of 0.05, which corresponds to z = 1.65,

$$z = \frac{x - \mu}{\sigma}$$

$$1.65 = (x - 8)/1.5$$

solving for x yields 5.525 years. Thus the firm can afford to specify a guarantee period of as high as 5 years.

5.

   a. MTBF = (10)(0.01) + $\cdots$ + (80)(0.14) = 54.2 hours.

   b. Cost of breakdown repair = Number of breakdowns expected × Repair costs = (4,000/54.2) × \$350 = \$25,830.

c. The cost of preventive maintenance policy of every 10 hours:

Preventive maintenance cost = (4,000 hours/10 hours) × $150 = $60,000

Breakdown cost = (4,000/10)(0.01)($350) =   1,400

    Total $61,400

d.

Cost Computation for Preventive Maintenance

(1) Time Between Inspections	(2) Number of Inspections per Year	(3) Probability of Failure Before Next Inspection	(4) Inspection Costs ($)	(5) Failure Costs ($)	Total Costs ($)
10	400	0.01	60,000	1,400	61,400
20	200	0.06	30,000	4,200	34,200
30	133	0.21	19,950	9,776	29,726
40	100	0.36	15,000	12,600	27,600
50	80	0.51	12,000	14,280	26,280
60	67	0.66	10,000	15,477	25,477
70	57	0.86	8,571	17,157	25,728

Preventive maintenance policy every 60 hours gives the lowest total costs.

6. David sets the cost of buy equal to the cost of make and solves for the break-even quantity. In other words,

$$\$5x = \$3x + \$10,000$$

$$\$2x = \$10,000$$

$$x = 5,000 \text{ units}$$

The break-even quantity is 5,000 units. At this quantity, buying or making costs the same. If annual quantity is less than 5,000 units, it is less costly to buy the part; otherwise, make it in-house.

7. Because of the price discount, we buy over 10,000 units. We need to compute two break-even crossover points, one comparing each purchase price with in-house manufacturing costs:

$$\$1.55x = \$3,500 + \$1x$$

$$\$0.55x = \$3,500$$

$$x = 6,364 \text{ units}$$

$$\$1.30x = \$3,500 + \$1x$$

$$\$0.30x = \$3,500$$

$$x = 11,667 \text{ units}$$

Because there is no start-up cost involved and no machine to buy, buying the part would always be less costly for all small quantities. Figure 4.12 indicates that although buying would be less costly up to 6,364 units, making it is less costly thereafter. The volume–price discount at the 10,000-unit mark complicates matters. For quantities just over 10,000, again it pays to buy but only up to 11,667 units, after which it again is profitable to make (see Figure 4.12).

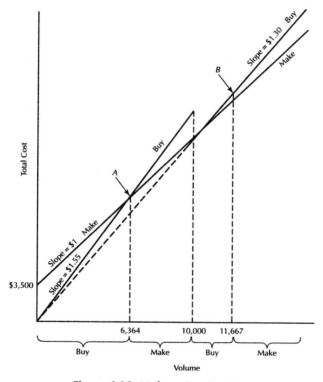

Figure 4.12. Make-or-Buy Decisions

8.

  a. Effective capacity = Capacity of most limited component in the line = 23 titles per day

  b. Efficiency = 19 titles per day/23 titles per day = 82.6%

  c. Utilization = 19/39 = 48.7%

9.

    a. See Figure 4.13.

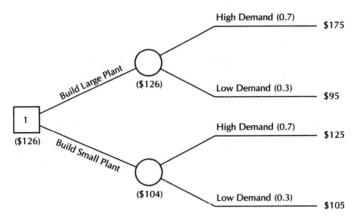

Figure 4.13. Decision Tree

    b. The decision tree indicates that the optimal decision is to build the large plant, and this alternative has an expected net benefit of $101 million.

Build large plant: $(150)(0.7) + (70)(0.3) = 105 + 21 = 126$;
Expected net benefit $= 126 - 25 = 101$

Build small plant: $(110)(0.7) + (90)(0.3) = 77 + 27 = 104$;
Expected net benefit $= 104 - 15 = 89$

5
FACILITY
LOCATION

KEY TERMS

center-of-gravity method quantitative approach to locating a facility that minimizes the distance or cost of transportation weighted by the volume of goods moved.

factor ratings procedure in which each alternative site is rated according to each factor relevant to the decision, and each factor is rated according to importance.

locational break-even analysis technique that compares potential locations on an economic basis by estimating the variable and fixed costs and then graphing them for a representative sales or production volume at each location.

transportation LP problem problem of determining how much to ship from each origin to each destination in order to minimize total shipping costs.

In its strategy formulation, a company determines what types of goods or services it will offer and in what markets it will compete. It makes demand forecasts to estimate the demand that can be found in various markets. Part of the company's strategy consists of selecting the location from which potential markets will be served. The location of a service operation helps determine how conveniently customers can conduct business with the company.

Location of production and service operations can have a great impact on investment and operating costs, thereby affecting profits and perhaps the price at which goods or services can be offered, as well as some aspects of the production system design. Even though location is a factor of importance, ordinarily many alternative locations can be equally good. Normally plant location is considered or reconsidered consciously only periodically, but in some sense broad alternatives are considered whenever an expansion or contraction is necessary.

FACTORS IN LOCATION

Rational decisions concerning plant location are intended to minimize relevant costs. Normally, however, we are thinking of not only operating costs but also costs in the longer term. Thus, differences in operating costs might be compensated for in the longer term by differences in capital investment.

A wide variety of subjective factors can influence location decisions. Therefore, it is common to rate alternative locations on such subjective factors as

- Labor supply

- Type of labor

- Labor union activity

- Community attitude

- Appearance

- Transportation

- Availability of utilities

- Recreational facilities

Even though these factors are subjective, we are really thinking of long-term costs in attempting to rate alternative locations on the basis of these dimensions. Thus, a tight labor supply or heightened union activity could mean higher labor costs in the future. A community attitude oriented against industry could mean a future tax loading on intruding business.

One of the most important subjective factors in location analysis is the personal preference of the owners and managers. In fact, personal preference may well dominate as a factor in the location of single-plant enterprises. Multiplant enterprises are much more likely to be influenced primarily by objective and subjective economic factors.

SITE SELECTION

Given a general area for location, a site within the area must then be chosen. The following requirements must be met:

- A site zoned for the activity contemplated.

- A site large enough to accommodate present floor plan needs and room for expansion, parking, transportation facilities, and the like. Normally a site size five times the actual plant area is regarded as the minimum.

- Provision for necessary transportation facilities, utilities, and waste disposal.

- A soil structure that can carry the required bearing foundation loads.

Alternative sites also need to be studied from the point of view of the relation of investment versus operating cost effects. The concept of break-even analysis can be used to compare various sites on the basis of total costs relative to the volume of operation. Thus, a site that may require large capital expenditure but that makes possible low operating costs may be a more economical site than one that has the reverse cost characteristics.

MULTIPLANT LOCATION

When the addition of a proposed plant produces a multiplant situation, then each alternative plant location must be considered in the framework of a production–distribution system. In such a situation, the linear programming models (discussed in Chapter 2) and transportation linear programming (to be discussed later in the chapter) represent a valid conceptual framework. Each alternative location would produce a different allocation of shipments to distribution points, depending on the relative costs of production and distribution in the network. Thus, the location that produces the minimum cost for the system would be the one favored in objective terms.

For the multiplant situation, locational dynamics affect the operation of plants from period to period as markets change. For example, if overall demand were to decline, it might be more economical to close one plant and operate the other plants at higher capacities, even using more costly capacity units, such as overtime. Again, linear programming distribution methods are a value in appraising the various alternatives.

SPECIAL CONSIDERATIONS IN LOCATION DECISIONS

Over the last decade many factors have shifted in relative importance regarding the location decision process. New emphasis is being placed on energy availability, energy costs, and pollution problems. Often companies that have a history of pollution or that manufacture products that generate pollutants by known production processes have met with community resistance when they sought to locate plants in a given geographical area. Consequently, the added costs of pollution control equipment, state environmental compliance, disposal of toxic by-products, and monitoring efforts must be considered part of the overall cost determination.

The rapid growth of energy costs and national efforts to reduce dependence on foreign energy sources has an impact on the location decision. A company must determine whether the available public utilities are capable of supplying its energy needs on an uninterrupted basis and must consider the possibility of alternative approaches to generating power, such as solar energy and energy recycling. Coupled with energy considerations are the attitudes of personnel working in Sunbelt versus non-Sunbelt locations. Extreme climatic conditions that cause excessive energy use and delays in the distribution and receipt of materials are being avoided.

Another factor that must be considered is the taxes of the community and state in which the plant could be located. These taxes include not only normal taxes on business profits but also requirements for contribution to unemployment compensation, taxes on inventories, and local taxes.

Many communities offer a wide variety of help to companies that plan to locate in them. This help ranges from supplying detailed information on site locations, land costs, and the like, to direct subsidies, financed by industrial revenue bond issues, to defray the cost of plant production. Because many of these bond issues are tax-free municipal bonds, their use lowers the cost of capital for plant construction. In some cases, communities build plants to specifications and lease them to companies over an extended period, thereby allowing the companies to avoid the high expenditures associated with plant construction.

LOCATION DECISIONS

Several methods that help management decide on a location for facilities include

- Locational break-even analysis

- Factor ratings

- The center-of-gravity method

- Transportation linear programming

LOCATIONAL BREAK-EVEN ANALYSIS

Potential locations can be compared on an economic basis by estimating the variable and fixed costs and then graphing them for a representative sales or production volume at each location. Assuming equal revenues from all locations considered, you would select the location with lowest total cost; otherwise, revenue figures must be also included in your analysis. Comparisons should be made on the basis of profit (total revenue minus total cost) at each location.

EXAMPLE 1

Management is considering three potential sites for plant facilities, which have the following cost structure for a product expected to sell for $200. Find the most economical location for an expected sales volume of 5,000 units per year.

Potential Location	Variable Cost per Unit ($)	Fixed Cost per Year ($)
Cambridge (X)	75	150,000
Austin (Y)	50	200,000
San Jose (Z)	40	400,000

For each location, compute and plot the fixed cost (costs at zero volume) and total costs (TC) at the expected volume Q. See Figure 5.1.

$$TC = FC + V \cdot Q$$

X: TC = $150,000 + $75 (4,000) = $450,000

Y: TC = $200,000 + $50 (4,000) = $400,000

Z: TC = $400,000 + $25 (4,000) = $500,000

The most economical site is Y because it is the least expensive.

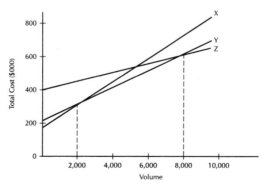

Figure 5.1. Locational Break-Even Chart

From the chart, note that the best location is X for up to 2,000 units, Y for 2,000–8,000 units, and Z for volume greater than 8,000 units.

FACTOR RATINGS

Factor ratings is a procedure in which each alternative site is rated according to each factor relevant to the decision, and each factor is rated according to importance. Weights may total 1.00. We score each location and multiply the scores by the weights. Then we total the points for each location and choose the location with the maximum points. The technique is popular because it enables managers to bring diverse locational considerations into the evaluation process and it fosters consistency of judgment about location alternatives.

EXAMPLE 2

A firm is considering two sites, A and B, for its research laboratory. The following list of factors is to be considered along with their associated weights and ratings.

Factors	Weights	A Score	A Weighted Score	B Score	B Weighted Score
Labor Supply	0.33	40	13.20	30	9.90
Markets	0.25	80	20.00	80	20.00
Environment	0.20	70	14.00	45	9.00
Material Supply	0.05	70	3.50	50	2.50
Site and Construction Cost	0.02	60	1.20	90	1.80
Operating Cost	0.15	90	13.50	50	7.50
Total Score			65.40		50.70

Based on the total weighted score, A should be chosen.

CENTER-OF-GRAVITY METHOD

The center-of-gravity method is a method used to determine the location of a distribution center that will minimize transportation costs. The method treats shipping cost as a linear function of the distance and the quantity shipped. We assume, however, that the quantity to be shipped to each destination is fixed. The coordinates of the center of gravity (i.e., the location of the distribution center) can be obtained by finding the *weighted* average of the x coordinate and the *weighted* average of the y coordinate, with weights being the quantities to be shipped. In other words,

$$\bar{x} = \sum x_i Q_i \Big/ \sum Q_i$$

$$\bar{y} = \sum y_i Q_i \Big/ \sum Q_i$$

where Q_i = quantity to be shipped to location i
  x_i = x coordinate of destination i
  y_i = y coordinate of destination i
Note: If the quantities shipped are equal, simple averages will do with Q_i terms.

EXAMPLE 3

Given the following data:

Destination	(x, y)	Quantity
A	3, 5	800
B	5, 1	900
C	6, 7	200
D	8, 4	100

The center of gravity can be determined as follows:

$$\bar{x} = \sum x_i Q_i \Big/ \sum Q_i = \frac{3(800) + 5(900) + 6(200) + 8(100)}{800 + 900 + 200 + 100} = \frac{8900}{2000} = 4.45$$

$$\bar{y} = \sum y_i Q_i \Big/ \sum Q_i = \frac{5(800) + 1(900) + 7(200) + 4(100)}{800 + 900 + 200 + 100} = \frac{6700}{2000} = 3.35$$

The idea behind this method is to pick the site close to the center of gravity.

TRANSPORTATION LINEAR PROGRAMMING

Transportation linear programming is useful in location planning. This method may be helpful especially after the initial screening phase has narrowed the feasible alternative sites. The remaining candidates can then be evaluated on the basis of the criterion, which is typically minimum overall transportation cost.

The *transportation LP method* is a special form of linear programming whose objective is to assign sources to destinations so as to minimize total shipping costs. To use this method, follow these steps:

1. **Set up the transportation table** so that the total number of shipments available equals the number of shipments needed.

2. **Develop an initial feasible solution** by using

   Northwest corner rule or

   Vogel's approximation method (VAM).

3. **Test the solution for improvement** using

   MODI (modified distribution) method or

   stepping-stone method.

4. **Repeat steps 3 and 4 until no further improvement is possible.**

YOU SHOULD REMEMBER

Initial Solutions	Optimal Solutions
Northwest corner rule	Stepping-stone method
Vogel's approximation method	Modified distribution method

• *NORTHWEST CORNER RULE*

1. Starting with the far left-hand side corner, set the level of this route at either the requirements or the availability, whichever is smaller.

2. Proceed across the table in a general northwest-to-southeast direction, exhausting the availabilities of one row before moving down to the next and exhausting the requirements of one column before moving on to the next.

EXAMPLE 4

	A	B	C	D	Supply
1	2	4	1	3	300
2	8	2	6	5	300
3	6	1	4	2	200
Demand	200	200	300	100	800

Using the northwest corner rule yields the following initial feasible solution:

	A	B	C	D	Supply
1	2 / 200	4 / 100	1	3	300
2	8	2 / 100	6 / 200	5	300
3	6	1	4 / 100	2 / 100	200
Demand	200	200	300	100	800

For this solution, the cost is 200(2) + 100(4) + 100(2) + 200(6) + 100(4) + 100(2) = $2,800.

• *VOGEL'S APPROXIMATION METHOD*

1. For each row or column, compute a penalty cost, which is the difference *between* the unit cost of the second best route in the row or column *and* the best route in the row or column.

2. Identify the row or column with the highest penalty cost and assign as many units as possible to the *best* cell or route in the identified row or column.

3. Reduce the row supply and the column demand by the amount assigned to the cell.

4. If the row supply is zero, eliminate the row; if the column demand is zero, eliminate the column; if both are zero, eliminate both the row and column.

5. Compute the new row and column penalty costs after the step 4 reduction and return to step 2 until the initial feasible solution is obtained.

EXAMPLE 5

Going back to Example 4, we apply the Vogel's approximation method as follows:

The first solution:

	A	B	C	D	Supply	Column Penalty
1	2	4	1	3	300	1
2	8	2	6	5	300	3
3	6	1	4	2	200	1
Demand	200	200	300	100	800	
Row Penalty	④	1	3	1		

The second solution:

	A	B	C	D	Supply	Column Penalty
1	200 2	4	1	3	300	2
2	8	2	6	5	300	③
3	6	1	4	2	200	1
Demand	200	200	300	100	800	
Row Penalty	x	1	③	1		

The third solution:

	A	B	C	D	Supply	Column Penalty
1	200 ²	4	100 ¹	3	300	x
2	8	2	6	5	300	③
3	6	1	4	2	200	1
Demand	200	200	300	100	800	
Row Penalty	x	1	2	③		

The fourth solution:

	A	B	C	D	Supply	Column Penalty
1	200 ²	4	100 ¹	3	300	x
2	8	200 ²	6	5	300	1
3	6	1	4	2	200	2
Demand	200	200	300	100	800	
Row Penalty	x	x	2	③		

The final solution by VAM:

	A	B	C	D	Supply
1	200 ²	4	100 ¹	3	300
2	8	200 ²	100 ⁶	5	300
3	6	1	100 ⁴	100 ²	200
Demand	200	200	300	100	800

The cost for this solution is 200(2) + 200(2) + 100(1) + 100(6) + 100(4) + 100(2) = $2,100.

• *MODIFIED DISTRIBUTION METHOD*

1. Set up $u_i + v_i = c_{ij}$ for all the occupied cells.

2. Solve the system by setting an initial $u = 0$.

3. Compute $c_{ij} - u_i - v_i$ for unoccupied cells (i.e., x_{ij} is nonbasic). If it is *negative*, further improvement is possible. If all indices are greater than or equal to zero, the optimal solution has been obtained. Otherwise, go to step 4.

4. Select the unused cell with the largest negative index. Trace the closed path for the unused cell having the largest negative index. Develop an improved solution using the Stepping-Stone Method. Repeat steps 1–3 for the improved solution.

EXAMPLE 6

In Example 5, to see if the Vogel solution is optimal, we set up the following equations for occupied cells:

$$u_1 + v_1 = 2$$
$$u_1 + v_3 = 1$$
$$u_2 + v_2 = 2$$
$$u_2 + v_3 = 6$$
$$u_3 + v_3 = 4$$
$$u_3 + v_4 = 2$$

To solve, we initially set $u_1 = 0$ and find $u_1 = 0$, $v_1 = 2$, $v_3 = 1$, $u_2 = 5$, $v_2 = -3$, $u_3 = 3$, and $v_4 = -1$. Using these values, we compute $c_{ij} - u_i - v_i$ for unoccupied cells:

$$c_{21} - u_2 - v_1 = 8 - 5 - 2 = 1$$
$$c_{31} - u_3 - v_1 = 6 - 3 - 2 = 1$$
$$c_{22} - u_2 - v_2 = 4 - 5 - (-3) = 2$$
$$c_{32} - u_3 - v_2 = 1 - 3 - (-3) = 1$$
$$c_{14} - u_1 - v_4 = 3 - 0 - 1 = 2$$
$$c_{24} - u_2 - v_4 = 5 - 5 - (-3) = 1$$

These are all positive, so no further improvement is possible. The Vogel's solution is optimal. The cost of the final solution is 200(2) + 200(2) + 100(1) + 100(6) + 100(4) + 100(2) = $2,100.

• *STEPPING-STONE METHOD*

1. Place a + sign in the cell you wish to evaluate.

2. Move horizontally (or vertically) to a completed cell. Choose a cell that will permit your next move to another completed cell. Assign a – sign to the cell.

3. Change direction and move to another completed cell. Again, choose one that will permit your next move. Assign a + sign to the cell.

4. Continue this process of moving to completed cells and alternating + and − signs until you complete a closed path back to the original cell. Make only horizontal and vertical moves.

Note: You may find it helpful to place a small dot or checkmark in cells that have been evaluated to help keep track of them.

EXAMPLE 7

We will start with the northwest corner rule's initial feasible solution and attempt to improve with the stepping-stone method:

	A	B	C	D	Supply
1	2 200	4 100	1	3	300
2	8	2 100	6 200	5	300
3	6	1	4 100	2 100	200
Demand	200	200	300	100	800

Evaluation of the closed path corresponding to the unoccupied cell 1C shows the following:

$$
\begin{array}{ll}
1C & +1 \\
1B & -4 \\
2C & -6 \\
2B & \underline{+2} \\
& -7
\end{array}
$$

The cost will decrease by $7 for every unit added to cell 1C.

	A	B	C	D	Supply
1	2 200	4	1 100	3	300
2	8	2 200	6 100	5	300
3	6	1	4 100	2 100	200
Demand	200	200	300	100	800

The solution is optimal. The cost of the final solution is 200(2) + 200(2) + 100(1) + 100(6) + 100(4) + 100(2) = $2,100.

• SPECIAL PROBLEMS

Two cases associated with the transportation problem need special attention.

- *The unbalanced problem.*

  (a) If demand is less than supply, create a fictitious destination (or dummy destination).

  (b) If demand is greater than supply, create a dummy plant having a capacity exactly equal to the additional demand.

- *Degeneracy.*

In this situation, (a) there may be an excessive number of used cells in a solution or (b) there may be an insufficient number of unused cells in a solution. When degeneracy exists, a very simple "patch-up" will solve the problem. We simply place ε (epsilon), an exceedingly small number, in some cells. The cells with this in them can be used as stepping stones but have no effect on the cost of a solution. Consequently, if epsilon is still in the final solution, it can be ignored.

YOU SHOULD REMEMBER

The steps to be followed in a facility location decision follow:

1. Define the location goals and associated factors.

2. Identify the decision criteria—quantitative (e.g., cost) or qualitative (intangible).

3. Choose a decision model (e.g., break-even or factor ratings).

4. Select the location that best meets the criteria.

KNOW THE CONCEPTS

DO YOU KNOW THE BASICS?

1. In what ways can the location decision have an impact on the productive system?

2. How do manufacturing and service location decisions differ?

3. List basic approaches to location decisions.

4. What is a location factor rating and how does it work?

5. List the assumptions behind the center-of-gravity method. How does it work?

6. How do location problems for service facilities differ from those in manufacturing?

7. What information is needed to use the transportation method?

8. Why does a dummy row or a dummy column become necessary? Explain briefly.

9. How is the transportation method useful in location decisions?

10. Briefly explain the northwest corner rule.

TERMS FOR STUDY

center-of-gravity method
factor ratings
locational break-even analysis
modified distribution (MODI)
  method

northwest corner rule
stepping-stone method
transportation LP problem
Vogel's approximation method
  (VAM)

PRACTICAL APPLICATION

1. Dry Seal, Inc., is trying to decide between two location sites, A and B. The following data applies to A and B.

Potential Location	Revenue per Unit ($)	Variable Cost per Unit ($)	Fixed Cost per Year ($)
A	50	32	60,000
B	48	29	80,000

Variable cost includes direct material, direct labor, and transportation cost.

a. Which site would yield the higher profit at an annual volume of 9,000 units?

b. At what volume would the company be indifferent between the two alternative sites in terms of annual profits?

2. Angela is considering two location alternatives, A and B. The relevant data follow:

Potential Location	Variable Cost per Unit ($)	Fixed Cost per Year ($)
A	63	300,000
B	32	800,000

Sales volume is estimated to be 25,000 units per year. Which location is most attractive?

3. Given the data on scores of three location sites:

		Location		
Factor	Weight	X	Y	Z
Raw Materials	0.4	80	70	80
Market	0.2	40	60	80
Transportation Cost	0.1	90	70	50
Labor Cost	0.2	70	70	60
Construction Cost	0.1	90	80	60

Which site would you choose? Why?

4. Determine the optimum location for a distribution center to serve the following locations. Shipments to each location will be about equal.

Destination	(x, y)
A	2, 2
B	5, 6
C	6, 3
D	7, 5

5. For the destinations and shipping quantities shown below, determine the center-of-gravity location:

Destination	(x, y)	Quantity
A	3, 5	600
B	5, 1	400
C	6, 7	300
D	8, 4	500

6. Given the transportation program below, use MODI to determine if it is optimal. If not optimal, obtain the optimal solution.

	X	Y	Z	Supply
1	4 10	7	1	10
2	3 20	8 20	4	40
3	5	6 30	2 20	50
Demand	30	50	20	100

7. Given the following transportation program:

	A	B	C	D	Supply
1	10	15	8	20	7
2	3	2	7	15	5
3	8	11	12	18	3
Demand	4	2	3	6	15

a. Determine the shipping program by the northwest corner rule. What is the total shipping cost for this solution?

b. Determine the shipping program by the VAM. What is the total shipping cost for this solution?

c. See if the VAM solution is optimal.

ANSWERS

DO YOU KNOW THE BASICS?

1. Location decisions can have an impact on access to markets; costs of materials, labor, rent, and transportation; quality of work life; and growth potential.

2. Manufacturing firms are more concerned with location of raw materials, transportation costs, availability of infrastructure, and the like, whereas service operations focus more on convenience, access to markets, traffic flow, and customer service.

3. Four popular methods used in location decisions are locational break-even analysis, factor ratings, center-of-gravity method, and transportation LP method.

4. Factor rating is a qualitative technique used to develop an overall composite index for relative attractiveness. It involves identifying relevant factors, assigning relative weights to these factors, and rating each alternative site with respect to the factors.

5. The assumptions are that shipping between locations costs are constant and that demands are constant. The method aims at minimizing the weighted distance between the warehouse and its supply/distribution points.

6. In manufacturing, distribution costs and service times are the important factors, while for services the location with respect to demand and competition as well as response time are the crucial factors.

7. The following information is needed: (a) supply available from each origin (plant), (b) demand at each destination (market), and (c) transportation cost per unit for each origin/destination combination.

8. A dummy is added to supply or demand, whichever is lower.

9. The transportation LP method can be used to compare the total cost of alternative locations in terms of their shipping costs.

10. The northwest corner rule works as follows: (a) starting with the far left-hand side corner, set the level of this route at either the requirements or the availability, which is smaller, and (b) proceed across the table in a general northwest-to-southeast direction, exhausting the availabilities of one row before moving down to the next and exhausting the requirements of one column before moving on to the next.

PRACTICAL APPLICATION

1.
   a. Total profit = Total revenue – Total cost
   For site A: $50(9,000 units) – $32(9,000) – $60,000 = $102,000.
   For site B: $48(9,000 units) – $29(9,000) – $80,000 = $91,000.
   The answer is site A.

   b. $50Q – $32Q – $60,000 = $48Q – $29Q – $80,000$, or
   $18Q – $60,000 = $19Q – $80,000$. Solving for Q we obtain $Q = 20,000$ units.

2. At the expected demand of 25,000 units, total costs for the alternatives are:

   For site A: $63(25,000) + $300,000 = $1,875,000.
   For site B: $32(25,000) + $800,000 = $1,600,000.

   Location B is more attractive, although annual fixed costs are much higher than for A.

3. Composite scores are: X = 72, Y = 69, and Z = 71, as shown in the following table. Choose X because it gives the highest composite.

Factor	Weight	X Score	X Weighted Scores	Y	Y Weighted Scores	Z	Z Weighted Scores
Raw Material	0.4	80	32	70	28	80	32
Market	0.2	40	8	60	12	80	16
Transportation Cost	0.1	90	9	70	7	50	5
Labor Cost	0.2	70	14	70	14	60	12
Construction Cost	0.1	90	9	80	8	60	6
			72		69		71

4.

$$\bar{x} = (2 + 5 + 6 + 7)/4 = 20/4 = 5$$

$$\bar{y} = (2 + 6 + 3 + 5)/4 = 16/4 = 4$$

The optimum location is at (5, 4) of x and y coordinates.

5.

$$\bar{x} = \frac{3(600) + 5(400) + 6(300) + 8(500)}{600 + 400 + 300 + 500} = \frac{9600}{1800} = 5.33$$

$$\bar{y} = \frac{5(600) + 1(400) + 7(300) + 4(500)}{600 + 400 + 300 + 500} = \frac{7500}{1800} = 4.17$$

The center of gravity is at 5.33, 4.17.

6.

$$u_1 + v_1 = 4$$

$$u_2 + v_1 = 3$$

$$u_2 + v_2 = 8$$

$$u_3 + v_2 = 6$$

$$u_3 + v_3 = 2$$

Setting $u_1 = 0$ yields $v_1 = 4$, $u_2 = -1$, $v_2 = 9$, $v_3 = 5$, and $u_3 = -3$.
Using these values, we compute $c_{ij} - u_i - v_i$ for unoccupied cells:

$$c_{12} - u_1 - v_2 = 7 - 0 - 9 = -2$$

$$c_{13} - u_1 - v_3 = 1 - 0 - 5 = -4$$

$$c_{23} - u_2 - v_3 = 4 - (-1) - 5 = 0$$

$$c_{31} - u_3 - v_1 = 5 - (-3) - 4 = 4$$

Thus, the initial solution is not optimal. One improvement (moving 10 units to 1Z) gives an optimal solution. Actually, there are two optimal solutions to this problem:

a. 1Z = 10, 2X = 30, 2Y = 10, 3Y = 40, and 3Z = 10; total transportation cost = $440.

b. 1Z = 10, 2X = 30, 2Z = 10, and 3Y = 50 with the same total transportation cost.

7.

a.

	A	B	C	D	Supply
1	10 4	15 2	8 1	20	7
2	3	2 2	7 3	15 3	5
3	8	11	12	18 3	3
Demand	4	2	3	6	15

Total shipping cost is $191.

b.

	A	B	C	D	Supply	Column Penalty
1	10	15	8	20	7	2
2	3	2	7	15	5	1
3	8	11	12	18	3	3
Demand	4	2	3	6	15	
Row Penalty	5	(9)	1	3		

	A	B	C	D	Supply	Column Penalty
1	10	15	8	20	7	2
2	3	2 2	7	15	5	4
3	8	11	12	18	3	4
Demand	4	2	3	6	15	
Row Penalty	(5)	x	1	3		

	A	B	C	D	Supply	Column Penalty
1	10	15	8	20	7	2
2	3 3	2 2	7	15	5	4
3	8	11	12	18	3	4
Demand	4	2	3	6	15	
Row Penalty	(5)	x	1	3		

	A	B	C	D	Supply	Column Penalty
1	10	15	8	20	7	2
2	3 3	2 2	7	15	5	x
3	8	11	12	18	3	4
Demand	4	2	3	6	15	
Row Penalty	2	x	4	2		

	A	B	C	D	Supply	Column Penalty
1	10	15	3 8	20	7	(10)
2	3 3	2 2	7	15	5	x
3	8	11	12	18	3	(10)
Demand	4	2	3	6	15	
Row Penalty	2	x	x	2		

The final solution by VAM is:

	A	B	C	D	Supply
1	10 1	15	8 3	20 3	7
2	3 3	2 2	7	15	5
3	8	11	12	18 3	3
Demand	4	2	3	6	15

The cost is $1(10) + 3(8) + 3(20) + 3(3) + 2(2) + 3(18) = \$161$.

c. Requiring that $u_i + v_j = c_{ij}$ for all the occupied cells leads to a system of six equations and seven variables:

for 1A, $u_1 + v_1 = 10$
for 1C, $u_1 + v_3 = 8$
for 1D, $u_1 + v_4 = 20$
for 2A, $u_2 + v_1 = 3$
for 2B, $u_2 + v_2 = 2$
for 3D, $u_3 + v_4 = 18$

Setting $u_1 = 0$ and solving the value of the other variables yields: $v_1 = 10$, $v_3 = 8$, $v_4 = 20$, $u_2 = -7$, $v_2 = 9$, and $u_3 = -2$.

The computation for net change, $c_{ij} = u_i - v_j$ for all other unoccupied cells follows:

for 1B, $c_{12} - u_1 - v_2 = 15 - 0 - 9 = 6$

for 2C, $c_{23} - u_2 - v_3 = 7 - (-7) - 8 = 6$

for 2D, $c_{24} - u_2 - v_4 = 15 - (-7) - 20 = 2$

for 3A, $c_{31} - u_3 - v_1 = 8 - (-2) - 10 = 0$

for 3B, $c_{32} - u_3 - v_2 = 11 - (-2) - 9 = 4$

for 3C, $c_{33} - u_3 - v_3 = 12 - (-2) - 8 = 6$

Because they are all positive, the VAM solution is optimal.

6
DESIGN OF THE WORK SYSTEM AND WORK MEASUREMENT

KEY TERMS

job design determination of specific job tasks and responsibilities, the work environment, and work methods.

learning curve effect reduction in labor hours as the cumulative production doubles, ranging typically from 10% to 20%.

motion study analysis of manual task in order to improve productivity.

MTM (methods time measurement) system of predetermined motion-time data used to develop standards for highly repetitive tasks.

operation chart often called right-handed, left-handed chart; chart used to describe simultaneous motions of hands when performing a task.

time standard amount of time required to perform a task by a trained operator working at a normal pace and using a prescribed method.

time study development of standards through stopwatch observation.

work measurement process of estimating the amount of worker time required to generate one unit of output.

work sampling work measurement technique involving the sampling of the nature of the activity in which the worker is involved; used for the broader problem of determining production standards.

One of the greatest assets a company has is its human resources. Because the largest portion of a company's employees often are found in the operation function, it is important to consider the jobs or work people perform within operations. The changing nature of work has been influenced most significantly by the advancement of technology. The majority of work now consists of some form of interface between people and machines. This relationship has significantly changed the nature of workers' tasks. Therefore, a large part of the operations manager's concern with the design of a work system will center around people, machines, and their relationship. Work design is primarily concerned with examination and evaluation of existing or proposed methods of performing work. Job design consists of developing the best way the individual tasks or jobs within the work system can be performed.

In this chapter, we examine some aspects of job and work design. In the latter part of the chapter, we address the related subjects such as how to measure work and how to determine performance standards. Learning curve phenomena can be incorporated into determining production standards.

WORK AND JOB DESIGN

One of the important aspects of the design of the physical system is the design of the jobs. Job design results in part from the preceding phase of facility layout, and the layout configuration results in part from job design. As noted in Chapter 7 on facility layout, the overall organization of work must be considered at the time of layout, and any given organization of activities has a particular impact on the layout. Conversely, if the technology is considered dominant, basic layout configurations are decided on, and job design is affected. Thus, there is an interaction between the design of the technological system and the design of the social or man system to produce a unified sociotechnical system design. Within this process, one particular dimension has received a great deal of attention since the days of Adam Smith. That dimension is the degree to which division of labor will be used. Job enlargement represents an opposing view of work organization, using job satisfaction as its major criterion. American business and industry, however, regard job satisfaction as a very important subcriterion, with economic considerations being dominant.

MAN–MACHINE SYSTEMS

The entire spectrum of work from the purely manual to the completely automatic can be conceptualized within the framework of man–machine systems. In fact, one of the important tasks of job design is to allocate to humans and machines the activities to which they are each best suited. In performing work, human functions fall into three classifications:

- Receiving information through the various sense organs.
- Making decisions based on information received and stored in the human memory.
- Taking action based on decisions.

Note how man's functions neatly fall within the general structure of a closed-loop automated system.

When humans and machines are viewed outside an economic basis for allocating tasks to them, it appears that the kinds of tasks most appropriate for humans and machines fall within the following general guidelines:

- Humans appear to surpass existing machines in their ability to

    detect small amounts of light and sound,

    receive and organize patterns of light and sound,

    improvise and use flexible procedures,

    store large amounts of information for long periods and recall relevant facts at the appropriate time,

    reason inductively,

    exercise judgment, and

    develop concepts and create methods.

- Existing machines appear to surpass humans in their ability to

    respond quickly to control signals,

    apply great force smoothly and precisely,

    perform repetitive and routine tasks,

    store information briefly and then erase it completely,

    perform rapid computations, and

    perform many different functions simultaneously.

CONCEPTS

People and machines perform similar functions in doing work, although they each have comparative advantages. The functions they perform are divided into the four basic classes: sensing, information storage, information processing, and action. In completely manual systems, all the functions are performed by humans. At the other end of the spectrum, in completely automatic systems, all the functions are performed by machines. In the common situation between the two extremes, involving teamwork between humans and machines, the functions are allocated and/or shared between men and machines, and such systems may be semiautomatic. Thus, in conceptualizing man–machine systems, it is useful to establish the classifications manual, semiautomatic, and automatic systems, noting that in all three classifications the basic closed-loop feedback structure is operating.

Manual systems involve humans, commonly with mechanical aids or hand tools. Humans are the power source, and they act as controllers of the process, using the tools to help multiply their efforts.

Semiautomatic systems involve men mainly as controllers of processes where they interact with the machine by sensing information about the processes, interpreting it, and manipulating controls. The power source is usually supplied by the machine or is shared in some combination between humans and machine.

Automatic systems combine all the functions of sensing, information storage and processing, and action within the machine system. If the machine is truly automatic, then it must be fully programmed to sense and take required action in all possible situations, and this is not usually economically justified. Man, therefore, normally functions as a monitor to assist with process control.

All three types of man–machine systems operate in some kind of working environment, which is a combination of temperature, humidity, noxious gases, noise, vibration, and other factors.

In a sense, the semiautomatic kind of operation is fully representative of the general range of activities found in man–machine systems. In such a situation, man is receiving and interpreting information about the process from information displays, manipulating mechanisms for control, and maintaining a general surveillance. The machine responds to these control actions to convert input to output. Thus, manipulative activity represents the dominant features of manual systems; information input, sensing, and controlling activities are representative of both semiautomatic and automatic systems; and information input and general monitoring activities are representative of automatic systems. The environmental and physical relationships of man to the work flow and workplace arrangement apply to all man–machine systems. Therefore, it is useful to divide the material dealing with man–machine systems into the following main headings: information input, human manipulative and control activities, and the work environment.

INFORMATION INPUT

In man–machine systems, human sensing can be direct, but it is becoming increasingly indirect, placing emphasis on encoding and information display systems. The design of these display systems for information input to humans is important if operations are to be effective. Although input to the human eyes is most common, auditory and tactual input is also used.

• *VISUAL DISPLAYS*

A guideline for designing visual displays follows:

- Dials should be about 2.75–3 inches in diameter for a reading distance of up to 30 inches.

- Dial marks should be located at the 0, 5, 10, 15, etc., positions. The marks at the 0, 10, 20, etc., positions should be longer than the others and should be the only ones numbered.

- The distance between numbered markers on dials should be about 0.5 inch.

- The separation between scale markers should be uniform around the dial.

- There should be a gap between the beginning and the end of the scale.

- Values on the scale should increase in a clockwise direction.

- Banks of dials should be oriented in a pattern so that normal readings are in the 9 or 12 o'clock positions.

• *AUDITORY AND TACTUAL DISPLAYS*

Auditory displays have particular value as warning devices or as devices to attract attention. They are also used when vision is impaired. Tactual displays are sometimes used to code control knobs by shape so that they can be identified by touch.

HUMAN MANIPULATIVE AND CONTROL ACTIVITIES

Given information input by direct or indirect means, the human operator of man–machine systems responds by performing work in the physical sense. He may be assembling objects, manipulating controls, and in general using his body to accomplish the required tasks within the objectives of the system.

• *ANALYSIS OF MANUAL ACTIVITY*

The analytical methods commonly used for manual activity are charts and graphs that display how the activity is carried out. Flow charts have been developed for use in various specific situations.

The principles of motion economy are a set of general statements concerning the arrangement of work, the use of the human hands and body, and the design and use of tools. These guides to job design have general applicability, even though they are not in fact principles in the strict sense of the word.

• *ANALYSIS OF CONTROL ACTIVITY*

A great deal of research concerning manual control activity has been performed. It may be summarized under the following headings:

- A knowledge of the forces that humans can exert in various positions and with different parts of the body.

- Data on the speed and accuracy of various kinds of positioning movements.

- Data concerning positioning through settings of dials, cranks, and handwheels.

- Coding of controls by color, size, shape, or location.

- Work area limits.

- Chair and table heights.

THE WORK ENVIRONMENT

• *TEMPERATURE, HUMIDITY, AND AIRFLOW*

The sensation of warmth is affected by each of these factors and has been combined into a single psychological scale called *effective temperature*. Effective temperature is the temperature of still, saturated air that gives the same sensation of warmth or cold as various combinations of air temperature, humidity, and air movement would. Elevated effective temperature has a marked effect on both mental and physical work.

• *NOISE*

Research data show that hearing loss with age is characteristic of the general population, even of persons not exposed to high-noise environments. However, the severity of hearing loss depends on the intensity of exposure. It appears that the effects of noise on work performance are minimal.

• *LIGHT*

Various lighting criteria have been used in research studies. However, critical illumination levels seem to be preferable for performance types of criteria. The critical level of illumination for a given task is that level beyond which there is practically no increase in performance for increases in illumination intensity. Lighting standards based on critical illumination levels have been set for a wide variety of generalized tasks.

• *CONTAMINANTS AND HAZARDS*

A large number of fumes, dusts, gases, liquids, and solids have proved harmful to workers. These, together with the general mechanical hazards from machine moving parts, traffic from material transportation, falling objects, and the like, form a part of the work environment.

WORK MEASUREMENT AND PRODUCTION STANDARDS

Standards are highly desirable for almost every kind of organized work. Managers need to have some idea of how long work will take, how many employees will be needed, and what it will cost. Only with this information can they make intelligent decisions about schedules, facilities, people needed, costs, and selling prices. Work measurement is the methodology by which production standards are determined. Production standards, in turn, are the basis for judging what represents a "fair day's work."

PRODUCTION STANDARDS

• *USES OF STANDARDS*

Production standards provide basic data for many decision-making problems as well as for many day-to-day operating problems. They are particularly important where labor cost is a predominant factor. Some of their uses follow:

- Assessing the labor component for decision problems such as make versus buy, equipment replacement, and process selection.

- Conducting day-to-day operations in the scheduling or loading of machines, giving promised delivery dates, providing bid prices to customers, and the like.

- Establishing the basis for labor cost control and incentive wage payment systems.

• *THE ESSENCE OF THE STANDARDS DETERMINATION PROBLEM*

Actually, in order to set production standards, it would be necessary to know the distribution of performance times (or production rates) for the entire working population for each specific job. If we knew the distribution for each job, it would be a simple matter to establish the standard at some particular point in the distribution, (e.g., either at the average of the distribution or possibly at a level that would accommodate perhaps 95% of the working population). Ordinarily, however, there may be only one or two individuals on the job whose work can be measured. The problem, therefore, is to estimate the nature of the entire distribution based on sample data from only one or two workers on the job. This is done by measuring the time actually taken during work performance while rating that performance. The actual time is then adjusted by the performance rating to produce the so-called normal time. The normal time is then augmented by allowances for personal time, delays, and fatigue to produce the standard time.

• *PERFORMANCE RATING*

The crucial element in the methodology is, then, the performance rating process because it enters standards determination as a factor and is based on judgment and experience. The process follows: a pace or performance level is selected as standard, and the analyst observes this pace, comparing it with other paces and learning to judge pace level in percent of the standard pace.

EXAMPLE 1

If for a certain job normal pace were associated with a cycle time of 0.48 minutes, a pace of work 25% faster would require proportionately less time per cycle, or $0.48/1.25 = 0.384$ minutes. A skilled analyst observing the working pace and measuring the cycle time, 0.384 minutes, would rate the performance at 125% of normal. By multiplying his observed time by the performance rating in decimals, he would obtain the normal time for the job ($0.384 \times 1.25 = 0.48$ minutes).

All formal measurement systems require the input of the performance rating in some way.

• *RATING AS A MEASUREMENT SYSTEM*

Two things are needed to be able to measure anything:

- An accepted standard for comparison.

- A scale or unit of measurement.

Performance rating meets these two requirements in the following ways.

Standards for comparison have been developed for a large number of different kinds of factory and clerical operations in the form of motion-picture films. In each instance, various working paces are shown. The films have been rated by thousands of experienced analysts, and their judgments concerning the selection of normal working pace have been pooled. The films are then used as a basis for training time study of personnel and for retraining them.

Two different scales have been adopted and are in common use. Both are calibrated in percent of normal, although one of them selects normal performance to be at the mean of the distribution, whereas the other establishes normal performance at a level that can be exceeded by approximately 95% of the working population.

Commonly accepted figures for the accuracy of performance rating by experienced analysts are ±5%. Controlled studies in which films have been rated indicate a standard deviation of 7–10%. Given the strong element of judgment in the process, these limits of accuracy are fairly good.

WORK MEASUREMENT SYSTEMS

There are two major work measurement systems designed to determine normal time by somewhat different methods: nonengineered and engineered standards. Nonengineered standards are less costly and more frequently used. They include historical (statistical) data and technical estimate. Engineered time standards are determined scientifically, with great precision. They include time study (stopwatch methods), work sampling, predetermined standards, and standard data systems.

TIME STUDY (STOPWATCH) METHODS

Time study methods are the most commonly used and employ a stopwatch coupled with a performance rating to determine normal time. The general procedure follows:

1. Standardize methods of operation, and record the resulting standard practice.

2. Select an operator experienced and trained in the standard methods.

3. Compute cycle time (CT)—time each task element over a number of cycles (repetitions). The average time for each task element is its cycle time.

4. Determine a performance rating (PR), a rating of the pace at which the employee performed each task element. For example, if the pace was 10% faster than normal, a performance rating assigned is 1.1 or 110%.

5. Compute normal time (NT).

6. Determine allowances (A) for personal time, delays, and fatigue. If allowances as a percentage of total time come out to be 10%, the A value is 0.10.

7. Compute standard time (ST).

The number of cycles times is a function of the variability of observed times, the desired accuracy, and the desired level of confidence for the estimated job time. The desired accuracy is often stated as a percentage of the average of the observed time. The sample size needed to achieve a certain level of accuracy can be computed using the formula:

$$n = \left(\frac{zs}{a\bar{x}} \right)^2$$

where s = sample standard deviation of representative observed times for a work element

a = desired accuracy as a proportion of the true value

$\bar{x}$ = sample mean of select time for a work element

z = number of normal standard deviations needed to achieve desired confidence

Typical values of z used in this computation are

Desired Confidence Percent	z value
90	1.65
95	1.96
99	2.58

Of course, the value of z for any desired confidence can be obtained from the normal distribution table.

An alternative formula used when the desired accuracy is expressed as n amount is

$$n = \left(\frac{zs}{e} \right)^2$$

where e = desired accuracy (e.g., within one minute of the true mean)

EXAMPLE 2

A time study analyst wished to estimate the time required to perform a certain job. A preliminary work showed a mean of 6 minutes and a standard deviation of 2 minutes. The desired confidence is 95%. What's the sample size needed if the desired error is (a) ± 10% and (b) 0.5 minute of the sample mean?

a. Note that $s = 2$, $\bar{x} = 6$, $z = 1.96$, and $a = 10\%$.

$$n = \left(\frac{zs}{\bar{a}}\right)^2 = \left(\frac{1.96(2)}{0.1(6)}\right)^2 = 42.68$$

b. $e = 0.5$

$$n = \left(\frac{zs}{e}\right)^2 = \left(\frac{1.96(2)}{0.5}\right)^2 = 61.47$$

Developing a time standard involves computing the observed time or cycle time (CT), the normal time (NT), and the standard time (ST).

$$CT = \Sigma \text{ Times}/n \text{ cycles}$$

$$NT = CT \times PR$$

$$ST = NT \times A$$

Note: There are two cases for allowances. If allowances are a percentage of the work (job) time: $A = 1 + A_{work}$. If allowances are a percentage of the total (workday) time: $A = 1/(1 - A_{total})$.

EXAMPLE 3

A time study revealed the following observed times for a job:

Observation	1	2	3	4	5
Time, x (minutes)	1.15	1.16	1.12	1.15	1.12

The analyst gave a performance rating of 1.2 for this job. Determine the appropriate standard time for this operation, assuming allowances for personal needs, delays, and fatigue total 15%.

n = 5, PR = 1.2, A = 0.2

a. The cycle time = Σ Times/n cycles = 5.7/5 = 1.14.

b. The normal time = CT × PR = 1.14(1.2) = 1.37 minutes.

c. The standard time (ST) = NT × A = NT(1 + A_{work}) = 1.37(1.15) = 1.58 minutes. In an eight-hour day, a worker would produce 8 × 60/1.58, or 304 units. This implies 304 minutes working and 480 − 304 = 176 minutes for allowances. Using the total work period, ST = NT[1/(1 − A_{total})] = 1.37 [(1/(1 − 0.15)] = 1.61 minutes. In the same eight-hour day, 8 × 60/1.61, or 298 units are produced with 298 working minutes and 182 minutes for allowances. Depending on which equation is used, there is a difference of 6 minutes in the daily allowance time.

WORK SAMPLING

Work sampling is a random sampling technique designed originally as a methodology for estimating delay allowances. Later, it was applied to the determination of normal time as well. The technique involves observing the worker at many randomly selected moments and observing the proportion of time the worker is actively working or idle. When the worker is observed to be idle, the reason for idleness can be recorded in order to identify and eliminate problems. The fundamental principle that allows the conversion of these kinds of observations to percentage delay allowances and normal time is the fact that the *number* of observations is proportional to *the amount of time spent* in the working or idle state.

• *DETERMINING SAMPLE SIZE*

Tables and charts are available for finding the proper size sample for the desired level of accuracy, with a given percentage of occurrences of the activity being studied, at the 95% confidence level. Such tables have been derived by using the following formulas:

$$e = z \sqrt{ \bar{p}(1 - \bar{p})/n }$$

where

$$\bar{p} = \frac{x}{n} = \frac{\text{Number observed in classification}}{\text{Total number of observations}}$$

where $\bar{p}$ is the percentage of occurrence of any class of observations being studied (i.e., working, delay).

For example, to maintain a precision in the estimate of $\bar{p}$ of ±1.0 percentage point at 95% confidence, 10,000 observations are required if $\bar{p}$ is in the neighborhood of 50%. By contrast, if $\bar{p}$ is only 10% and the tolerance on $\bar{p}$ is 2 percentage points, then the sample size required for 95% confidence is only approximately 900. Even though the sample sizes seem large, the observation required is simply a recognition of whether the employee is working or idle.

The appropriate sample size can be determined by solving the formula for n:

$$n = \left(\frac{z}{e}\right)^2 \bar{p}(1 - \bar{p})$$

EXAMPLE 4

To illustrate work sampling, assume that a study is made of an operation to determine the percentage of time a worker or group of workers are working. The observations are made at random, and a simple tally is made to indicate whether the operator was working or idle when each observation was made. A sample of the resultant tally of 60 observations made in a given day is given below.

State	Total	Percent
Working	49	81.7
Idle	11	18.3
Total	60	100

Note that the operator was working during 49 observations, or 81.7% of the time, and idle during 11 observations, or 18.3%.

To determine the sample size with an accuracy of +2%, and a confidence level of 95%, substitute into the formula, with $\bar{p}$ = 11/60 = 18% (rounded), as follows:

$$n = \left(\frac{z}{e}\right)^2 \bar{p}(1 - \bar{p}) = \left(\frac{1.96}{0.02}\right)^2 (0.18)(1 - 0.18) = 1{,}417.55 \text{ observations}$$

• *DETERMINATION OF STANDARDS*

If in the preceding procedure we had collected some additional data, we could also compute normal time. The additional data are the number of units produced during the total time of the study and the performance rating for each observation of the work time.

$$CT = \frac{\text{(Total time of study in minutes)} \times \text{(Work time \% from work sampling study)}}{\text{Total number of units produced}}$$

Studies indicate that production standards determined by work sampling and stopwatch methods are approximately equivalent.

The normal time and standard time would then be computed as follows:

$$NT = CT \times PR$$

$$ST = NT(1 + A)$$

EXAMPLE 5

A work-sampling of customer service representatives in a telephone company office revealed that a receptionist was working 84% of the time at 1.05 performance rating. This receptionist handles 200 customers during a 8-hour study period. Company policy is to give allowances of 10% of total on-the-job time. The CT, NT, and ST are

$$CT = \frac{480 \times 0.84}{200} = 2.02 \text{ minutes per customer}$$

$$NT = 2.02 \times 1.05 = 2.12 \text{ minutes per customer}$$

$$ST = 2.12(1.1) = 2.33 \text{ minutes per customer}$$

PREDETERMINED STANDARDS

Tables of predetermined standards for micromotions are available from the Methods Time Measurement (MTM) Association. These tables include micromotions such as reach, grasp, turn, release, and eye travel and focus. Tedious work is required by the analyst to select all the motions and link them together to describe a specific task.

STANDARD DATA

Standard times for particular tasks have been developed in certain industries. There are two kinds of standard data systems: universal data based on minute elements of motion (microdata) and standard data for job families (macrodata or element standard data).

- ## *UNIVERSAL STANDARD DATA*

Universal standard data give time values for motion elements, and cycle times are then synthesized by specifying the motions required to perform a given task. The time values associated with given motion elements were built up by measuring in conjunction with performance ratings the times taken for such elements in a wide variety of tasks. Therefore, the performance rating enters the system in that it is used in originally constructing the data. On the other hand, individual performance ratings are not required in order to estimate normal times for jobs. Universal standard data systems are known by various trade names: Methods Time Measurement (MTM), Work Factor, and Basic Motion Time Study.

- ## *STANDARD DATA FOR JOB FAMILIES*

These data give normal time values for major elements of jobs and are often called macrostandard data. Unlike universal standard data, these time values have been based on actual previous stopwatch studies within the job family. Recall that one of the reasons for the elemental breakdown in a stopwatch study is to provide data concerning the job families. Given a large number of studies, we may find how the normal time for some particular element varies with size, depth of cut, type of material, the way the workpiece is held in the machine, and the like.

HISTORICAL STANDARDS AND TECHNICAL ESTIMATES

Much work is variable and nonstandard. Frequently, historical averages of times to do different jobs are used. Sometimes, technical expertise is used to "guesstimate" task times.

YOU SHOULD REMEMBER

Work measurement systems designed to determine normal time include: time study (stopwatch) methods, work sampling, predetermined standards, standard data systems, historical (statistical) data, and technical estimates.

LEARNING CURVE

The learning curve is based on the proposition that labor hours decrease in a definite pattern as labor operations are repeated. More specifically, it is based on the statistical findings that as the cumulative production doubles, the cumulative average time required per unit will be reduced by some constant percentage, ranging typically from 10% to 20%. By convention, learning curves are referred to in terms of the complements of their improvement rates.

For example, an 80% learning curve denotes a 20% decrease in unit time with each doubling of repetitions. As an illustration, a project is known to have an 80% learning curve. It has just taken a laborer 10 hours to produce the first unit. Then each time the cumulative output doubles, the time per unit for that amount should be equal to the previous time multiplied by the learning percentage. An 80% learning curve is shown in Figure 6.1.

Unit	Unit Time (hours)
1	10
2	0.8(10) = 8
4	0.8(8) = 6.4
8	0.8(6.4) = 5.12
16	0.8(5.12) = 4.096

The learning curve model is

$$y_n = an^{-b}$$

where y_n = time for the nth unit

a = time for the first unit (in this example, 10 hours)

b = the index of the rate of increase in productivity during learning (Log learning rate/log 2)

To be able to use linear regression, we need to convert this power (or exponential) function form into a *linear* form by taking a log of both sides, which yields

$$\text{Log } y_n = \log a - b \log n$$

The learning rate, which is indicated by b, is estimated using a *least-squares regression*, with the sample data on y and n Note that

$$b = \frac{\log (\text{learning rate})}{\log 2}$$

which means

$$\log (\text{learning rate}) = b \times \log 2$$

The unit time (i.e., the number of labor hours required) for the nth can be computed using the estimated model:

$$y_n = an^{-b}$$

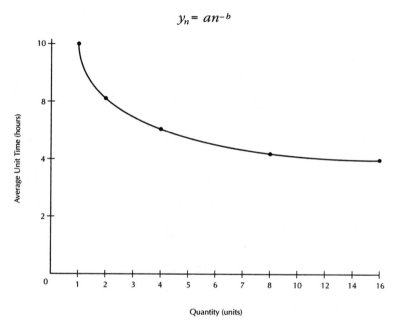

Figure 6.1. An 80% Learning Curve

YOU SHOULD REMEMBER

This learning phenomenon is observed in the behavior of labor and labor-driven overhead. Material costs per unit may also be subject to this effect if less scrap and waste occur as a result of learning.

EXAMPLE 6

For an 80% curve with $a = 10$ hours, the time for the third unit would be computed as

$$y_3 = 10 \ (3^{-\log 0.8/ \log 2}) = 10 \ (3^{0.3219}) = 7.02$$

Fortunately, it is not necessary to grid through this model each time a learning calculation is made; values (*nb*) can be found using Table 4 of Appendix II. The time for the *n*th unit can be quickly determined by multiplying the table value by the time required for the first unit.

EXAMPLE 7

NB Contractors, Inc., is negotiating a contract involving the production of 20 jets. The initial jet required 200 labor-days of direct labor. Assuming an 80% learning curve, we will determine the expected number of labor-days for (a) the 20th jet and (b) all 20 jets. Using Table 4 in Appendix II with *n* = 20 and an 80% learning rate, we find Unit = 0.381 and Total = 10,485. Therefore,

   a. Expected time for the 20th jet = 200(0.381) = 76.2 labor-days.

   b. Expected total time for all 20 jets = 200(10.485) = 2,097 labor-days.

YOU SHOULD REMEMBER

The learning curve theory has found useful applications in many areas, including

Budgeting, purchasing, and inventory planning

Scheduling labor requirements

Setting incentive wage rates

Pricing new products

Negotiating purchases

Evaluating suppliers' price quotations

Example 8 illustrates the use of the learning curve theory for the pricing of a contract.

EXAMPLE 8

Big Mac Electronics Products, Inc., finds that new product production is affected by an 80% learning effect. The company has just produced 50 units of output at 100 hours per unit. Costs were as follows:

Materials 50 units @ $20	$1,000
Labor and labor-related costs:	
Direct labor—100 hours @ $8	800
Variable overhead—100 hours @ $2	200
	$2,000

The company has just received a contract calling for another 50 units of production. It wants to add a 50% markup to the cost of materials and labor and labor-related costs. To determine the price for this job, the first step is to build up the learning curve table.

Quantity	Total Time (hours)	Average Time (per unit)
50	100	2 hours
100	160	1.6 (0.8 × 2 hours)

Thus, for the new 50 unit job, it takes 60 hours in total. The contract price is

Materials 50 units @ $20	$1,000
Labor and labor-related costs:	
Direct labor—60 hours @ $8	480
Variable overhead—60 hours @ $2	120
	$1,600
50% markup	800
Contract price	$2,400

KNOW THE CONCEPTS

DO YOU KNOW THE BASICS?

1. Distinguish between job design and work design.
2. Why is job design important? List the important factors that must be addressed in job design.

3. What are some of the reasons that methods analyses are needed?
4. How are devices such as flow process charts and man–machine charts useful?
5. List the various approaches to work measurement.
6. What is a time standard? What factors must be taken into account when developing standards?
7. What are some of the main uses of time study information?
8. What is the procedure for developing a time study?
9. Give some examples of learning curve applications.
10. Why might practicing managers and industrial engineers be skeptical about the job enrichment and sociotechnical approaches to job design?

TERMS FOR STUDY

flow process chart
job design
learning curve effect
motion study
MTM (Methods Time Measurement)

multiple-activity chart
operation chart
time standard
time study
work sampling

PRACTICAL APPLICATION

1. An analyst observed 28-week cycles, for which the average cycle time was 5 minutes and the performance rating was 1.05. Allowance for the department is 25% of job time. Determine the appropriate standard time for this job.
2. Given the following time study data conducted by continuous time measurement, compute the standard time. Use an allowance of 15%.

Cycle of Observation

Activity	1	2	3	4	5	Performance Rating (PR)
Get casting	0.21	0.21	0.21	0.23	0.20	0.95
Fix into fixture	0.27	0.28	0.25	0.26	0.25	0.90
Drilling operation	1.04	1.05	1.00	1.04	1.04	1.00
Unload	0.21	1.19	0.25	0.20	0.22	0.95
Inspect	0.25	0.26	0.24	0.21	0.25	0.80
Replace	0.12	0.12	0.10	0.12	0.13	1.10

3. Comfort Faucet Manufacturing wants to have a 90% probability that the value of the sample mean provides a sampling error of 0.01 minute or less. The estimated standard deviation from historical experience is 0.02. Determine the sample size that will provide the required precision.

4. The manager of a small supermarket chain wishes to estimate the proportion of time store clerks spend making price changes on previously marked merchandise. The manager wants a 95% confidence that the resulting estimate will be within 5% of the true value. Based on her previous experience, she believes that the proportion will be approximately 30%.

   a. What sample size would the manager need in order to achieve her goal?

   b. If the manager uses a sample size of 400 observations, what is the maximum possible error that will be associated with the estimate?

5. A work-sampling was made of a cargo-loading operation with the aim toward developing a standard time. During the total 160 minutes of observation, the worker was working 85% of the time and loaded 60 pieces of cargo. The performance was rated at 100%. The company wants to incorporate a 10% allowance factor for fatigue, delays, and personal time. What is the standard time for this operation in minutes per piece?

6. The typed examinations have just arrived from the word processing center after being collated in the proper page order. These sheets have to be stapled, a computer scoring sheet inserted in between, and a serial number has to be written on both the test sheets and the computer scoring sheet. If the number is odd, the sheet has to be placed in the bin on the left; if it is even, it has to be stored in a bin on the right. The layout is given in Figure 6.2.

7.

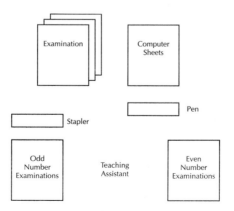

Figure 6.2. The Layout for Midterm Exams Activity

Construct an operation chart for the activity of preparing midterm examinations.

8. A worker is operating two semiautomatic machines matching similar components. The loading and unloading times are 20 seconds and the operating time is 45 seconds.

   a. Construct a multiple activity chart for this case.

   b. Calculate the utilization of the operator and the total output per hour.

9. Assembly of a transistor unit has a learning curve of 80%. Estimated time to build the second unit is 64 hours. Calculate about how much time will be required for:

   a. the eighth unit.

   b. the first ten units.

10. The first P/OM problem Allison did in a set of similar problems took her 1 hour, and the ninth problem took 24 minutes.

    a. Determine Allison's learning curve.

    b. How long did it take Allison to do her set of ten problems?

11. Carson, Inc., uses a learning curve of 80% for all new products it develops. A trial run of 500 units of a new product shows total labor-related costs (direct labor, indirect labor, and fringe benefits) of $120,000. Management plans to produce 1,500 units of the new product during the next year.

    a. Compute the expected labor-related costs for the year to produce the 1,500 units.

    b. Find the unit cost of production for next year for labor-related costs.

ANSWERS

DO YOU KNOW THE BASICS?

1. Work design is primarily concerned with examination and evaluation of existing or proposed methods of performing work. Job design consists of developing the best way the individual tasks or jobs within the work system can be performed.

2. Job design is important because it has a significant impact on the efficiency and productivity of workers. The factors that need to be addressed in job design are design of work methods, work measurement,

design of physical workplace, and design of the physical, social, and psychological environment.

3. The need for methods analysis can come from changes in tools and equipment, changes in product or service design, introduction of new products, changes in methods and procedures, and changes in government regulations or contractual agreements.

4. The approaches to work measurement include historical data, time study, predetermined data, standard data, and work sampling.

5. Flow process charts and man–machine charts are useful in reviewing and analyzing operations in terms of sequence and workflow. They provide a visual mode of the work.

6. A time standard reflects the length of time a given task should take a qualified worker who works at a sustainable rate, using given methods and equipment, given material inputs, and a given workplace arrangement.

7. The information provided by time study is useful for scheduling, budgeting, manpower planning, cost and time estimation, designing incentive systems, and the like.

8. The procedure for developing a time study is to divide the task into smaller work elements, observe the time to perform each element several times, rate the performance of each work element, determine the normal element time, determine allowance, and determine the standard time.

9. The learning curve theory has found useful applications in many areas, including budgeting, purchasing, and inventory planning; scheduling labor requirements; setting incentive wage rates; pricing new products; and evaluating suppliers' price quotations.

10. Job enrichment by definition moves away from specialization, which, from a purely mechanical standpoint, is the most efficient way of work. Sociotechnical approaches include job enrichment as a design strategy and in addition emphasize worker and work group autonomy. Thus, managers and industrial engineers have legitimate concerns about the implications of these approaches on output, planning and control.

PRACTICAL APPLICATION

1. CT = 5 minutes, PR = 1.05, A = 25%. So, NT = 5 × 1.05 = 5.25 minutes; ST = 5.25(1.25) = 6.5625 minutes.

2.

Cycle of Observation

Activity	1	2	3	4	5	Average	Performance Rating (PR)	Normal Time
Get casting	0.21	0.21	0.21	0.23	0.20	0.21	0.95	0.201
Fix into fixture	0.27	0.28	0.25	0.26	0.25	0.26	0.90	0.236
Drilling operation	1.04	1.05	1.00	1.04	1.04	1.03	1.00	1.034
Unload	0.21	1.19	0.25	0.20	0.22	0.41	0.95	0.393
Inspect	0.25	0.26	0.24	0.21	0.25	0.24	0.80	0.194
Replace	0.12	0.12	0.10	0.12	0.13	0.12	1.10	0.130

Normal time = 2.188

Plus allowance (15%) = 2.516

3. Note that $s = 0.02$, $z = 1.645$, and $e = 0.01$.

$$n = \left(\frac{zs}{e}\right)^2 = \left(\frac{1.645(0.02)}{0.01}\right)^2 = 10.8$$

A sample size of 11 (or more) will provide the required precision.

4.

a.

$$n = \left(\frac{z}{e}\right)^2 \bar{p}(1 - \bar{p}) = \left(\frac{1.96}{0.05}\right)^2 (0.3)(0.7) = 322.69 \text{ or } 323 \text{ observations}$$

b.

$$e = z \sqrt{\bar{p}(1 - \bar{p})/n} = 1.96 \sqrt{(0.3)(0.7)/400} = 1.96(0.0327) = 0.064$$

5. The NT is

$$\text{Normal time} = \frac{160 \times 0.85 \times 1.0}{60} = 2.27 \text{ minutes per piece}$$

$$ST = 2.27 \times 1/(1 - 0.01) = 2.50 \text{ minutes per piece}$$

6. See Figure 6.3.

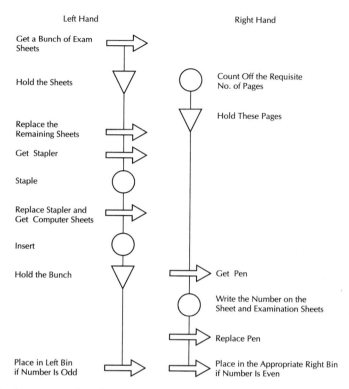

Figure 6.3. Operation Chart for the Activity of Preparing Midterm Examinations

7. See Figure 6.4.

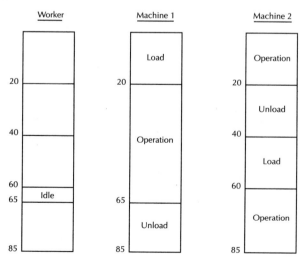

Figure 6.4. Multiple Activity Chart

   a. Operator utilization = 80/86 = 93.7%

   b. Total output = 2 pieces in 85 seconds, or (3,600/85) × 2 = 84.7 pieces per hour

8. The time for the initial unit is 64/.8 = 80 hours. Using Table 4 in Appendix II we find:

   a. Unit time for eighth unit: 80 × 0.512 = 40.96 hours

   b. Total time for ten units: 80 × 6.315 = 505.2 hours

9.

   a. Before going to Table 4 in Appendix II, we determine the factor 24 minutes/60 minutes = 0.4, which corresponds to the 4.02 in the table. Thus, there is approximately a 75% learning percentage.

   b. The total time for 10, using 75% is 60(5.589) = 335.34 minutes, or about 6 hours.

10.

   a. The 80% learning theory says that as cumulative quantities double, average time per unit falls to only 80% of the previous time. Therefore, the following data can be constructed:

Quantity (units)	Time Cost ($)	Average Cost Per Unit ($)
500	120,000	240
1,000	192,000	192 (80% x $240)
2,000	308,000	154 (80% x $192)

Thus,

Quantity	Total Cost ($)
2,000	308,000
500	120,000
1,500	188,000

Thus expected labor-related costs for the 1,500 units of output is $188,000.

   b. $125.33 per unit ($188,000/1,500 units)

7

FACILITIES DESIGN AND LAYOUT

Selection of a site does not complete all location considerations. After a site has been determined, the focus narrows to the location of various functions inside the work facility. Locating functions within a facility is called layout, plant layout, facility design, or facility management. *Layout* refers to the efforts involved in selecting specific locations for each department, process, machine, support functions, and other activity that will be a part of the operations at a facility. The need for a layout may arise for one or more reasons such as the following:

- A new process or method becomes available.

- The volume of business changes.

- A new product or service is offered.

- A new facility is to be built, or an outdated one is to be remodeled.

- The demanded mix of goods or services changes.

- Existing products or services may be redesigned, changing operations at a facility.

LAYOUT OF FACILITIES

In planning any operations system, no matter what type (intermittent, continuous, or batch), the major concern of the manager is to facilitate the flow of inputs. The layout of the processing facilities is a key to the achievement of this goal. This involves determining the best location of the equipment within the physical facilities to make the flow as close as optimal as possible.

The major goals of a good layout are to

Minimize materials-handling costs,

Reduce bottlenecks in moving material or people,

Provide flexibility,

Provide ease of supervision,

Utilize available space effectively and efficiently,

Reduce hazards to people, and

Facilitate ergonomics, coordination, and communications wherever appropriate.

MATERIAL-HANDLING METHODS

Because of the nature of product line layout, some direct means of transportation between operations is required. Thus, quite often, conveyors, industrial trucks, cranes and hoists, or gravity chutes can be used effectively. Where possible, the functions of internal transportation, processing, and storage can be integrated, all being accomplished on conveyor lines, as in many assembly operations.

Like the processing equipment itself, material-handling equipment in product layout tends to be special purpose, often designed for the specific situation.

CLASSICAL LAYOUT TYPES

The activities involved in production or service operations may be grouped and arranged in a variety of ways. Several popular types of layout are product layout, process layout, and fixed-position layout or a combination of them. In the product layout, the product and its flow dictate the design. In the process layout, the basic organization of technology is around processes. In the fixed-position layout, the construction of a large product is accomplished in one place.

PRODUCT LAYOUT

Product layout, also called *mass production layout, line layout,* and *straight-line layout,* is employed when the product is produced through a continuous process. Here the raw material enters the production line, and operations are performed on it in sequence until it goes out as a finished product. The product moves continuously, perhaps down a conveyor line past successive workstations where men and machines perform the necessary operations in sequence. Automobile and home appliance lines are examples of this type of layout. A schematic illustration of the nature of the product layout is shown in Figure 7.1.

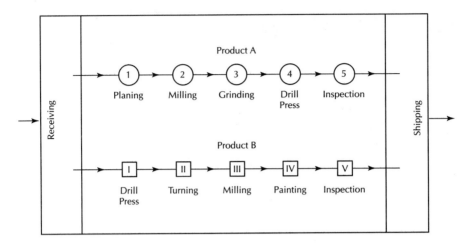

Figure 7.1. Schematic Representation of a Product Layout

When the conditions for product layout are met, we have a low-cost, highly specialized, very productive system. The requirements follow:

- An adequate volume that makes possible reasonable equipment use.

- Stable product demand.

- Product standardization.

- Part interchangeability.

- Continuous material supply.

The main advantage of product layout is its low production cost per unit. Production control is relatively simple, because product designs are stable and routes through the system are standardized.

The disadvantages of product layout are that the investment in single-purpose equipment is high, and the system is therefore open to obsolescence if product designs change. Also, if a machine in the sequence breaks down or men are absent, not only is the process immediately affected delayed but perhaps the entire line is delayed. Thus, seemingly minor stoppages or material shortages could be very costly. Also, the highly repetitive nature of the work has resulted in low job satisfaction and morale in many instances.

Product layout is most commonly used with assembly operations. Fabrication lines are less common because of the difficulty in attaining balance between operations. A common combination is for fabrication operations to be organized on a process basis and assembly on a product or fixed position basis.

PROCESS LAYOUT

In process layout, often called *functional* and *job lot layout,* all machines or processes of the same generic type are grouped together in what are commonly called machine centers or departments. The departments are technologically specialized in such processes as turning, grinding, heat treating, painting, assembly, castings, accounts receivable, and typing. This layout is suitable for batch or intermittent production. Workshops producing small quantities of products or factories producing batches of made-to-order products are examples of this type of plant layout.

The great advantages of process layout lie in the use of highly skilled workmen and/or very expensive equipment. The machines themselves are usually general purpose so that a wide variety of products, parts, sizes, and the like can be accommodated. Also, the items being processed may follow diverse paths through the various departments. Thus, flexibility is the watchword: flexibility of path, flexibility of product design, flexibility of lot size. If one machine breaks down, work can be transferred to a nearby machine that can do similar work, and the delay will rarely interfere with the progress of other orders through the plant. Process layout is particularly adaptable to parts and products made in relatively small batches because the machines and men are flexible.

The disadvantages of process layout stem from the general-purpose nature of the equipment and the great flexibility of the system. Orders moving through a process layout are likely to take considerable time. Work routing, scheduling, material handling and transportation, and cost accounting are relatively expensive because each order is treated as a unit. A schematic representation of a process layout is shown in Figure 7.2.

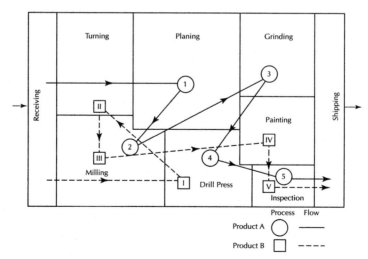

Figure 7.2. Schematic Representation of a Process Layout

The major economic problem of process layout lies in determining the relative location of the departments. Ordinarily, there are many possible combinations of relative arrangements; for example, for ten departments there would be 36,288 possible arrangements (10 factorial). Therefore, enumeration of each possibility is impossible.

GROUP LAYOUT

Group layout is a hybrid approach combining the features of product layout in a process layout context. It is used in more structured job shops.

CELLULAR LAYOUT

This is also a product-oriented layout and is useful when volumes do not warrant a specialized line to produce one product. Several operations are grouped together to produce one item or a family of goods, which use the same sequential set of operations. Cells are often formed by "stealing" equipment from various process-oriented areas, and personnel are cross-trained for several jobs. This is typical of just-in-time (JIT) manufacturing.

FIXED-POSITION LAYOUT

In a fixed-position layout, very large items such as large aircraft or residential construction product stay in a fixed location, and all the equipment and personnel are brought to it.

YOU SHOULD REMEMBER

	Advantages	Disadvantages
Product Layout	High utilization of equipment	Lack of process flexibility
	Reduced material handling	High-cost specialized equipment
	Less in-process inventory	Worker monotony
	Simplified production planning and control	Interdependent operations
Process Layout	Flexibility of equipment and worker	Costly material handling
	Low-cost general-purpose equipment	Low equipment use
	Higher job satisfaction	Complex control and supervision
	Low work breakdowns	High-cost skilled labor

	Advantages	Disadvantages
Fixed-Position Layout	Lower movement of the work item More continuity of assigned work force	Need of skilled and versatile workers Costly movement of equipment Low equipment use

MINIMIZATION OF MATERIAL-HANDLING COST

The major criterion for selecting good arrangements is material-handling cost. Because each product may take a different route through the system, the relative location chosen can result in a very large material-handling cost or a relatively small cost. Our objective, then, is to minimize the total incremental material handling cost C. In other words,

$$C = \sum_i \sum_j A_{ij} X_{ij} = \text{minimum}$$

where A_{ij} is the number of loads per unit of time transported between departments i and j, and X_{ij} is the distance between departments i and j. Thus, it is only the distance-related material-handling cost with which we are concerned. The pickup and set-down costs are presumed to be the same for all alternative arrangements.

SYSTEMATIC LAYOUT PLANNING

Systematic layout planning is a generalized approach to layout that indicates nearness priorities, taking into account factors other than transportation cost. Developed by Richard Muther, the method uses a half matrix or a similar equivalent grid to display the relative importance of the distance between locations such as departments (see Figure 7.3). The diamond-shaped boxes on the right-hand side of the figure are used to indicate the desired relationships between the two departments that intersect. A letter (a, e, i, o, or x) is used to depict the desired relationship, and a number is used to indicate a reason for the relationship.

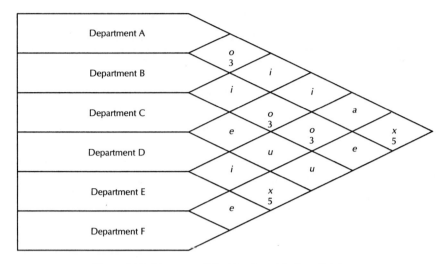

Figure 7.3. Nearness Priorities in a Muther Grid

Nearness Priority Code	Degree of Importance	Reason Code	Possible Reasons
a	Absolutely necessary	1	Use same equipment
e	Very important	2	Use same records or personnel
i	Important	3	Work flow facilitated
o	OK, ordinary importance	4	Ease of communication or supervision
u	Unimportant	5	Unsafe conditions
x	Undesirable		

The *a* in the matrix indicates that it is absolutely necessary that departments E and A be near each other. The *e*s indicate that department F should be near department E and B and that department C should be near D. The *x*s indicate that department F should not be near D or A. An example layout of a facility that meets these conditions is shown in Figure 7.4.

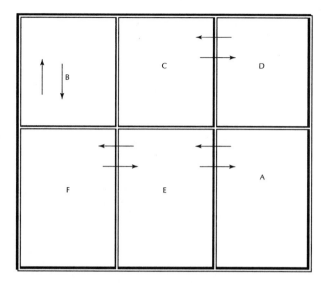

Figure 7.4. A Layout That Meets the Priorities of Figure 7.3

COMPUTERIZED PLANT LAYOUTS

The number of possible layout designs, even with a small number of departments, is so large that evaluating a considerable number of possibilities requires the aid of a computer. Several computer software programs are available for developing and analyzing process layouts, including the ALDEP (automated layout design program), CORELAP (computerized relationship layout planning) and CRAFT (computerized relative allocation of facilities technique) programs. The first two programs rank the desirability of closeness of departments to each other, whereas the CRAFT program uses the quantitative measure of minimizing the total transportation costs between them and material-handling costs.

YOU SHOULD REMEMBER

Computer-generated layout plans may not be implemented directly. Constraints such as the shape of departments, existing ventilation and sewage systems, natural lighting requirements, and the like must be superimposed upon these results.

PRODUCT LAYOUT AND LINE BALANCING

Because all operations are geared to the flow of the product in product layout, the central problem in design is to divide the necessary operations in such a way that smooth flow results. We attempt to assign the work in a manner that minimizes the number of work stations and labor and other resources to perform all the operations. This attempt will therefore minimize idle time.

Balance refers to the equality of output at each stage in the sequence of a line. If the outputs are all equal, balance is assumed to be perfect, and if they are unequal, we know that the maximum possible output for the line as a whole will be determined by the slowest operation in the line, the bottleneck operation. Thus, where imbalance exists, we have idle capacity in all other operations except the bottleneck operation.

Given a solution to the line balance problem for a particular application, the necessary detailed layout of lines and support areas, aisles, service area, and the like, must follow.

THE LINE BALANCE PROBLEM

Line balancing is the process of distributing the work loads evenly, that is to group and/or subdivide activities or tasks in such a way that all job stations have an equal amount of work to do in terms of the time required to perform the tasks. The idea is to obtain the desired level of output with the minimum input of labor and other resources.

In order to start with the greatest flexibility in alternatives to achieve balance for a specified rate of output, we need to know the performance times for the smallest possible whole units of activity called tasks, (e.g., tightening a nut, attaching a wire, or soldering a wire). We also need to know the technological constraints that may require certain sequences of these activities. Simple examples of these technological sequence constraints are a hole that must be drilled before it can be reamed, before it can be tapped; a washer that must go on the bolt before the nut; and wheel nuts that must be assembled and tightened before the hub cap can be placed. But not all tasks have restricted sequences, and this represents the remaining flexibility.

Figure 7.5 shows a network drawing of a *precedence* relationship given in Table 7.1.

Table 7.1. Work Tasks Sequence

Task	Immediate Predecessor	Task Time
a	—	0.3
b	a	0.9
c	a	1.0
d	b,c	0.4
e	d	0.8

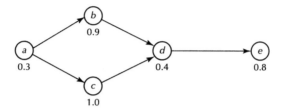

Figure 7.5. Network

The network suggests, for example, that task *b* cannot be started until *a* is completed; *b* must be done before *d* can be started; and *b* can occur either before or after *c*. The numbers below the nodes give the average task performance time in minutes. Consider now the assignment of the tasks to work stations. The total time available at each station depends on the required output of the process, which in turn depends on the expected sales or usage rate of the output.

EXAMPLE 1

In Figure 7.5, suppose that a unit must be produced every 1 minute. A quick examination of the network reveals that no two tasks could be combined within a single station. Tasks *a* and *d*, if combined, would fall within the 1-minute time limit. They cannot be assigned to the same station, however, because tasks *b* and *c* must be performed between tasks *a* and *d*. Thus, the job would require five separate work stations. This results in a rather low labor utilization level. The total amount of actual work accomplished is equal to the sum of the task times, or 3.4 minutes. However, five workers are occupied for 1 minute each for a total labor time of 5 minutes or a labor utilization rate of 3.5/5 = 0.7 = 70%.

Despite the problem of balancing the line, the continuous process has economic advantages, such as reduced materials handling, smaller facility and tool investment, and lower skill requirements that can be achieved when sales volume is sufficiently large.

For line balancing, two important pieces of information are required:

- The sum of the task times, indicating the *maximum* cycle time of the line.
- The length of the longest elemental task, indicating the *minimum* possible cycle time.

These are important because they can be used to determine the upper and lower bounds on a line's output potential.

We will need to compute the following:

- Daily capacity:

$$\text{Output} = \frac{OT}{CT}$$

where OT = operating time per day and CT = cycle time.

- The minimum number of stations necessary to provide a specified rate of output:

$$N = \frac{D\Sigma t}{OT}$$

where N = minimum number of stations, D = desired output rate, Σt = sum of task times, and OT = operating time.

- The cycle time needed to obtain a desired level of output:

$$CT = \frac{OT}{D}$$

where OT = operating time per day and D = desired output rate.

- Idle time per cycle per station:

$$\text{Idle time per station} = \text{Cycle time} - \text{Station time}$$

- The percentage of idle time:

$$\text{Percentage of idle time} = \text{Idle time per cycle}/(N \times CT)$$

EXAMPLE 2

Suppose that the work required to fabricate a certain product can be divided up into five elemental tasks, with the task times (in minutes) and precedent relationships as shown here:

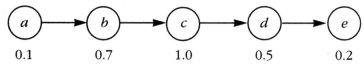

a	b	c	d	e
0.1	0.7	1.0	0.5	0.2

Assume that the line will operate for 8 hours per day (480 minutes). With a cycle time of 1 minute,

$$\text{Output} = \frac{\text{OT}}{\text{CT}} = 480 \text{ minutes per day} / 1 \text{ minute per unit}$$

$$= 480 \text{ units per day}$$

Suppose that the desired rate of output is the maximum of 480 units per day. The minimum number of stations required to achieve this goal is

$$N = \frac{{}_D\Sigma t}{\text{OT}}$$

$= (480 \text{ units per day} \times 2.5 \text{ minutes per unit})/480 \text{ minutes per day per station}$

$$= 2.5 \text{ stations.}$$

Because 2.5 stations is *not* feasible, we usually *round up* to 3 stations.
Combining the five tasks into 3 workstations with a cycle time of 1 minute results in the following assignments:

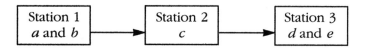

The idle times follow:

Station	Station Time	Station Idle Time
1	0.8 (0.1 + 0.7)	0.2 (1 − 0.8)
2	1.0	0 (1 − 1)
3	0.7 (0.5 + 0.2)	0.3 (1 − 0.7)
	Total	0.5

Percentage of idle time = Idle time per cycle/$(N \times \text{CT})$ = 0.5/3(1.0) = 16.7%

BALANCING TECHNIQUES

Much work has been done to develop models that produce optimally balanced lines. There have been a large number of proposals for theoretical and practical methods for solving the line balance problem. Some of the proposals have been attempts to deal with large-scale balance problems, particularly those involving 75 to 100 tasks or more and line lengths involving 10 to 15 stations or more. We will discuss first a method useful in handling problems of moderate size, called *heuristic line balancing* and then a model for handling very large problems, known as the *COMSOAL technique*, which is a computer-based sampling methodology.

THE HEURISTIC LINE-BALANCING TECHNIQUE

The heuristic line-balancing technique involves the generation of a precedence diagram (technological sequencing requirements) in a particular way, which indicates the flexibility available for shifting tasks from column to column to achieve the desired balance. The heuristic rules are effective in reducing the number of alternatives that must be considered, but they do not guarantee an optimal solution. The heuristic method has been applied to television assembly line problems with 45 and 133 tasks and has achieved excellent results.

Some of the most widely used heuristic rules are:

- Assign tasks to work stations, longest tasks first, and continue until all tasks have been assigned.

- Assign tasks in order of most number of following tasks.

- Assign tasks in order of most number of preceding tasks.

- Assign tasks according to *positional weights*, which is the sum of a task's time and the times of all the following tasks.

EXAMPLE 3

Consider the tasks in the following table. Management wishes to balance the line with the intent of minimizing idle time. Assume an output rate of 275 units and 440 minutes available per day. Task times are in minutes.

Task	Immediate Predecessor	Task Time
a	—	0.3
b	—	0.6

Task	Immediate Predecessor	Task Time
c	a	0.4
d	b	1.2
e	c	0.2
f	d	0.6
g	e	0.1
h	g	0.5
i	h	0.3

The precedent diagram looks like this:

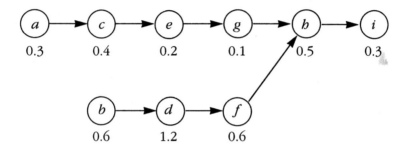

The appropriate cycle time is

$$CT = \frac{OT}{D} = 440 \text{ minutes per day}/275 \text{ units per day} = 1.6 \text{ minutes}$$

The minimum number of stations required is

$$N = \frac{D\Sigma t}{OT} = (275 \text{ units per day} \times 4.2)/ 440 \text{ minutes per day} = 2.6 \text{ (rounded to 3)}$$

For illustrative purposes, we will assign tasks using the positional weight rule. That is, assign tasks with highest following times (including its own time) first and, in case of a tie, use the greatest number of the following tasks.

Station	Task	Time Remaining	Feasible Next Task
1	b	3.2	a
	a	1.8	c
	c	1.5	None
2	d	2.6	c
	c	1.1	g
	g	0.9	None
3	f	1.4	h
	h	0.8	i
	i	0.3	None

The resulting assignments are

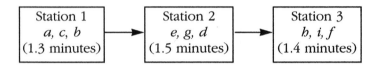

Note that the time needed to produce 275 units will be 275 × 1.5 minutes = 412.5 minutes. With 440 minutes per day available, this leaves 27.5 minutes of "slack." This time could be used for work breaks, for equipment maintenance, or to produce additional units.

THE COMSOAL TECHNIQUE

COMSOAL uses a computer routine, which generates a fairly large number of feasible solutions through a biased sampling method. The best solutions in the set become alternative solutions to the line-balancing problem. The universe from which we are sampling is, of course, all the possible feasible solutions to the particular line-balancing problem. There is a finite probability that we can turn up optimal solutions in this fashion, a slightly large probability that we can turn up the next best solutions, and so on. The probability of developing excellent solutions is related to the size of the sample. Obviously, the trick is to generate feasible solutions rapidly and to bias the generation of these solutions toward the better ones rather than to simply generate feasible solutions at random. The COMSOAL technique has been implemented by Chrysler Corporation and other concerns. It has been applied to a hypothetical line with 1,000 tasks and a known optimum of 200 stations with zero idle time, and a sequence requiring 203 stations resulting in 1.48% idle time.

AUXILIARY BALANCING TECHNIQUES

If the bottleneck operation is substantially out of balance, careful motion studies and/or the design of special tools may result in a time reduction. Also, when there are operations with large idle time, which cannot be combined into a single station, as is often true for machine operations, material banks before and after the fast operations may be required. These operations may then be run for only a small portion of the day, and where the work is compatible, a single operator can man them all by a schedule. The material banks provide work for the subsequent operations when the fast operations are shut down.

YOU SHOULD REMEMBER

Line-balancing solutions offered by the heuristic approach are abstract and for real problems. The grouping of tasks requires consideration of factors other than precedence relationships (e.g., space limitations, technical problems, and incompatible operations) that complicate the problem and restrict alternatives.

A PLANT LAYOUT DECISION

As discussed earlier, many plants use a combination of process and product layouts. The most common types of layouts found in industry are process and product layouts. There is a less common but basic type of layout known as a fixed-position layout. In this type of layout, the product being manufactured remains in a fixed position whereas machine, employees, materials, and supporting services are brought to it.

Fixed-position layouts, process layouts, and product layouts can be compared in terms of fixed costs and variable costs. Typically, fixed-position layouts have the lowest fixed costs, process layouts have higher fixed costs, and product layouts have the highest fixed costs. Offsetting this situation is the fact that the situation is usually the opposite with respect to variable costs.

Because of these cost relationships, the break-even point increases as one moves from fixed-position layouts to process layouts to product layouts. Further, the volume at which a product layout becomes more economical than a process layout is higher than the volume at which a process layout becomes more economical than a fixed-position layout.

EXAMPLE 4

The Levy Furniture Company is contemplating a new production facility for its Distressed Products line. A fixed-position layout involves a fixed cost of $15,000 and a variable cost of $50 per unit. A process layout involves a higher fixed cost of $24,000. However, variable costs are only $30 per unit. A product layout has the highest fixed cost at $32,500, but variable costs are only $20 per unit. The selling price is $150 per unit. Using the break-even analysis discussed in Chapter 4, the break-even point can be computed as follows:

Recall that

$$X_{be} = \frac{FC}{(P - V)}$$

where X_{be} = break-even point, P = price or average revenue per unit, V = unit variable cost, and FC = total fixed costs.

For a fixed-position layout, $X_{be} = 15,000/(150 - 50) = 150$ units.

For a process layout, $X_{be} = 24,000/(150 - 30) = 200$ units.

For a product layout, $X_{be} = 32,500/(150 - 20) = 250$ units.

The fixed-position layout is most economical. The process layout is best when production exceeds 450 units, and the product layout is best when production exceeds 850 units. These production levels are derived as follows:

$$24,000 + 30X = 15,000 + 50X$$

$$X = 450$$

$$32,500 + 20X = 24,000 + 30X$$

$$X = 850$$

These relationships are plotted and compared in Figure 7.6.

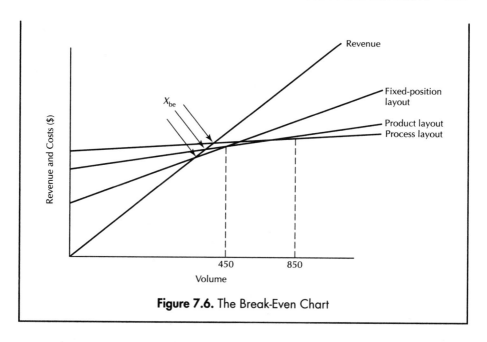

Figure 7.6. The Break-Even Chart

KNOW THE CONCEPTS

DO YOU KNOW THE BASICS?

1. Describe the goals of process design and layout. Give some of the reasons why such studies are initiated.
2. List the major types of facilities layouts used in production.
3. Discuss some of the problems associated with designing production lines.
4. Discuss the concept of group technology and its importance in production.
5. What kind of layout is used in a physical fitness center?
6. What is the objective of assembly line balancing? How would you deal with the situation where one worker, although trying hard, is 20% slower than the other ten people on a line?
7. What information of particular importance do route sheets and process charts provide to the layout planner?
8. Discuss JIT in a job-shop layout and in a line layout.

TERMS FOR STUDY

fixed-position layout
flow process chart
group layout
group technology
layout

line balancing
material handling
process layout
product layout

PRACTICAL APPLICATION

1. A small part can be made (1) on an ordinary general-purpose lathe, which is easy to set up but not very efficient in production; (2) on a turret lathe, which is more costly but produces at lower unit cost once it is set up; or (3) with automatic screw machines where volume begins to count and where setup costs are much higher but operating costs are much lower. It costs $2.50 to set up an ordinary lathe, after which operating, material, and scrap cost is $0.45 per unit; turret lathes cost $5.00 to set up and $0.20 per unit; and automatic screw machines cost $15.00 to set up but only $0.04 per unit. Determine the crossover point among lathes, turret lathes, and automatic screw machines.

2. Given the following data:

Station	Station Time (minutes)
1	4.2
2	4.7
3	4.4
4	4.8

Cycle time = 5.1 minutes.

   a. Compute the station idle time and the total idle time per cycle.

   b. Determine the percentage idle time.

3. Determine the minimum number of workstations needed for the following data:

   Operating time = 480 minutes per day

   Desired output = 80 units per day

   The sum of task times (Σt) = 56 minutes

4. Consider the tasks in the following table. Management wishes to balance the line with the intent of minimizing idle time. Assume an output rate of 400 units in an 8-hour work day. Task times are in minutes.

Task	Immediate Predecessor	Task Time
a	—	0.2
b	a	0.2
c	—	0.8
d	c	0.6
e	b	0.3
f	d,e	1.0
g	f	0.4
h	g	0.3
		$\Sigma t = 3.8$

a. Draw the network.

b. Calculate the cycle time needed to obtain the desired output.

c. Find the minimum number of workstations required.

d. Assign tasks to workstations using the rule: (1) assign tasks according to the greatest number of the following tasks and (2) in case of a tie, use the longest task time first.

e. Can the solution obtained in part d be improved?

5. Departments A, C, D, and E should be 40 feet × 40 feet. Department B should be 40 feet × 80 feet. Arrange these five departments in an 80-feet × 12-feet space so that the layout meets the conditions specified in the matrix.

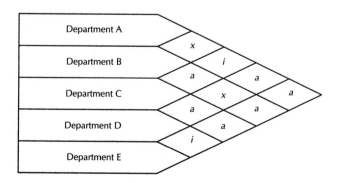

6. Given the following layout of six different departments and the frequency of movements among them along with the distance between each department, determine if less material handling is achieved by switching Department D and F. Assume the diagonal distance to be 2 units and the horizontal/vertical distances between adjacent departments to be 1.

To From	A	B	C	D	E	F
A	0	10	—	5	5	10
B	5	0	—	5	10	5
C	2	10	0	5	5	1
D	5	10	2	0	5	5
E	10	5	0	0	0	5
F	0	10	5	0	5	0

Present Layout	
A	B
C	D
E	F

Proposed Layout	
A	B
C	F
E	D

ANSWERS

DO YOU KNOW THE BASICS?

1. The objectives of process design and layout are to improve the flow and control of work, reduce costs resulting from handling and inventory, minimize facilities investment, improve space utilization, and improve worker morale. Such studies are initiated when a new facility is built, a change in production volume arises, new products are introduced, or new processes or equipment is installed.

2. They are product layout, process layout, fixed-position layout, and group layout.

3. There are a number of design alternatives and several types of material-handling equipment to choose from. Furthermore, the performance of a system design is often unpredictable because of the complex interaction of equipment and parts in process.

4. Group technology is designed to use mass production layout and production techniques for small batch systems in order to reduce setups and handling. The idea is to group families of parts requiring similar operations and treats them as a batch of similar parts.

5. In process layout similar equipment or functions are grouped together; for example, rowing machines are in one area and weight machines in another. The exercise enthusiasts move through the fitness center, following an established sequence of operations.

6. The goal is to create an efficient balance between the tasks and workstations to minimize idle time. If the employee is deemed valuable, training may enhance his/her speed. It is also possible to place a worker in the "choice" job (i.e., that workstation that has most idle time) to adjust for the slowness. Also faster workers may assist the slowpoke if the balance and physical features of the line permit.

7. Route sheets and process charts tell the layout planner the sequence of steps and the processing times. This is critical to planning effective use of plant facilities.

8. JIT can be applied in a variety of organizational process flows. Even though the pure JIT applications are often thought of as a line improvement, JIT can work in services or in job shops. In a job shop, any repetitive work can be organized and arranged as a line flow. This visibility of the process allows application of JIT.

PRACTICAL APPLICATION

1. The cost formulas for making this part on these three kinds of machines are (with x being the quantity to be made each time the machine is set up):

Lathes	$ 2.50 + 0.45x$
Turret lathes	$ 5.00 + 0.20x$
Automatic screw machine	$15.00 + 0.04x$

To find the exact crossover points, it is necessary to set the equations for the two methods being compared and solve for x. For example, the comparison of lathes to turret lathes is

$$\$ 2.50 + \$0.45x = \$5.00 + \$0.20x$$

$$\$0.25x = \$2.50$$

$$x = 10 \text{ units}$$

Similar calculations comparing lathes to automatic screw machines and turret lathes to automatic screw machine yield the other two crossover points at 30 units and at 63 units, respectively.

So, for orders under 10 units, use a lathe; for 10 to 63 units, use a turret lathe; and above 63, use an automatic screw machine.

2.

a.

Station	Station Time (minutes)	Station Idle Time (minutes)
1	4.2	0.9
2	4.7	0.4
3	4.4	0.7
4	4.8	0.3
Total	18.1	2.3

b. Percentage of idle time = Idle time per cycle/($N \times$ CT) = 2.3 minutes/4(5.1 minutes) = 11.27%

3. The minimum number of stations required is

$$N = \frac{D\Sigma t}{\text{OT}}$$

= (80 units per day × 56 minutes per unit)/480 minutes per day per station

= 9.33   (rounded to 10 stations)

4.

a. The precedent diagram looks like this:

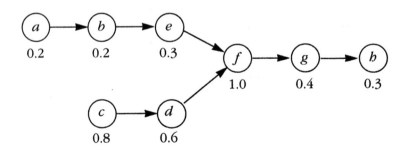

b. The appropriate cycle time CT is

$$CT = \frac{OT}{D} = 480 \text{ minutes per day}/400 \text{ units per day} = 1.2 \text{ minutes per cycle}$$

c. The minimum number of stations required is

$$N = \frac{D\Sigma t}{OT} = (400 \text{ units per day} \times 3.8)/\ 480 \text{ minutes per day} = 3.17$$
$$\text{(rounded to 4)}$$

Station	Task	Time Remaining (Minutes)	Feasible Next Task	Task with Most Followers
1	a	1	b,c	Tie
	c	0.2	b,d	b
	b	0	None	
2	d	0.6	e	e
	e	0.3	None	
3	f	0.2	None	
4	g	0.8	h	h
	h	0.5	None	

The resulting assignments follow

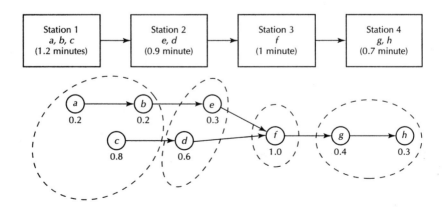

e. Yes. It can be improved upon by moving task *b* to station 2. This would reduce the idle time of the system.

5.

```
┌─────────────────────────────────────┐
│                                     │
│                  B                  │
│                                     │
├──────────────────┬──────────────────┤
│                  │                  │
│        C         │        E         │
│                  │                  │
├──────────────────┼──────────────────┤
│                  │                  │
│        D         │        A         │
│                  │                  │
└──────────────────┴──────────────────┘
```

6.

Present Layout

From	A = (10)(1) + 5(2) + 5(2) + 10(3) =	60
	B = 5 + 5 + 30 + 10 =	50
	C = 2 + 20 + 5 + 5 + 2 =	34
	D = 10 + 10 + 2 + 10 + 5 =	37
	E = 20 + 15 + 5 =	40
	F = 20 + 10 + 5 =	35
		256

Proposed Layout

From	A = 10 + 15 + 10 + 20 =	55
	B = 5 + 10 + 30 + 5 =	50
	C = 2 + 20 + 10 + 5 + 1 =	38
	D = 15 + 20 + 4 + 5 + 5 =	49
	E = 20 + 15 + 10 =	45
	F = 10 + 5 + 10 =	25
		262

There are no savings in material handling. There will be an increase of 6 units for the proposed layout.

8

AGGREGATE PLANNING AND MASTER SCHEDULING

KEY TERMS

aggregate production planning establishment of aggregate production and inventory levels over a medium range time horizon.

assignment problem problem of determining how the assignments should be made in order to minimize total costs.

chase plan aggregate production plan that adjusts capacity in response to seasonal demand.

due date promised delivery date.

Johnson's rule technique that can be used to minimize the completion time for a group of jobs that are to be processed on two machines or at two successive work centers.

level plan aggregate production plan that maintains a uniform output rate.

loading allocating work loads to specific work.

master production schedule (MPS) time-phased statement of how many finished items are to be manufactured. It is obtained by disaggregating the production plan and is the primary input to material requirement planning (MRP).

priority rules simple heuristics used to select the order in which the jobs will be processed.

rough-cut capacity planning analysis of the master production schedule to determine the feasibility with respect to capacity limitations (e.g., warehouse facilities, equipment, labor).

---

scheduling assignment of work to a facility and the specification of the sequence and timing of the work.

sequencing determination of the order in which a facility is to process a set of jobs.

SPT (shortest processing time) scheduling rule that chooses jobs in order of shortest processing time first.

tardiness amount by which completion time exceeds the due date.

Production planning and master scheduling involve the determination of future production levels over a time horizon of several months to one year. The production plan sets an intermediate-range goal for the company's products and capacity utilization in total, whereas the master schedule provides the input for detailed scheduling and control at the operational level. Poor production planning can lead to excessive inventory levels or back orders and thus increase cost or reduce customer service. Therefore, production planning is important in helping a firm to achieve its productivity goals. In this chapter, we discuss basic concepts and tools used in aggregate production planning and master scheduling. This provides the basis for material requirements planning (MRP), which is discussed in Chapter 10.

THE PRODUCTION PLANNING PROCESS

Aggregate production planning is the development of monthly or quarterly production requirements that will meet the estimates of demand. Gross capacity considerations must be taken into account during production planning.

Once a production plan is made, it must be desegregated into time-phased requirements for individual products. This plan is called the *master production schedule (MPS)*. The MPS usually states weekly product requirements over a 6- to 12-month time horizon. The MPS is not a forecast but rather a schedule of when production should be completed. Operating personnel make detailed plans for the procurement of materials, the production of components, and the final assembly of the finished goods using the MPS.

The final element of the production planning process is called *rough-cut capacity planning*. This involves analyzing the MPS to determine if sufficient capacity is available at critical points in the production process and any potential bottlenecks might occur. This provides a rapid determination of the feasibility of the MPS. Rough-cut capacity planning generally covers a 3-month time horizon. Figure 8.1 illustrates the essential elements of the production/operations planning and scheduling process.

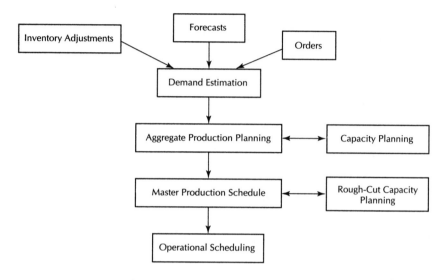

Figure 8.1. The Operations Planning and Scheduling Process

AGGREGATE PLANNING

Aggregate production planning and scheduling deals with the overall planning and scheduling of the use of various sources of capacity in relation to demand. Stated slightly differently, it deals with the allocation of the various sources of capacity to demand over some planning horizon. The various sources of capacity to which we refer are

- Variations in the size of the work force.
- Variations in the production rate, including the number of hours worked (overtime and undertime).
- Variations in inventory level, including the possibility of negative inventory (lost sales and/or back orders).
- Variable use of subcontracting.
- Combinations of two or more of the above.

Thus, aggregate planning and scheduling is an expression of the policies and procedures by which the enterprise will absorb fluctuations in demand.

A few methods of aggregate planning are listed next and are grouped in the four major categories.

- Trial-and-error method
- Methods attempting to model cost and selecting the least-cost program

  Transportation method of linear programming

  Linear decision rule (LDR)

- Heuristic decision rules

  Management coefficients model

  Search decision rule (sdr)

- Rough-cut capacity planning

TRIAL-AND-ERROR METHOD

A graphic development of a master production plan and schedule serves to illustrate the nature of the problem. Table 8.1 shows a year's forecast of production requirements for a seasonal product. Figure 8.2 shows the production requirements graphs in relation to available production days and illustrates schematically the impact of the seasonal demand.

Table 8.1. Production Requirements

Month	Monthly Demand Forecast (units)	Cumulative Demand Forecast	Normal Production Days in Month	Cumulative Normal Production Days
April	1,600	1,600	21	21
May	1,400	3,000	22	43
June	1,200	4,200	22	65
July	1,000	5,200	21	86
August	1,500	6,700	23	109
September	2,000	8,700	21	130
October	2,500	11,200	21	151
November	2,500	13,700	20	171
December	3,000	16,700	20	191
January	3,000	19,700	20	211
February	2,500	22,200	19	230
March	2,000	24,200	22	252
Total	24,200		252	

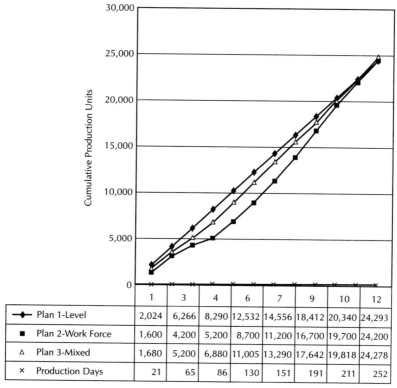

		1	3	4	6	7	9	10	12
◆	Plan 1-Level	2,024	6,266	8,290	12,532	14,556	18,412	20,340	24,293
■	Plan 2-Work Force	1,600	4,200	5,200	8,700	11,200	16,700	19,700	24,200
△	Plan 3-Mixed	1,680	5,200	6,880	11,005	13,290	17,642	19,818	24,278
×	Production Days	21	65	86	130	151	191	211	252

Production Days

Figure 8.2. Cumulative Production Versus Cumulative Production Days

For planning purposes, plotting the requirements on a cumulative basis is simpler and more effective. Figure 8.2 also shows the graph of cumulative production requirements and cumulative maximum requirements, together with three feasible production programs.

We will use an example to discuss trial-and-error method of aggregate planning. This example considers three alternative operating strategies:

- Uniform output rate (level) plan

- Variable output rate (chase) plan

- A mixed strategy

We assume the following data for Giant Sail Company, a maker of boat sails:

- The typical sail requires 20 hours to make.

- Each employee's working hours is 8 per day.

- 1,000 units of inventory will be on hand at the start of the planning horizon (i.e., April).

- The costs of hire and layoff are $300 and $200, respectively.

- The cost of holding an item in inventory is $6 per month for the average amount in inventory, including work-in-process.

- The number of employees at the beginning of the planning year will be set equal to the number of employees at the end.

• PLAN 1—UNIFORM OUTPUT RATE (LEVEL) PLAN (VARYING THE INVENTORY LEVEL)

The uniform output rate (level) plan considers maintaining a uniform (level) production rate so that all the variation in demand is accommodated by inventory that will be accumulated during part of the year. This strategy thus keeps constant labor force. This strategy is indicated by the line with diamonds in Figure 8.2. Note that this plan is feasible if backordering is permitted or if inventory is held.

Because the company needs to make 24,200 units in 252 days, it must produce at an average rate of at least 96.03 units per day. A work force of 241 employees will be required, which will provide a production rate of 96.4 units per day. The monthly inventory levels and the resulting cost of $209,266 are developed in Table 8.2.

Table 8.2. Calculation of Cost to Use Inventory and a Uniform Production Rate

Month	Monthly Demand Forecast (units) (1)	Cumulative Demand Forecast (2)	Normal Production Days in Month (3)	Cumulative Normal Production Days (4)	Cumulative Production (5) = (4) × 96.4	Ending Inventory (6) = (5) – (2) + 1000*	Inventory Holding Cost = $6 (Beginning + Ending)/2
Apr	1,600	1,600	21	21	2,024	1,424	$ 7,273
May	1,400	3,000	22	43	4,145	2,145	$10,709
June	1,200	4,200	22	65	6,266	3,066	$15,634
July	1,000	5,200	21	86	8,290	4,090	$21,469
Aug	1,500	6,700	23	109	10,508	4,808	$26,694
Sept	2,000	8,700	21	130	12,532	4,832	$28,919
Oct	2,500	11,200	21	151	14,556	4,356	$27,565
Nov	2,500	13,700	20	171	16,484	3,784	$24,422
Dec	3,000	16,700	20	191	18,412	2,712	$19,490
Jan	3,000	19,700	20	211	20,340	1,640	$13,058
Feb	2,500	22,200	19	230	22,172	972	$ 7,837
Mar	2,000	24,200	22	252	24,293	1,093	$ 6,194
	24,200		252				$209,266

*Note: 1,000 units will be on hand at the start of the planning horizon.

• PLAN 2—VARIABLE OUTPUT RATE (CHASE) PLAN (VARYING THE WORK FORCE)

The variable output rate (chase) plan is a plan that changes period-to-period output to match capacity with the demand fluctuation by hiring additional employees in periods of high demand and cutting the labor force in low-demand periods. It assumes that employees with the necessary skills can be employed when they are needed and that they will be hired or laid off to keep the direct labor hours that are available equal to the demanded production hours. When graphed, the cumulative production curve coincides with the cumulative demand curve and is indicated by the line with squares in Figure 8.2. The cost of implementing this plan is developed in Table 8.3 and is estimated to be $199,976.

Table 8.3. Cost to Vary Work Force in Accordance with Monthly Production Requirements[a]

Month	Monthly Demand Forecast (units) (1)	Production Hours Needed (2)= (1) × 20 hrs	Normal Production Days in Month (3)	Production Hours per Employee During Month (4) = (3) × 8 hrs	Direct Employee Needed During Month Rounded (5) = (2) / (4)	Employees Added at Start of Month (6)	Employees Laid Off at Start of Month (7)	Cost of Changing Employment Load (8) = $300 × (6) + $200 × (7)
Apr	1,600	32,000	21	168	190		37	7,359
May	1,400	28,000	22	176	159		31	6,277
June	1,200	24,000	22	176	136		23	4,545
July	1,000	20,000	21	168	119		17	3,463
Aug	1,500	30,000	23	184	163	44		13,199
Sept	2,000	40,000	21	168	238	75		22,516
Oct	2,500	50,000	21	168	298	60		17,857
Nov	2,500	50,000	20	160	313	15		4,464
Dec	3,000	60,000	20	160	375	63		18,750
Jan	3,000	60,000	20	160	375		0	0
Feb	2,500	50,000	19	152	329		46	9,211
Mar	2,000	40,000	22	176	227		102	20,335
	24,200		252			256	256	127,976[b]

[a] *Note:* It is assumed that the firm would have 227 direct employees at the beginning of the planning if this strategy were used.

[b] Total cost is:

Cost of changing employment level =	$127,976
Cost of maintaining 1,000 units of inventory =	72,000
	$199,976

• *PLAN 3—A MIXED STRATEGY*

A mixed strategy assumes a combined strategy—to set a relatively low but uniform production rate for the first part of the year and a higher but uniform rate for the latter part of the year. The first month demand of 1,600 units would require a minimum production rate of 76 units per day (1,600/21 days). If the production rate were set at 80 units per day for the early part of the planning horizon, it would require 200 employees (80 units × 20 hours per day, divided by 8 hours per day per person). At the end of 109 days, the company would have produced 8,720 units (80 units × 109 days).

Note that at the end of production day 252, the company needs to have a total production of 24,200 units. This means that Giant will need to make 15,480 units during the last 143 days, or an average of about 108.3 units per day. The work force required for this rate of production is about 272 employees, which will provide a production rate of 108.8 units per day. Thus, 72 employees should be hired at the beginning of September and laid off at the end of the year to achieve these employment levels and end the year with the same employment level.

The cost of this mixed strategy, which is developed and presented in Table 8.4, is estimated to be $180,979. Notice that the cost of this strategy is lower than using only inventory changes (Plan 1) or only work force changes (Plan 2). This strategy is indicated by the line with triangles in Figure 8.2.

Table 8.4. Cost of Mixed Strategy to Change Work Force and Use Inventory

Month	Monthly Demand Forecast (units) (1)	Cumulative Demand Forecast (2)	Normal Production Days in Month (3)	Cumulative Normal Production Days (4)	Production Rate (units/day) (5)[a]	Normal Production (6) = (3) × (5)	Cumulative Production (7)	Ending Inventory (8) = (7) − (2) + 1000[b]	Inventory Holding Cost = $6 (Beginning + Ending)/2 (8)	Cost of Changing Work Force (9)	
Apr	1,600	1,600	21	21	80.0	1,680	1,680	1,080	$ 6,240		
May	1,400	3,000	22	43	80.0	1,760	3,440	1,440	$ 7,560		
June	1,200	4,200	22	65	80.0	1,760	5,200	2,000	$ 10,320		
July	1,000	5,200	21	86	80.0	1,680	6,880	2,680	$ 14,040		
Aug	1,500	6,700	23	109	80.0	1,840	8,720	3,020	$ 17,100		
Sept	2,000	8,700	21	130	108.8	2,285	11,005	3,305	$ 18,974	$ 21,600	(72 × $300)
Oct	2,500	11,200	21	151	108.8	2,285	13,290	3,090	$ 19,183		
Nov	2,500	13,700	20	171	108.8	2,176	15,466	2,766	$ 17,566		
Dec	3,000	16,700	20	191	108.8	2,176	17,642	1,942	$ 14,122		
Jan	3,000	19,700	20	211	108.8	2,176	19,818	1,118	$ 9,178		
Feb	2,500	22,200	19	230	108.8	2,067	21,885	685	$ 5,407		
March	2,000	24,200	22	252	108.8	2,394	24,278	1,078	$ 5,290	$ 14,400	(72 × $200)
	24,200		252						$ 144,979	$ 36,000	

[a]80 units means 200 employees (80 units × 20 hours per unit divided by 8 hours per employee day)
108.8 units means 272 employees (108.8 × 20 hours per unit divided by 8 hours per employee day)
[b]*Note* : 1,000 units will be on hand at the start of the planning horizon.
Total cost is = $144,979 + $36,000 = $180,979.

CHOOSING A CAPACITY STRATEGY—LEVEL PLAN VERSUS CHASE PLAN

In devising a master plan (i.e., deciding on what capacity strategy is more appropriate, chase demand or level), five major considerations need to be taken into account:

- Demand variability

- Training cost

- Level of skills required

- Inventoriability of products

- Concern for quality

With these criteria in mind, the following table presents a recommended capacity strategy for some selected businesses:

Business	Recommended Strategy	Demand Variability	Training Cost	Level of Skilled Required	Inventoriable?	Quality Concern
Burger King (a fast food restaurant)	Chase	Highly variable	Low	Low	No	High
Intel (a high-tech chip maker)	Level	Predictable	High	High	Yes	High
School districts	Level	Steady and stable	High	High	No	High
H&R Block (a tax preparation firm)	Chase	Highly seasonal	Medium	Medium	No	Medium

YOU SHOULD REMEMBER

	Level-Output Strategy	Chase-Output Strategy
Advantages	Lower hiring, layoff, and training costs Retain skilled employees	No need to backlog Low costs of carrying inventory Impossible to build inventories of most services
Disadvantages	Must build costly inventories and/or backlog or refuse orders	High costs of hiring and layoffs High training costs Loss of skilled employees Quality and productivity problems.

METHODS ATTEMPTING TO MODEL COST AND SELECTING THE LEAST-COST PROGRAM

Several methods attempt to model cost and select the least-cost program. These include the transportation LP method and linear decision rule.

• *TRANSPORTATION LP METHOD*

The goal here is to minimize the sum of costs associated with regular labor time, overtime, subcontracting, inventory carrying costs, and costs related to changing the size of the work force. Constraints involve capacities of work force, inventories, and outsourcing. The problem can be formulated in terms of a transportation-type programming model as a way to obtain aggregate plans that would match capacities with demand requirements and minimize costs.

EXAMPLE 1

Using the following data, we will show the formulation in a transportation format and the final solution.

	Period		
	January	February	March
Demand	550	700	750
Capacity			
Regular	500	500	500
Overtime	50	50	50
Subcontracting	120	120	120

Costs:

Regular time:	$60
Overtime:	$80
Subcontracting:	$90
Carrying:	$ 1
Backorder:	$ 3

Beginning inventory: 100 units

Because supply (capacity) and demand must be equal, a "dummy" (unused capacity in this example) column has been added to satisfy this requirement. The costs associated with these columns are obviously zeros.

Supply from		Demand for			Unused Capacity (Dummy)	Total Capacity Available (Supply)
		January	February	March		
Period	Beginning Inventory	0*	1	2	0	
		100				100
January	Regular	60	61	62	0	
		450	50			500
	Overtime	80	81	82	0	
			50			50
	Subcontract	90	91	92	0	
			30		90	120

		Period 1	Period 2	Period 3		Capacity
February	Regular	63 **500**	60	61	0	**500**
	Overtime	83 **50**	80	81	0	**50**
	Subcontract	93 **20**	90	91 **100**	0 **90**	**120**
March	Regular	66	63 **500**	60	0	**500**
	Overtime	86	83	80	0	**50**
	Subcontract	96	93	90 **100**	0	**100**
Demand		550	700	750	90	2,090

*Costs are shown in the upper right-hand corner of each cell in this table.

The total cost is

$(100 \times \$0) + (450 \times 60) + (50 \times 61) + (50 \times 81) + (30 \times 91) + (500 \times 60) + (50 \times 80) + (20 \times 90) + (100 \times 91) + (500 \times 60) + (50 \times 90) + (100 \times 90) =$ $124,730

• *LINEAR DECISION RULE*

Another optimizing technique, the *linear decision rule (LDR)*, was developed in 1955 and applied initially at the Pittsburgh Paint Company. The LDR would be classed as a quadratic programming approach to the aggregate planning problem. The cost model for the company is the sum of four cost functions: (1) regular payroll, (2) hiring and layoff, (3) overtime costs, and (4) inventory holding, back ordering, and machine setup costs. With the exception of the regular payroll, these cost functions are idealized as quadratic in form. The equations for each of the cost functions state each cost function in terms of the size of the work force and/or the production rate. The mathematical methodology is then based on the fact that the total incremental cost equation (which is the sum of the four cost functions) is subjected to partial differentiation with respect to work force (W) and with respect to production rate (P), the resulting functions being set to 0 in order to derive the minimum or optimum point. The result is two optimum linear decision rules, one to compute production rate. These two rules require as inputs the forecast for each period of the planning horizon in aggregate terms, the ending size of the work force, and the inventory level in the last period. Once the two rules have been developed for a specific situation, the computations required to produce the decisions recommended by the model require only a few minutes by manual methods.

The advantages of LDR are that it is optimizing and that the two decision rules, once derived, are simple to apply. Also, the model is dynamic and represents the multistage decision system, which we outlined. The principal disadvantage of LDR is that the quadratic cost structure may not represent the actual cost structure very well. In addition, there are no constraints on the size of the work force, overtime, inventory, and capital, and it is possible to generate decisions that are not feasible from some points of view.

HEURISTIC DECISION RULES

Two methodologies result in heuristic decision rules: the management coefficients model and the search decision rule.

• *THE MANAGEMENT COEFFICIENTS MODEL*

The management coefficients methodology attempts to establish the form of decision rules for aggregate planning through rigorous analysis. It establishes the coefficients for the decision rules through statistical analysis of management's own past decisions. This is in contrast to the LDR, in which both the form and the coefficients are determined by mathematical analysis. The rules are rooted in the assumption that management is actually sensitive to the same criteria used in analytical models and that management's behavior tends to be highly variable rather than off center. In theory, then, management's performance using the decision rules can be improved considerably by applying the rules more consistently, because in terms of the usual dish-shaped criterion function, variability in applying decision rules is much more costly than being slightly off center from optimum decisions, but it is consistent in those decisions.

• *SEARCH DECISION RULE*

The search decision rule (SDR) approach was an attempt to overcome the dilemma one faces in attempting to expand the realism contained in mathematically optimum aggregate planning models. Small incremental improvements in model realism seem to require almost exponential increases in mathematical complexity. It appears that the lack of realism exhibited by mathematically optimum models is an inevitable consequence of the limitation of the solution methodologies. In order to use most of the common optimal solution techniques, the model builder is forced to design his cost model so that it precisely matches the requirements of the particular solution technique. This forced fit generally involves reducing the number of cost relationships and decision variables and/or assuming that they are linear, quadratic, or some other specified shape.

The net result is usually a mathematically optimum solution technique to a grossly oversimplified cost model. The SDR programming system consists of a main program and two subroutines containing the search routine and the cost model. The operating sequence of the system follows. The main program initializes all variables and reads in the sales forecast, the initial starting decision vector, and the initial state vector. The main program then calls the search routine, which, in turn, systematically explores the response surface until the cost model evaluation is reached or a better point cannot be found. At the conclusion of the search, control is returned to the main program for printing out the final decision vector and other information relating to the operation of the cost model.

YOU SHOULD REMEMBER

Some Advantages and Limitations of Aggregate Planning Methods

Method	Solution Approach	Advantages	Limitations
Trial and error	Alternative plans through trial and error	Simple to develop and easy to understand	Nonoptimal
Transportation LP method	Optimizing	Will find optimum solution to stated problem	Actual problem may not fit the linear model; assume constant work force
Linear decision rule	Optimizing	Will find optimum solution to stated problem	Actual problem may not fit the quadratic cost model; complex to use
Management coefficients	Heuristic	Use multiple regression to incorporate past managerial performance into a model	Nonoptimal
Search decision techniques	Heuristic	Does not constrain mathematical form of problem	Search may be tricked into selecting local instead of global minimum; complicated to develop; nonoptimal

| Simulation of master schedule | Trial and error | "Scenario" or "what if" analysis; tests aggregate plans developed by other methods | Assume a computer-based production system |
| Rough-cut capacity planning | Trial and error | Simple to understand and apply; intuitively appealing | Relies on judgment to determine the most desirable master schedule; does not guarantee optimum solution |

MASTER SCHEDULING

Master scheduling involves planning the production of individual products or services to fill orders and meet forecasts of other demand. A master schedule, often called a *master production schedule (MPS)*, is a schedule of planned completion of finished items. That means that it is concerned only with the final product (planning the production of parts and components will be left for detailed plans to follow). In services, the appointment book serves as the master schedule.

ROUGH-CUT CAPACITY PLANNING

The first step in master scheduling is to make a trial master schedule. Rough-cut capacity planning is the process of testing whether certain key resources are adequate to produce this schedule. If not, the trial MPS is revised until it is feasible. The first choice would be to try to move some of the production to an earlier period, so as to not disappoint customers. When a workable plan is found, it becomes the final master schedule.

EXAMPLE 2

Zeller Wood Company produces several types of furniture-grade plywood to stock. It wants to test its trial master schedule to see whether it might overload the laminating machine, which has been an occasional bottleneck in the plant. The laminating machine can laminate a high-density plastic surface to 4×8 sheets of particle board at a rate of 12 sheets per hour. The trial MPS for the next five weeks follows:

Week	1	2	3	4	5
Sheets of 4 × 8 laminates	290	420	600	380	500

The number of sheets that can be run on five 8-hour shifts is 480 sheets per week (5 shifts × 8 hours × 12 sheets). So we can shift production from weeks 3 and 5 to earlier weeks, so that no week exceeds 480 sheets. The company's final MPS follows:

Week	1	2	3	4	5
Sheets of 4 × 8 laminates	350	480	480	400	480

COMPUTERIZED SCHEDULING SYSTEMS

In many cases computer software packages for master production scheduling are an integral part of a large manufacturing information system—cost analysis, inventory information, and scheduling. IBM's Communications Oriented Production and Control System (COPICS) is an example of such a system. The system integrates forecasting, scheduling, inventory, and purchasing decisions into one large information system, planning and controlling all facets of the production system. Many computer programs also perform "what-if" (or sensitivity) analysis, which allows a production planner to determine how the production schedule would change with different assumptions concerning demand forecasts or cost figures.

Some recent computerized scheduling systems are gaining in popularity. Noteworthy among those are Optimized Production Technology (OPT), Disaster, and Q-Control, all of which concentrate their scheduling efforts on bottleneck operations. Dr. Eli Goldratt in Israel developed the first two and William E. Sandman developed the third one.

OPERATIONS SCHEDULING

Master scheduling is concerned only with end-items such as finished goods or sometimes major components and only with completion dates. Operations scheduling, which is also called detailed scheduling, or simply scheduling, is concerned with starts and completion of each part or component through each operation.

A schedule is a time table for performing activities, using resources, or allocating facilities. Examples include a physician's appointment schedules, class schedules at a university, hospital admission scheduling, surgery scheduling, airline scheduling, or bus scheduling. The purpose of scheduling is to

- Desegregate the general production plan into time-phased weekly, daily, or hourly activities.

- Specify in precise terms the planned workload on the production system in the very short run.

Some of the goals that must be considered for scheduling the job shop are to

- Minimize the average lateness.

- Minimize idle labor and facilities.

- Minimize setup costs.

- Deliver the maximum number of jobs before the due date.

All these criteria that may conflict with each other can not be achieved at the same time. A tradeoff among these conflicting goals exists. But scheduling and control must take place while keeping some goal or goals in mind. In general, two steps are involved in scheduling: loading and sequencing.

LOADING

Loading involves allocating work loads to specific work. A number of approaches are used for loading, especially *Gantt charts* and the *assignment method* of linear programming.

• *GANTT CHARTS*
Gantt charts are a visual aid. They are useful in organizing and classifying the actual or intended use of resources in a time framework. In most cases, a time scale is represented horizontally and resources to be scheduled are listed vertically. There are two kinds of Gantt charts: the load chart, which depicts the loading and idle times of a group of machines or departments, and the schedule chart, which is used to monitor the progress of jobs.

• *ASSIGNMENT METHOD*

The problem with the assignment method is to determine how the assignments should be made in order to minimize total costs.

1. **For each row, select the smallest number in that row and then subtract it from every element in that row.** Repeat this step for all rows, entering the results in a new matrix.

2. **For each column, select the smallest number in that column and then subtract it from every element in that column.** Repeat this step for all columns, entering the results in a new matrix.

3. **Search for a solution having all zero-cost assignments.** If one is found, it is an optimal solution. Otherwise, draw a set of lines through rows or columns (each line covering one row or one column) such that all zero elements are covered using as *few lines* as possible. Let m = the minimum number of lines that cover all zero elements at least once. If $m < n$, then a solution with all zero-cost elements is not yet present.

4. **Select the smallest uncovered element, subtract it from all uncovered elements, and add it to *all twice-covered elements*.** Do not change the singly covered elements. Return to step 3.

EXAMPLE 3

Consider an assignment problem having three jobs and three facilities. The costs of all possible assignments are given in the following cost matrix.

		Job		
		J1	J2	J3
Facility	F1	5	4	6
	F2	9	3	7
	F3	3	2	1

Step 1 gives the following table, often called an *opportunity cost matrix*.

1	0	2
6	0	9
2	1	0

Step 2 yields

0	0	2
5	0	4
1	1	0

In step 3, *W* found all zero-cost assignments in step 2:

0*	0	2
5	0*	4
1	1	0*

The optimal solution is: F1-J1; F2-J2, and F3-J3 with a total cost of $9.

EXAMPLE 4

Consider the following assignment problem:

3	5	7	1
9	8	12	10
13	8	14	2
5	7	10	6

After doing step 1, row and column substations, we have the following opportunity cost matrix:

2	4	2	0
1	0	0	2
11	6	8	0
0	2	1	1

The zero elements of this matrix can be covered by three lines but *not* by two. Hence, *m* = 3, whereas *n* = 4. Step 3 concludes with the knowledge that a zero-cost solution is *not yet* present. Hence, we must go to step 4 and select the smallest uncovered element. Subtract it from all uncovered elements. Add it to *all twice-covered elements.* Do not change the singly covered elements. Return to step 3.

0	2	0*	0
1	0*	0	4
9	4	6	0*
0*	2	1	3

Now we found a zero-cost solution: F1-J3; F2-J2; F3-J4, and F4-J1 with a total cost of $22.

SEQUENCING

Operations sequencing is the situation in which one or several products must go through one particular machine or process. Sequencing involves determining the sequence in which operations are to be performed. It indicates the order in which the jobs waiting at a given work center are to be processed. Here the objective is to decide on the order in which several jobs should be scheduled on the same machine in an optimum manner. There are two basic rules:

- Priority rules
- Johnson's rules

• *PRIORITY RULES*

Priority rules are simple heuristics used to select the order in which the jobs will be processed. Some common rules follow:

- *First come, first served (FCFS):* Jobs are processed in the order that they arrive at a machine or work center.

- *Shortest processing time (SPT):* Jobs are processed according to processing time at a machine, (i.e., shortest jobs first).

- *Due date (DD):* Jobs are selected according to due date, that is, earliest due date first.

- *Least slack (LS):* Defined as time until due date minus remaining time to process. The job with the least slack goes first.

- *Rush:* Emergency or preferred customers first.

Performance measures that can be used to compare different priority rules are:

- *Average completion time* (average flow time): the average time each job spends at the work center.

- *Average job lateness* (tardiness)

- *Average number of jobs in the system*

EXAMPLE 5

Consider the following jobs and their processing times and due dates:

Job	Processing Time (days)	Due Date (days)
A	2	7
B	8	16
C	4	4
D	10	17
E	5	15
F	12	18

Assume that job setup costs and times are independent of processing sequence.

a. The FCFS sequence is simply A-B-C-D-E-F. Assume jobs arrived in the alphabetical order.

Job	Processing Time (days) (1)	Flow Time (days) (2)	Due Date (days) (3)	Days Late (2) − (3)
A	2	2	7	0
B	8	10	16	0
C	4	14	4	10
D	10	24	17	7
E	5	29	15	14
F	12	41	18	23
Total	41	120		54

Average completion time: 120/6 jobs = 20 days

Average job lateness (tardiness): 54/6 jobs = 9 days

Average number of jobs in the system: 120/41 = 2.93 jobs

b. Using the SPT rule, the sequence is A-C-E-B-D-F.

Job	Processing Time (days) (1)	Flow Time (days) (2)	Due Date (days) (3)	Days Late (2) – (3)
A	2	2	7	0
C	4	6	4	2
E	5	11	15	0
B	8	19	16	3
D	10	29	17	12
F	12	41	18	23
Total	41	108		40

Average completion time: 108/6 = 18 days

Average job lateness (tardiness): 40/6 = 6.67 days

Average number of jobs in the system: 108/41 = 2.63 jobs

c. Using the DD rule, the sequence is C-A-E-B-D-F.

Job	Processing Time (days) (1)	Flow Time (days) (2)	Due Date (days) (3)	Days Late (2) – (3)
C	4	4	4	0
A	2	6	7	0
E	5	11	15	0
B	8	19	16	3
D	10	29	17	12
F	12	41	18	23
Total	41	110		38

Average completion time: 110/6 = 18.33 days

Average job lateness (tardiness): 38/6 = 6.33 days

Average number of jobs in the system: 110/41 = 2.68 jobs

d. Using the LS, the sequence is C-A-F-D-B-E.

Job	Processing Time (days) (1)	Flow Time (days) (2)	Due Date (days) (3)	Slack (days) (3) – (1)	Days Late (2) – (3)
C	4	4	4	0	0
A	2	6	7	5	0
F	12	18	18	6	0
D	10	28	17	7	11
B	8	36	16	8	20
E	5	41	15	10	26
Total	41	133			57

Average completion time: 133/6 – 22.17 days

Average job lateness (tardiness): 57/6 = 9.5 days

Average number of jobs in the system: 133/41 = 3.24 jobs

• *JOHNSON'S RULE*

Johnson's rule is a technique that can be used to minimize the completion time for a group of jobs that are to be processed on two machines or at two successive work centers. Using this rule saves time because it is impractical to enumerate all possible sequences.

Determination of the optimum sequence involves the following steps:

1. List all jobs with their corresponding times on both work centers.

2. Find the minimum time among all listed times.

3. If this time belongs to the first work center, schedule the corresponding job first; if the time is at the second center, schedule the job last. Break ties arbitrarily. In either case, eliminate the job from further consideration.

4. Go to steps 2 and 3 and continue this process until all jobs are scheduled.

EXAMPLE 6

Processing times for six jobs in two work centers follow:

Job	Processing Time (hours) WC1	WC2
A	5	5
B	4	3
C	8	9
D	2	7
E	6	8
F	12	15

Steps 1 and 2:

1st	2nd	3rd	4th	5th	6th
D					B

Step 3: The remaining jobs and their times follow:

Job	Processing Time (hours) WC1	WC2
A	5	5
C	8	9
E	6	8
F	12	15

Repeating steps 1, 2, and 3, we obtain:

1st	2nd	3rd	4th	5th	6th
D	E	C	F	A	B

The following chart displays the throughput time and idle times at two work centers:

Time	0	2	8	16	28	33	37
WC1	D	E	C	F	A	B	
WC2		D	E	C	F		

Idle = ▉

The group will take 51 hours to complete. The WC2 will wait 2 hours for its first job. WC1 will be finished in 37 hours.

KNOW THE CONCEPTS

DO YOU KNOW THE BASICS?

1. Briefly explain the production planning process.
2. Why is aggregate planning much more difficult with seasonal demand?
3. List the basic controllable variables (strategies) of a production planning problem. What are the four major costs?
4. What is a master production schedule? Why is it necessary?
5. Define level output strategy. How does it differ from the chase plan in aggregate production planning?
6. Briefly discuss the conditions under which you would be better off using the LP simplex method rather than the period model in aggregate planning.
7. How important is forecast accuracy to the practical application of the aggregate planning models?
8. What are the objectives of scheduling?
9. How does a job shop differ from a flow shop?
10. Discuss the importance of managing bottlenecks in job shop scheduling.
11. Describe the conditions under which the assignment method is appropriate.

TERMS FOR STUDY

aggregate production planning
assignment problem
chase plan
Johnson's rule
level plan
loading
master production schedule (MPS)

operations scheduling
planning horizon
priority rules
rough-cut capacity planning
trial-and-error method of
    aggregate planning

PRACTICAL APPLICATION

1. A firm producing one product is scheduling (allocating) its January–March production capabilities. Part of the decision involves scheduling overtime work. A unit produced on overtime costs an

extra $300. Similarly, a unit made one month before it is needed incurred an inventory carrying cost of $100; two months costs $200 per unit. The units delivered according to this schedule follows:

January	80 units
February	120 units
March	150 units

Production capacities follow:

	Regular Time	Overtime
January	100	50
February	100	40
March	100	30

Formulate the production scheduling problem as a transportation problem and solve it by the northwest corner rule.

2. Given the following data, use the transportation method to develop an optimal aggregate plan.

	Period		
	1	2	3
Demand	130	160	140
Capacity			
Regular	100	100	100
Overtime	20	20	20
Subcontracting	30	30	30

Costs:

Regular time:	$10
Overtime:	15
Subcontracting:	20
Carrying:	2
Backorder:	5

3. The production planner of Omega Research, a maker of industrial lenses, devised the following level output aggregate plan for the next four periods.

Period	Demand Forecast	Planned Production	Beginning Inventory	Ending Inventory
1	40,000	48,000	9,000	
2	70,000	48,000		
3	30,000	48,000		
4	55,000	48,000		

Calculate the projected beginning and ending inventory for each period. Possible backorders may be shown by a negative number.

4. Refer to problem 3.

   a. Develop a chase demand strategy that gradually increases the inventory level to 14,000 units by the end of period 4. Show the effect of the plan on inventory level for each period.

   b. Assume that the company currently has 10 employees and each employee, on average, can produce 4,000 units per period. Develop a staffing plan showing the number of employees that should be hired or laid off at the beginning period, using the following worksheet format.

Period	Required Work Force	Required Number of Employees	Available at the End of Previous Period	Hire	Layoff
1					
2					
3					
4					

5. Refer to problem 3. The company wishes to develop a master production schedule for the next four periods. The trial MPS allocates the planned production (48,000 units) equally (12,000 units per week). Even though the company has sufficient employee time to carry out the schedule, the capacity of an automatic machine that polishes the lenses may not be adequate. The machine is scheduled for regular maintenance and has a maximum capacity of 13,200 units per week.

   a. Check the feasibility of the trial MPS.

   b. If this trial MPS exceeds the available capacity of the polishing machine in any week, devise a feasible MPS.

6. The costs to do each of the three jobs on three alternate pieces of equipment are given in the following table.

Determine a job–equipment combination that will minimize total cost.

Job	Equipment		
	A	B	C
1	8	7	4
2	9	6	9
3	12	5	8

7. Consider the following assignment problem:

Facility	Job		
	X	Y	Z
A	25	31	35
B	15	20	24
C	22	19	17

Find an optimal assignment.

8. Consider the following jobs and their processing time and due dates:

Job	Processing Time (days)	Flow Time (days)	Due Date (days)
A	4	4	6
B	17	21	20
C	14	35	18
D	9	44	13
E	11	55	12

Assume that jobs arrived in alphabetical order.

a. Determine processing sequence using the FCFS and average completion time, average job lateness, and average number of jobs in the system.

b. Determine the same using the SPT rule.

c. Determine the same using the DD rule.

d. Determine the same using the LS rule.

9. For the following six jobs:

Job	Processing Time (hours)	
	WC1	WC2
A	4	6
B	9	8
C	10	5
D	6	9
E	9	7
F	12	10

   a. Determine the processing sequence using Johnson's rule.
   b. Chart total throughput time.
   c. Can total time be reduced by splitting any jobs? If so, how much?

ANSWERS

DO YOU KNOW THE BASICS?

1. First, estimate demand including demand forecasts and customer orders. Next, develop monthly or quarterly production plans on an aggregate basis and then desegregate into time-phase requirements for individual products (the master production schedule MPS) over a 6–12 month planning horizon. Perform rough-cut capacity planning to determine if sufficient capacity is available at critical points in the production process. The MPS may then have to be adjusted.

2. With seasonal demand, it is more difficult to control inventory levels and shortage conditions.

3. Basic controllable variables are production rate, work force levels, and inventories. Major costs involved are production costs (fixed and variable), production rate change costs, inventory holding costs, and backlogging costs.

4. An MPS states how many finished products are to be produced and when. This is necessary in order to make specific plans and schedules at shop floor level, establish delivery dates, and plan short-term capacity adjustments.

5. Level output strategy focuses on holding production constant over a period of time. It is more like a combination of strategies in that for the period it keeps the work force constant and inventory low and depends on a demand backlog to pull products through.

6. The basic simplex model is needed if changes in work force size (hiring/firing) is an option over the planning horizon.

7. An accurate forecast encourages the use of deterministic techniques such as LP which in turn permits the development of near optimal plans. Any reduction in uncertainty enhances the likely accuracy of any production planning method.

8. Operations scheduling is intended to meet due dates, minimize lead times, minimize setup times and cost, minimize work-in-process inventory, and maximize machine use.

9. A job shop may have flow of products going in any direction between departments. A flow shop has a flow going in one direction only between departments and work centers within each department.

10. The bottlenecks constrain capacity and limit throughput. Poor bottleneck management can lead to large works in process.

11. The assignment method is appropriate when there are n "things" to be distributed to n "destinations," each thing must be assigned to one and only one destination, and only one evaluation criterion can be used.

PRACTICAL APPLICATION

1.

Supply from		Demand for			Unused Capacity (Dummy)	Total Capacity Available (Supply)
		January	February	March		
January	Regular	80	20			100
	Overtime		50			50
February	Regular		50	50		100
	Overtime			40		40

Supply from		Demand for January	Demand for February	Demand for March	Unused Capacity (Dummy)	Total Capacity Available (Supply)
March	Regular			60	40	100
	Overtime				30	30
Demand		80	120	150	70	420

Supply from		Demand for 1	Demand for 2	Demand for 3	Unused Capacity (Dummy)	Total Capacity Available (Supply)
1	Regular	10 / 100	12	14	0	100
	Overtime	15 / 20	17	19	0	20
	Subcontract	20 / 10	22 / 20	24	0	30
2	Regular	15	10 / 100	12	0	40
	Overtime	20	15 / 20	17	0	20
	Subcontract	25	20 / 20	22 / 10	0	30
3	Regular	20	15	10 / 100	0	100
	Overtime	25	20	15 / 20	0	20
	Subcontract	30	25	20 / 10	0 / 20	30
Demand		130	160	140	20	450

Total costs = $5,360.

3.

Period	Demand Forecast	Planned Production	Beginning Inventory	Ending Inventory
1	40,000	48,000	9,000	17,000
2	70,000	48,000	17,000	–5,000
3	30,000	48,000	–5,000	13,000
4	55,000	48,000	13,000	6,000

Note that Ending Inventory = Beginning inventory + Planned production – Demand forecast.

4.

a. Inventory is increased by 1250 units in each period, (14,000 – 9,000)/4.

Period	Demand Forecast	Planned Production	Beginning Inventory	Ending Inventory
1	40,000	41,250	9,000	10,250
2	70,000	71,250	10,250	11,500
3	30,000	31,250	11,500	12,750
4	55,000	56,250	12,750	14,000

b.

Period	Required Work Force	Required Number of Employees	Available at the End of Previous Period	Hire	Layoff
1	41,250/4,000 = 10.3	10	10		
2	71.250/4,000 = 17.8	18	10	8	
3	31,250/4,000 = 7.8	8	18		10
4	56,250/4,000 = 14.1	14	8	6	

5.

a.

Week	1	2	3	4
Trial MPS	12,000	12,000	12,000	12,000
Capacity	13,200	13,200	11,000	13,200

The trial MPS exceeds the capacity of the polishing machine, which is a bottleneck in week 3. The machine runs only for 5 days and can produce 11,000 units (13,200 × 5/6).

b. The 1,000 units shortage in week 3 may be produced in an earlier week preferably in week 2. A revised MPS may look like:

Week	1	2	3	4
Trial MPS	12,000	13,000	11,000	12,000
Capacity	13,200	13,200	11,000	13,200

6.

8	7	4	
9	6	9	row reduction
12	5	8	⟶

Using row and column reductions we obtain the following opportunity cost matrices.

4	3	0	
3	0	3	column reduction
7	0	3	⟶

1	3	0*
0*	0	3
4	0*	3

So we found a zero-cost solution, which is optimal:

1 to C; 2 to A; 3 to B with a total cost of $18.

7. Using Step 1 we obtain the following opportunity cost matrix:

0	6	10
0	5	9
5	2	0

We cannot find a zero-cost solution, so we go to step 2, which gives

0	4	10
0	3	9
5	0	0

Since $m = 2 < n = 3$, we go to step 4.

0*	1	7
0	0*	6
8	0	0*

Note that $m = n = 3$, we find an optimal solution:

A to X	$25
B to Y	20
C to Z	17
	$62

8.

    a. Using the FCFS rule, the sequence is A-B-C-D-E.

Job	Processing Time (days) (1)	Flow Time (days) (2)	Due Date (days) (3)	Days Late (2) – (3)
A	4	4	6	0
B	17	21	20	1
C	14	35	18	17
D	9	44	13	31
E	11	55	12	43
	55	159		92

Average completion time: 159/5 jobs = 31.8 days

Average job lateness (tardiness): 92/5 jobs = 18.4 days

Average number of jobs in the system: 159/55 = 2.89 jobs

    b. Using the SPT rule, the sequence is A-D-E-C-B.

Job	Processing Time (days) (1)	Flow Time (days) (2)	Due Date (days) (3)	Days Late (2) – (3)
A	4	4	6	0
D	9	13	13	0
E	11	24	12	12
C	14	38	18	20
B	17	55	20	35
	55	134		67

Average completion time: 134/5 jobs = 26.8 days

Average job lateness (tardiness): 67/5 jobs = 13.4 days

Average number of jobs in the system: 134/55 = 2.44 jobs

c. Using the DD rule, the sequence is A-E-D-C-B, which is the same as the one by the SPT rule.

Job	Processing Time (days) (1)	Flow Time (days) (2)	Due Date (days) (3)	Days Late (2) – (3)
A	4	4	6	0
E	11	15	12	3
D	9	24	13	11
C	14	38	18	20
B	17	55	20	35
	55	136		69

Average completion time: 136/5 jobs = 27.2 days

Average job lateness (tardiness): 69/5 jobs = 13.8 days

Average number of jobs in the system: 136/55 = 2.47 jobs

d. Using the LS rule the sequence is: E-A-B-C-D (or E-A-B-D-C)

Job	Processing Time (days) (1)	Flow Time (days) (2)	Due Date (days) (3)	Slack (3) – (1)	Days Late (2) – (3)
E	11	11	12	1	0
A	4	15	6	2	9
B	17	32	20	3	12
C	14	46	18	4	24
D	9	55	13	4	42
Total	55	159			87

Average completion time: 159/5 jobs = 31.8 days

Average job lateness (tardiness): 87/5 jobs = 17.4 days

Average number of jobs in the system: 159/55 = 2.89 jobs

9.

a. The sequence is A-D-F-B-E-C.

Steps 1 and 2:

1st	2nd	3rd	4th	5th	6th
A					C

Step 3: The remaining jobs and their times follow:

	Processing Time (hours)	
Job	WC1	WC2
B	9	8
D	6	9
E	9	7
F	12	10

Repeating steps 1, 2, and 3, we obtain the following:

1st	2nd	3rd	4th	5th	6th
A	D	F	B	E	C

b. The following chart displays the throughput time and idle times at two work centers.

c. Yes, by splitting job C, total time can be reduced to 52.5 hours.

9
INVENTORY MANAGEMENT

KEY TERMS

ABC analysis inventory control system that divides the inventory into three classes—A, B, and C—depending on the value and importance of the item.

cycle time length of time between the placing of two consecutive orders.

economic order quantity (EOQ) order quantity that minimizes total annual inventory costs.

independent demand demands for various items are unrelated to each other and therefore determined separately and independently.

lead time time between the placing of an order and its receipt in the inventory system.

marginal approach inventory marginal analysis to determine the optimal stock level.

quantity discount model inventory model that takes into account the price varying with the order size.

reorder point inventory level that triggers a new order.

safety stock inventory carried to ensure that the desired service level is met.

service level probability of no stockouts during the lead time.

One of the most common problems facing operations managers is inventory planning. This is understandable because inventory usually represents a sizable portion of a firm's total assets and, more specifically, on the average, more than 30% of total current assets in U.S. industry. Excessive money tied up in inventory is a drag on profitability.

Inventories may contain materials that have either dependent demand or independent demand. *Dependent demand* inventories consist of items whose demand depends on the demands for other items also held in inventory. Demand (or usage) of subassemblies and component parts is derived from the number of finished units that will be assembled. A classic example is demand for wheels for new automobiles. *Independent demand* items are the finished goods or other end-items. Its demand is independent of the demand for any other item carried in inventory.

This chapter focuses on management of independent demand items. The next chapter deals with inventory systems for dependent demand.

ECONOMIC ORDER QUANTITY AND REORDER POINT

The purpose of inventory planning is to develop policies that will achieve an optimal investment in inventory. This objective is achieved by determining the optimal level of inventory necessary to minimize inventory related costs.

Inventory-related costs fall into three categories:

- *Ordering costs,* which include all costs associated with preparing a purchase order.

- *Carrying (holding) costs,* which include storage costs for inventory items plus the cost of money tied up in inventory.

- *Shortage (stockout) costs,* which include those costs incurred when an item is out of stock. These include the lost contribution margin on sales plus the lost customer goodwill.

Many inventory planning models are available. They all try to answer basically the following two questions:

- How much to order?

- When to order?

They include the economic order quantity model, the reorder point, and the determination of safety stock.

BASIC ECONOMIC ORDER QUANTITY MODEL

The economic order quantity (EOQ) determines the order quantity that results in the lowest sum of carrying and ordering costs. The EOQ is computed as:

$$EOQ = \sqrt{\frac{2DO}{C}}$$

where C = carrying cost per unit, O = ordering cost per order, D = annual demand (requirements) in units.

If the carrying cost is expressed as a percentage of average inventory value (say, 12 % per year to hold inventory), then the denominator value in the EOQ formula would be 12% times the price of an item.

EXAMPLE 1

Assume that the Los Alamitos Store buys sets of steel at $40 per set from an outside vendor. It will sell 6,400 sets evenly throughout the year. The store's carrying cost is $8 per unit per year. The ordering cost is $100 per order. Therefore,

$$EOQ = \sqrt{\frac{2(6,400)(\$100)}{\$8}} = \sqrt{160,000} = 400 \text{ sets}$$

$$\text{Total number of orders per year} = \frac{D}{EOQ} = \frac{6,400}{400} = 16 \text{ orders}$$

Total inventory costs = Carrying cost + Ordering cost

$$= C \times \frac{EOQ}{2} + O\frac{D}{EOQ}$$

$$= (\$8.00)\left(\frac{400}{2}\right) + (\$100)\left(\frac{6,400}{400}\right)$$

$$= \$1,600 + \$1,600 = \$3,200$$

Based on these calculations, the Los Alamitos Store's inventory policy should be the following:

- The store should order 400 sets of steel each time it places an order and order 16 times during a year.

This policy will be most economical and cost the store $3,200 per year.

YOU SHOULD REMEMBER

When an item is made instead of purchased, the EOQ model is used to determine the economic production run size where O = setup cost per setup.

REORDER POINT

The reorder point (ROP), which answers when to place a new order, requires a knowledge about the lead time, which is the time interval between placing an order and receiving delivery. The reorder point can be calculated as follows:

ROP = (Average demand per unit of lead time × lead time) + Safety stock

First, multiply the average daily (or weekly) demand by the lead time in days (or weeks) yielding the lead time demand. Then add safety stock to this to provide for the variation in lead time demand to determine the reorder point. If average demand and lead time are both certain, no safety stock is necessary and should be dropped from the formula.

EXAMPLE 2

Assume in Example 1 that the lead time is constant at one week, and that there are 50 working weeks in a year. Then the reorder point is 128 sets = (6,400 sets/50 weeks) × 1 week. Therefore, when the inventory level drops to 128 sets, the new order should be placed. Suppose, however, that the store is faced with variable demand for its steel and requires a safety stock of 150 additional sets to carry. Then the reorder point will be 128 sets plus 150 sets, or 278 sets.

Figure 9.1 shows this inventory system when the order quantity is 400 sets and the reorder point is 128 sets.

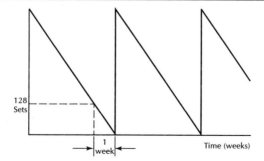

Figure 9.1. Basic Inventory System with EOQ and ROP

ASSUMPTIONS AND APPLICATIONS

The EOQ model makes the following strong assumptions:

- Demand is fixed and constant throughout the year.
- Lead time is known with certainty.
- No quantity discounts are allowed.
- No shortages are permitted.

YOU SHOULD REMEMBER

The assumptions may be unrealistic; however, the model still proves useful in inventory planning for many firms. In fact, many situations exist where a certain assumption holds or nearly holds. For example, subcontractors who must supply parts on a regular basis to a primary contractor face a constant demand. Even where demand varies, the assumption of uniform demand is not unrealistic. Demand for automobiles, for example, varies from week to week over a season, but the weekly fluctuations tend to cancel out each other so that seasonal demand can be assumed constant.

EOQ WITH NONINSTANTANEOUS REPLENISHMENT

So far we have assumed that the inventory replenishment is instantaneously received. Now we consider the case where the inventory is being manufactured while demands are being met. We make the following assumptions:

- The product held in inventory is not purchased from an outside source but rather is manufactured.
- Units are continuously being added to inventory during the production run.
- When this inventory is completely depleted, a new production run is started.

Let S = setup cost, D = annual demand, p = production rate, u = usage rate, and $p > u$.

The costs associated with operating this system are the carrying costs and the production setup costs (instead of ordering costs). Note that during a production run, inventory accumulates at a rate of $(p - u)$ units per period. Afterwards it is depleted at a rate of u units. The situation is depicted in Figure 9.2.

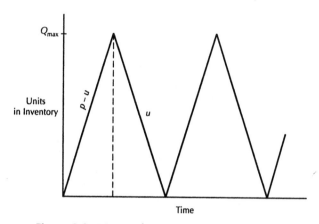

Figure 9.2. EOQ with Noninstantaneous Replenishment

$$\text{Setup costs} = O\,\frac{D}{Q}$$

Maximum inventory level = Inventory buildup rate × Period of delivery

$$= (p - u)\left(\frac{Q}{p}\right)$$

Minimum inventory level = 0

$$\text{Average inventory level} = \frac{\text{Maximum inventory} + \text{Minimum inventory}}{2}$$

$$= \left(\frac{1}{2}\right)\left[(p - u)\left(\frac{Q}{p}\right) + 0\right] = \left(\frac{Q}{2}\right)\left[\frac{(p - u)}{p}\right]$$

$$\text{Total annual inventory costs} = C\frac{Q}{2}\left[\frac{(p - u)}{p}\right] + S\left(\frac{D}{Q}\right).$$

Using calculus yields

$$\text{EOQ} = \sqrt{\frac{2DS}{C}\left[\frac{p}{(p - u)}\right]} = \sqrt{\frac{2DS}{C\left(1 - \dfrac{u}{p}\right)}}$$

EXAMPLE 3

Jog Plumbing, Inc., developed the following estimates for the #123 valves. $D = 800$ valves per year, $C = \$.05$ per valve per year, $S = \$1.00$ per order or setup, $p = 100$ valves per week, and $u = 60$ valves per week. Then

$$\text{EOQ} = \sqrt{\frac{2DS}{C} \ \frac{p}{(p-u)}} = \sqrt{\frac{2(800)(1)}{(0.05)} \ \frac{100}{(100-60)}} = 283 \ \text{valves}$$

$$\text{Maximum inventory level} = (p-u)\left(\frac{Q}{p}\right) = (100-60)\left(\frac{283}{100}\right) = 113.2 \ \text{valves}$$

$$\text{Total annual inventory costs} = C\frac{Q}{2}\left[(p-u)p\right] + S\left(\frac{D}{Q}\right)$$

$$= \$.05\left(\frac{283}{2}\right)\left[\frac{(100-60)}{100}\right] + \$1\left(\frac{800}{283}\right)$$

$$= \$2.83 + \$2.83 = \$5.66 \ \text{per year}$$

The production run time (the production phase of the cycle) = EOQ/p = 283 valves/100 valves per week = 2.83 weeks. Thus, each run will require 2.83 weeks to complete. The cycle time (the time between orders or between the beginnings of runs) = EOQ/u = 283 valves/60 valves per week = 4.72 weeks. Thus, a run of valves will be made every 4.72 weeks.

EOQ WITH QUANTITY DISCOUNTS

The EOQ model does not take into account quantity discounts, which is not realistic in many real-world cases. Usually, the more you order, the lower the unit price you pay. Quantity discounts are price reductions for large orders offered to buyers to induce them to buy in large quantities. If quantity discounts are offered, the buyer must weigh the potential benefits of reduced purchase price and fewer orders that will result from buying in large quantities against the increase in carrying costs caused by higher average inventories. Hence, the buyer's goal in this case is to select the order quantity that will minimize total costs, where total cost (TC) is the sum of carrying cost, ordering cost, and product cost:

$$\text{TC} = \text{Carrying cost} + \text{Ordering cost} + \text{Product cost}$$

$$= C\left(\frac{Q}{2}\right) + O\left(\frac{D}{Q}\right) + PD$$

where P = unit price and Q = order quantity.

There are two general cases:

- Carrying costs are constant.
- Carrying costs are stated as a percentage of purchase price.

When carrying costs are constant. there will be a single EOQ that is the same for all the cost curves. When carrying costs are stated as a percentage, each curve will have a different EOQ.

CONSTANT CARRYING COSTS

A step-by-step approach for computing EOQ with quantity discounts follows:

1. Compute the common EOQ when price discounts are ignored.

2. Only one of the curves will have the EOQ in its feasible range. Identify that curve.

If the feasible EOQ is the lowest-price curve, this is the overall EOQ.

If the EOQ is on any other curve, compute the total cost for the EOQ and for the quantities for which price reductions will occur.

3. Select the value of Q that will result in the lowest total cost.

EXAMPLE 4

In Example 1, assume that the ABC Store was offered the following price discount schedule:

Order Quantity, Q	Unit Price, P
1 to 499	$40.00
500 to 999	39.90
1000 or more	39.80

First, the EOQ with no discounts is computed as follows:

$$EOQ = \sqrt{\frac{2(6,400)(\$100)}{\$8}} = \sqrt{160,000} = 400 \text{ sets}$$

Total cost = $8(400/2) + $100(6,400/400) + $40(6,400)

$$= \$1,600 + 1,600 + 256,000 = \$259,200$$

We see that the value that minimized the sum of the carrying cost and the ordering cost but not the purchase cost was EOQ = 400 sets. The farther we move from the point 400, the greater will be the sum of the carrying and ordering costs. Thus, 400 is obviously the only candidate for the minimum total cost value within the first price range. Q = 500 is the only candidate within the $39.90 price range, and Q = 1,000 is the only candidate within the $39.80 price bracket. These three quantities are evaluated in Table 9.1 and illustrated in Figure 9.3.

Table 9.1. Annual Costs with Varying Order Quantities

	Order Quantity, Q ($)		
	400	500	1,000
Purchase price (P)	40	39.90	39.80
Carrying cost (C × Q/2) = $8 × (Order quantity/2)	$1,600	$2,000	$4,000
Ordering cost (O × D/Q) = $100 × (6,400/Order quantity)	1,600	1,280	640
Product cost (PD) Unit price × 6,400	256,000	255,360	254,720
Total cost	259,200	258,640	259,360

Note that C = $8, O = $100, and D = 6,400 for all possible orders.

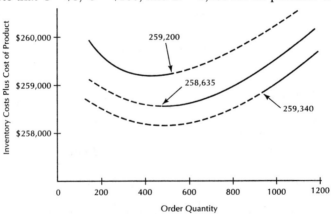

Figure 9.3. Inventory Cost and Quantity

The EOQ with price discounts is 500 sets. Hence, ABC store is justified in going to the first price break but the extra carrying cost of going to the second price break more than outweighs the savings in ordering and in the cost of the product itself.

CARRYING COSTS STATED AS A PERCENTAGE OF PURCHASE PRICE

The procedure for computing carrying costs stated as a percentage of purchase price follows:

1. Calculate EOQs for each price. Reject any EOQ that is not within the allowable quantity range for the price used.

2. Calculate total annual cost for feasible EOQs

If the feasible EOQ is the lowest price curve, this is the overall EOQ.

If the EOQ is not the lowest price range, compute the total cost for the EOQ and for the next quantities for which price reductions will occur.

3. Select the value of Q that will result in the lowest total cost.

EXAMPLE 5

Discount Plumbing Industries, Inc., a maker of the No. 510 valve, has offered quantity discounts. The volumes and prices follow:

Order Quantity, Q	Unit Price, P
1 to 399	$2.20
400 to 699	2.00
700 or more	1.80

The company developed the following estimates: D = 10,000 valves per year, S = \$5.50 per order, and C = 20% of unit price (P). First, the EOQs are computed for each of the prices:

$$EOQ_{2.20} = \sqrt{2[10,000(5.5)/0.2(2.20)]} = 500 \text{ (reject—too large)}$$

$$EOQ_{2.00} = \sqrt{2[10,000(5.5)/0.2(2.00)]} = 524.4 \text{ (feasible)}$$

$$EOQ_{1.80} = \sqrt{2[10,000(5.5)/0.2(1.80)]} = 552.8 \text{ (reject—too small)}$$

Therefore, the total annual cost at two quantities is investigated: 524.2 and 700 units per order:

At $Q = 524.4$, total annual cost

$$= (0.2)(\$2)(524.4/2) + \$5.5(10,000/524.4) + \$2(10,000)$$

$$= \$104.88 + \$104.88 + \$20,000$$

$$= \$20,209.76.$$

At $Q = 700$, total annual cost

$$= (0.2)(\$1.8)(700/2) + \$5.5(10,000/700) + \$1.8(10,000)$$

$$= \$126 + \$78.57 + \$18,000$$

$$= \$18,204.57.$$

700 valves are a more economical order quantity because the total annual cost is lower that that associated with the EOQ. This case is depicted in Figure 9.4.

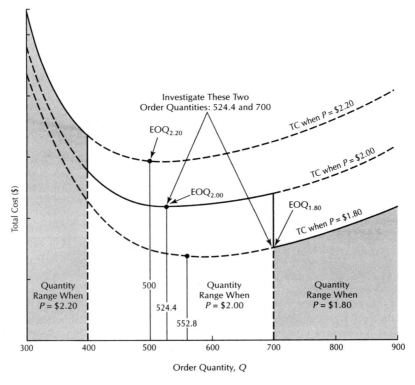

Figure 9.4. Quantity Discount Curves

DETERMINATION OF SAFETY STOCK

When lead time and demand are not certain, the firm must carry extra units of inventory, called *safety stock,* as protection against possible stockouts. To determine the appropriate level of safety stock size, you must consider the service level or stockout costs.

Service level can be defined as the probability that demand will not exceed supply during the lead time. Thus, a service level of 90% implies a probability of 90% that demand will not exceed supply during lead time. Figure 9.5 shows a service level of 90%.

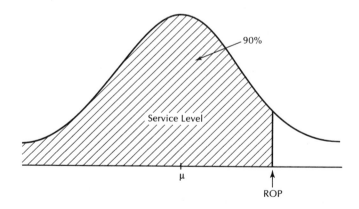

Figure 9.5. Service Level of 90%

To determine the optimal level of safety stock size, you might also want to measure the costs of not having enough inventory, or stockout costs.

Here are four cases for computing the safety stock. The first three do not recognize stockout costs; the fourth case does.

KNOWN MAXIMUM DEMAND RATE, CONSTANT LEAD TIME

A simple way to determine the size of safety stock is to deduct *average demand* from the *maximum demand* that can reasonably be expected during a period and then multiply the difference by the lead time.

EXAMPLE 6

Assume that the economic order quantity is 500 units, that the lead time is 4 weeks, that the average weekly demand is 60 units, and that the maximum expected weekly demand is 70 units. The owner of a small manufacturing business would compute a safety stock as follows:

Maximum expected demand	70 units
Average demand	60
Excess	10 units
Lead time	× 4 weeks
Safety stock	40 units

ROP = Expected demand during lead time + Safety stock

= Lead time × Average demand per unit of time + Safety stock

= 4 weeks × 60 + 40

= 240 + 40 = 280 units

VARIABLE DEMAND RATE, CONSTANT LEAD TIME

ROP = Expected demand during lead time + Safety stock

$$= \overline{d}\,\text{LT} + z\,\sqrt{\text{LT}}\,(\sigma_d)$$

where

$$\overline{d} = \text{average demand}$$

LT = lead time

σ_d = standard deviation of demand rate

z = standard normal variate [See Table 3 (Normal Distribution Table) in Appendix II]

EXAMPLE 7

Norman's Pizza uses large cases of tomatoes at an average rate of 50 cans per day. The demand can be approximated by a normal distribution with a standard deviation of 5 cans per day. The lead time is 4 days. Thus,

$$\overline{d} = 50 \text{ cans per day}$$

$$LT = 4 \text{ days}$$

$$\sigma_d = 5 \text{ cans}$$

How much safety stock is necessary for a service level of 99%? And what is the ROP?

For a service level of 99%, z = 2.33 [from Table 3 (Normal Distribution Table) in Appendix II]. Thus,

$$\text{Safety stock} = 2.33 \sqrt{4} \, (5) = 23.3 \text{ cans}$$

$$ROP = 50(4) + 23.3 = 223.3 \text{ cans}$$

Figure 9.6 shows a service level of 99%.

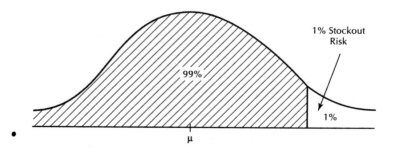

Figure 9.6. Service Level of 99%

CONSTANT DEMAND, VARIABLE LEAD TIME

ROP = Expected demand during lead time + Safety stock

$$= d \, \overline{LT} + zd \, (\sigma_{LT})$$

where

d = constant demand

$\overline{LT}$ = average lead time

σ_{LT} = standard deviation of lead time

EXAMPLE 8

SVL's Hamburger Shop uses 10 gallons of cola per day. The lead time is normally distributed with a mean of 6 days and a standard deviation of 2 days. Thus,

d = 10 gallons per day

$\overline{LT}$ = 6 days

σ_{LT} = 2 days

How much safety stock is necessary for a service level of 99%? And what is the ROP?

For a service level of 99%, z = 2.33. Thus,

Safety stock = 2.33 (10)(2) = 46.6 gallons

ROP = 10(6) + 46.6 = 106.6 gallons

INCORPORATION OF STOCKOUT COSTS

The case where stockout costs are incorporated specifically recognizes the cost of stockouts or shortages, which can be quite expensive. Lost sales and disgruntled customers are examples of external costs. Idle machine and disrupted production scheduling are examples of internal costs. We will illustrate the probability approach to show how the optimal safety stock can be determined in the presence of stockout costs.

EXAMPLE 9

In Examples 1 and 2, suppose that the total demand over a one-week period is expected to be:

Total Demand	Probability
78	0.2
128	0.4
178	0.2
228	0.1
278	0.1
	1.00

Suppose further that a stockout cost is estimated at $12 per set. Recall that the carrying cost is $8 per set.

Table 9.2 shows the computation of safety stock. The computation shows that the total costs are minimized at $1,200, when a safety stock of 150 sets is maintained. Therefore, the reorder point is 128 sets + 150 sets = 278 sets.

THE SINGLE PERIOD INVENTORY PROBLEM—MARGINAL ANALYSIS

Unlike the basic EOQ model, the marginal approach to inventory introduces the concept of uncertainty. The basic rule is to add inventory as long as the expected reduction in penalty cost for a shortage is greater than the expected cost of stocking the unit. Define:

p = probability of selling an additional unit

Table 9.2. Computation of Safety Stock

Safety Stock Levels (units)	Stockout and Probability	Average Stockout (units)	Average Stockout Costs ($)	Number of Orders	Total Annual Stockout Costs ($)	Carrying Costs ($)	Total ($)
0	50 with 0.2 100 with 0.1 150 with 0.1	35[a]	420[b]	16	6,720[c]	0	7,140
50	50 with 0.1 100 with 0.1	15	180	16	2,880	400[d]	3,280
100	50 with 0.1	5	60	16	960	800	1,760
150	0	0	0	16	0	1,200	1,200

[a]50(0.2) + 100(0.1) + 150(0.1) = 10 + 10 + 15 = 35 units
[b]35 units × $12.00 = $420
[c]$420 × 16 times = $6,720
[d]50 units × $8.00 = $400

MP = marginal profit from selling a unit

$(1 - p)$ = probability of not selling a unit

ML = marginal loss from turning away a customer.

As long as the expected marginal (incremental) profit is greater than the expected marginal (incremental) loss, the order quantity will be added. Net profits will be maximized when

$$p(MP) = (1 - p)(ML)$$

for the last unit in order. Solving for p, we obtain

$$p = \frac{ML}{ML + MP}$$

The probability of selling a unit must be at least ML/(ML + MP) in order to justify the stocking of the unit.

EXAMPLE 10

Home Holiday Store wishes to stock Christmas wreaths for sale during the holiday season. Assume that the store knows the probability distribution of demand to be as follows:

Demand	Probability of Demand Equal to the Given Number	Probability of at Least the Given Number
6	0.05	1.00
7	0.15	0.95
8	0.20	0.80
9	0.40	0.60
10	0.10	0.20
11	0.10	0.10
	1.00	

The store pays $2 for each item and sells it for $6. It must dispose of each item not sold by December 25 at a cost of $0.50 per wreath. The ordering cost is fixed for all courses of action.

Note that MP = $6 − $2 = $4, and ML = $2 + $.50 = $2.50.

$$p = \frac{ML}{ML + MP} = \frac{\$2.50}{\$2.50 + \$4.00} = 0.385$$

way, a manager may ask a series of "what-if" questions about the system. An advantage of this process is that we can use simulation to analyze systems and problems that are too complex for other mathematical techniques. An example is a system in which we would like to explore the effect of the interactions of several probability distributions. Simulation involves the following steps:

1. Determine the distribution that describes the statistical property of concern.

2. Convert the probability distribution to a cumulative probability distribution.

3. Sample at random (using the random number table) from the cumulative probability distribution to produce outcomes.

4. Simulate the process.

A simulation of an elementary inventory problem is used to illustrate how this one type of simulation model works.

INVENTORY SIMULATION

A company is faced with a problem of determining the size of orders and when to reorder, but in the face of sales that vary randomly from day to day. The company studied sales records for 500 days and found that demand varied between 17 and 26 units per day according to the frequency shown in Table 9.3. The number of days on which each level of demand occurred was converted into relative frequencies in column 3, and because management felt that this same pattern of demand would continue for the immediate future, these relative frequencies were taken to be the probabilities of occurrence. From Table 9.3, we find that 0.15 is the probability for a demand of 19 units on any given day.

• *MONTE CARLO PROCESS*

We can simulate sales that vary randomly according to this pattern by the Monte Carlo process. The Monte Carlo process is a technique of selecting numbers randomly from a probability distribution. In the last column of Table 9.3, we assigned sets of two-digit numbers to each demand. One number (01) is assigned to a demand of 17 because it has a 0.01 probability of occurrence; thirteen numbers (02–14) are assigned to a demand of 18 units because it has a 0.13 probability of occurrence; and so forth.

Table 9.3. Probability Distribution *F* Daily Demand

Number of Units Demanded	Number of Occurrences	Probability of Occurrence	Cumulative Probability of Occurrence	Corresponding 2-Digit Numbers
17	5	0.01	0.01	01
18	65	0.13	0.14	02–14
19	75	0.15	0.29	15–29
20	140	0.28	0.57	30–57
21	60	0.12	0.69	58–69
22	50	0.1	0.79	70–79
23	40	0.08	0.87	80–87
24	40	0.08	0.95	88–95
25	15	0.03	0.98	96–98
26	10	0.02	1.00	99–00
Total	500	1.00		

Average demand = 20.1 units per day.

We now obtain two-digit random numbers by some means such as rolling dice, drawing numbers from a hat, generating them on a computer, or selecting them from a table of uniformly distributed random numbers like the one in Appendix II. We use them to select demands from the distribution of demands in the table. If the number selected is 60, the demand would be 21 because 60 falls into the 57–68 set of numbers in the last column of the table. In Table 9.4 we have drawn five random numbers and use them to determine simulated demand for five days. If we repeat this process many times, we would have a randomly varying pattern of demands which would occur with the relative frequencies shown in Table 9.4.

Table 9.4. Simulated Demand for Five Days

Day Number	Random Number	Demand (units)
1	60	21
2	18	19
3	10	18
4	85	23
5	55	20

The company is concerned with another probability distribution. That is the distribution of lead times, or the time between placing an order and receiving the goods, as indicated in Table 9.5. Mathematical analysis of this type of problem is difficult because of the interaction between the demand and lead time probability distributions, but we can simulate the behavior of this system using the Monte Carlo method and determine the cost of various purchasing policies. We could simulate this situation by hand using the method described earlier, but the amount of calculation required to simulate, say, a year's operation of the system would be rather tedious. This is the type of calculation for which a digital computer is suited.

Table 9.5. Probability Distribution of Lead Times

Lead Time (days)	Probability of Occurrence	Cumulative Probability of Occurrence
6	0.10	0.10
7	0.20	0.30
8	0.30	0.60
9	0.25	0.85
10	0.15	1.00

YOU SHOULD REMEMBER

Simulation has been applied to a wide variety of operations management activities, such as maintenance operations, service facilities scheduling, corporate planning, distribution systems, location of facilities, personnel planning, and facilities investment decisions. Using a computer is often the only feasible way of performing simulation. Many special-purpose simulation languages such as SIMSCRIPT, GPSS, and GASP have been developed and are suitable for queuing and scheduling problems.

USING THE ABC SYSTEM FOR INVENTORY CONTROL

ABC analysis focuses on the most critical items—gross profitability, sensitive price or demand patterns, and supply excesses or shortages. The ABC method requires the classification of inventory into one of three groups—A, B, or C—according to the potential savings associated with a proper level of inventory control. Class A items, needing close control, are the high-dollar-volume group. They may include 80% of total inventory cost but only 1% of total items stocked. Class B is an intermediate-dollar-volume group—perhaps 15% of dollars and 30% of items. Class C is the rest—5% of dollars and 69% of items. Table 9.6 illustrates an ABC distribution.

Table 9.6. ABC Inventory Distribution

Inventory Classification	Population (%)	Dollar usage (%)
A	1	80
B	30	15
C	69	5

To institute the ABC method:

1. Compute annual dollar volume by inventory type anticipated (annual demand times unit cost).

2. Segregate merchandise into components based on annual dollar value.

3. Rank inventory in terms of annual dollar volume, ranging from high to low (e.g., As in the top 80%, Bs in the next 15%, and Cs in the last 5%).

4. Tag inventory with the appropriate classification and record the classifications in the inventory records.

The following example illustrates the ABC system.

EXAMPLE 11

Garner Auto Supply Company has arranged its ten inventory items in order of annual dollar volume. Figure 9.7 shows the ordered list, with dollar volume expressed in percentages. The ordered list is examined in order to arrive at an ABC classification of the items.

Table 9.8 shows the same ten items grouped into classes A, B, and C. The two A items account for over 80%—almost five times as much annual dollar-volume as the two B items—whereas the two B items account for almost six times as much as the five C items. Figure 9.7 graphically illustrates the ABC classification for this example.

Table 9.7. Inventory Items in Annual Dollar Volume Order

Item Number	Annual Dollar Usage	Percent of Total Dollar Usage
113	130,000	47.5
103	90,000	32.9
123	31,000	11.3
134	14,500	5.3
301	6,200	2.3

Item Number	Annual Dollar Usage	Percent of Total Dollar Usage
721	650	0.2
764	525	0.2
402	325	0.1
520	300	0.1
Total	273,500	100.0

Table 9.8. ABC Classification

Classification	Item Number	Annual Dollar Usage	Percent of Total Dollar Usage	Number of Items	Percent of Total Number of Items	Cumulative Percent of Total Number
A	103, 113	220,000	80.5	2	22.2	22.2
B	123, 134	45,500	16.6	2	22.2	44.4
C	301, 721, 520, 402, 764	8,000	2.9	5	55.6	100.0
Total		273,500	100.0	9	100.0	

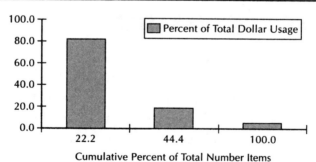

Figure 9.7. ABC Classification Percent Versus Percent of Items

It is clear that A items should receive major attention, B items moderate attention, and C items little attention. Perpetual inventory records should be maintained for class A items, which require accuracy and frequent, often daily, attention. Class B items are less expensive than A items but are still important and require intermediate control. Class C items include most of the inventory items. Because they are usually less expensive and less used, they require less attention.

> There is usually a high safety stock level for C items. Blanket purchase orders should exist for A items and only "spot buys" for Bs and Cs.

Examples of inventory controls that may be based on ABC classification follow:

- *Purchasing.* A purchase order for a class A item might be signed by the president, for a class B item by the head of the purchasing department, and for a class C item by any purchasing agent.

- *Physical Inventory Check.* Count A items monthly, B items twice a year, and C items annually.

- *Forecasting.* Forecast A items by several methods with resolution by a prediction committee, B items by simple trend projection, and C items by best guess of the responsible purchasing agent.

- *Safety Stock.* No safety stock for A items, one month's supply for B items, and three months' supply for C items.

KNOW THE CONCEPTS

DO YOU KNOW THE BASICS?

1. List inventory-related costs. Explain each briefly.
2. What are two basic questions regarding inventory management?
3. Distinguish between independent demand and dependent demand.
4. What is the reorder point? How do you determine this?
5. Write down the economic order quantity formula.
6. Describe the basic steps to finding EOQ with quantity discounts in the case where the carrying cost is stated as a percentage of the unit price.
7. List four cases of safety stock determination.
8. Explain how ABC analysis works. List some of the control strategies.
9. Discuss the marginal approach to determining the optimal stock size.
10. What is simulation?
11. List the steps involved in simulation.

TERMS FOR STUDY

ABC analysis
economic order quantity (EOQ)
independent demand
lead time
marginal approach to inventory

Monte Carlo simulation
quantity discount model
reorder point
safety stock

PRACTICAL APPLICATION

1. The following information relates to the Janie Company:

Units required per year	30,000
Cost of placing an order	$400
Unit carrying cost per year	$600

    Assuming that the units will be required evenly throughout the year, what is the economic order quantity?

2. Pierce, Inc., has to manufacture 10,000 blades for its electric lawn mower division. The blades will be used evenly throughout the year. The setup cost every time a production run is made is $80, and the cost to carry a blade in inventory for the year is $0.40. Pierce's objective is to produce the blades at the lowest cost possible. Assuming that each production run will be for the same number of blades, how many production runs should Pierce make?

3. Politan Company manufactures bookcases. Setup costs are $2. Politan manufactures 4,000 bookcases evenly throughout the year. Using the EOQ approach, find the cost of carrying one bookcase in inventory for one year when the optimal production run is 200.

4. No-nonsense Engineering, a maker of the No. 562 valve, has offered quantity discounts. The volumes and prices follow:

Order quantity, Q	Unit Price, P
1–99	$10.00
100–499	$ 9.50
500 or more	$ 9.00

    The company developed the following estimates: D = 2,000 valves per year, S = $30 per order, and C = 35% of unit price (P). Determine the company's true EOQ.

5. The Robney Company is a restaurant supplier that sells a number of products to various restaurants in the area. One of their products is a special meat cutter with a disposable blade. The blades are sold in packages of 12 blades for $20 per package. After a number of years, it has been determined that the demand for the replacement blades is at a constant rate of 2,000 packages per month. The packages cost the Robney Company $10 each from the manufacturer and require a three-day lead time from the date of order to date of delivery. The ordering cost is $1.20 per order and the carrying cost is 10% per annum.

   a. Calculate the economic order quantity, the number of orders needed per year, and the total cost of buying and carrying blades for the year.

   b. Assuming there is no safety stock and that the present inventory level is 200 packages, when should the next order be placed? (Use 360 days in one year.)

   c. Discuss the problems that most firms would have in attempting to apply this formula to their inventory problems.

6. The Orpra Company buys raw materials from an outside supplier at $40 per unit; total annual needs are 6,400 units. The material is used evenly throughout the year. Order costs are $100 per order, and carrying costs for the year are $8 per unit in stock. The firm carries a safety stock of 50 units, has a lead time of one week, and works 50 weeks per year. Determine the economic order quantity and the re-order point.

7. The purchasing agent responsible for ordering cotton underwear for Barr Retail Stores has come up the following information:

Maximum daily demand	100 packages
Average daily demand	80 packages
Lead time	9 days
Economic order quantity	3,500 packages

   a. Compute the safety stock.
   b. Calculate the reorder point.

8. The Bolger Company has obtained the following costs and other data pertaining to one of its materials:

Working days per year	250
Average use per day	500 units
Maximum use per day	600 units

Lead time	5 days
Cost of placing one order	$36
Carrying cost per unit per year	$1

a. Calculate the economic order quantity.

b. Determine the safety stock.

c. Compute the reorder point.

9. Harrington & Sons, Inc., would like to determine the safety stock to maintain for a product so that the lowest combination of stockout cost and carrying cost would result. Each stockout will cost $75; the carrying cost for each safety stock unit will be $1; the product will be ordered five times a year. The following probabilities of running out of stock during an order period are associated with various safety stock levels:

Safety Stock Level (units)	Probability of Stockout (%)
10	40
20	20
40	10
80	5

Using the expected value approach, determine the safety stock level.

10. McCormick Company, a regional supermarket chain, orders 480,000 cans of frozen orange juice per year from a California distributor. A 2-dozen-can case of frozen juice delivered to McCormick's central warehouse costs $4.80, including freight charges. The company borrows funds at a 10% interest rate to finance its inventories. The McCormick Company's purchasing agent has calculated that it costs $15 to place an order for frozen juice and that the annual carrying expense (electricity, insurance, handling) is $0.08 for each can of juice.

a. What is the economic order quantity?

b. How would you change your answer in part a if the California distributor offered a 10% discount off the delivery price for minimum orders of 72,000 cases?

11. DKT Electronics, Inc., makes part number 562 for one of its computers. The annual demand is 10,000 units. The annual carrying cost is $10 per unit, and the cost of preparing an order and making production setup for the order is $100. The firm operates 250 days per year. The machine used to make this part has a production rate of 200 units per day.

a. Calculate the economic production run size.

b. How many lots are to be produced in a year?

c. What is the annual cost of setups?

d. What is the average inventory?

e. What is the annual cost of carrying inventory of part 562?

12. Davidson's Restaurant uses cooking oil at an average rate of 15 gallons per day. The demand can be approximated by a normal distribution with a standard deviation of 2 gallons per day. Lead time is eight days. The restaurant wants to achieve a service level that is seven times the risk of a stockout. If cooking oil can be ordered as needed, what re-order point should be used if lead time is eight days?

13. Constas Hamburger Shop uses 20 gallons of cola per day. The lead time is normally distributed with a mean of five days and a standard deviation of two days. Determine the level of safety stock and optimal reorder point. Assume a service level of 99%.

14. XYZ Store wishes to stock refrigerators for sale. Assume that the store knows that the probability distribution of demand is as follows:

Demand	Probability of Demand Equal to the Given Number	Probability of at Least the Given Number
6	0.1	1.00
7	0.3	0.9
8	0.4	0.6
9	0.2	0.2
	1.00	

The store pays $650 for each item and sells it for $1,000. There is no disposal cost. The ordering cost is fixed for all courses of action. How many items should the store stock?

15. The following data for an inventory item is given:

Demand Per Hour (units)	Probability
0	0.2
1	0.4
2	0.3
3	0.1

Beginning inventory	5 units
Order quantity	4 units

Lead time   2 hours
Reorder point (checked at the end of each hour) 3 units

Simulate 10 hours of operation for demand, beginning and ending inventories, and order placements and arrivals, using the following random digits: 07 34 35 23 17 20 72 59 05 68.

ANSWERS

DO YOU KNOW THE BASICS?

1. Inventory-related costs fall into three categories: (a) ordering costs, which includes all costs associated with preparing a purchase order, (b) carrying (holding) costs, which include storage costs for inventory items plus the cost of money tied up in inventory, and (c) shortage (stockout) costs, which include those costs incurred when an item is out of stock. These include the lost contribution margin on sales plus lost customer goodwill.

2. Many inventory planning models are available. They basically try to answer the following two questions: (a) how much to order? and (b) when to order?

3. Dependent demand inventories consist of items whose demand depends on the demands for other items held in inventory. Independent demand items are the finished goods or other end-items. Its demand is independent of the demand for any other item carried in inventory.

4. The ROP answers when to place a new order, and requires a knowledge of the lead time, which is the time interval between placing an order and receiving delivery. ROP can be calculated as follows:

= Average demand per unit of lead time × lead time + Safety stock

5. The EOQ is computed as:

$$EOQ = \sqrt{\frac{2DO}{C}}$$

where C = carrying cost per unit, O = ordering cost per order, and D = annual demand (requirements) in units.

6. The procedure is as follows: (a) calculate EOQs for each price; rejecting any EOQ that is not within the allowable quantity range for the

price used; (b) calculate total annual cost for feasible EOQs. (i) if the feasible EOQ is the lowest price curve, this is the overall EOQ and (ii) if the EOQ is not the lowest price range, compute the total cost for the EOQ and for the next quantities for which price reductions will occur, and (c) select the value of Q that will result in the lowest total cost.

7. There are four cases: (a) known maximum demand rate, constant lead time, (b) variable demand rate, constant lead time, (c) constant demand, variable lead time, and (d) incorporation of stockout costs.

8. ABC analysis involves the following steps: (a) compute annual dollar volume by inventory type anticipated (annual demand times unit cost); (b) segregate merchandise into components based on annual dollar value; and (c) rank inventory in terms of annual dollar volume, ranging from high to low (e.g., As in top 80%, Bs in next 15% and Cs in last 5%). Examples of inventory controls that may be based on ABC classification are *purchasing* (e.g., a purchase order for a class A item might be signed by the president, for a class B item by the head of the purchasing department, and for a class C item by any purchasing agent), *physical inventory check* (e.g., Count A items monthly, B items twice a year, and C items annually), *forecasting* (e.g., forecast A items by several methods with resolution by a prediction committee, B items by simple trend projection, and C items by best guess of the responsible purchasing agent), and *safety stock* (e.g., no safety stock for A items, one month's supply for B items, and three months' supply for C items).

9. Unlike the basic EOQ model, the marginal approach to inventory introduces the concept of uncertainty. The basic rule is to add inventory as long as the expected reduction in penalty cost for a shortage is greater than the expected cost of stocking the unit.

10. Simulation refers to the use of a numerical model that represents the dynamic relationships in a system to predict the behavior of the system.

11. Simulation involves the following steps: (a) determine the distribution that describes the statistical property of concern; (b) convert the probability distribution to a cumulative probability distribution; (c) sample at random (using the random number table) from the cumulative probability distribution to produce outcomes, and (d) simulate the process.

PRACTICAL APPLICATION

1.

$$EOQ = \sqrt{\frac{2DO}{C}}$$

where C = carrying cost per unit, O = ordering cost per order, and D = annual demand in units.

$$EOQ = \sqrt{\frac{2(\$400)(30,000)}{\$600}} = \sqrt{40,000} = 200$$

2.

$$Economic\ run\ size = \sqrt{\frac{2OD}{C}}$$

$$\sqrt{\frac{2(\$80)(10,000)}{\$0.40}} = \sqrt{4,000,000} = 2,000$$

where C = carrying cost per unit, O = setup cost per order, and D = annual requirements in units.

If each production run is to be 2,000 units and a total of 10,000 units are needed, there will have to be 5 runs (10,000/2,000).

3.

$$\sqrt{\frac{2(\$2)(4,000)}{Carrying\ cost}} = 200$$

Note that 200 × 200 = 40,000.

$$40,000 = \frac{\$16,000}{Cost\ of\ carrying\ one\ unit\ for\ one\ period}$$

The cost of carrying one unit for one period = $0.40.

4. First, the EOQs are computed for each of the prices:

$$EOQ_{10.00} = \sqrt{2(2,000)(30)/0.35(10.00)} = 185\ (reject—too\ large)$$

$$EOQ_{9.50} = \sqrt{2(2,000)(30)/0.35(9.50)} = 190\ (feasible)$$

$$EOQ_{9.00} = \sqrt{2(2,000)(30)/0.35(9.00)} = 195 \text{ (reject—too small)}$$

The total annual cost at two quantities is therefore investigated: 190 and 500 units per order.

At $Q = 190$,

total annual cost $= (0.35)(\$9.50)(190/2) + \$30(2,000/190) + \$9.50(2,000)$

$$= \$315.88 + \$315.79 + \$19,000 = \$19,631.67.$$

At $Q = 500$,

total annual cost $= (0.35)(\$9.00)(500/2) + \$30(2,000/500) + \$9.00(2,000)$

$$- \$787.50 + \$120 + \$18,000 = \$18,907.50.$$

500 valves is a more economical order quantity because the total annual cost is lower that that associated with the EOQ.

5.

a. The economic order quantity is

$$EOQ = \sqrt{\frac{2(\$1.20)(24,000)}{(\$10)(10\%)}} = \sqrt{57,600} = 240$$

The number of orders needed per year is

$$\frac{\text{Annual requirements}}{EOQ} = \frac{24,000}{240} = 100 \text{ orders per year}$$

The total cost of buying and carrying blades for the year is

$$\frac{EOQ}{2} \text{ (Holding cost per unit)} + \frac{\text{Annual requirements}}{EOQ} \text{ (Ordering cost per order)}$$

$$= \frac{240}{2} (\$10.00 \times 10\%) + \frac{24,000}{240} (\$1.20) = \$240$$

b. The optimal reorder point is

$$\text{Lead time} \times \text{Average daily demand}$$

$$= 3 \text{ days} \times (24,000 \text{ packages}/360) = 200 \text{ packages}$$

Because the company has 200 packages now, it should place the next order immediately.

c. Applying the EOQ formula to inventory problems can cause some of the following problems:

- Inventory is not always used at a constant rate, and the constant demand assumption is implicit in the EOQ formula.

- The EOQ formula requires estimates of annual sales, ordering costs, purchase price per unit, and cost of carrying inventories. These estimates may be extremely difficult to obtain.

6.

$$EOQ = \sqrt{\frac{2(\$100)(6,400)}{\$8.00}} = \sqrt{160,000} = 400$$

ROP = Average demand during lead time + Safety stock

= 1 week × (6,400/50 weeks) + 50 units

= 128 units + 50 units = 178 units

7.

a. The safety stock is computed as follows:

Maximum daily demand	100 packages
Average daily demand	80
Excess	20
Lead time	× 9 days
Safety stock	180 packages

b. ROP = Average demand during lead time + Safety stock

= 80 packages × 9 days + 180 packages = 720 + 180 = 900 packages

8.

a.

$$EOQ = \sqrt{\frac{2(\$36)(125,000)}{\$1}} = \sqrt{9,000,000} = 3,000$$

b.

Maximum use per day	600 units
Average use per day	500
Safety stock	100 units × 5 days of lead time = 500 units

c.

Average use per day (500) × Days of lead time (5)	2,500 units
Safety stock	500
Reorder point	3,000 units

9.

Annual Number of Orders ×	Probability of Stockout =	Expected Annual Stockouts ×	Cost Per Stockout ($) =	Annual Stockout Cost ($) +	Annual Safety Stock Carrying Cost ($1/unit) =	Total Cost ($)
5	0.4	2	75	150.00	10	160.00
5	0.2	1	75	75.00	20	95.00
5	0.1	0.5	75	37.50	40	77.50
5	0.05	0.25	75	18.75	80	98.75

The recommended level of safety stock is 40 units.

10.

a.

$$EOQ = \sqrt{\frac{2(\$15)(480,000)}{[(\$4.80/24)(0.1)] + \$0.08}} = \sqrt{144,000,000} = 12,000 \text{ cans}$$

or 12,000/24 = 500 cases

b. McCormick should decide to order in quantities of 72,000 cans, based on the following computations:

	12,000 cans	72,000 cans
Order size	12,000 cans	72,000 cans
Number of orders per year	40	6(2/3)
Average inventory	6,000 cans	36,000 cans
Cost of placing orders @ $15	$600	$100
Cost of carrying inventory:		

$0.08 \times 6,000$	480	
$0.08 \times 36,000$		2,880
$[6,000 \times (\$4.80/24)] \times 0.10$	120	
$[36,000 \times (\$4.80/24)] \times 0.10$		720
Product cost:		
($4.8/24) $\times$ 480,000 cases	96,000	
($4.32/24) $\times$ 480,000 cases		86,400
Total cost including product cost	97,200	90,100

11. O = setup cost = $100 per setup, C = carrying cost = $10 per unit, D = annual demand = 10,000 units, p = production rate = 200 units, and u = usage rate 40 units (10,000 units/250 working days).

a.

$$\text{EOQ} = \sqrt{\frac{2DS}{C} \frac{p}{(p-u)}} = \sqrt{\frac{2(10,000)(100)}{10} \frac{200}{(200-40)}} = 500 \text{ units}$$

b. Number of lots per year = D/Q = 10,000/500 = 20 lots.

c. Annual setup costs = $S(D/Q)$ = (100)(10,000/500) = $2,000.

d. Average inventory level = $Q/2[(p-u)p]$ = (500/2)[(200 − 40)/200] = 200 units.

e. Annual cost of carrying this inventory = 200 units $\times$ $10 per unit = $2,000.

12.

ROP = Expected demand during lead time + Safety stock

$$= \overline{d}\text{LT} + z\sqrt{\text{LT}}\,(\sigma_d)$$

where $\overline{d}$ = 15 gallons per day, LT= 8 days, and σ_d = 2 gallons per day. Service level is 7/8 = 0.875 [from Table 3 (Normal Distribution Table) in the Appendix II, z = 1.15]

Safety stock = $1.15\sqrt{8}(2)$ = 6.8 gallons
ROP = 15(8) + 6.8 = 126.8 gallons

13.

ROP = Expected demand during lead time + Safety stock

$$= d \; \overline{LT} + zd \, (\sigma_{LT})$$

where d = 20 gallons per day, $\overline{LT}$ = 5 days, and σ_{LT} = 2 days.
For a service level of 99%, z = 2.33. Thus,

Safety stock = 2.33 (20)(2) = 93.2 gallons

ROP = 20(5) + 93.2 = 193.2 gallons

14.

Note that MP = $1,000 – $650 = $350, ML = $650 – 0 = $650.

$$p = \frac{ML}{ML + MP} = \frac{\$650}{\$650 + \$350} = 0.65$$

The probability of selling a unit must be 0.65 in order to justify the
stocking of the unit. From the demand distribution, the best course of
action is to stock 7 units.

15.

Demand per Hour (units)	Probability	Cumulative Probability	Corresponding Random 2-digits
0	0.2	0.2	1–19
1	0.4	0.6	20–59
2	0.3	0.9	60–89
3	0.1	1.0	90–99

Based on the random digits assigned, we obtain demand units in the
second column.

Hours	Demand	Beginning Inventory	Ending Inventory	Order Point[a]	Order Arrivals[a]
1	0	5	5		
2	1	5	4		
3	1	4	3	4	
4	1	3	2		
5	0	2	2		4
6	1	6	5		
7	2	5	3	4	
8	1	3	2		
9	0	2	2		4
10	2	6	4		

[a]end of hour

10

MATERIAL REQUIREMENTS PLANNING AND JUST-IN-TIME

KEY TERMS

bill of materials (BOM) structured parts list that shows the manner in which the product is actually put together.

capacity requirements planning (CRP) system for determining if a planned production schedule can be accomplished with available capacity and, if not, making adjustments as necessary.

inventory status file file indicating how much inventory is on hand or on order.

just-in-time production approach to manufacturing in which items are produced only when needed in production.

Kanban Japanese information system for coordinating production orders and withdrawals from in-process inventory to realize just-in-time production.

manufacturing resource planning (MRP II) integrated information system that steps beyond first-generation MRP to synchronize all aspects (not just manufacturing) of the business.

material requirements planning (MRP) computerized data processing system whose function is to schedule production and control the level of inventory for components with dependent demand.

time bucket a time period used in the master schedule.

The previous chapter focused on independent-demand inventories, which enable a company to respond to demand from outside the production system more quickly than it could if it had to buy or produce an item before selling it. The extent of external demand is usually not known ahead of time; it must be forecast, and some uncertainty is inherent in these forecasts. Quite often, safety stock is required to ensure that sufficient quantities of these items will be available.

Many types of organizations such as make-to-stock manufacturers, hospitals, wholesale distributors, and retail businesses must keep independent-demand items on hand. On the other hand, many manufacturers deal with dependent-demand inventories. *Dependent-demand items* are those components that are assembled to become part of some parent item or in some similar way become part of a set of components. Dependent-demand inventories typically are consumed within the production system, not by some outside demand.

In this chapter, we present material requirements planning, a system that works backwards from the scheduled quantities and need dates for end-items specified in a master production schedule to determine the requirements for components needed to meet the MPS. In a latter part of the chapter we will discuss the just-in-time (JIT) system of inventory, a Japanese contribution.

MATERIAL REQUIREMENTS PLANNING

Material requirements planning (MRP) is a flow-control system design to ensure that parts and components (items with dependent demand) are available in the period when they are needed, with little or none present at other times. The theme of MRP is "getting the right component parts and materials to the right place at the right time." Figure 10.1 depicts an MRP computer system.

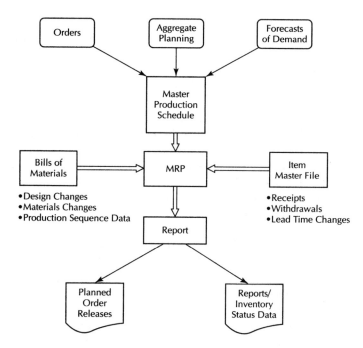

Figure 10.1. An MRP Computer System

The overall objective of MRP is to provide a more effective, responsive, and disciplined approach to determining the material requirements of the organization. Employed properly, MRP may serve as a communication device as well as a planning tool, allowing various subfunctions of the firm to operate with a common, integrated plan. Fundamentally, MRP attempts to answer the following questions (given a master production schedule):

- What material is needed?

- When is the material needed?

- How much is needed?

- When should orders be placed?

Correct answers to these questions are vital for effective operations in the manufacturing context.

SYSTEM LOGIC

Fundamental is the concept of dependent demand. Demands for end-items (final products) create demands for assemblies, which in turn create demands for components, and so on. Take telephone stands, for example. Demands for stands create demands for legs; sills are then manufactured; these parts create demands for the basic raw material, wood, in several different forms. Additionally, demand for the end-items or final products will occur as a function of scheduled production and customer demands. Therefore, it is not necessary to forecast independently the need for parts and components, because the "exploding" of the end-item will provide this information. *Exploding* simply means the breaking down of final items into component parts that can be individually planned and scheduled. The amount of material available for use in the production process is a function of material on hand and material on order (pipeline inventory). MRP operates on a perpetual inventory concept. The key to the use of MRP is an understanding of the netting process. The principle is illustrated in Table 10.1.

Table 10.1. Netting Process[a]

	Inventory Units
W: End-item	25
X: Assembly X	100
Y: Subassembly Y	50
Z: Part Z	10

[a]Assume 1:1 relationships.

EXAMPLE 1

If the demand for end-item W is 200 units and the current inventory equals 25 units, the netting process would operate as follows:

Net requirement for W = Gross requirement (W) – Inventory (W)

$$= 200 - 25 = 175 \text{ units}$$

If the net requirement for W is 175 units, then the gross requirement for assembly X would also be 175 units:

Net requirement for X = Gross requirement (X) – Inventory (X)

$$= 175 - 100 = 75 \text{ units}$$

The net requirement for assembly X becomes the gross requirement for subassembly Y; substituting:

Net requirement for Y = Gross requirement (Y) – Inventory (Y)

$$= 75 - 50 = 25 \text{ units}$$

The net requirement for subassembly Y becomes the gross requirement for part Z; substituting:

Net requirement for Z = Gross requirement (Z) – Inventory (Z)

$$= 25 - 10 = 15 \text{ units}$$

The netting process is based on the fact that, for example, a subassembly contains all the parts or items that define it as a subassembly. Therefore, if we have a stock of subassemblies on hand, we must also count (consider) the parts in that subassembly, in effect, netting out these parts from the computations to avoid double counting. Double counting would occur if the inventory levels of W, X, Y, and Z were simply subtracted from the gross requirement of W, as shown in Table 10.2.

Table 10.2. Impact on Requirements With and Without Netting

	With Netting	Without Netting
W	175	175
X	75	100
Y	25	150
Z	15	190

SYSTEM COMPONENTS

The components of the MRP system in its simplest form are shown in Figure 10.1. Here, the MRP component parts feed into the MRP processor—the computer program. Yet each component plays a vital role.

The *bill of materials (BOM) file* tells what a finished product is composed of. It provides the basic relationships among parts, assemblies, subassemblies, and end-items. Thus, each product has its own BOM. The listing is hierarchical. It shows that the quantity of each item needed to complete one unit of the next-highest level of assembly. The product-structure tree shows this relationship (see Figure 10.2). The final product is assigned a level 0 designation. Levels 1...n indicate the relationship between items. For example, subassembly 1 is composed of parts 1 and 2. The bill of materials also specifies the quantities required to make each item. These values are shown in parentheses.

The *master schedule* tells how much a finished product is desired and when. It states (a) which end items are to be produced, (b) when these end items are needed, and (c) what quantities are needed. Generally master production schedules are developed for periods ranging from 26 to 104 weeks, with revisions or updates on a weekly or biweekly basis. Master schedules are set forth in standard planning periods called time buckets and are most commonly specified in weeks.

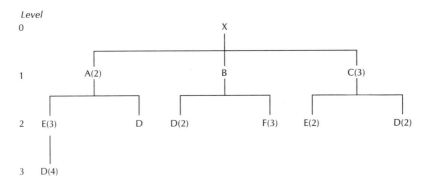

Figure 10.2. Product-Structure Tree

The *inventory status file* indicates how much inventory is on hand or on order. It contains such information as gross requirements, scheduled receipts, expected amount on hand, and other information such as supplier, lot size, and lead times for acquisition of purchased parts and internal operations on these parts plus the waiting time between operations.

MRP COMPUTER PROGRAM

The MRP processor itself performs the explosion process and the netting process and offsets the lead times to provide reports on what to buy, when to buy, and when to expedite, deexpedite, cancel, and increase or decrease orders. It involves taking the end-item requirements that are specified by the master schedule and "exploding" them into *time-phased* requirements for the components using the bill of materials offset by lead times. The net requirement of each material are computed as follows:

Net material requirement = Gross material requirements – Inventory on hand (available at the beginning of the period) – Planned order receipts (or scheduled receipts)

Scheduled receipts, sometimes called *open orders,* are orders that have been placed but not yet completed. *Planned receipts* are new orders not yet released to the shop or the supplier. Planning for receipt of these new orders will keep the projected on-hand balance from dropping below the desired safety stock level. A planned receipt indicates the amount to order or to start producing in each period in order to be available for the next level of production or assembly. This entire computer procedure results in inventory transaction data (orders released, changes in orders, and so on), which are used to update the inventory status file, the primary output reports, and secondary output reports. Note that normally,

Inventory on hand (available at the beginning of the next period)
= In stock – Safety stock – Inventory allocated to other uses

$$\text{On hand}_t = \text{On hand}_{t-1} - \text{Gross requirements}_t + \text{Scheduled receipts}_t + \text{Planned order receipts}_t$$

EXAMPLE 2

Donna is the MRP manager for Gadgets, Inc. An MPS is given to her showing gross requirements for 250 units of the Model A gadget in week 4 and 100 units in week 6. These are the only items on the MPS. The following is a product structure diagram based on the bill of materials.

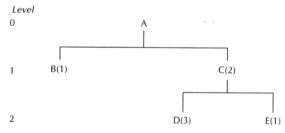

The Item Master File shows the inventory levels and other planning data for every item.

Item Master File[a]

	In Stock	Safety Stock	Allocated	Lead Time (weeks)	Lot Size	Scheduled Receipts Amount	Scheduled Receipts Week
A	150	50	0	1	200		
B	200	100	100	2	500		
C	400	100	0	1	300		
D	400	200	100	2	2,000	2,000	2
E	100	50	0	1	500		

[a]Note: Safety stock is a reserve and not available for planned use. Allocated is committed to another use and hence not available for planned use. Lot size is the minimum order quantity; one may order more for the current period, but not less. Scheduled receipts is the order that has already been released.

Donna adheres to the following routine:

1.

Inventory on hand = In stock − Safety stock − Inventory allocated to other uses

For example, beginning inventory on hand for item A: 150 − 50 − 0 = 100.

On hand$_t$ = On hand$_{t-1}$ − Gross requirements$_t$ + Scheduled receipts$_t$ + Planned order receipts$_t$

For example, inventory on hand for item A in week 4: 100 − 250 + 0 + 200 = 50.

2.

Net material requirement = Gross material requirements − Inventory on hand − Planned order receipts (or scheduled receipts)

For example, net material requirement for item A in week 4: 250 − 100 − 0 = 150.

3. Planned order receipts. Plan to receive order of the amount of net requirement (more if required by lot size).

4. Planned order release. This is the same amount as the planned order receipt, except that it is offset by lead time. For example, units of A (lead time = 1 week) required in week 4 must be ordered in week 3. Note also that a planned order release for the parent generates gross requirements in the same week for the "children" (lower level). For example, order releases for A in weeks 3 and 5 generate gross requirements for B and C in those weeks; order releases for C in weeks 2 and 4 generate gross requirements for D and E in those weeks. Note also that gross requirements for "children" are dictated by the bill of materials amount. For example, gross requirements for D is 900 units (planned order release units of 300 for C × 3 units of D required for each unit of C).

Item Code	Level Code	Lead Time	On Hand	Safety Stock	Allocated		Week 1	Week 2	Week 3	Week 4	Week 5	Week 6
A	0	1	150	50	0	Gross requirements	100	100	100	250	50	100
						Scheduled receipts						
						On hand **100**						
						Net requirements						
						Planned order receipts						
						Planned order releases						
B	1	2	200	100	100	Gross requirements				100		150
						Scheduled receipts				150		50
						On hand **0**						
						Net requirements			200		200	
						Planned order receipts					200	200
						Planned order releases			200	200		
C	1	1	400	100	0	Gross requirements				300	100	100
						Scheduled receipts						
						On hand **300**		0	0			
						Net requirements			200			
						Planned order receipts			500			
						Planned order releases	500					
D	1	2	400	200	100	Gross requirements		300	300	300	300	100
						Scheduled receipts		900		900		
						On hand **100**						
						Net requirements		100	100		200	
						Planned order receipts			1,200	1,200	200	
						Planned order releases	300	2,000	300			
E	1	1	100	50	0	Gross requirements		250		250		450
						Scheduled receipts		50		50		
						On hand **50**						
						Net requirements	50		250		450	
						Planned order receipts		500		500		
						Planned order releases	500		500			

Donna has completed her MRP plan. She plans to release the following orders:

Week 1: 500 units of B and 500 units of E

Week 2: 300 units of C

Week 3: 200 units of A and 500 units of E

Week 4: 300 units of C

Week 5: 200 units of A

Week 6: None

YOU SHOULD REMEMBER

Questions Addressed in MRP Processing

Questions	Remarks
(1) What do we want to produce and when?	Input to the MRP program through the master schedule
(2) What components are required to make and how many does it take?	Provided by the bill of materials
(3) How many are already scheduled to be available in each future period?	Obtained from the inventory status file
(4) How many more do we need to obtain for each future period?	Subtract (3) from (2), if (2) is larger
(5) When do we need to order these amounts so that they will be available when needed?	Move earlier in time by the production or procurement lead time for each time

OUTPUTS OF MRP

The outputs of MRP systems dynamically provide the schedule of materials for the future—amount of each material required in each time period to support the master planning schedule. Two primary outputs result:

- *Planned order schedule.* A plan of the quantity of each material to be ordered in each time period.

- *Changes in planned orders.* Modification of previous planned orders.

The secondary MRP outputs provide the following information:

- *Exception reports.* Reports that flag items requiring management attention in order to provide the right quantity of materials in each time period, (e.g., reporting errors, out-of-bound situations, and excessive scrap).

- *Performance reports.* Reports that indicate how well the system is operating, (e.g., inventory turns, percentage of delivery promises kept, and stockout incidences).

- *Planning reports.* Reports to be used in future inventory planning activities, [e.g., inventory forecasts, purchase commitments report, traces to demand sources (pegging), and long-range material requirements planning].

INVENTORY DECISION RULES FOR MRP

Many decision rules (lot-sizing rules) can be employed for lot sizing under MRP.

Rule 1. Lot-size ordering—minimum order quantity needed.

Rule 2. Lot-for-lot (LFL) ordering—ordering the exact quantity to satisfy the requirements of each time period (usually a week).

Rule 3. Period order quantities (POQ)—selection of a fixed time interval over which to purchase and determine requirements.

Rule 4. Economic order quantity—using the standard EOQ formula, the annual usage is determined by proportioning.

Rule 5. Least total cost method—attempts to select the quantity to order that balances the cost of possession and the cost of acquisition.

Additional rules can be used, including least unit cost, period order quantity, and dynamic programming plus variations on these. Which is best is impossible to say because they all have the major constraint of discontinuous (lumpy) demand for items.

BENEFITS AND LIMITATIONS OF MRP

The benefits of MRP include:
- The reduction of inventory investment

- The reduction of shortages

- The achievement of more reliable delivery schedules

- The improvement of work flow

But MRP is not without shortcomings. It may use outdated bills of materials, not incorporating design changes. Further, MRP may lack accurate and up-to-date master schedules.

MANUFACTURING RESOURCE PLANNING

Manufacturing resource planning (MRP II or "closed loop" MRP) is an integrated information system that steps beyond first-generation MRP to synchronize all aspects (not just manufacturing) of the business. The MRP II system coordinates sales, purchasing, manufacturing, finance, and engineering by adopting a focal production plan and by using one unified database to plan and update all systems.

MRP II enables managers to test what-if scenarios by using simulation. Management can project the dollar value of shipments, product costs, overhead allocations, inventories, backlogs, and profits. The system reports can help managers in production, purchasing, marketing, finance, and engineering develop and monitor the overall business plan and recognize sales objectives, production capabilities, and cash flow limitations.

JUST-IN-TIME MANUFACTURING

The inventory control problem occurs in almost every type of organization. It exists whenever products are held to meet some expected future demand. In most industries, cost of inventory represents the largest liquid asset under the control of management. Therefore, it is very important to develop a production and inventory planning system that will minimize both purchasing and carrying costs. During the 1960s and 1970s, material requirements planning (MRP) was adopted by many U.S. manufacturing companies as the key component of their production and inventory planning systems. Although success has not been universal, users typically agreed that the inventory approach inherent in an MRP system generally is more effective than the classical approach to inventory planning. Aside from the manufacturing aspects, the purchasing function also is of major importance to the overall success of the system. Even though MRP has received a great deal of attention, effective purchasing and management of materials is still a high-priority activity in most manufacturing firms. Material cost, as a proportion of total product cost, has continued to rise significantly during the last few years and, hence, is a primary concern of top management.

Competing on the basis of both price and quality, the Japanese have demonstrated the ability to manage their production systems effectively. Much of their success has been attributed to what is known as the *just-in-time (JIT)* approach to production and inventory control, which has generated a great deal of interest among practitioners. The Kanban system—as the Japanese call it—has been a focal point of interest, with its dramatic impact on the inventory performance and productivity of the Japanese auto industry.

This section provides an overview of the JIT approach. It also highlights the impact that JIT implementation might have on inventory control, the purchasing function, and production costs.

WHAT IS JUST-IN-TIME?

JIT is a demand–pull system. Demand for customer output (not plans for using input resources) triggers production. Production activities are pulled, not pushed, into action. JIT production, in its purest sense, is buying and producing in very small quantities just in time for use. The basic idea has its roots in Japan's densely populated industrial areas and its lack of resources, both of which have produced frugal personal habits among the Japanese people. The idea was developed into a formal management system by Toyota in order to meet the precise demands of customers for various vehicle models and colors with minimum delivery delays.

As a philosophy, JIT targets inventory as an evil presence that obscures problems that should be solved. JIT suggests that, by contributing significantly to costs, large inventories keep a company from being as competitive or profitable as it otherwise might be. Practically speaking, JIT has as its principal goal the elimination of waste, and the principal measure of success is how much or how little inventory there is. Virtually anything that achieves this end can be considered a JIT innovation.

Furthermore, the little inventory that exists in a JIT system must be of good quality. This requirement has led to JIT purchasing practices uniquely able to deliver high-quality materials. JIT systems integrate five functions of the production process—sourcing, storage, transportation, operations, and quality control—into one controlled manufacturing process. In manufacturing, JIT means that a company produces only the quantity needed for delivery to dealers or customers. In purchasing, it means suppliers deliver subassemblies just in time to be assembled into finished goods. In delivery, it requires selecting a transportation mode that will deliver purchased components and materials in small-lot sizes at the loading dock of the manufacturing facilities just in time to support the manufacturing process.

The Japanese believe that human error, machine breakdowns, and defective parts can be prevented and that inventory simply hides these problems and keeps companies from achieving their goals. During the 1950s, the Japanese recognized that they needed to upgrade their manufacturing expertise significantly if they were to make additional inroads in world markets. The targeted goals were quality and the elimination of waste. Development of new techniques occurred, among which JIT is the most publicized. It (Kanban) uses simple tags to track the flow of work-in-process inventory. The word *Kanban* literally means signboard or ticket in Japanese. Tickets control the flow of materials through the system. The goal in using Kanban is to have each material arrive just in time for its use in the production operation. The ability of Kanban to achieve this goal depends upon the characteristics of the environment in which it operates. These characteristics have been divided into major categories in Table 10.3.

The flow of materials is always associated with the relationship between two work centers; this interrelationship is crucial to the efficient flow of materials. The consuming work center is independent of the producing department for its necessary components. The notion of a producing work center likewise is extended to the distribution system for the finished product. All communication is accomplished through the movement of Kanban tickets that identify products, routing, and order quantity information. All activities dealing with materials flow or conversion are associated with Kanbans. Thus, the total quantity of material is controlled by the number of Kanbans in the system. A reduction in the number of Kanbans circulating in the system will result in a reduction in the inventory. No material-based activity is permitted without an attached Kanban card.

Table 10.3. Major Characteristics of the Japanese Just-in-Time System

Technical Factors	Behavioral/Environmental Factors
Group technology	Factory—unions
Minimized setup times	Focused factory
Smoothing of master production schedule/aggregate plan	Quality at source
Flow-type shop employment	Job security/lifetime
Visible control, pull-up/ management	Group decision making/bottom-up system with Kanban
Automation	Supporting supplier network
Total preventive maintenance	

Figure 10.3 illustrates the flow of materials in a simple Kanban system. Material flows from work station Wn through an intermediate storage area to work station Wn_{+1}; all material is moved in standardized containers, with each holding approximately one-tenth of one day's usage quantity. Each container has a Kanban attached and cannot be removed until a material handler arrives with a conveyance Kanban (used to control the flow of material within the shop). Once this occurs, the production Kanban is removed and returned to the producing department. This serves as an authorization to replace the material just removed.

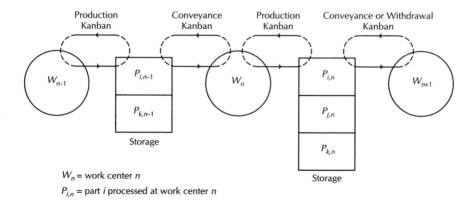

W_n = work center n

$P_{i,n}$ = part i processed at work center n

Figure 10.3. Flow of Materials with Kanbans

The conveyance Kanban attached to the container moves to the consuming department. The conveyance Kanban cannot be used to acquire additional stock until the material within the container is actually used. Hence, not only is the total amount of inventory controlled by the Kanban cards, but the production of additional inventory is also delayed until current inventory is used. To make the Kanban system work, a smoothed daily production rate is essential. This means that the aggregate production schedule and the master production schedule must be adjusted smoothly on a daily basis. Because the production lot size is defined by a standardized container, a typical production lot size in the Kanban system is inherently smaller than lot sizes used in a typical MRP system, which uses a weekly time bucket. This also means that more frequent production setups are required under the Kanban system and that minimizing the setup time becomes a very important feature of the system.

Group technology employs the principal of grouping parts with common processing characteristics to reduce processing variety and hence to increase manufacturing productivity. Application of group technology justifies the use of flow-shop processing modes with increased automation because a larger volume of parts can use the common processes. Preventive maintenance supports uninterrupted flow of material and parts through the manufacturing system.

BEHAVIORAL AND ENVIRONMENTAL FACTORS

In what follows, the major behavioral characteristics listed in Table 10.3 will be briefly discussed. The fact that Japanese labor unions are organized not by trade but by factory tends to foster cooperation between management and union. Both parties can deal with specific problems in a particular factory or company that affect both the worker and the company.

The focused factory concept is part of a larger strategy designed to have a limited number of products or items manufactured under the responsibility of a single profit center or cost center. This concept tends to reduce the complexity in planning and controlling production and inventory management activities. It also tends to delineate specific management responsibilities.

The Japanese system emphasizes the quality at source concept. This simply means that a worker who makes an item also has the responsibility for the quality of the item. The same worker must check the quality and, if necessary, has the authority to stop the production process if it is malfunctioning. The result tends to be improved quality levels, with an emphasis on preventive and corrective actions rather than on the identification of defective items after the production process is completed. Many Japanese companies subscribe to the life-long employment concept. Although the practice does not cover all employees, this long-term relationship is generally extended to the core employees of the company. This culturally embedded practice stimulates management to think in terms of long-term objectives and performance. It also helps the company secure loyal and committed employees. Even for those employees who have not achieved lifetime status, it serves as a major motivating force.

A final important point is the fact that the Japanese emphasize group consensus in the decision making process. Usually, this generates a bottom-up management style that encourages participation and commitment by all parties in any significant decision. An illustration of this practice is the much publicized Quality Circle concept. Although it might take longer to reach agreement, execution of the decision typically is easier because much of the resistance to change has already been dissipated.

PURCHASING ASPECTS OF JIT

The basic objectives of a JIT production control system is to minimize work-in-process and raw materials inventories by providing each work center with the exact quantity of parts or materials at the precise time they are needed. Therefore, the ideal state of JIT production would be a stockless production system in which each unit of output is produced as it is needed at each succeeding work station.

Implementation of such a production system, however, requires heavy involvement of the purchasing function which, in reality, is the starting point for the materials flow cycle. The concept of JIT purchasing is very similar to the JIT production system previously described. Under the JIT purchasing system, suppliers are required to deliver a small quantity of required parts of materials to the buyer's plant as they are needed. This can mean daily or sometimes twice a day deliveries of purchased items. The critical elements of JIT purchasing are

- Reduced order quantities
- Frequent and reliable delivery schedules
- Reduced and highly reliable lead times
- Consistently high quality levels for purchased materials

On the surface, the JIT purchasing concept may appear to be a drastic departure from the conventional and traditional inventory and purchasing management. Close examination of fundamental inventory and purchasing theories, however, indicates that the JIT purchasing concept is well founded in existing theory.

Traditional inventory theory states that the order quantity Q should be determined on the basis of relationships between material usage rate u, inventory carrying costs C, and incremental ordering or setup costs O. The relationship is expressed as

$$Q = f(u, C, O)$$

All existing techniques to determine order quantity values represent variations of this generalization. The basic objective of these techniques is to find the economic order quantity that minimizes the total cost associated with materials, with a given set of parameters. Under this condition, in order to reduce the order quantity, the unit ordering cost must be relatively low compared with the unit inventory carrying cost.

Too often, application of traditional inventory theory treats the unit ordering cost as a fixed value that is assumed to be constant. In reality, however, this is often an incorrect assumption. Under the JIT purchasing system, for example, the ordering cost (or setup cost) can be and is reduced sufficiently for conventional EOQ analysis (discussed in Chapter 9) to produce a smaller optimum order quantity. Figure 10.4 is an illustration of this phenomenon.

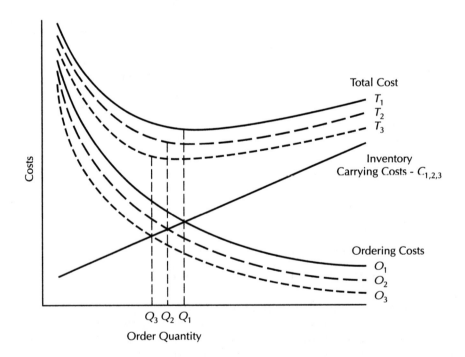

Figure 10.4. Impact of Reduced Ordering Cost on Order Quantity

In a traditional reorder point system, the inventory reorder point is determined by three factors:

- The usage rate u

- The replenishment lead time "LT"

- The safety stock level

Order frequency is determined by the usage rate u and the order quantity Q. These general expressions can be expressed as

$$\text{ROP} = f(u, \text{LT, and Safety stock})$$

and

$$\text{Order frequency} = f(u, Q)$$

The reorder point typically is set at a level that reflects the demand value during lead time $(\text{DDLT} = u \times \text{LT})$ plus the safety stock value. At the same time, the size of DDLT and safety stock are directly related to the length of lead time and to variations in the lead time usage rate. Therefore, in order to reduce the reorder point under a given demand condition, the replenishment lead time must be reduced.

Replenishment lead time typically is determined by the supplier's manufacturing lead time and the length of time required for transportation. The supplier's manufacturing lead time is a function of that firm's available capacity and work load commitments. These general relationships can be expressed as follows:

$$\text{Replenishment LT} = f(\text{Supplier's manufacturing LT, Transit time})$$

and

$$\text{Supplier's manufacturing LT} = f(\text{Available capacity, Work loads})$$

and

$$\text{Work loads} = \text{Sum of orders } (Q) \text{ to be processed}$$

The JIT purchasing concept attempts to reduce replenishment lead time by using suppliers close to the using plant and by ordering in small quantities, which in turn reduces the supplier's work load per period.

From this simple analysis of basic theory, it is clear that, if implemented properly, the JIT purchasing concept is in substantial harmony with conventional purchasing and inventory theory. The important feature is that the JIT purchasing concept takes variables that are often considered uncontrollable in conventional applications and treats them as true decision variables. The major action focuses on attempts to reduce the ordering cost and replenishment lead time values.

REDUCTION OF ORDERING COSTS AND REPLENISHMENT LEAD TIME

The costs associated with a purchase order can be divided into the following six components:

- Negotiating cost
- Costs incurred in converting a planned order to an open order
- Expediting costs
- Receiving count costs
- Receiving inspection costs
- Premium cost for transportation if the least cost transportation method is not used

In the JIT purchasing environment, a vendor who meets the JIT purchasing requirements is set into a different classification than the rest of the vendors. A JIT vendor can be exempted from normal qualification processing checks. As a result, four major components of ordering cost can be eliminated, and the negotiating transportation cost components also can be reduced significantly so that the new total ordering cost is substantially lower than before. It follows that the larger reduction in ordering cost makes it possible to order more often, perhaps even daily. These reductions are made possible by introducing a fundamental change in purchasing practice as it is conducted in many American companies today. The fundamental philosophical change requires the buying firm to emphasize the development of long-term vendor relationships, rather than consistently seeking short-term price breaks. As vendors' capacity capabilities, process capabilities, and quality performance levels become known, the first five components of the purchasing order costs can be reduced dramatically. The premium for transportation can be reduced by ordering a "family" of parts from a given vendor, such that truckload and carload can still be ordered. Costs can also be minimized by giving preference to suppliers located within close geographical proximity to the using plant.

Replenishment lead time can be analyzed in a similar manner. The four major factors of the replenishment lead time are:

- Paperwork time required to convert an order from a planned order to an open order

- Manufacturing lead time for the vendor

- Transportation time for the vendor

- Average receiving time

Clearly, for a vendor with whom a long-term relationship has been estimated, the first three components can be reduced dramatically; further, if preference is given to vendors within close geographical proximity, the transportation time requirement can also be reduced.

JIT COMPARED WITH TRADITIONAL MANUFACTURING

JIT manufacturing is a demand–pull approach, rather than the traditional push approach. The philosophy underlying JIT manufacturing is to produce a product when it is needed and only in the quantities demanded by customers. Demand pulls products through the manufacturing process. Each operation produces only what is necessary to satisfy the demand of the succeeding operation. No production takes place until a signal from a succeeding process indicates a need to produce. Parts and materials arrive just in time to be used in production. To understand the differences between pull and push systems of material control, consider the example of a fast food restaurant.

"At McDonald's, the customer orders a hamburger, the server gets one from the rack, the hamburger maker keeps an eye on the rack and makes new burgers when the number gets too low. The manager orders more ground beef when the maker's inventory gets too low. In effect, the customer's purchase triggers the pull of materials through the system. . . . . In a push system, the caterer estimates how many steaks are likely to be ordered in any given week. He/she reckons how long it takes to broil a steak: he/she can figure out roughly how many meals are needed in a certain week. . . . "

• *REDUCED INVENTORIES*

The primary goal of JIT is to reduce inventories to insignificant or zero levels. In traditional manufacturing, inventories result whenever production exceeds demand. Inventories are needed as a buffer when production does not meet expected demand.

• *MANUFACTURING CELLS AND MULTIFUNCTION LABOR*

In traditional manufacturing, products are moved from one group of identical machines to another. Typically, machines with identical functions are located together in an area referred to as a department or process. Workers who specialize in the operation of a specific machine are located in each department. JIT replaces this traditional pattern with a pattern of manufacturing cells or work centers. Robots supplement people to do many routine operations.

Manufacturing cells contain machines that are grouped in families, usually in a semicircle. The machines are arranged so that they can be used to perform a variety of operations in sequence. Each cell is set up to produce a particular product or product family. Products move from one machine to another from start to finish. Workers are assigned to cells and are trained to operate all machines within the cell. Thus, labor in a JIT environment is multifunction labor, not specialized labor. Each manufacturing cell is basically a minifactory or a factory within a factory. A comparison of the physical layout of JIT with the traditional system is shown in Table 10.4.

• *TOTAL QUALITY CONTROL*

JIT has a stronger emphasis on quality control. A defective part brings production to a grinding halt. Poor quality simply cannot be tolerated in a stockless manufacturing environment. In other words, JIT cannot be implemented without a commitment to *total quality control (TQC)*. TQC is essentially an endless quest for perfect quality. This approach to quality is opposed to the traditional belief, called *acceptable quality level (AQL)*. AQL allows defects to occur provided they are within a predetermined level.

• *DECENTRALIZATION OF SERVICES*

JIT requires easy and quick access to support services, which means that centralized service departments must be scaled down and their personnel assigned to work directly to support production. For example, with respect to raw materials, JIT calls for multiple stock points, each one near where the material will be used. There is no need for a central warehouse location.

• *SUPPLIERS AS OUTSIDE PARTNERS*

The most important aspects of the JIT purchasing concept focus on new ways of dealing with suppliers and a clear-cut recognition of the appropriate purchasing role in developing corporate strategy. Suppliers should be viewed as "outside partners" who can contribute to the long-run welfare of the buying firm rather than as outside adversaries.

• *BETTER COST MANAGEMENT*

Cost management differs from cost accounting in that it refers to the management of cost, whether or not the cost has direct impact on inventory or the financial statements. The JIT philosophy simplifies the cost accounting procedure and helps managers manage and control their costs, which will be discussed in detail later in the chapter.

JIT recognizes that with simplification comes better management, better quality, better service, and better cost control. Traditional cost accounting systems have a tendency to be very complex, with many transactions and involved data reporting. Simplification of this process will transform a cost accounting system into a cost management system that can be used to support management's needs for better decisions about product design, pricing, marketing, and mix and to encourage continual operating improvements.

Table 10.4. Physical Layout—Traditional Versus JIT Manufacturing

Traditional Manufacturing[a]		
Department A	Department B	Department C
<P1> X X	< P1> Y Y	< P1> Z Z
<P2>	< P2>	< P2>

JIT Manufacturing[b]	
Product 1 (P1)	Product 2 (P2)
Manufacturing Cell 1	Manufacturing Cell 2
Y	Y
<P1> X Z	<P2> X Z

Symbols: X = Machine A, Y = Machine B, Z = Machine C, P1 = Product 1, P2 = Product 2.

[a]Each product passes through departments that specialize in one process. Departments process multiple products.

[b]Each product passes through its own cell. All machines necessary to process each product are placed within the cell. Each cell is dedicated to the production of one product or one subassembly.

YOU SHOULD REMEMBER

Comparison of JIT and Traditional Manufacturing

JIT	Traditional
Pull system	Push system
Insignificant or zero inventories	Significant inventories
Manufacturing cells	"Process" structure
Multifunction labor	Specialized labor
Total quality control (TQC)	Acceptable quality level (AQL)
Decentralized services	Centralized services
Complex cost accounting	Simple cost accounting

BENEFITS OF JIT

The potential benefits of JIT are numerous. First, JIT practice reduces inventory levels, which means lower investments in inventories. Because the system requires only the smallest quantity of materials needed immediately, it reduces the overall inventory level substantially. In many Japanese companies that use the JIT concept, inventory levels have been reduced to the point that makes the annual working capital turnover ratio much higher than that experienced by U.S. counterparts. For instance, Toyota reported inventory turnover ratios of 41 to 63, whereas comparable U.S. companies reported inventory turnover ratios of 5 to 8.

Second, because purchasing under JIT requires a significantly shorter delivery lead time, lead time reliability is greatly improved. Reduced lead time and increased reliability also contribute to a significant reduction in the safety stock requirements.

Third, reduced lead times and setup times increase scheduling flexibility. The cumulative lead time, which includes both purchasing and production lead times, is reduced. Thus, the firm schedule within the production planning horizon is reduced. This results in a longer "look-ahead" time that can be used to meet shifts in market demand. The smaller lot size production, made possible by reduced setup time, also adds flexibility.

Fourth, improved quality levels have been reported by many companies. When the order quantity is small, sources of quality problems are quickly identifiable and can be corrected immediately. In many cases, employee quality consciousness also tends to improve, producing an improvement in quality at the production source.

Fifth, the costs of purchased materials may be reduced through more extensive value analysis and cooperative supplier development activities. Sixth, other financial benefits reported include:

- Lower investments in factory space for inventories and production
- Less obsolescence risk in inventories
- Reduction in scrap and rework
- Decline in paperwork
- Reduction in direct material costs through quantity purchases

Table 10.5 lists typical performance measures under the traditional and JIT systems.

Table 10.5. Performance Measures—Traditional Versus JIT

Traditional	JIT
Direct labor efficiency	Total head-count productivity
Direct labor use	Return on assets
Direct labor productivity	Days of inventory
Machine use	Group incentives
	Lead time by product
	Response time to customer feedback
	Number of customer complaints
	Cost of quality
	Setup reduction

MRP VERSUS JIT SYSTEMS

In general, although MRP (a push system) and JIT (a pull system) work well in certain environments, they may not work well in others. The nature of the production process determines the appropriate system. For line flows, order releases don't change from week to week, so JIT works well. In job shop environments, where material flows are complex and demands are highly variable, MRP is the system of choice. The material flows are too complex for a JIT system, and pull techniques can't cope with the demand and lead time variability. MRP II systems are good at overall materials planning and data management and can be used to support the informational needs of various functional areas in the firm. MRP systems can be used effectively to understand the implications of lot-sizing decisions and master scheduling changes on overall inventories and capacity. In contrast, JIT systems are a less expensive, more effective way to control material flows on the shop floor. A Kanban system can be used to maintain low levels of inventory and to adjust production rates over time.

Is a choice between the MRP and JIT systems necessary? The choice of a system can affect inventory levels and customer service. Actually, these methods aren't mutually exclusive, and the best solution often is a hybrid of the strengths of both approaches.

COMPUTERIZED JIT

Using *electronic data exchange (EDI)* can greatly enhance JIT implementation, especially when internal business partners are involved. Notable computer software for JIT includes:

- HP Manufacturing Management II, which supports multilocation tracking and JIT component ordering, extensive MRP and inventory control, and interactions with budgeting, costing, and CDA/CAM applications.

- Control Manufacturing by Cincom Systems, which supports multiple location JIT inventory control, MRP, financial management, and production scheduling.

VALUE ANALYSIS (OR VALUE ENGINEERING)

Value analysis (VA) or value engineering (VE) is a systematic effort to reduce the cost or improve the performance of items either purchased or produced. This effort is used to rethink the design of a part, product, or service, to eliminate anything that does not add value. VA attempts to define, as simply as possible, the purpose or function of the item and then to search for the simplest way to accomplish that function. Good "partnership" suppliers often initiate value analysis, suggesting ways to make an item better and cheaper, thereby benefiting both buyer and supplier, and ultimately the final customer. This strategy is considered a major part of supply chain management as a global competitive strategy, which was introduced in Chapter 1.

KNOW THE CONCEPTS

DO YOU KNOW THE BASICS?

1. Distinguish between independent and dependent demand.
2. When is MRP appropriate?
3. Briefly explain the requirements of effective MRP.
4. List some of the main advantages and limitations of MRP.
5. Define planned order release in MRP.
6. How important is the master production schedule in an MRP system?
7. Distinguish between advanced versions of MRP (MRP II) and the basic system.
8. Compare MRP II and a Kanban system.
9. Describe the roles of suppliers and customers in a JIT system.
10. Discuss how cards are used in a Kanban system.
11. How does MRP relate to computer-integrated manufacturing?
12. What is the objective of value analysis (or value engineering)? What types of questions should be addressed?

TERMS FOR STUDY

bill of materials (BOM)
capacity requirements planning (CRP)
dependent demand
gross requirements
inventory-status file
just-in-time (JIT)
Kanban
lot-for-lot ordering
manufacturing resource planning (MRP II)

material requirements planning (MRP)
net requirements
planned order releases
product structure file
scheduled receipts
time bucket
value analysis (or value engineering)

PRACTICAL APPLICATION

1. The following is a list of the components required to produce one unit of end-item P:

    P: 2 As, 3Bs, 3Cs

    A: 5 Ms, 2 Rs

    B: 1 D, 3 Ns

    C: 1 T, 4 Ns

    M: 1 N

    a. Draw the product-structure tree.

    b. Determine the number of Ns that will be needed to make 60 Ps in each of these cases:

    (1) There are currently 10 Ps on hand.

    (2) On-hand inventory consists of 15 Ps, 10 As, 20 Bs, 10 Cs, 100 Ns, 300 Ts and 200 Ms.

2. Consider the following product structure:

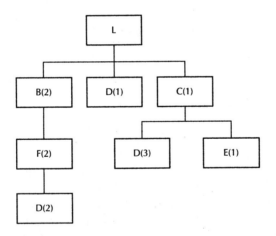

    How many pieces of each item are required to make 100 units of L?

3. End-item P is composed of three subassemblies—K, L, and W. K is assembled using 3 Gs and 4 Hs; L is made of 2 Ms and 2 Ns; and W is made using 3 Zs. On-hand inventories are: K, 10; L, 20; and Z, 200. One hundred Ps are to be shipped at the start of week seven. Lead times are two weeks for subassemblies and one week for components (e.g., G, H, M). Final assembly of P requires two weeks.

a. Determine a product-structure tree.

b. Determine a master schedule for P.

c. Determine a material requirements plan for K, G, and H.

4. The product structures for end-items M and N follow. All items have a one-week lead time. Presently, there are 20 units of M available, 15 units of N, and 90 units of C. The standard lot sizes are 50 for M, 35 for N, and 100 for C. The MPS calls for 20 units of item M and 15 units of item S for each of the next five weeks. An open order for 100 units of item C is scheduled for receipt in week 1. Develop the MRP records for items M, N, and C.

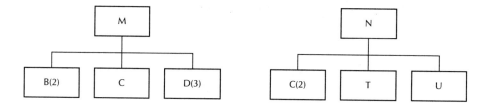

5. A product structure diagram based on the bill of materials for end-item A follows.

Emily, a product manager, wishes to determine the material requirements for ordered-part C that will be needed to complete 120 units by the start of week 5. Lead times for items are: one week for level 0 items, one week for level 1 items, and two weeks for level 2 items. There is a scheduled receipt of 60 units of B in week 2 and 100 units of C in week 1. The lot-for-lot ordering rule is used.

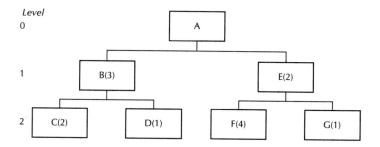

6. Haesoo is the MRP manager for Golf-Crazy, Inc. A MPS is given to him showing gross requirements for 350 units of the golf cart in week 5. The following product structure diagram is based on the bill of materials.

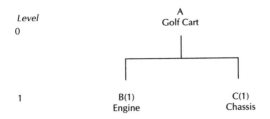

The item master file shows the inventory levels and other planning data for every item.

Item Master File

	In Stock	Safety Stock	Allocated	Lead Time (weeks)	Lot Size	Scheduled Receipts Amount	Scheduled Receipts Week
A	0	0	0	1	LFL [a]		
B	50	0	0	1	LFL [a]	50	1
C	0	0	0	1	100		

[a] LFL = lot-for-lot (as needed).

Prepare detailed MRP records.

7. Part of the item master file relating to a computer desk (model ABJ-510) as well as the bill of material follows.

Item Master File

	In Stock	Safety Stock	Allocated	Lead Time (weeks)	Lot Size	Scheduled Receipts Amount	Scheduled Receipts Week
ABJ-510	30	20	0	1	LFL [a]		
A	45	20	0	2	500		
B	10	0	0	1	100	150	2

[a] LFL = lot-for-lot (as needed).

According to the MPS, 100 units of ABJ-510 in week 5 and 120 units in week 7 are required. Prepare MRP records to determine planned order release.

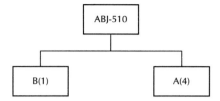

ANSWERS

DO YOU KNOW THE BASICS?

1. Independent demand refers to demand for end-items and is thus often random and unpredictable, whereas dependent demand is derived from demand for end-items and is somewhat predictable.

2. MRP is appropriate when inventory requirements planning must be accomplished for dependent demand.

3. Effective MRP requires accurate inputs (master schedule, bills of materials, and inventory status). It also requires a computer to process information and generate material requirement plans and related reports.

4. Advantages of MRP include low levels of in-process inventories and the ability to track material requirements for derived demand. Unfortunately, it takes much longer and costs much more than expected to implement MRP when there are inaccurate or outdated records and/or personnel problems.

5. A planned order release is planning to meet the schedule. This does not mean that the order will actually be released that period. It may be released earlier or later; the order quantity may be rounded to some even number or lot size. The planned order may be combined with net requirements in other periods to a larger order size.

6. The master production schedule drives the system. It states the planned due dates for end-items. MRP computer runs, however, involve an iterative process. The master production schedule proposes or hypothesizes a tentative schedule. After the MRP run with this schedule, the shop scheduler examines the MRP plan for impractical loads on the productive system—either by stating excessive demands on personnel or equipment or in excessive idle time. Then the master production schedule is revised, and the program is run again.

7. Many of the advanced versions such as manufacturing resources systems (MRP II) and closed loop MRP are more comprehensive in that they are used to plan and control all aspects of the manufacturing firm. This might include design, CIM, financial, personnel, planning, and purchasing systems. Newer systems use EDI with MRP systems that include client/server architecture, relational databases with structured query language, graphical user interfaces, decision support systems, multiple platforms, and user-friendly programming interfaces.

8. The goals of MRP II and Kanban are essentially the same (i.e., to improve customer service, reduce inventories, and increase productivity). MRP II is basically a computerized system, handling complex planning and scheduling, whereas Kanban is a manual system involving very small lot sizes, short lead times, and a high-quality output.

9. JIT involves customers and suppliers as integral parts of the process. Customers provide product enhancement, modification, and usage data. Suppliers work with the manufacturing organization to coordinate delivery and raw material or other input production. Both groups may sit on JIT teams and participate in improvement activities because all groups will benefit from changes.

10. Cards in a Kanban system represent a visual work order. As material is moved from the line to the customer, the last operator in the process goes to the next work station up the line and pulls a bin of work for further processing. This employee removes a card from the bin and leaves it at the previous station. This card represents a work order for this station to make or process more products. This sequence continues in a backward fashion through the line and back even to the supplier.

11. CIM replaces the conventional areas of product and process design, planning and control, and manufacturing with six new areas—computer-aided design, group technology, manufacturing planning and control systems, automated materials handing, computer-aided manufacturing, and robotics. MRP's position in the CIM scheme is primarily in the manufacturing planning and control systems, which plan and schedule operations, compare alternatives, update data, monitor operations, and project operating results. This can include order-entry, shop floor control, purchasing, and cost accounting. Other effects on the MRP system occur because of other parts of CIM (e.g., group technology affects the routing and sequencing for MRP); aspects of computer aided manufacturing change MRP (e.g., flexible manufacturing systems simplify MRP because an FMS cell can do a variety of processes).

12. VA or VE is used to rethink the design of a part, product, or service, eliminating anything that does not add value. It involves asking questions

such as: What is the function of the item? Is the function necessary? Can a lower-cost part that serves the purpose be identified? Can the item be simplified to achieve a lower price?

PRACTICAL APPLICATION

1.

a. The product-structure tree follows:

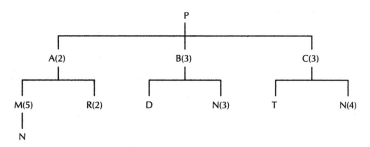

(1)

A leg: 2 As × 5 Ms = 10 Ns

B leg: 3 Bs × 3 Ns = 9 Ns

C leg: 3 Cs × 4 Ns = <u>12 Ns</u>

31 Ns × (60 As − 10 As on hand) = 1,550 Ns

(2) 45 Ps needed:

A leg: A: 2 × 45 − 10 = 80. M: 80 × 5 − 200

= 200. N: 200 − 100 on hand

= 100

B leg: B 3 × 45 − 20 = 115. N: 3 × 115 = 345

C leg: C: 3 × 45 − 10 = 125. N: 4 × 125 = 600

Thus, 100 + 345 + 600 = 1,045 Ns needed.

2.

Item B: 100 × 2 = 200

Item C: 100 × 1 = 100

Item E: 100 × 1 = 100

Item F: 200 × 2 = 400

Item D: (100 × 2 × 2 × 2) + (100 × 1) + (100 × 1 × 3) = 1,200

3.

a.

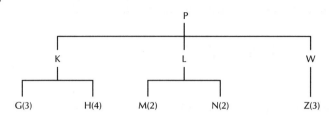

b.

	1	2	3	4	5	6	7
Master schedule for P							100

c.

Item: P, LT = 2 weeks

	1	2	3	4	5	6	7
Gross requirements							100
Schedule receipts							
On-hand							0
Net requirements							100
Planned order receipts							
Planned order release					100		

Item: K, LT = 2 weeks

	1	2	3	4	5	6	7
Gross requirements					100		
Schedule receipts							
On-hand					10		
Net requirements					90		
Planned order receipts					90		
Planned order release			90				

Item: G, LT = 1 week

	1	2	3	4	5	6	7
Gross requirements			270				
Schedule receipts							
On-hand			40				
Net requirements			230				
Planned order receipts			230				
Planned order release		230					

Item: H, LT = 1 week

	1	2	3	4	5	6	7
Gross requirements			360				
Schedule receipts							
On-hand			0				
Net requirements			360				
Planned order receipts			360				
Planned order release		360					

4.

Item: M, LT = 1 week

		1	2	3	4	5
Gross requirements		20	20	20	20	20
Schedule receipts						
On-hand	**20**		30	10	40	20
Net requirements						
Planned order receipts			50		50	
Planned order release		50		50		

Item: N, LT = 1 week

		1	2	3	4	5
Gross requirements		15	15	15	15	15
Schedule receipts						
On-hand	**15**		20	5	25	10
Net requirements						
Planned order receipts			35		35	
Planned order release		35		35		

Item: C, LT = 1 week

		1	2	3	4	5
Gross requirements		120[a]		120		
Schedule receipts		100				
On-hand	**90**	70	120	70		
Net requirements						
Planned order receipts				100		
Planned order release			100			

[a] $120 = (50 \times 1) + (35 \times 2)$

5.

	1	2	3	4	5
Master schedule for A					120

Item: A, LT = 1 week

	1	2	3	4	5
Gross requirements					120
Schedule receipts					
On-hand	**0**				
Net requirements					120
Planned order receipts					120
Planned order release				120	

Item: B, LT = 1 week

	1	2	3	4	5
Gross requirements				360[a]	
Schedule receipts		60			
On-hand	**0**	60	60		
Net requirements					
Planned order receipts				300	
Planned order release			300		

[a]360 = 120 × 3 units of B.

Item: C, LT = 1 week

	1	2	3	4	5
Gross requirements			600[a]		
Schedule receipts	100				
On-hand	**0**	100	100	100	
Net requirements			500		
Planned order receipts			500		
Planned order release	500				

[a]600 = 300 × 2 units of C.

Item Code	LT	On Hand	Safety Stock	Allocated		1	2	3	4	5
A	1	0	0	0	Gross requirements					350
					Scheduled receipts					
					On hand **0**					
					Net requirements					350
					Planned order receipts					350
					Planned order releases				350	

Item Code	LT	On Hand	Safety Stock	Allocated		1	2	3	4	5
B	1	50	0	0	Gross requirements				350	
					Scheduled receipts	50				
					On hand	**50**	100	100	100	
					Net requirements				250	
					Planned order receipts				250	
					Planned order releases			250		
C	1	0	0	0	Gross requirements				350	
					Scheduled receipts					
					On hand	**0**			50	50
					Net requirements				350	
					Planned order receipts				400	
					Planned order releases			400		

7.

Item Code	LT	On Hand	Safety Stock	Allocated		1	2	3	4	5	6	7
ABJ-510	1	30	20	0	Gross requirements					100		120
					Scheduled receipts							
					On hand	**10**	10	10	10	10	10	0	0
					Net requirements							120
					Planned order receipts					90		120
					Planned order releases				90		120	
A	2	45	20	0	Gross requirements			360		480		
					Scheduled receipts							
					On hand	**25**	25	25	25	165	165	165	185
					Net requirements			335		315		
					Planned order receipts			500		500		
					Planned order releases	500		500				
B	1	10	0	0	Gross requirements					90		120
					Scheduled receipts		150					
					On hand	**10**	10	160	160	70	70	70	50
					Net requirements			100			50	
					Planned order receipts			300			100	
					Planned order releases				100			

11

FACILITIES INVESTMENT DECISIONS

KEY TERMS

capital budgeting process of making long-term planning decisions and evaluating capital expenditures decisions.

discounted cash flow (DCF) techniques methods of selecting and ranking investment proposals such as the net present value and internal rate of return methods where time value of money is taken into account.

equivalent uniform annual cost annualized sum of all relevant costs (e.g., an installment loan payment).

internal rate of return (IRR) rate earned on a proposal; the rate of interest that equates the initial investment with the present value of future cash inflows.

net present value (NPV) method method widely used for evaluating investment projects, the present value of all cash inflows from the project is compared against the initial investment.

payback period length of time required to recover the amount of an initial investment.

Operations managers frequently have discretionary power over certain expenditures from their capital budgets. Higher investments for operations equipment may require the approval of top management. Facilities investment decisions, more often called *capital budgeting,* is the process of planning for and evaluating long-term capital expenditure decisions. In addition to facilities investment decisions, the firm must make many other investment decisions in order to grow. Examples of capital budgeting applications are selecting a product line, deciding whether to keep or sell a business segment or to lease or buy an auto, and evaluating which asset to invest in.

WHAT ARE THE FEATURES OF INVESTMENT PROJECTS?

Long-term investments have three important features:

- They typically involve a large amount of initial cash outlays which tend to have a long-term impact on the firm's future profitability. Therefore, this initial cash outlay needs to be justified on a cost–benefit basis.

- There are expected recurring cash inflows (e.g., increased revenues, savings in cash operating expenses) over the life of the investment project. This frequently requires considering the time value of money.

- Income taxes could make a difference in the accept or reject decision. Therefore, income tax factors must be taken into account in every capital budgeting decision.

UNDERSTANDING THE CONCEPT OF TIME VALUE OF MONEY

A dollar now is worth more than a dollar to be received later. This statement sums up an important principle: money has a time value. The truth of this principle is not that inflation might make the dollar received at a later time worth less in buying power. The reason is that you could invest the dollar now and have more than a dollar at the specified later date.

Time value of money is an important consideration in making facilities investment decisions. Discounted cash flow methods require discounting future cash flows. Discounting (present value) is the opposite of compounding.

WHAT IS PRESENT VALUE—HOW MUCH MONEY IS WORTH NOW?

Present value is the value today of future cash flows. The computation of present values (discounting) is the opposite of determining the compounded future value. The interest rate i is referred to as the *discount rate*. The discount rate we use is more commonly called the *cost of capital,* which is the minimum rate of return required by the investor.

$$F_n = P(1 + i)^n$$

Therefore,

$$P = \frac{F_n}{(1 + i)^n} = F_n\left(\frac{1}{(1 + i)^n}\right) = F_n \cdot T_1(i, n)$$

where $T_1(i, n)$ represents the present value of $1 and is given in Table 1 (Present Value of $1) in Appendix II.

EXAMPLE 1

You have the option of receiving $60,000 6 years from now. If you earn 15% on your money, how much should you pay for this investment? To answer this query, you need to compute the present value of $60,000 to be received 6 years from now at a 10% rate of discount. F_6 is $60,000, i is 15%, and n is 6 years. $T_1(15\%, 6)$ from Table 1 in Appendix II is 0.432.

$$P = \$60,000\left(\frac{1}{(1 + 0.15)^6}\right) = \$60,000 \ T_1(15\%, 6) = \$60,000(0.432) = \$25,920$$

This means that you can earn 15% on your money, and you would be indifferent to receiving $25,920 now or $60,000 6 years from today because the amounts are time equivalent. Stated another way, you could invest $25,920 today at 15% and have $60,000 in 6 years.

PRESENT VALUE OF AN ANNUITY

Interest received from notes, bonds, pension funds, and insurance contracts involve annuities. To compare these financial instruments, the present value of each must be determined. The present value of an annuity (P_n) is solved as follows:

$$P_n = A + A \cdot \frac{1}{(1+i)^1} + A \cdot \frac{1}{(1+i)^2} + \dots + A \cdot \frac{1}{(1+i)^n}$$

$$= A \left(\frac{1}{(1+i)^1} + \frac{1}{(1+i)^2} + \dots + \frac{1}{(1+i)^n} \right)$$

$$= A \cdot \sum_{t=1}^{n} \frac{1}{(1+i)^t} + \frac{1}{i}\left(1 - \frac{1}{(1+i)}\right) = A \cdot T_2(i, n)$$

where $T2(i, n)$ represents the present value of an annuity of $1 discounted at i percent for n years and is found in Table 2 (Present Value of an Annuity of $1) in Appendix II.

EXAMPLE 2

Assume an annuity of $10,000 for 3 years. Then the present value is

$$P_n = A \cdot T2(i, n)$$

$$P_3 = \$10,000 \ T2(10\%, 3 \text{ years}) = \$10,000 \ (2.487) = \$24,870$$

YOU SHOULD REMEMBER

Many financial calculators contain preprogrammed formulas to perform many present value and future value applications. Furthermore, spreadsheet software such as Microsoft's Excel and Lotus 1-2-3 have built-in financial functions to perform many such applications.

HOW DO YOU EVALUATE FACILITIES INVESTMENT PROJECTS?

Several popular methods of evaluating investment projects follow:

- Payback period
- Net present value
- Internal rate of return
- Equivalent uniform annual cost

PAYBACK PERIOD

The payback period measures the length of time required to recover the amount of initial investment. It is computed by dividing the initial investment by the cash inflows through increased revenues or cost savings.

EXAMPLE 3

Assume that

Cost of investment	$18,000
Annual after-tax cash savings	$ 3,000

Then, the payback period is

$$\text{Payback period} = \frac{\text{Initial investment}}{\text{Cost savings}} = \frac{\$18,000}{\$3,000} = 6 \text{ years}$$

Decision rule. Choose the project with the shorter payback period. The rationale behind this choice is: The shorter the payback period, the less risky the project, and the greater the liquidity.

The advantages of using the payback period method of evaluating an investment project are that it is simple to compute and easy to understand and that it handles investment risk effectively.

The shortcomings of this method are that it does not recognize the time value of money and that it ignores the impact of cash inflows received after the payback period. Note that, essentially, cash flows after the payback period determine profitability of an investment.

NET PRESENT VALUE

Net present value (NPV) equals the present value (PV) of cash inflows from a proposal less the initial investment (I):

$$NPV = PV - I$$

The present value of future cash flows is determined using the cost of capital (or minimum required rate of return) as the discount rate. When cash inflows are equal, the present value would be

$$PV = A \cdot T_2 \, (i, \, n)$$

where A is the amount of the annuity.

Decision rule. If NPV is positive, accept the project; otherwise, reject it.

EXAMPLE 4

Consider the following investment:

Initial investment	$37,910
Estimated life	5 years
Annual cash inflows after taxes	$10,000
Cost of capital (minimum required rate of return)	8%

Present value of the cash inflows is:

$PV = A \cdot T_2(i, \, n)$

$= \$10,000 \cdot T_2(8\%, \, 5 \text{ years})$

$= \$10,000 \, (3.993)$	$39,930
Initial investment (I)	37,910
Net present value (NPV = PV − I)	$ 2,020

Because the NPV of the investment is positive, the investment should be accepted.

The advantages of the NPV method are that it obviously recognizes the time value of money and that it is easy to compute whether the cash flows form an annuity or vary from period to period.

YOU SHOULD REMEMBER

If cash inflows are different from year to year, you should compute the present value separately year by year using Table 1 in Appendix II.

INTERNAL RATE OF RETURN

Internal rate of return (IRR), a project's yield or real return, is defined as the rate of interest that equates I with the PV of future cash inflows. In other words, at IRR

$$I = \text{PV} \quad \text{or} \quad \text{NPV} = 0$$

Decision rule. Accept the project if the IRR exceeds the cost of capital; otherwise, reject it.

EXAMPLE 5

Assume the same data given in Example 4, and set the following equality ($I = \text{PV}$):

$$\$37,910 = \$10,000 \cdot T_2(i, 5 \text{ years})$$

$$T_2(i, 5 \text{ years}) = \frac{\$37,910}{\$10,000} = 3.791$$

which is right on 10% in the 5-year line of Table 2 in Appendix II. Because the IRR of the investment is greater than the cost of capital (8%), accept the project.

The advantage of using the IRR method is that it does consider the time value of money and, therefore, it gives a more exact and realistic yield on the project. The shortcomings of this method are that it is time-consuming to compute and that it fails to recognize the varying sizes of investment in competing projects.

YOU SHOULD REMEMBER

It is extremely tedious to compute the IRR, especially when the cash inflows are not even. Most financial calculators and PCs have a key to calculate IRR.

EQUIVALENT UNIFORM ANNUAL COST

A replacement decision typically involves two mutually exclusive projects. When these two mutually exclusive projects have significantly different lives, an adjustment would be necessary. It may require a comparison of annual costs, which means the conversion of cash flows into an equivalent uniform annual series. This procedure may be thought of as the inverse of finding present values. The so-called capital recovery factor, which is the reciprocal of the present value of an annuity factor (T_2), is used for this purpose. We calculate uniform annual cost (UAC) by using the following formula:

$$\text{UAC} = \{I - S_N [T_1 (i, T)]\} \text{CRF}(i, N) + c$$

where $\quad S_N$ = salvage value at terminal period N

$\quad\quad\quad$ CRT(i, N) = capital recovery factor = $1/T_2$

$\quad\quad\quad$ c = uniform operating cost

EXAMPLE 6

A company considers two equipment modules: Plan A and Plan B. Plan A, which requires an initial investment of $44,000, has expected annual operating costs of $24,400 and no terminal salvage value. Plan B, which requires an initial investment of $70,000, is expected to reduce operating costs to $20,900 per year and has a salvage value of $9,500. Both equipment modules have a useful life of ten years. We assume that the firm has determined a cost of capital of 22%.

Using the UAC formula gives the following results:

$$\text{UAC}_A = \{\$44,000 - 0 \,[T_1 (22\%, 10)]\} \,\text{CRF}(22\%, 10) + \$24,400$$

$$= \$44,000 \,(1/T_2(22\%, 10) + \$24,400$$

$$= \$44,000 \,(1/3.923) + \$24,400$$

$$= \$44,000 \,(0.255) + \$24,400 = \$35,620$$

$$\text{UAC}_B = \{\$70,000 - \$9,500 \,[T_1 (22\%, 10)]\} \,\text{CRF}(22\%, 10) + \$20,900$$

$$= [\$70,000 - \$9,500 \,(.137)] \,(1/T_2(22\%, 10) + \$20,900$$

$$= (\$70,000 - \$1,302) \,(1/3.293) + \$20,900$$

$$= \$68,698 \,(0.255) + \$20,900 = \$38,418$$

Based on an equivalent uniform annual cost comparison, Plan A is more economical than Plan B.

YOU SHOULD REMEMBER

Equivalent uniform annual cost is the annualized sum of all relevant costs. It is like the amount of an installment loan payment. Uniform annual cost is also called equivalent annual cost (EAC) in some production/operations management texts.

HOW DO INCOME TAXES AFFECT INVESTMENT DECISIONS?

Income taxes have to be considered when making capital budgeting decisions. The project that looks good on a before-tax basis may have to be rejected on an after-tax basis and vice versa. Income taxes usually have an impact on both the amount and the timing of cash flows. Because net income, not cash inflows, is subject to tax, after-tax cash inflows are different from after-tax net income. To calculate after-tax cash flows, depreciation, which is not a cash outlay, must be added to net income after taxes. That is,

After-tax cash inflows = After-tax net income + Depreciation

EXAMPLE 7

The Navistar Company estimates that it can generate sales of $67,000 and incur annual cost of operations of $52,000 for the next ten years if it buys a special-purpose machine at a cost of $100,000. No residual value is expected. Depreciation is by straight-line. (Note that depreciation by straight-line is $100,000/10 = $10,000 per year.) Assume that the income tax rate is 30%, and the after-tax cost of capital (minimum required rate of return) is 10%. After-tax cash inflows can be calculated as follows:

After-tax cash inflows = After-tax net income + Depreciation

$$= (\$67,000 - \$52,000)(1 - 0.3) + \$10,000$$

$$= \$15,000 \ (0.7) + \$10,000$$

$$= \$10,500 + \$10,000 = 20,500$$

To see if this machine should be purchased, calculate the net present value:

$$PV = \$20,500 \; T_2(10\%, \; 10 \text{ years}) = \$20,500 \; (6.145) = \$125,972.50$$

Thus,

$$NPV = PV - I = \$125,972.50 - \$100,000 = \$25,972.50$$

Because NPV is positive, the machine should be bought.

EXAMPLE 8

The treasurer of a small appliance maker estimates the cash inflows, outflows, and net cash flows before taxes shown in columns 1, 2, and 3 of the following table, if it buys a high-tech machine at a cost of $1,000,000. No residual value is expected. Life is 5 years. Depreciation is by straight-line. Assume that the income tax rate is 35% and that the after-tax cost of capital (minimum required rate of return) is 10%. The process of arriving at net cash flow after taxes is shown in columns 4–8.

Year	Cash Inflow ($) (1)	Cash Outflow ($) (2)	Net Cash Flow Before Taxes ($) (3) = (1) − (2)	Depreciation (Noncash Expense) ($) (4) = 0.2 × 1,000,000	Net Income Before Taxes ($) (5) = (3) − (4)	Income Taxes ($) (6) = 0.35 × (5)	Net Income After Taxes ($) (7) = (5) − (6)	Net Cash Flow After Taxes ($) or (7) + (4)
1	1,000,000	625,000	375,000	200,000	175,000	61,250	113,750	313,750
2	900,000	610,000	290,000	200,000	90,000	31,500	58,500	258,500
3	925,000	635,000	290,000	200,000	90,000	31,500	58,500	258,500
4	930,000	605,000	325,000	200,000	125,000	43,750	81,250	281,250
5	825,000	557,000	268,000	200,000	68,000	23,800	44,200	244,200

EXAMPLE 9

The NPV of the machine can be calculated using Table 1 in Appendix II as shown here.

Year	Net Cash Flow After Taxes ($)	T_1 at 10% Table Value ($)	Present Value ($)
0	(1,000,000)	1.000	(1,000,000)
1	313,750	0.909	285,199
2	258,500	0.826	213,521
3	258,500	0.751	194,134
4	281,250	0.683	192,094
5	244,200	0.621	151,648
		NPV =	36,596

KNOW THE CONCEPTS

DO YOU KNOW THE BASICS?

1. Define capital budgeting.
2. What is the payback period? Give two advantages of this method.
3. How would you define the internal rate of return of a capital project?
4. What is the definition of the net present value of a project? What is the decision rule under the NPV method?
5. What role does the cost of capital play in the IRR method and in the NPV method?
6. What is uniform annual equivalent cost? What is the major use of this concept.
7. How do you compute after-tax cash flows?

TERMS FOR STUDY

after-tax cash inflows
after-tax net income
capital budgeting
equivalent uniform annual cost

internal rate of return
net present value
payback period
time value of money

PRACTICAL APPLICATION

1. The following data are given for Barron's Aluminum Company:

Initial cost of proposed equipment	$80,000
Estimated useful life	7 years
Estimated annual savings in cash operating expenses (after taxes)	$20,000
Cost of capital after taxes	12%

    a. Compute the payback period.

    b. Compute the present value of estimated annual savings.

    c. Compute the net present value.

    d. Compute the internal rate of return.

2. The Travis Company is considering a capital outlay of $75,000. Net annual cash inflows after taxes are estimated at $15,000 for 10 years. Straight-line depreciation is to be used, with no residual value.

    a. Compute the net present value, assuming a cost of capital after tax of 12%.

    b. Compute the internal rate of return.

3. Horn Corporation invested in a four-year project. Horn's cost of capital after taxes is 8%. Additional data about the project follows:

Year	Cash Inflow from Operations After Taxes ($)	Present Value of $1 at 8%
1	3,000	0.926
2	3,500	0.857
3	2,400	0.794
4	2,600	0.735

Assuming a positive net present value of $500, what was the amount of the original investment?

4. Gene, Inc., bought equipment with a useful life of eight years and no residual value. Straight-line depreciation is used. It was anticipated to result in cash inflow from operations, net of income taxes, of $4,000. The present value of an ordinary annuity of $1 for eight periods at 10% is 5.335. The present value of $1 for eight periods at 10% is 0.467. Assume that Gene used an internal rate of return of 10%. How much was the amount of the initial investment?

5. Two new machines are being evaluated for possible purchase. Forecasts relating to the two machines follow:

	Machine 1	Machine 2
Purchase price	$50,000	$60,000
Estimated life (straight-line depreciation)	4 years	4 years
Estimated scrap value	None	None
Annual cash benefits before income tax:		
Year 1	$25,000	$45,000
Year 2	25,000	19,000
Year 3	25,000	25,000
Year 4	25,000	25,000
Income tax rate	40%	40%

Compute the net present value of each machine. Assume a cost of capital after taxes of 8%.

6. The Nomo Company estimates that it can generate sales of $70,000 and incur annual cost of operations of $50,000 for the next ten years if it buys a special-purpose machine at a cost of $90,000. No residual value is expected. Depreciation is by straight-line. Assume that the income tax rate is 30% and that the after-tax cost of capital (minimum required rate of return) is 10%. Should the company buy the machine? Use the NPV method.

7. The JS Company is considering buying a machine at a cost of $800,000, which has the following cash flow pattern. No residual value is expected. Depreciation is by straight-line. Assume that the income tax rate is 40% and that the after-tax cost of capital (minimum required rate of return) is 10%. Should the company buy the machine? Use the NPV method.

Year	Cash Inflow ($) (1)	Cash Outflow ($) (2)
1	800,000	550,000
2	790,000	590,000
3	920,000	600,000
4	870,000	610,000
5	650,000	390,000

8. A piece of equipment has an installed cost of $32,000, estimated annual operating cost of $4,500 over its expected life of seven years, and an estimated salvage value of $3,000. Compute the equivalent uniform annual cost of this equipment of 12%.

9. A popular material for roofing a building has an estimated life of eight years and an initial cost of $2,500. A heavier grade of roof costs $825 more but has an estimated life of twelve years. The installed cost for either roof is $1,200. If the cost of capital is 10%, which roof is cheaper on a uniform equivalent annual cost basis?

ANSWERS

DO YOU KNOW THE BASICS?

1. Capital budgeting is the process of evaluating alternative capital projects and selecting alternatives that provide the most profitable return on available funds.

2. The payback period is the length of time required to pay back the amount of initial investment. The advantages of using the payback period method of evaluating an investment project are that it is simple to compute and easy to understand and it handles investment risk effectively.

3. The internal rate of return is the rate of return that equates the present value of future expected cash inflows from an investment with the cost of the investment; it is the rate at which the net present value of the project is zero.

4. The NPV of a project is given by the present value of the expected cash inflows that it will generate minus the initial cost. Projects are acceptable if their NPVs are greater than zero.

5. Under the IRR method, the cost of capital is a cut-off point for deciding which projects are acceptable for further consideration. Under the NPV method, the cost of capital is the discount rate used to calculate the present value of the cash inflows.

6. The uniform annual equivalent cost method is used to compare mutually exclusive projects with significantly different lives. It may require a comparison of annual costs, which means the conversion of cash flows into an equivalent uniform annual series.

7. To calculate after-tax cash flows, depreciation, which is not a cash outlay, must be added to net income after taxes; that is, after-tax cash inflows = after-tax net income + depreciation.

PRACTICAL APPLICATION

1.

   a. Payback period = Initial investment ($80,000) / Annual savings ($20,000) = 4 years.

   b. $20,000 × T_2(12%, 7 years) = $20,000 × 4.564 = $91,280.

   c. NPV = PV − I = $91,280 − $80,000 = $11,280.

   d. At IRR, I = PV. Thus, $80,000 = $20,000 × T_2(i, 7 years). T_2(i, 7 years) = $80,000 / $20,000 = 4.00, which is, in the seven-year line, somewhere between 16% and 18% in Table 2 in Appendix II.

2.

   a.   NPV = PV of cash inflows after taxes

[discounted at the cost of capital (12%)] − Initial investment = PV − I

= $15,000 × T_2(12%, 10 years) − $75,000 = $15,000 (5.650) − $75,000 = $9,750

   b. IRR is the rate that equates the amount invested with the present value of cash inflows generated by the project. Therefore, we set the following equation:

$$\$75,000 = \$15,000 \ T_2(i, \ 10 \ \text{years})$$

$$T_2(i, \ 10 \ \text{years}) = \$75,000 \ / \ \$15,000 = 5$$

which stands between 14% and 16%.

	Table Value	
14%	5.216	5.216
True rate		5,000
16%	4.833	
Difference	0.383	0.216

Using interpolation,

IRR = 14% + [(5.216 – 5.0000) / (5.216 – 4.833)] (16% – 14%)

= 14% + [(0.216) / (0.383)] (2%)

= 14% + (0.564)(2%) = 14% + 1.13% = 15.13%

3. Because NPV = PV – I, I = PV – NPV:

Year	Cash Inflow ($)	Present Value of $1	Total PV ($)
1	3,000	0.926	2,778
2	3,500	0.857	3,000
3	2,400	0.794	1,906
4	2,600	0.735	1,911
PV of future inflows			9,595
NPV			500
Initial outlay (1)			9,095

4. By definition, at IRR, PV = I or NPV = 0. To determine the amount of initial investment, all that is needed is to compute the present value of $4,000 a year for eight periods.

PV = $4,000 × 5.335 = $21,340

5. After-tax cash benefit follows:

Year	Cash Benefit ($) (a)	Depreciation ($)	Taxable Income ($)	Income Tax ($) (b)	Net After-Tax Cash Inflow ($) (a) − (b)
			Machine 1		
1	25,000	12,500	12,500	5,000	20,000
2	25,000	12,500	12,500	5,000	20,000
3	25,000	12,500	12,500	5,000	20,000
4	25,000	12,500	12,500	5,000	20,000
			Machine 2		
1	45,000	15,000	30,000	12,000	33,000
2	19,000	15,000	4,000	1,600	17,400
3	25,000	15,000	10,000	4,000	21,000
4	25,000	15,000	10,000	4,000	21,000

Net present value:

Year	Cash (Outflow) Inflow ($)	Present Value of $1 at 8%	Net Present Value of Cash Flow ($)
		Machine 1	
0	(50,000)	1.000	(50,000)
1–4	20,000	3.312	66,240
		NPV	16,240
		Machine 2	
0	(60,000)	1.000	(60,000)
1	33,000	0.926	30,558
2	17,400	0.857	14,912
3	21,000	0.794	16,674
4	21,000	0.735	15,435
		NPV	17,579

6. After-tax cash inflows can be calculated as shown here. Note that depreciation by straight-line is $90,000/10 = $9,000 per year. Thus,

After-tax cash inflows = After-tax net income + depreciation

$$= (\$70,000 - \$50,000)(1 - 0.3) + \$9,000$$

$$= \$20,000 \ (0.7) + \$9,000$$

$$= \$14,000 + \$9,000 = \$23,000$$

To see if this machine should be purchased, calculate NPV.

$$PV = \$23,000 \ T_2(10\%, \ 10 \ \text{years}) = \$23,000 \ (6.145) = \$141,335$$

Thus,

$$NPV = PV - I = \$141,335 - \$90,000 = \$51,335$$

Because NPV is positive, the machine should be bought.

7.

Net Cash Flow After Taxes Calculation

Year (1)	Cash Inflow ($) (1)	Cash Outflow ($) (2)	Net Cash Flow Before Taxes ($) (3) = (1) – (2)	Depreciation (Noncash Expense) ($) (4) = 0.2 × 800,000	Net Income Before Taxes ($) (5) = (3) – (4)	Income Taxes ($) (6) = 0.4 × (5)	Net Income After Taxes ($) (7) = (5) – (6)	Net Cash Flow After Taxes ($) (7) + (4)
1	800,000	550,000	250,000	160,000	90,000	36,000	54,000	214,000
2	790,000	590,000	200,000	160,000	40,000	16,000	24,000	184,000
3	920,000	600,000	320,000	160,000	160,000	64,000	96,000	256,000
4	870,000	610,000	260,000	160,000	100,000	40,000	60,000	220,000
5	650,000	390,000	260,000	160,000	100,000	40,000	60,000	220,000

NPV is computed as follows:

Year	Net Cash Flow After Taxes ($)	T_1 at 10% Table Value	Present Value ($)
0	(800,000)	1.000	(800,000)
1	214,000	0.909	194,526
2	184,000	0.826	151,984
3	256,000	0.751	192,256
4	220,000	0.683	150,260
5	220,000	0.621	136,620
		NPV =	25,646

The company should buy the machine because NPV is positive ($25,646).

8.

$$\text{UAC} = \{I - S_N [T_1 (i, T)]\} \text{ CRF}(i, N) + c$$

$$\text{UAC} = \{\$32,000 - \$3,000 [T_1 (12\%, 7)]\} \text{ CRF}(12\%, 7) + \$4,500$$

$$= [\$32,000 - \$3,000 (0.452)] (1/T_2(12\%, 7) + \$4,500$$

$$= (\$32,000 - \$1,356) (1/4.564) + \$4,500$$

$$= \$30,644 (0.219) + \$4,500 = \$6,711.04 + \$4,500 = \$11,211.04$$

9.

$$\text{UAC} = \{I - S_N [T_1 (i, T)]\} \text{ CRF}(i, N) + c$$

The popular roof has a total initial cost of $2,500 + $1,200 = $3,700.

$$\text{UAC}_A = \{\$3,700 - 0 [T_1 (10\%, 8)]\} \text{ CRF}(10\%, 8) + 0$$

$$= \$3,700 (1/T_2(10\%, 8) + 0$$

$$= \$3,700(1/5.335) + 0$$

$$= \$3,700(0.187) + 0 = \$691.90$$

The heavier grade has a total initial cost of $2,500 + $825 + $1,200 = $4,525.

$$\text{UAC}_B = \{\$4,525 - 0 [T_1 (10\%, 12)]\} \text{ CRF}(10\%, 12) + \$3,325$$

$$= \$4,525 (1/T_2(10\%, 12) + 0$$

$$= \$4,525(1/6.814) + 0$$

$$= \$4,525(0.147) + 0 = \$665.18$$

The heavier grade at $665.18 per year is cheaper than the lighter grade at $691.90 per year.

12
PROJECT MANAGEMENT

KEY TERMS

backward pass calculation procedure that moves backward through the network determining the latest start and latest finish times for each activity.

beta distribution probability distribution often used to describe activity times.

crashing process of reducing an activity time by adding resources and hence usually cost.

critical path longest sequence of activities in a project management network.

dummy activity fictitious activity with zero activity time used to represent precedence or used whenever two or more activities have the same starting and ending nodes.

earliest finish time earliest time at which an activity may be completed.

earliest start time earliest time at which an activity may begin.

Gantt chart graphical representation of a schedule used to plan or monitor progress.

latest finish time latest time at which an activity must be completed without holding up the complete project.

latest start time latest time at which an activity must begin without holding up the complete project.

nodes intersection or junction points of a network.

PERT/cost also known as the Critical Path Method (CPM); technique designed to assist in the planning, scheduling, and controlling of project costs.

slack length of time an activity can be delayed without affecting the project completion date.

Project management involves planning and scheduling. *Project planning* includes all activities that result in a course of action for a project. Goals for the project must be set and their priorities established. Goals include resources to be committed, completion times, and activities. Areas of responsibility must be identified and assigned. Time and resource requirements to perform the work activities must be projected and budgeted. Compared to project planning, project scheduling is more specific. Scheduling establishes time and sequences of the various phases of the project.

PROJECT SCHEDULING MODELS

There are various methods for scheduling projects. Presented in this chapter are two popular scheduling models—Gantt charting and the Program Evaluation and Review Technique. Both are schematic models, but PERT also is a mathematical model.

GANTT CHARTS

A *Gantt chart* is a bar chart that depicts the relationship of activities over time. Table 12.1 provides the symbols frequently used in a Gantt chart. An open bracket indicates the scheduled start of the activity, and a closing bracket indicates the scheduled completion. The symbol [—] indicates the currently completed portion of the activity. A caret at the top of the chart indicates current time.

Table 12.2 shows a Gantt chart of a business student preparing for final exams. Project activities are listed down the page and time appears across the top of the page. The project activities are studying for exams in Human Resource Management (HRM), Marketing, Operations Management (OM), and Information Systems (IS). OM is broken into two subactivities—studying concepts new since the last exam and studying concepts covered on previous exams for review. By examining the horizontal time axis, we see that all activities must be completed in three and one-half weeks.

Studying HRM, for example, is scheduled to start at the beginning of week 1 and end after one and one-half weeks. The check mark at the top indicates that one and one-half weeks have already passed. The heavy lines show how much of each activity has already been done. Students can use this chart to visualize their progress and to adjust their study activities. As you can see, one of the strengths of project scheduling with Gantt charts is the simplicity of the schematic model.

Table 12.1. Gantt Chart Symbols

Symbol	Meaning
[	Start of an activity
]	End of an activity
[—]	Actual progress of the activity
v	Point in time where the project is now

Table 12.2. Gantt Chart for Project Scheduling

Project Activity	Week 1	Week 2 ✓	Week 3	Week 4
Study HRM	[———————	]		
Study Marketing		[———————	]	
Study OM				
Study concepts new since last exam		[—	]	
Study concepts covered on previous exams			[ ]	
Study IS				[ ]

PROGRAM EVALUATION AND REVIEW TECHNIQUE

Program Evaluation and Review Technique (PERT) is a useful management tool for planning, scheduling, costing, coordinating, and controlling complex projects such as the construction of buildings, installation of computers, assembly of a machine, research and development activities, and development of a new product.

Questions to be answered by PERT include:

- When will the project be finished?

- What is the probability that the project will be completed by any given time?

PERT involves the diagrammatic representation of the sequence of activities comprising a project by means of a network. The network visualizes all the individual tasks (activities) to complete a given job or program; points out interrelationships; and consists of activities (represented by arrows) and events (represented by circles).

- *Arrows.* Arrows represent tasks or activities, which are distinct segments of the project, consuming time and resources.

- *Nodes (circles).* Nodes symbolizes events or milestone points in the project representing the completion of one or more activities and/or the initiation of one or more subsequent activities. An event is a point in time and does not consume any time in itself as does an activity.

RULES OF NETWORK CONSTRUCTION

Fundamental to PERT is the construction of a network. The rules for its construction follow:

Rule 1. Each arrow should represent only one activity.

Rule 2. The length of the arrow is determined only by convenience and clarity, and is not related to the time needed for that activity.

Rule 3. Each activity, except the first, must have an activity preceding it.

Rule 4. Each activity, except the last, must have an activity following it.

Rule 5. For any activity to begin, all preceding activities must be completed.

EXAMPLE 1

Consider the activities, A, B, C, D, E, F, and G. The following network

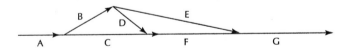

is interpreted as:

1. Perform activity A.

2. Start B and C after A is performed. B and C can be performed concurrently.

3. Start D and E after B is completed.

4. Start F only after C *and* D are completed.

5. Start G only after E *and* F are completed.

YOU SHOULD REMEMBER

It is evident that a network can represent the most complex relationship of activities conceivable and yet permit the tracking of all activities with little trouble.

An additional important rule must be noted:

Rule 6. No two activities can have the same origin and ending.

EXAMPLE 2

Assume that we are to perform A and B concurrently. Because of Rule 6, the following network is illegal:

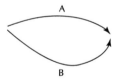

Because of Rule 4, the following network is illegal as it stands:

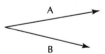

However, the problem can be resolved by a *dummy activity* in the following way:

A dummy activity represents *no* work but permits observance of Rules 4 and 6.

In a real-world situation, the estimates of completion times of activities will seldom be certain. To cope with the uncertainty in activity time estimates, the PERT proceeds by estimating three possible duration times for each activity. As shown in Figure 12.1, the numbers appearing on the arrows represent these three time estimates for activities needed to complete the various events. These time estimates are:

- the most optimistic time, labeled *a*

- the most likely time, labeled *m*

- the most pessimistic time, labeled *b*

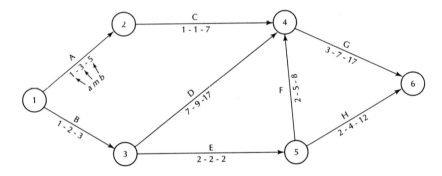

Figure 12.1. Network Diagram

For example, the optimistic time for completing activity H is 2 days, the most likely time is 4 days, but the pessimistic time is 12 days. The next step is to calculate an expected time, which is determined as follows:

$$t_e \text{ (expected time)} = (a + 4m + b) / 6$$

For example, for activity H, the expected time is

$$(2 + 4(4) + 12) / 6 = 30 / 6 = 5 \text{ days}$$

Note that this formula is based on the assumption that the uncertain activity times are best described by a *beta probability distribution*. This distribution assumption, which was judged to be reasonable by the developers of PERT, provides the time distribution for activity H as shown in Figure 12.2.

As a measure of variation (uncertainty) about the expected time, the standard deviation is calculated as follows:

$$\sigma = (b - a) / 6$$

For example, the standard deviation of completion time for activity H is

$$\sigma = (12 - 2) / 6 = 10 / 6 = 1.67 \text{ days}$$

Note: This formula is based on the notion that a standard deviation is approximately 1/6 of the difference between the extreme values of the distribution.

Expected activity times and their standard deviations are computed in this manner for all the activities of the network and arranged in the tabular format as shown in Table 12.3.

Table 12.3. Computations of Expected Time and Standard Deviation

Activity	Predecessors	a	m	b	t_e	σ
A	None	1	3	5	3.0	0.67
B	None	1	2	3	2.0	0.33
C	A	1	1	7	2.0	1.00
D	B	7	9	17	10.0	1.67
E	B	2	2	2	2.0	0.00
F	E	2	5	8	5.0	0.67
G	C, D, F	3	7	17	8.0	2.33
H	E	2	4	12	5.0	1.67

To answer the first question, we need to determine the network's critical path. A path is a sequence of connected activities. In Figure 12.1, 1-2-4-6 would be an example of a path. The critical path for a project is the path that takes the longest amount of time. The sum of the estimated times for all activities on the critical path is the total time required to complete the project. These activities are critical because any delay in their completion will cause a delay in the project.

The time to do all the activities on the critical path represents the minimum amount of time needed for the completion of the project. Thus, to speed up the project, the activities along this path must be shortened. Activities not on the critical path are not critical because they will be worked on simultaneously with critical path activities and their completion could be delayed up to a point without delaying the project as a whole.

An easy way to find the critical path involves the following two steps:

1. Identify all possible paths of a project and calculate their completion times.

2. Pick the one with the longest amount of completion time, which is the critical path.

In the example, we have the following paths and completion times:

Path	Completion Time
A-C-G	13 days (3 + 2 + 8)
B-D-G	20 days (2 + 10 + 8)
B-E-F-G	17 days (2 + 2 + 5 + 8)
B-E-H	9 days (2 + 2 + 5)

The critical path is B-D-G, which means that it takes 20 days to complete the project.

STEPS TO BE FOLLOWED IN DETERMINING THE CRITICAL PATH

When the network is large and complex, it is tedious to find the critical path by listing all the paths and picking the longest one. We need a more systematic and efficient approach, which is explained next.

1. **Find the earliest start (ES) and earliest finish (EF) times for the activities.** (See Figure 12.3.) This is done by assigning a start time (usually zero) for the initial job(s) and determining the earliest possible start time for each of the activities in the network. The rule is: since a job cannot be started until all preceding jobs have been finished, the earliest start time of an activity is the maximum of the earliest finish times of the immediate predecessors. The earliest finish time for an activity is its earliest start time plus the activity duration time t. $EF = ES + t$.

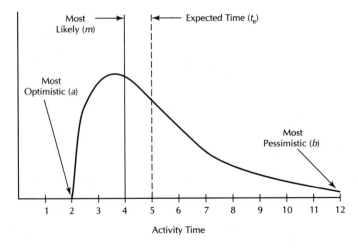

Figure 12.2. Activity Time Distribution for Activity H

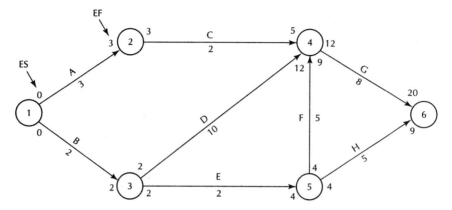

Figure 12.3. Earliest Start and Finish Times

2. **Compute the latest start (LS) and latest finish (LF) times for the activities.** (See Figure 12.4.) This is done by a *backward pass.* We begin this time at the completion point. The latest finish time is the latest time at which an activity can be completed without extending the completion time of the network. The rule is: the latest finish time for an activity is the minimum of the latest start time of the immediately succeeding activities. The latest start time is the latest at which an activity can begin without extending the completion time of the project. It is the latest finish time minus the activity duration, $LS = LF - t$.

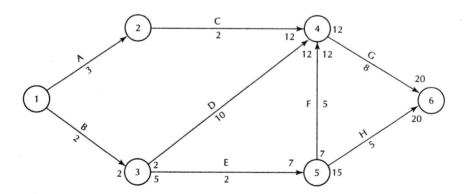

Figure 12.4. Latest Start and Finish Times

3. **Compute slack times for the activities.** The critical path of the project is made up of those activities with zero slack, as shown in Figure 12.5 by the dark line. The *slack* is the length of the time we can delay an activity without interfering with the project completion. Any delay in completing activities on the critical path will result in a lengthening of the project duration:

$$\text{Slack} = \text{ES} - \text{LS} \text{ or } \text{EF} - \text{LF}$$

In other words, we compare the earliest start time with the latest start time for any activity (i.e., we look at when it *can* be started and when it *must* be started to see how much free time, or slack, that activity has).

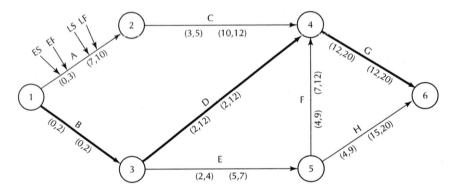

Figure 12.5. Critical Path

Table 12.4 illustrates how the critical path is determined using this approach.

Table 12.4. Determination of the Critical Path

Activity	ES	EF	LS	LF	Slack = ES – LS or EF – LF	Activity on Critical Path
A	0	3	7	10	7	
B	0	2	0	2	0	Yes
C	3	5	10	12	7	
D	2	12	2	12	0	Yes
E	2	4	5	7	3	
F	4	9	7	12	3	
G	12	20	12	20	0	Yes
H	4	9	15	20	11	

The next important information we want to obtain is the chance that the project will be completed within a contract time, say, 21 days. To secure this information, we introduce the standard deviation of total project time around the expected time, which is determined as follows:

$$\text{Standard deviation (project)} = \sqrt{\begin{array}{l}\text{Sum of the squares of the standard}\\ \text{deviations of all critical path activities}\end{array}}$$

Using this formula, the standard deviation of completion time (the path B-D-G) for the project is as follows:

$$\sqrt{(0.33)^2 + (1.67)^2 + (2.33)^2} = \sqrt{0.1089 + 2.7889 + 5.4289}$$

$$= \sqrt{8.3267} = 2.885 \text{ days}$$

Using the standard deviation and table of areas under the normal distribution curve (Table 3 in Appendix II), the probability of completing the project within any given time period can be determined. Assume that the expected delivery time is, say, 21 days. The first step is to compute z, which is the number of standard deviations from the mean represented by our given time of 21 days. The formula for z is

$$z = \frac{(\text{Delivery time} - \text{Expected time})}{\text{Standard deviation}}$$

Therefore,

$$z = \frac{(21 \text{ days} - 20 \text{ days})}{2.885 \text{ days}} = 0.35$$

The next step is to find the probability associated with the calculated value of z by referring to a table of areas under a normal curve.

From Table 3 in Appendix II, we see the probability is 0.6368, which means that there is close to a 64% chance that the project will be completed in less than 21 days.

To summarize, we have determined that

- The expected completion time of the project is 20 days.

- There is a better than 60% chance of finishing before 21 days.

Note: We can also obtain the chances of meeting any other deadline if we wish. All we need to do is change the delivery time and recalculate the z value.

- Activities B-D-G are on the critical path; they must be watched more closely than the others because the whole project will fall behind if they fall behind.

- If extra effort is needed to finish the project on time or before the deadline, we must borrow resources (e.g., money and labor) from any activity not on the critical path.

It is possible to reduce the completion time of one or more activities, which will require an extra expenditure of cost. The benefit from reducing the total completion time of a project by accelerated efforts on certain activities must be balanced against the extra cost of doing so. A related problem is to determine which activities must be accelerated to reduce the total project completion time. The Critical Path Method (CPM), also known as PERT/COST, is widely used to deal with this subject.

SUMMARY OF PERT PROCEDURE

In analyzing any project using PERT, we perform the following steps:

1. **Develop a list of activities that make up the project, including immediate predecessors and draw a network corresponding to the activity list developed.**

2. **Estimate the expected activity time and the variance for each activity.**

3. **Using the expected activity time estimates, determine the earliest start time and the earliest finish time for each activity.** The earliest finish time for the complete project corresponds to the earliest finish time for the last activity. This is the expected project completion time.

4. **Using the project completion time as the latest finishing time for the last activity, work backward through the network to compute the latest start and latest finish time for each activity.**

5. **Compute the slack associated with each activity.** The critical path activities are the activities with *zero* slack.

6. **Use the variability in the activity times to estimate the variability of the project completion date; then, using this estimate, compute the probability of meeting a specified completion date.**

THE CRITICAL PATH METHOD MODEL: PERT/COST

If the project duration (length of critical path) exceeds the allowable deadline, options include changing the deadline or "crashing" the project. *Crashing* means speeding up one or more activities along the critical path. This may involve shifting more resources (money) to those activities or perhaps outsourcing some of the work.

The critical path method (CPM) model, also known as PERT/COST, argues that most activities can be reduced in duration if extra resources (e.g., men, machines, money) are assigned to them. The cost for getting the job done may increase, but if other advantages outweigh this added cost, the job should be expedited or crashed. The CPM model attempts to determine which jobs to crash and by how much.

The *normal time* is similar to the most likely time estimate in PERT. This could be viewed as the most efficient time to complete the project. The *crash time* is the time required when extra resources are added to complete the project in the minimum possible time. Using the crash time results in added costs for the project. A simplified view of the relationship between the normal and the crash times is seen in Figure 12.6. This represents a linear cost-time relationship. A nonlinear relationship is also possible and may be more realistic. However, to illustrate the model, only the simplified linear relationship will be used. The slope of the cost–time line for any activity can be determined by the following:

$$\text{Slope} = \text{Cost per day} = \frac{\text{Crash cost} - \text{Normal cost}}{\text{Normal time} - \text{Crash time}}$$

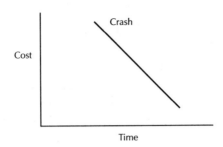

Figure 12.6. Linear Cost–Time Relationship

The slope of these lines actually measures the increase in cost per unit increase in time. Therefore, all such slopes are negative. The minus sign can be ignored and only absolute values considered, however.

To illustrate the CPM model, assume a simple project, as represented by the network diagram in Figure 12.7. The time, cost, and cost slope data for this project are shown in Table 12.5.

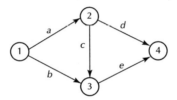

Figure 12.7. Network Diagram for CPM Illustration

NORMAL SOLUTION

From the foregoing information, the normal time solution can be developed. This solution is shown in Figure 12.8, with the appropriate normal time estimates indicated on the activity arrows. The critical path for this solution, as indicated by the heavy arrows, is a-c-e = 15 days. The total cost of the normal time solution is $3,900.

Table 12.5. CPM Project Time and Cost Data

| Activity | Time/Days | | Cost ($) | | Slope |
	Normal	Crash	Normal	Crash	
a	4	3	400	800	400
b	8	5	600	2,400	600
c	6	5	1,000	1,200	200
d	9	8	700	1,400	700
e	5	2	1,200	2,700	500
Total cost			3,900	8,500	

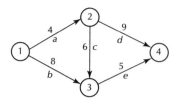

Figure 12.8. Normal Time Solution CPM Network

CRASH SOLUTION

The crash time solution can also be determined from the information in the same way. This solution is found in Figure 12.9. The critical path can be determined as a-d = 11 days, with a cost of $8,500.

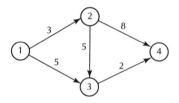

Figure 12.9. Crash Time Solution CPM Network

DETERMINATION OF MINIMUM-COST CRASH SOLUTION

The crash solution already set forth indicated that this project can be completed in 11 days at a cost of $8,500. The next question for management to answer is whether the project can be completed in this same period of time for a lower cost.

The CPM (PERT/COST) model involves the following steps:

1. **Find the critical path.**
2. **Look at all the slopes (crash costs per unit of time) for all activities on the critical path.**
3. **Pick the activity on the critical path with the lowest cost increase per unit of time.** If there is a tie, pick one of the ties activities at random.
4. **Using crash time on this activity, compute the expected total time and the total cost, and determine the new critical path.**

5. Repeat the process until either the expected total time is equal to or less than the required time, there are no more possible time savings, *or* the total cost exceeds available funds.

Now we apply these steps to the example. First, we list all paths:

Path	Length
a-c-e	15 ◀——— critical path
b-e	13
a-d	13

Next, we determine the critical path activities in the order of lowest crashing cost and the number of days that can be crashed.

Activity	Slope	Available Days
c	200	1
a	400	1
e	500	3

Shorten c and a one day apiece at a cost of $600 ($200 + $400). The length of the path a-c-e becomes 13 days, which is the same as the length of paths b-e and a-d. Because all three paths are now critical, further improvements will necessitate shorting one activity on each.

Path	Length
a-c-e	13 ◀——— critical path
b-e	13 ◀——— critical path
a-d	13 ◀——— critical path

Path	Activity	Slope
a-c-e	a	No reduction possible
	c	No reduction possible
	e	$500
b-e	b	$600
	e	No reduction possible
a-d	a	No reduction possible
	d	$700

The following three activities can be crashed:

Activity	Slope	Available Days
e	500	3
b	600	3
d	700	1

Shortening activity e two days for $1,000 ($500 × 2) and d one day ($700) would lead to the critical paths a-c-e and a-d of 11 days for $6,200. Even though activity b can be crashed, their crashing does not reduce project duration. The minimum time of the project is 11 days at a cost of $6,200. At this point, no additional improvement is possible.

To summarize, consult the following table:

Project Time	Crashing Options	Least Cost Option	Project Cost ($)	Critical Paths
15 days			3,900	a-c-e
13	−1 at c & a ($200 + 400)	c & a	4,500	a-c-e; b-d; a-d
11	−2 at e ($500 × 2) & −1 at d ($700)	e & d	6,200	a-c-e; a-d

MANAGEMENT USE OF CPM

The CPM network has the primary goal of aiding management in the control of costs as well as of time. In these models, this goal is accomplished by providing management with a technique whereby the various time–cost tradeoffs in a project can be evaluated. The process involves the determination of the lowest cost, longest completion time solution; and the shortest time, highest cost solution. From these two solutions, various alternatives can be established. For example, the lowest cost possible for the shortest completion time can be found. In addition, a variety of alternatives involving reduction in completion time and the added cost of each can be ascertained. Thus, the time and cost of completing the project under normal conditions and the amount of time that can be saved by the expenditure of more money on various activities are determined. Management can then make a decision about the project after a consideration of all of the time–cost options. The lowest cost option, the shortest time option, and the interim alternatives with the appropriate cost and schedule data will be available.

COMPUTER SOFTWARE FOR PROJECT MANAGEMENT

Most project management applications today use computers extensively. The management of projects is enhanced by tools such as Gantt charting, PERT, and CPM. These tools are easily computerized, and indeed there are dozens of commercial packages on the market. The user inputs activity time estimates and procedure information, program output slack for each activity, duration and variance for critical paths, and other useful project management information. Some popular packages are listed next.

Harvard Project Manager by Harvard Software, Inc.

Pertmaster by Westminster Software, Inc.

PMSII/RMS II by North America Mica, Inc.

Pimavera by Primavera Systems, Inc.

Project Scheduler 5000 by Scitor Corporation

Pro-Jet 6 by Soft-Corp, Inc.

Project Manager Workbench by Applied Business Tech Corporation

Project by Microsoft Corporation

MacProject & LisaProject by Apple Computer Corporation

VisiSchedule by Paladin Software Corporation

KNOW THE CONCEPTS

DO YOU KNOW THE BASICS?

1. Define project management.
2. What are the underlying assumptions of minimum cost scheduling? Are they equally realistic?
3. Describe the key elements of the project-planning process.
4. Why is a network diagram used in project management?
5. Differentiate between an event and an activity.
6. Discuss why Gantt charts are a useful aid to an operations manager.

7. What options are available if the project duration (length of critical path) exceeds the allowable deadline?

8. What is the difference between the normal time and the crash time?

9. Briefly describe PERT/cost? What is it also known as?

TERMS FOR STUDY

backward pass	earliest start time
beta distribution	Gantt chart
crashing	latest finish time
critical path	latest start time
critical path method (CPM)	nodes
dummy activity	PERT/cost
earliest finish time	

PRACTICAL APPLICATION

1. Laurie, an operator at Charles Speedy printshop, has three jobs that she must get out today. Each job must be type set, printed, and folded, and the jobs must be done in the order shown here.

Job	Type Setting (hours)	Printing (hours)	Collating (hours)
X	1	3	1.5
Y	4	3	0.5
Z	2.5	2	1

Construct a Gantt chart of her day's work.

2. Jane is the owner of a general contracting company that specializes in the construction of single-family homes and small office buildings. She wants to construct a Gantt chart to monitor and control her home building project. The following table summarizes the activities involved in the project along with the precedence relationships among the activities.

Description	Time Required (days)	Immediate Predecessor Activity
Excavate	3	—
Lay foundation	4	A
Rough plumbing	3	B

Description	Time Required (days)	Immediate Predecessor Activity
Frame	10	B
Exterior	8	D
Install HVAC	4	D
Rough electric	6	D
Sheet rock	8	C, E, F, G
Carpentry	5	H
Paint	5	H
Final plumbing	4	Immediate
Final electric	2	J
Install flooring	4	K, L

3. Given the following project, what probability would you assign to a project duration of more than 8.5 weeks?

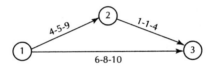

4. Given the following network diagram, determine the probability that the project will finish within 18 weeks of its start. Times on the diagram are in weeks.

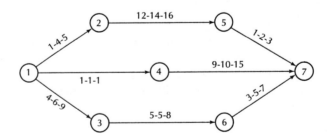

5. Given the following network diagram, note that the numbers on each row refer to the expected time (t_e) and standard deviation (σ) in weeks for that activity. For example, 14,4 indicates an expected time of fourteen and a standard deviation of four weeks.

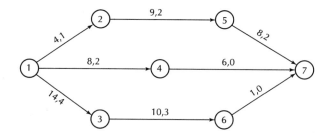

a. Determine the activities on the critical path.

b. Determine the expected project duration.

c. Determine the probability that the project will be completed in 29 weeks or less.

6. Consider the following:

Activity	Immediate Predecessor	a (weeks)	m (weeks)	b (weeks)
A	None	2	4	6
B	None	6	8	10
C	A	1	5	15
D	C	1	5	9
E	B	6	8	10

a. Compute the expected time and standard deviation of the time required to complete each activity.

b. Draw a network diagram and find the critical path by computing earliest start, latest start, and slack. What is the expected length of the critical path?

c. Assume that the time required to complete the project is normally distributed. Compute the probability that path ACD will be completed in less than 16 weeks.

d. What is the probability that the project will be completed in less than 16 weeks?

7. Given the following network of a project:

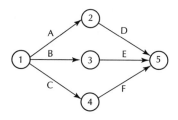

   a. Determine the critical path of the network by enumerating all paths.

   b. Determine the critical path of the network by computing the slacks of the activities.

8. Refer to the network of problem 4 and the following table:

Activity	Normal Time (day)	Normal Cost ($)	Crash Time (day)	Crash Cost ($)
A	3	70	1	300
B	1	250	1	250
C	4	80	3	130
D	2	220	1	420
E	7	700	3	1,400
F	3	150	2	240

   a. Compute the normal cost of the project.

   b. Perform a time–cost tradeoff analysis to reduce project duration.

9. Using the following information, develop an optimum time–cost solution.

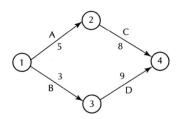

Activity	Normal Time (day)	Crash Time (day)	Crash Cost per Day ($)
A	5	3	2.5
B	3	2	4
C	8	6	3.5
D	9	7	1

10. Given the following network diagram and related information, develop an optimum time–cost solution.

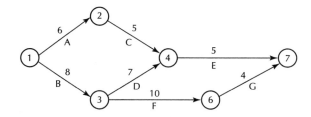

Activity	Normal Time (day)	Cost ($)	Crash Time (day)	Cost ($)	Cost Slope ($)
A	6	500	3	800	100
B	8	400	6	800	200
C	5	200	4	250	50
D	7	300	5	900	300
E	5	400	4	550	150
F	10	1,000	5	1,400	80
G	4	700	2	900	100
		3,500		5,600	

ANSWERS

DO YOU KNOW THE BASICS?

1. Project management involves the planning, directing, and controlling of resources (people, equipment, material) to meet the technical cost and time constraints of the project.

2. The assumptions underlying minimum cost scheduling are that it costs money to expedite a project activity and it costs money to sustain or lengthen the completion time of the project. It is often possible, however, that there is little or no cash expenditures associated with sustaining a project. Labor is often shifted between projects, and in the short run there may be no incentive to complete a project in normal time.

3. Project planning involves project definition, resource definition, project scheduling, and project control.

4. The network diagram provides an easily understood graphical description of the project and how activities must be sequenced.

5. Events correspond to points in time at which activities begin or end. Activities consume time and resources.

6. Gantt charts allow an operations manager to schedule activities over time in a graphical manner. A Gantt chart is readily understood and updated, and it is useful in determining the status of a project at any point in time.

7. If the project duration (length of critical path) exceeds the allowable deadline, options include changing the deadline or crashing the project.

8. The normal time is similar to the most likely time estimate in PERT. This could be viewed as the most efficient time to complete the project. The crash time is the time required when extra resources are added to complete the project in the minimum possible time. Use of the crash time results in added costs for the project.

9. PERT/cost, also known as CPM, is a technique designed to assist in the planning, scheduling, and controlling project costs.

PRACTICAL APPLICATION

1.

					Hours							
Activity	*1*	*2*	*3*	*4*	*5*	*6*	*7*	*8*	*9*	*10*	*11*	*12*
Type setting	[X] [		Y		] [		Z	]				
Printing		[	X	]		[		Y	] [	Z	]	
Collating				[X	]				[Y]	[	Z	]

2.

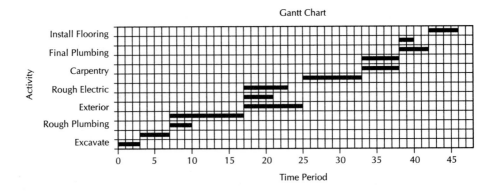

Gantt Chart

3.

Path	t_e	σ	z	$P(<8.5)$
1-2-3	7	0.972	+1.54	0.9382
1-3	8	0.667	+0.75	0.7734

The probability of both being less than 8.5 is (0.9382)(0.7734) = 0.7256. Thus, P(project > 8.5) = 1 − 0.7256 = 0.2744 = 27.44%.

4.

Path	t_e	σ	z	$P(<18)$
1-2-5-7	19.67	1.00	−0.33	0.3707
1-4-7	10.67	1.00	+7.33	1.0000
1-3-6-7	16.67	1.18	+1.13	0.8708

The probability that the project will finish in 18 weeks is (0.3707)(0.8708) = 0.3228 = 32.28%.

5.

Path	t_e	σ	z	$P(<29)$
1-2-5-7	21	3	+2.67	
1-4-7	14	2	+7.50	
1-3-6-7	25	5	+0.80	0.7881[a]

[a] $z = (29 − 25)/5 = + 0.80$; $P(<29) = 0.7881$.

   a. The critical path is 1-3-6-7.
   b. Expected project duration is 25 weeks.
   c. Except for the critical path, the project will easily finish on time due to their large z values.

The probability of critical path completion by week 29 is 0.7881 = 78.81%.

6.

   a.

Activity	t_e	σ	ES	LS	Slack
A	4	0.67	0	1	1
B	8	0.67	0	0	0
C	6	2.33	4	5	1
D	5	1.33	10	11	1
E	8	0.67	8	8	0

b.

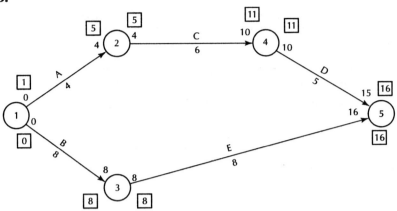

The critical path is B-E and the expected length is 8 + 8 = 16 days.

c. The path A-C-D = 4 + 6 + 5 = 15 days.

$$\sigma_{ACD} = \sqrt{(0.67)^2 + (2.33)^2 + (1.33)^2} = \sqrt{7.6467} = 2.76$$

To find the probability that path A-C-D will be completed in less than 16 weeks, define $Z = (16 - 15)/2.76 = 0.36$. From the normal distribution in Appendix II, we get 0.6406 or 64.06%.

d.

$$\sigma_{BE} = \sqrt{(0.67)^2 + (0.67)^2} = \sqrt{0.8978} = 0.947$$

Define $Z = (16 - 16)/0.947 = 0$. From Table 3 (Normal Distribution) in Appendix II, we get 0.50 or 50%, which is the probability the project will be completed in less than 16 weeks.

7.

a.

Path	Duration	Remark
A-D	3 + 2 = 5	
B-E	1 + 7 = 8	Critical Path
C-F	4 + 3 = 7	

b.

Activity	Duration	Immediate Predecessor	ES	EF	Predecessor of	LS	LF	Slack (LF − EF)
A	3	None	0	3	D	3	6	3
B	1	None	0	1	E	0	1	0
C	4	None	0	3	F	1	5	1
D	2	A	3	5	None	6	8	3
E	7	B	1	8	None	1	8	0
F	3	C	4	7	None	5	8	1

The critical path is B-E with zero slacks.

8.

    a. The normal cost is $1,470.

    b. Daily crash costs are as follows:

Activity	Slope = Daily Crash Cost ($)
A	(300 − 90)/(3 − 1) = 105
B	Cannot be crashed
C	(130 − 80)/(4 − 3) = 50
D	(420 − 220)/(2 − 1) = 200
E	(1400 − 700)/(7 − 3) = 175
F	(240 − 150)/(3 − 2) = 90

Project Time (days)	Crashing Options	Least Cost Option	Project Cost ($)	Critical Paths
8			1,470	B-E
7	−1 at E($175)	E	1,665	B-E; C-F
6	−1 at E & C($175 + $50)	E & C	1,890	B-E; C-F
	−1 at E & F($175 + $90)			
5	−1 at E & F($175 + $90)	E & F	2,155	A-D; B-E; C-F

Even though activities E, A, and D can be crashed, their crashing does not reduce project duration. The minimum time of the project is 5 days at a cost of $2,155.

9.

Activity	Normal Time (day)	Crash Time (day)	Crash Cost per Day ($)
A	5	3	2.5
B	3	2	4
C	8	6	3.5
D	9	7	1

Project Time (days)	Crashing Options	Least Cost Option	Crash Cost ($)	Critical Paths
13				A-C
12	−2 at A($2.5 × 2)	A	5	B-D
11	−2 at D($1 × 2)	D	7	A-C
10	−2 at C($3.5 × 2)	C	14	B-D
9	−1 at B($4)	B	18	A-C

10. The critical path is B-F-G for 22 days.

Path	Length
A-C-E	16
B-D-E	20
B-F-G	22 ◄──── critical path

You cannot crash C because its crashing does not reduce project duration. Crash activity F for 2 days for $160 ($80 × 2). We get the following results:

Path	Length
A-C-E	16
B-D-E	20 ◄──── critical path
B-F-G	20 ◄──── critical path

Now crash activity B for 2 days for $400 ($200 × 2) because it is on both critical paths. To summarize:

Project Time (days)	Crashing Options	Least Cost Option	Project Cost ($)	Critical Paths
22			3,500	B-F-G
20	–2 at F($160)	E	3,660	B-D-E; B-F-G
18	–2 at B($400)	B	4,060	B-D-E; B-F-G
	–2 at G, –1 at E, and			
	–1 at B($200 + 150 + 200)			

Total cost of completion of the project in 18 days = normal cost + additional crashing cost = $3,500 + 560 = $4,060.

13
WAITING LINES AND QUEUING

KEY TERMS

arrival rate number of customers or units arriving or entering the system in a given period of time.

channels number of waiting lines in a service system.

exponential distribution probability distribution used to describe the pattern or service times for some waiting lines.

GPSS, SIMSCRIPT specially designed computer programming languages used for simulation.

Monte Carlo simulation simulation using a random number procedure to create values for the probabilistic components.

multiple-channel line waiting line with two or more parallel identical servers.

Poisson distribution probability distribution used to describe the random arrival pattern for some waiting lines.

queue waiting line.

queue discipline rules that determine the order in which arrivals are serviced.

queuing (or waiting line) theory the study of waiting lines.

service rate number of customers or units that can be serviced by one server in a given period of time.

simulation technique to describe the behavior of a real-life system over time.

single-channel line waiting line with only one server.

utilization factor probability that the server is busy.

Queuing (waiting line) theory investigates the everyday hassle of waiting in line. Operations managers may apply this tool in performing their functions where waiting time is involved. Retailers and manufacturers know that waiting customers are often lost customers. However, improvements in this aspect of customer service are expensive in terms of extra attendants hired, whose pay must continue during slack hours. Coupled with this tradeoff problem of quick customer service versus expensive "standby" employees is the random nature of customer arrivals.

The analysis of waiting lines is of concern to operations managers because it affects design, capacity planning, layout planning, inventory management, and scheduling. Results from queuing analysis can provide helpful process design and layout information that will ensure proper operation when the new process is implemented.

In this chapter, we describe why waiting lines form, the uses of waiting line models in operations management, the structure of waiting line models, and how waiting line models can provide information about the characteristics of a process.

QUEUING OR WAITING LINE

There are a number of situations in which a customer of some sort arrive at a service facility of some sort. The only reason that a customer ever needs to wait for service is that for the moment, at least, the ability to provide service is not sufficient to satisfy the demand for that service.

Some examples of waiting for a service are:

Out-of-service industrial equipment waiting for a repairman.

Patients waiting in clinics.

Computer jobs waiting for processing

Airplanes waiting for a runway.

Cars waiting at toll booths.

More examples of waiting line (or queuing) situations are given in Table 13.

Table 13.1. Waiting Line (or Queuing) Situations

Types of Problem	Customer	Service	Service Facility	Queue Discipline
Teller windows	Person	Deposits and withdrawals	Teller and equipment	First-come, first-served (FCFS)
Telephone exchange	Incoming calls	Makes call connection	Operator and switchboard	Random
Machine repair	Disabled machines	Repair of machines	Repair crew	Priority
Tool crib	Machinist	Issues tools	Tool crib and attendants	FCFS
Market checkout stand	Customers with purchases	Ring up, collect, and wrap	Clerk, cash register, and wrappings	FCFS
Bus terminal	Buses	Arriving & departing	Loading area, dispatcher, driver	Schedule
Medical clinic	Patients	Medical treatment	Receptionist, nurse, doctor, equipment	FCFS or priority by appointment
Beauty shop	Patrons	Hair dressing	Beauty operator equipment	FCFS or priority by appointment

USING QUEUING ANALYSIS TO ANALYZE OPERATIONS

The goal of queuing is essentially to balance the cost of providing a level of service capacity and the customers waiting for service. Capacity costs relate to maintaining the ability to provide service. Examples include the number of repairmen to handle machine breakdowns, the number of checkouts in a retail store, and the number of bays in an auto repair garage.

This notion is illustrated in Figure 13.1. We expect a tradeoff between these two types of costs and total cost to be represented as a U-shaped curve. The optimal level of service capacity is the one in which total cost is minimized.

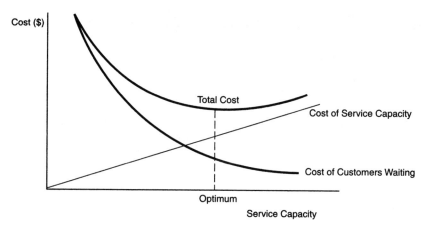

Figure 13.1. Optimal Service Capacity Determination

Many situations in productive systems are described conceptually by the general waiting line (queuing) model. How many shipping docks and receiving docks should be built for incoming and outcoming shipments? How many lift trucks should be provided to move products? How should machines be arranged to minimize waiting lines of products in process? How many teller windows should be open in a bank?

YOU SHOULD REMEMBER

Unlike in the case of the EOQ inventory model, the minimum cost is *not* usually obtained at the point where two cost curves intersect.

Operations managers can use queuing models to balance the gains that might be made by increasing the efficiency of the service system against the costs of doing so. Furthermore, managers should consider the costs of *not* making improvements to the system: long waiting lines or long waiting times may cause customers to balk or renege. Managers should therefore be concerned about the following characteristics of the system: line length, number of customers in the system, waiting time in line, total time in system, and service facility use.

Managers should relate these characteristics and their alternatives to dollars. Queuing models attempt to determine these operating characteristics.

STRUCTURE OF QUEUING (WAITING LINE) PROBLEMS

Four basic structures describe the general conditions at the service facility:

- *The single-channel, single-phase case* is the one in which arrival units form a waiting line and are serviced by a single service facility. The one-clerk parts department is illustrative.

Waiting Line   Service Facility

- *The multiple-channel, single-phase case* is illustrated by a two-or-more-clerks parts department since customers can be serviced by any of the clerks (channel).

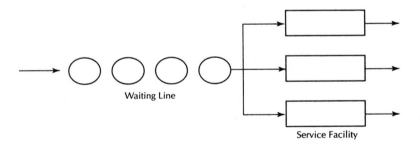

Waiting Line

Service Facility

- *The single-channel, multiple-phase case* is illustrated by a simple production line where there are a series of operations (phases) and the unit to be processed goes through the series for complete processing.

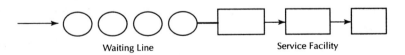

Waiting Line   Service Facility

- *The multiple-channel, multiple phase case* is illustrated by duplicate production lines in parallel.

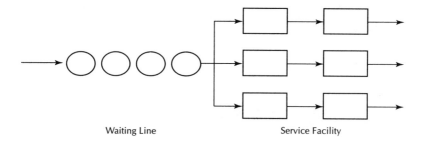

Waiting Line   Service Facility

Of course, a complex network of waiting lines could involve combinations of any or all the four basic structures.

YOU SHOULD REMEMBER

The layout analysis can effectively use queuing theory to find answers to such questions as the following:

How many customers will be waiting in line?

How long will these customers have to wait for service?

How many service facilities should be provided to minimize the costs and time involved?

How much idle time will the service facilities have?

ANALYTICAL MODELS FOR WAITING LINES

Depending on the size of source population of the inputs, waiting line models are based on whether the waiting line can theoretically become *infinite* or whether conditions limit the maximum waiting line to some *finite* value. Infinite waiting lines might be illustrated by automobile flow on a freeway. Finite waiting lines might be illustrated by the problem of a company with ten machines, such as looms: a unit "arrives" for service when a thread breaks, or the machine must be stopped for some other reason. The operator gives the needed service and starts the machine again. However, if there are only ten machines to be serviced, the maximum possible waiting line is ten.

Queue discipline, which is the order in which the units in the waiting line are selected for service, can be first-come, first-served (FCFS) or based on other priority rules. In a medical clinic, emergencies and patients with appointments are taken ahead of walk-in patients.

YOU SHOULD REMEMBER

The first-come, first-served rule is assumed in all four basic models. Because of the mathematical complexity involved, the systems involving queue disciplines other than the FCFS rule are typically analyzed using Monte Carlo simulation.

The most common waiting line analyses are based on the assumptions that *arrival rates* are represented by the Poisson distribution and that *service times* are represented by the negative exponential distribution. The formula for the Poisson distribution is

$$P(x) = \frac{e^{-\lambda}\lambda^x}{x!}$$

where x = the number of units arriving in one unit of time, $P(x)$ = probability of x arrivals, e = a constant equal to 2.71828, λ = the mean arrival rate, and $x! = x(x-1)(x-2)\cdots 1$. The Poisson is a discrete distribution. The example shown in Figure 13.2 is smoothed.

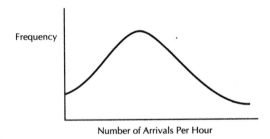

Number of Arrivals Per Hour

Figure 13.2. Example of Typical Poisson Distribution of Arrivals

The negative exponential distribution corresponds very closely to the Poisson. It is the distribution of the time intervals between arrivals where arrival times are the reciprocal of the arrival rates and indicates that the intervals of time are also random. The formula for the exponential distribution is

$$P(t) = e^{-\lambda t}$$

where t = the time between arrivals. An example of a negative exponential distribution is indicated in Figure 13.3.

Figure 13.3. Example of Typical Negative Exponential Distribution

---

YOU SHOULD REMEMBER

There are a few other standard distributions for which analytical solutions have been developed. Again, when the distribution assumptions are not valid, it is common to use simulation as the necessary mode of analysis.

QUEUING NOTATIONS

Define the following variables for queuing theory as shown:

λ = the mean arrival rate

μ = the mean service rate

$\dfrac{1}{\lambda}$ = the mean time between arrivals

$\dfrac{1}{\mu}$ = the mean time for service

ρ = utilization rate = $\dfrac{\lambda}{\mu}$ = the expected number being served

P_0 = probability of none in the system = $1 - \dfrac{\lambda}{\mu}$

P_n = probability of n units in the system at any point in time

L_q = expected number in the waiting line = expected length of the waiting line

L = expected number in the system = expected number in the waiting line plus the expected number being served = $L_q + \dfrac{\lambda}{\mu}$

W_q = expected waiting time in the queue = $L_q \left(\dfrac{1}{\lambda}\right) = \dfrac{L_q}{\lambda}$

W = expected waiting time in the system including service (i.e., total time in the system) = $\dfrac{L_q}{\lambda} = W_q + \dfrac{1}{\mu}$

The first three models are the case in which arrival units form a waiting line and are serviced by a single service facility. The population source being serviced is unlimited. Model 4 assumes multiple channels. The last model is appropriate when there exists a limited number of customers.

MODEL 1—THE SINGLE-CHANNEL WAITING LINE MODEL WITH POISSON ARRIVALS AND EXPONENTIAL SERVICE TIMES

Model 1 makes the following assumptions:

- Single-channel, single-phase case.
- Poisson arrival rates.
- Negative exponential service times.
- First-come, first-served queue discipline.
- Mean service rate greater than mean arrival rate $\mu > \lambda$.

Under these conditions, the following formulas apply.

The probability of none in the system = percentage of idle time:

$$P_0 = 1 - \dfrac{\lambda}{\mu}$$

The probability of n units in the system at any point in time:

$$P_n = \left(\frac{\lambda}{\mu}\right)^n P_0 = \left(\frac{\lambda}{\mu}\right)^n \left(1 - \frac{\lambda}{\mu}\right)$$

The probability of having to wait = probability of more than zero units in the system:

$$P(w) = 1 - P_0$$

The average number of units in the system, including the one being serviced:

$$L = \frac{\lambda}{(\mu - \lambda)}$$

The average time a unit spends in the system (waiting time plus service time):

$$W = \frac{1}{(\mu - \lambda)} = \frac{L}{\lambda}$$

The average number of units in the queue waiting for service:

$$L_q = \frac{\lambda^2}{\mu(\mu - \lambda)} = L - \frac{\lambda}{\mu}$$

The average time a unit spends in the queue waiting for service:

$$W_q = \frac{\lambda}{\mu(\mu - \lambda)} = \frac{L_q}{\lambda} = W - \frac{1}{\mu}$$

YOU SHOULD REMEMBER

Formulas used in operations management texts can be confusing. We also note the following relationships between W_q and W and L_q and L:

$$W_q = \text{Mean waiting time} = \frac{L_q}{\lambda}$$

$$L = \text{Mean number in waiting line} = L_q + \frac{\lambda}{\mu}$$

$$W = W_q + \frac{1}{\mu} = \frac{L}{\lambda}$$

These relationships are intuitively obvious, however.

EXAMPLE 1

Downey Bank is contemplating opening a drive-in window for customer service. It is estimated that customers will arrive for service at a rate of 15 per hour. The teller at the service window can serve customers at the rate of one every three minutes. Assuming Poisson arrivals and exponential service, the following can be computed:

Utilization rate of the teller = $\dfrac{\lambda}{\mu} = \dfrac{15}{20}$ = 75%

P_0 = probability of none in the system = $1 - \dfrac{\lambda}{\mu} = 1 - \left(\dfrac{15}{20}\right)$ = 25%

P_n = probability of, say, 2 units in the system at any point in time

$$= \left(1 - \dfrac{\lambda}{\mu}\right)\left(\dfrac{\lambda}{\mu}\right)^2 = 0.25\left(\dfrac{15}{20}\right)^2$$

= 0.14 = 14% L_q

= Mean number in waiting line = $\dfrac{\lambda^2}{\mu(\mu - \lambda)} = \dfrac{(15)^2}{20(20 - 15)}$

= 2.25 customers

L = Mean number in system, including the one being serviced

$$= \dfrac{\lambda}{(\mu - \lambda)} = \dfrac{15}{(20 - 15)} = 3 \text{ customers}$$

W_q = Mean waiting time = $\dfrac{\lambda}{\mu(\mu - \lambda)} = \dfrac{15}{20(20 - 15)}$

= 0.15 hour or 9 minutes

W = Mean time in system, including service = $\dfrac{1}{(\mu - \lambda)} = \dfrac{1}{(20 - 15)}$

= 0.2 hours or 12 minutes

EXAMPLE 2

Assume patients for the medical office of a very large plant arrive randomly following a Poisson process. The office can process patients at an average rate of 5 patients an hour and patients arrive at an average of 4 per hour. Assuming exponential service we can determine:

- The office will be idle 20% of the time and busy 80% of the time.

Utilization rate = $\dfrac{\lambda}{\mu}$ = $\dfrac{4}{5}$ = 80%

P_0 = Probability of none in the system = $1 - \dfrac{\lambda}{\mu}$ = $1 - \left(\dfrac{4}{5}\right)$ = 20%

- There will be an average of 3.2 persons in line and being served.

L_q = Mean number in waiting line = $\dfrac{\lambda^2}{\mu(\mu - \lambda)}$ = $\dfrac{(4)^2}{5(5 - 4)}$ = 3.2 patients

- There will be an average of 4 patients in line.

L = Mean number in system, including the one being serviced

$= \dfrac{\lambda}{(\mu - \lambda)}$ = $\dfrac{4}{(5 - 4)}$ = 4 patients

- The average waiting time of a patient is 0.8 of an hour or 48 minutes

W_q = Mean waiting time = $\dfrac{\lambda}{\mu(\mu - \lambda)}$

$= \dfrac{4}{5(5 - 4)}$ 0.8 hour or 48 minutes

- The average time a patient spends in the system, including service is 1 hour

W = Mean time in system, including service = $\dfrac{1}{(\mu - \lambda)}$ = $\dfrac{1}{(5 - 4)}$
= 1 hour

If we assume a 24-hour work day, there will be an average of 96 patients arriving per day (4 patients per hour × 24 hours), and the expected total lost time of patients waiting will be 76.8 hours (4 × 24 × 0.8). Assume that the cost of lost time to the company is $15 for each hour lost by a patient waiting. Then the average cost per day from waiting is $1,152 (76.8 hours × $15).

MODEL 2—THE SINGLE-CHANNEL WAITING LINE MODEL WITH POISSON ARRIVALS AND CONSTANT SERVICE TIMES

Model 2 is appropriate for the case of an automobile car wash, an automatic coffee machine in an office building, or a machine-controlled manufacturing operation.

Model 2 makes the following assumptions:

- Single-channel, single-phase case.
- Poisson arrival rates.
- Constant service times.
- First-come, first-served queue discipline.
- Mean service rate greater than mean arrival rate $\mu > \lambda$.

Then the average number waiting in line is as follows:

$$L_q = \frac{\lambda^2}{2\mu(\mu - \lambda)}$$

W_q = Mean waiting time $- \dfrac{L_q}{\lambda}$

L = Mean number in system, including the one being serviced $= L_q + \dfrac{\lambda}{\mu}$

W = Mean time in line and service $= W_q + \dfrac{1}{\mu} = \dfrac{L}{\lambda}$

EXAMPLE 3

Rossmore Car Wash is an automatic, five-minute wash operation with a single bay. On a typical Sunday morning, cars arrive at a mean rate of 8 per hour, with arrivals to follow a Poisson distribution. Note that $\lambda = 8$ cars per hour and $\mu = 12$ cars per hour (1 per 5 minutes).

Then the average number waiting in line is

$$L_q = \frac{\lambda^2}{2\mu(\mu - \lambda)} = \frac{(8)^2}{2(12)(12 - 8)} = 0.667 \text{ cars}$$

W_q = Mean waiting time $= \dfrac{L_q}{\lambda} = \dfrac{\lambda^2}{2\mu(\mu - \lambda)} = \dfrac{8}{2(12)(12 - 8)}$

$= 0.083$ hours or 4.98 minutes

L = Mean number in system, including the one being serviced

$= L_q + \dfrac{\lambda}{\mu} = 7.5 + \dfrac{8}{12} = 8.167 \text{ cars}$

W = Mean time in system, including service $= W_q + \dfrac{1}{\mu} = 0.083 + 0.083$

$= 0.166$ hours or 9.96 minutes

MODEL 3—THE SINGLE-CHANNEL WAITING LINE MODEL WITH POISSON ARRIVALS AND SERVICE TIMES NOT SPECIFIED

Model 3 makes the following assumptions:

- Single-channel, single-phase case.

- Poisson arrival rates.

- Service times not specified.

- First-come, first-served queue discipline.

- Mean service rate is greater than mean arrival rate $\mu > \lambda$.

Then the average number waiting in line L_q is as follows:

$$L_q = \frac{(\lambda\sigma)^2 + (\lambda/\mu)^2}{2(1 - \lambda/\mu)}$$

L = Mean number in system, including the one being serviced = $L_q + \lambda/\mu$

W_q = Mean waiting time = L_q/λ

W = Mean time in system, including service = $W_q + 1/\mu = L/\lambda$

EXAMPLE 4

Trucks arrive at the truck dock of a wholesale grocer at the rate of 8 per hour, and the distribution of arrivals is Poisson. The loading and/or unloading time averages 5 minutes, but the estimate of the standard deviation of service time (σ) is 6 minutes. Truckers are complaining that they must spend more time waiting than unloading, and the following information verifies their claim:

λ = 8 per hour; μ = 60/5 = 12 per hour; σ = 6/60 = 1/10 per hour

$$L_q = \frac{(\lambda\sigma)^2 + (\lambda/\mu)^2}{2(1 - \lambda/\mu)} = \frac{(8 \times 1/10)^2 + (8/12)^2}{2(1 - 8/12)} = 1.63 \text{ trucks in line}$$

L = Mean number in system, including the one being serviced

$\quad = L_q + \lambda/\mu = 1.63 + 8/12 = 2.3$ trucks in the system

W_q = Mean waiting time = L_q/λ = 1.63/8
= 0.204 hours, or 12.24 minutes in line waiting for service

W = Mean time in system, including service = L/λ = 2.3/8 = 0.288 hours, or 17.28* minutes in the system. Note also that $W = W_q + 1/\mu$ = 0.204 hours + 1/12 hours = 12.24 minutes + 5 minutes = 17.24* minutes.

Note: The discrepancy between 17.28 and 17.24 is due to rounding errors.

MODEL 4—THE MULTIPLE-CHANNEL WAITING LINE MODEL WITH POISSON ARRIVALS AND EXPONENTIAL SERVICE TIMES

The multiple-channel model is appropriate for the case of a toll road pay booth, bank teller window, and maintenance repair shop.
Model 4 makes the following assumptions:

- Multiple-channel.

- Poisson arrival rates and exponential service times.

- Services all work at the same rate.

- Customers form a single waiting line in order to maintain first-come, first-served processing.

Utilization rate is the expected number being served:

$$\rho = \lambda/M\mu$$

where M = number of servers (channels)

$$L_q = \frac{\lambda\mu(\lambda/\mu)^M}{(M-1)!(M\mu - \lambda)^2} P_o$$

The computation is very complicated. The procedure is to go to Table 13.2 with λ/μ and M.

EXAMPLE 5

Using the data from Example 2, consider the characteristics of the process if a second office is added. Each office can process 5 patients per hour, on average. Note that $M = 2$ and $\lambda/\mu = 0.8$. From the table we see $L_q = 0.152$ and $P_0 = 0.429$. We can determine the following:

W_q = Mean waiting time = $L_q/\lambda = 0.152/4 = 0.038$ hours

L = Mean number in system, including the one being serviced

$\quad = L_q + \lambda/\mu = 0.152 + 0.8 = 0.952$ patients

W = Mean time in system, including service = $W_q + 1/\mu = L/\lambda$

$\quad = 0.952/4 = 0.238$ hours

In Example 2, the expected time lost waiting one day with one office was 76.8 hours. With two offices, it is 3.65 hours ($4 \times 24 \times 0.038$). Again assuming a cost of $15 for each hour, the average cost of waiting per day is $54.75, which means a saving in expected cost of $1,097.25 ($1,152 – $54.75). If the cost of adding the second office is less than $1,097.25, then the decision should be to go from one to two offices.

Table 13.2. Infinite-Source Values for L_q and P_0 Given λ/μ and M

λ/μ	M	L_q	P_0	λ/μ	M	L_q	P_0	λ/μ	M	L_q	P_0
0.15	1	0.026	0.850		3	0.094	0.294		5	0.130	0.080
	2	0.001	0.860		4	0.016	0.300		6	0.034	0.082
0.20	1	0.050	0.800		5	0.003	0.301		7	0.009	0.082
	2	0.002	0.818	1.3	2	0.951	0.212	2.6	3	4.933	0.035
0.25	1	0.083	0.750		3	0.130	0.264		4	0.658	0.065
	2	0.004	0.778		4	0.023	0.271		5	0.161	0.072
0.30	1	0.129	0.700		5	0.004	0.272		6	0.043	0.074
	2	0.007	0.739	1.4	2	1.345	0.176		7	0.011	0.074
0.35	1	0.188	0.650		3	0.177	0.236	2.7	3	7.354	0.025
	2	0.011	0.702		4	0.032	0.245		4	0.811	0.057
0.40	1	0.267	0.600		5	0.006	0.246		5	0.198	0.065
	2	0.017	0.667	1.5	2	1.929	0.143		6	0.053	0.067
0.45	1	0.368	0.550		3	0.237	0.211		7	0.014	0.067
	2	0.024	0.633		4	0.045	0.221	2.8	3	12.273	0.016
	3	0.002	0.637		5	0.009	0.223		4	1.000	0.050
0.50	1	0.500	0.500	1.6	2	2.844	0.111		5	0.241	0.058
	2	0.033	0.600		3	0.313	0.187		6	0.066	0.060
	3	0.003	0.606		4	0.060	0.199		7	0.018	0.061
0.55	1	0.672	0.450		5	0.012	0.201	2.9	3	27.193	0.008
	2	0.045	0.569	1.7	2	4.426	0.081		4	1.234	0.044
	3	0.004	0.576		3	0.409	0.166		5	0.293	0.052
0.60	1	0.900	0.400		4	0.080	0.180		6	0.081	0.054
	2	0.059	0.538		5	0.017	0.182		7	0.023	0.055
	3	0.006	0.548	1.8	2	7.674	0.053	3.0	4	1.528	0.038
0.65	1	1.207	0.350		3	0.532	0.146		5	0.354	0.047
	2	0.077	0.509		4	0.105	0.162		6	0.099	0.049
	3	0.008	0.521		5	0.023	0.165		7	0.028	0.050
0.70	1	1.633	0.300	1.9	2	17.587	0.026		8	0.008	0.050
	2	0.098	0.481		3	0.688	0.128	3.1	4	1.902	0.032
	3	0.011	0.495		4	0.136	0.145		5	0.427	0.042
0.75	1	2.250	0.250		5	0.030	0.149		6	0.120	0.044
	2	0.123	0.455		6	0.007	0.149		7	0.035	0.045
	3	0.015	0.471	2.0	3	0.889	0.111		8	0.010	0.045
0.80	1	3.200	0.200		4	0.174	0.130	3.2	4	2.386	0.027
	2	0.152	0.429		5	0.040	0.134		5	0.513	0.037
	3	0.019	0.447		6	0.009	0.135		6	0.145	0.040
0.85	1	4.817	0.150	2.1	3	1.149	0.096		7	0.043	0.040
	2	0.187	0.404		4	0.220	0.117		8	0.012	0.041
	2	0.024	0.425		5	0.052	0.121	3.3	4	3.027	0.023
	4	0.003	0.427		6	0.012	0.122		5	0.615	0.033
0.90	1	8.100	0.100	2.2	3	1.491	0.081		6	0.174	0.036
	2	0.229	0.379		4	0.277	0.105		7	0.052	0.037
	3	0.030	0.403		5	0.066	0.109		8	0.015	0.037
	4	0.004	0.406		6	0.016	0.111	3.4	4	3.906	0.019
0.95	1	18.050	0.050	2.3	3	1.951	0.068		5	0.737	0.029
	2	0.277	0.356		4	0.346	0.093		6	0.209	0.032
	3	0.037	0.383		5	0.084	0.099		7	0.063	0.033
	4	0.005	0.386		6	0.021	0.100		8	0.019	0.033
1.0	2	0.333	0.333	2.4	3	2.589	0.056	3.5	4	5.165	0.015
	3	0.045	0.364		4	0.431	0.083		5	0.882	0.026
1.1	4	0.007	0.367		5	0.105	0.089		6	0.248	0.029
	2	0.477	0.290		6	0.027	0.090		7	0.076	0.030
	3	0.066	0.327		7	0.007	0.091		8	0.023	0.030
	4	0.011	0.367	2.5	3	3.511	0.045		9	0.007	0.030
1.2	2	0.675	0.250		4	0.533	0.074	3.6	4	7.090	0.011

MODEL 5—FINITE SOURCE MODEL

The fine-source model is appropriate when there exists a limited number of customers. An example is a situation where one repairman is servicing m machines. Essentially, arrivals are not independent; if $(N - J)$ are down for repairs, the set of potential arrivals is reduced to J. Because the derivation of the formulas for the finite-source model is quite complex and usually beyond the scope of the production and operations management course, finite queuing tables (Table 13.3) are often used to analyze these systems. A list of the key formulas and definitions follows.

Let:

$$X = \text{Service factor} = \frac{T}{(T + U)}$$

T = Average service time

U = Average time between customer service requirements per customer

M = Number of service channels

D = Probability that a customer will have to wait in line

= Probability of a delay

F = Efficiency factor = (1 − percentage waiting in line)

J = Average number of customers not in line or in service

H = Average number of customers being served

L_q = Average number of customers waiting for service

N = Number in population = Number of potential customers
= $J + L_q + H$

W = Average time customers wait in line

Then

Average number waiting = $L_q = N(1 - F)$

Average number running = $J = NF(1 - X)$

Average number being served = $H = FNX$

Average waiting time = $\dfrac{L_q(T + U)}{(N - L_q)} = \dfrac{T(1 - F)}{XF}$

Probability of not waiting = $1 - D$

Downtime = Waiting time + Service time

Table 13.3. Finite Queuing Tables

POPULATION 5 (N = 5)

X	M	D	F
0.012	1	0.048	0.999	0.005
0.019	1	0.076	0.998	0.010
0.025	1	0.100	0.997	0.015
0.030	1	0.120	0.996	0.020
0.034	1	0.135	0.995	0.025
0.036	1	0.143	0.994	0.030
0.040	1	0.159	0.993	0.035
0.042	1	0.167	0.992	0.045
0.044	1	0.175	0.991	0.045
0.046	1	0.183	0.990	0.050
0.050	1	0.198	0.989	0.055
0.052	1	0.206	0.988	0.060
0.054	1	0.214	0.987	0.065
0.056	2	0.018	0.999	0.005
	1	0.222	0.985	0.075
0.058	2	0.019	0.999	0.005
	1	0.229	0.984	0.080
0.060	2	0.020	0.999	0.005
	1	0.237	0.983	0.085
0.062	2	0.022	0.999	0.005
	1	0.245	0.982	0.090
0.064	2	0.023	0.999	0.005
	1	0.253	0.981	0.095
0.066	2	0.024	0.999	0.005
	1	0.260	0.979	0.105
0.068	2	0.026	0.999	0.005
	1	0.268	0.978	0.110
0.070	2	0.027	0.999	0.005
	1	0.275	0.977	0.115
0.075	2	0.031	0.999	0.005
	1	0.294	0.973	0.135
0.080	2	0.035	0.998	0.010
	1	0.313	0.969	0.155
0.085	2	0.040	0.998	0.010
	1	0.332	0.965	0.175
0.090	2	0.044	0.998	0.010
	1	0.350	0.960	0.200
0.095	2	0.049	0.997	0.015
	1	0.368	0.955	0.255
0.100	2	0.054	0.997	0.015
	1	0.386	0.950	0.250
0.105	2	0.059	0.997	0.015

X	M	D	F
	1	0.404	0.945	0.275
0.110	2	0.065	0.996	0.020
	1	0.421	0.939	0.305
0.115	2	0.071	0.995	0.025
	1	0.439	0.933	0.335
0.120	2	0.076	0.995	0.025
	1	0.456	0.927	0.365
0.125	2	0.082	0.994	0.030
	1	0.473	0.920	0.400
0.130	2	0.089	0.993	0.035
	1	0.489	0.914	0.430
0.135	2	0.095	0.993	0.035
	1	0.505	0.907	0.465
0.140	2	0.102	0.992	0.040
	1	0.521	0.900	0.500
0.145	3	0.011	0.999	0.005
	2	0.109	0.991	0.045
	1	0.537	0.892	0.540
0.150	3	0.012	0.999	0.005
	2	0.115	0.990	0.050
	1	0.553	0.885	0.575
0.155	3	0.013	0.999	0.005
	2	0.123	0.989	0.055
	1	0.568	0.877	0.615
0.160	3	0.015	0.999	0.005
	2	0.130	0.988	0.060
	1	0.582	0.869	0.655
0.165	3	0.016	0.999	0.005
	2	0.137	0.987	0.065
	1	0.597	0.861	0.695
0.170	3	0.017	0.999	0.005
	2	0.145	0.985	0.075
	1	0.611	0.853	0.735
0.180	3	0.021	0.999	0.005
	2	0.161	0.983	0.085
	1	0.638	0.836	0.820
0.190	3	0.024	0.998	0.010
	2	0.177	0.980	0.100
	1	0.665	0.819	0.905
0.200	3	0.028	0.998	0.010
	2	0.194	0.976	0.120
	1	0.689	0.801	0.995
0.210	3	0.032	0.998	0.010
	2	0.211	0.973	0.135

X	M	D	F
	1	0.713	0.783	1.085
0.220	3	0.036	0.997	0.015
	2	0.229	0.969	0.155
	1	0.735	0.765	1.175
0.230	3	0.041	0.997	0.015
	2	0.247	0.965	0.175
	1	0.756	0.747	1.265
0.240	3	0.046	0.996	0.020
	2	0.265	0.960	0.200
	1	0.775	0.730	1.350
0.250	3	0.052	0.995	0.025
	2	0.284	0.955	0.225
	1	0.794	0.712	1.440
0.260	3	0.058	0.994	0.030
	2	0.303	0.950	0.250
	1	0.811	0.695	1.525
0.270	3	0.064	0.994	0.030
	2	0.323	0.944	0.280
	1	0.827	0.677	1.615
0.280	3	0.071	0.993	0.035
	2	0.342	0.938	0.310
	1	0.842	0.661	1.695
0.290	4	0.007	0.999	0.005
	3	0.079	0.992	0.040
	2	0.362	0.932	0.340
	1	0.856	0.644	1.780
0.300	4	0.008	0.999	0.005
	3	0.086	0.990	0.050
	2	0.382	0.926	0.370
	1	0.869	0.628	1.860
0.310	4	0.009	0.999	0.005
	3	0.094	0.989	0.055
	2	0.402	0.919	0.405
	1	0.881	0.613	1.935
0.320	4	0.010	0.999	0.005
	3	0.103	0.988	0.060
	2	0.422	0.912	0.440
	1	0.892	0.597	2.015
0.330	4	0.012	0.999	0.005
	3	0.112	0.986	0.070
	2	0.442	0.904	0.480
	1	0.902	0.583	2.085
0.340	4	0.013	0.999	0.005
	3	0.121	0.985	0.075

POPULATION 10, (N = 10)

0.080	3	0.031	0.999	0.01	0.145	4	0.032	0.999	0.01	0.220	5	0.030	0.998	0.02
	2	0.177	0.990	0.10		3	0.144	0.990	0.10		4	0.124	0.990	0.10
	1	0.660	0.899	1.01		2	0.460	0.941	0.59		3	0.366	0.954	0.46
0.085	3	0.037	0.999	0.01		1	0.929	0.662	3.38		2	0.761	0.815	1.85
	2	0.196	0.988	0.12	0.150	4	0.036	0.998	0.02		1	0.993	0.453	5.47
	1	0.692	0.883	1.17		3	0.156	0.989	0.11	0.230	5	0.037	0.998	0.02
0.090	3	0.043	0.998	0.02		2	0.483	0.935	0.65		4	0.142	0.988	0.12
	2	0.216	0.986	0.14		1	0.939	0.644	3.56		3	0.400	0.947	0.53
	1	0.722	0.867	1.33	0.155	4	0.040	0.998	0.02		2	0.791	0.794	2.06
0.095	3	0.049	0.998	0.02		3	0.169	0.987	0.13		1	0.995	0.434	5.66
	2	0.237	0.984	0.16		2	0.505	0.928	0.72	0.240	5	0.044	0.997	0.03
	1	0.750	0.850	1.50		1	0.947	0.627	3.73		4	0.162	0.986	0.14
0.100	3	0.056	0.998	0.02	0.160	4	0.044	0.998	0.02		3	0.434	0.938	0.62
	2	0.258	0.981	0.19		3	0.182	0.986	0.14		2	0.819	0.774	2.26
	1	0.776	0.832	1.68		2	0.528	0.921	0.79		1	0.996	0.416	5.84
0.105	3	0.064	0.997	0.03		1	0.954	0.610	3.90	0.250	6	0.010	0.999	0.01
	2	0.279	0.978	0.22	0.165	4	0.049	0.997	0.03		5	0.052	0.997	0.03
	1	0.800	0.814	1.86		3	0.195	0.984	0.16		4	0.183	0.983	0.17
0.110	3	0.072	0.997	0.03		2	0.550	0.914	0.86		3	0.469	0.929	0.71
	2	0.301	0.974	0.26		1	0.961	0.594	4.06		2	0.844	0.753	2.47
	1	0.822	0.795	2.05	0.170	4	0.054	0.997	0.03		1	0.997	0.400	6.00
0.115	3	0.081	0.996	0.04		3	0.209	0.982	0.18	0.260	6	0.013	0.999	0.01
	2	0.324	0.971	0.29		2	0.571	0.906	0.94		5	0.060	0.996	0.04
	1	0.843	0.776	2.24		1	0.966	0.579	4.21		4	0.205	0.980	0.20
0.120	4	0.016	0.999	0.01	0.180	5	0.013	0.999	0.01		3	0.503	0.919	0.81
	3	0.090	0.995	0.05		4	0.066	0.996	0.04		2	0.866	0.732	2.68
	2	0.346	0.967	0.33		3	0.238	0.978	0.22		1	0.998	0.384	6.16
	1	0.861	0.756	2.44		2	0.614	0.890	1.10	0.270	6	0.015	0.999	0.01
0.125	4	0.019	0.999	0.01		1	0.975	0.549	4.51		5	0.070	0.995	0.05
	3	0.100	0.994	0.06	0.190	5	0.016	0.999	0.01		4	0.228	0.976	0.24
	2	0.369	0.962	0.38		4	0.078	0.995	0.05		3	0.537	0.908	0.92
	1	0.878	0.737	2.63		3	0.269	0.973	0.27		2	0.886	0.712	2.88
0.130	4	0.022	0.999	0.01		2	0.654	0.873	1.27		1	0.999	0.370	6.30
	3	0.110	0.994	0.06		1	0.982	0.522	4.78	0.280	6	0.018	0.999	0.01
	2	0.392	0.958	0.42	0.200	5	0.020	0.999	0.01		5	0.081	0.994	0.06
	1	0.893	0.718	2.82		4	0.092	0.994	0.06		4	0.252	0.972	0.28
0.135	4	0.025	0.999	0.01		3	0.300	0.968	0.32		3	0.571	0.896	1.04
	3	0.121	0.993	0.07		2	0.692	0.854	1.46		2	0.903	0.692	3.08
	2	0.415	0.952	0.48		1	0.987	0.497	5.03		1	0.999	0.357	6.43
	1	0.907	0.699	3.01	0.210	5	0.025	0.999	0.01	0.290	6	0.022	0.999	0.01
0.140	4	0.028	0.999	0.01		4	0.108	0.992	0.08		5	0.093	0.993	0.07
	3	0.132	0.991	0.09		3	0.333	0.961	0.39		4	0.278	0.968	0.32
	2	0.437	0.947	0.53		2	0.728	0.835	1.65		3	0.603	0.884	1.16
	1	0.919	0.680	3.20		1	0.990	0.474	5.26		2	0.918	0.672	3.28

YOU SHOULD REMEMBER

To use the finite-source model, do the following:

1. Compute the service factor $X = \dfrac{T}{(T + U)}$

2. Locate the section of Table 13.3 listing data for the population size N and the service factor.

3. Find the values D and F for the number of services M.

EXAMPLE 6

An employee loads and unloads a bank of five machines. Service time is exponential with a mean of 20 minutes per cycle. Machines run for an average of 80 minutes between loading and unloading, and this time is also exponentially distributed. Note that $M = 1$, $N = 5$, $T = 20$ minutes, and $U = 80$ minutes. Therefore, $X = T/(T + U) = 20/(20 + 80) = 0.200$. From Table 13.3, we see that $D = 0.689$ and $F = 0.801$

$$\text{Average number waiting} = L_q = N(1 - F) = 5(1 - 0.801)$$
$$= 0.995 \text{ machines}$$

$$\text{Average number running} = J = NF(1 - X) = 5(0.801)(1 - 0.2)$$
$$= 3.204 \text{ machines}$$

$$\text{Average number being served} = H = FNX = (0.801)(5)(0.2)$$
$$= 0.801 \text{ machines}$$

$$\text{Average waiting time} = \frac{L_q(T + U)}{(N - L_q)} = \frac{T(1 - F)}{XF}$$

$$\frac{L_q(T + U)}{(N - L_q)} = \frac{995(20 + 80)}{(5 - 0.995)} = 24.84 \text{ minutes}$$

or

$$\frac{T(1 - F)}{XF} = \frac{20(1 - 0.801)}{0.2(0.801)} = 24.84 \text{ minutes}$$

Machine downtime = Waiting time + Service time
$$= 24.84 \text{ minutes} + 20 \text{ minutes} = 44.84 \text{ minutes}$$

Probability of not waiting = $1 - D = 1 - 0.689 = 0.311$

COMPUTER SIMULATION FOR WAITING LINES

As we simulated inventory situations in Chapter 9, we can simulate waiting line situations that vary randomly according to this pattern by the Monte Carlo process.

EXAMPLE 7

Los Alamitos Memorial Hospital discovered that the pattern of arrivals of patients to the emergency room can be described by a Poisson distribution with a mean of 4 per hour. Simulate the number of patient arrivals for an 8-hour shift. Use the following three-digit random numbers: 036, 433, 453, 626, 048, 859, 037, 101. Directly from Table 8 (Poisson Distribution) in Appendix II, we get:

No. of Patients	0	1	2	3	4	5	6	7	8	9	10	11	12
Cumulative P(c)	0.018	0.092	0.238	0.433	0.629	0.785	0.889	0.949	0.979	0.992	0.997	0.999	1.000
Random Number Assigned	001–017	018–091	092–237	238–432	433–628	629–784	785–888	889–948	949–978	979–991	992–996	997–998	999–1,000

Using the three-digit random numbers given previously generates the following:

Hour	1	2	3	4	5	6	7	8
Random Number	036	433	453	626	048	859	037	101
No. of Patient Arrivals	1	4	4	4	1	6	1	2

KNOW THE CONCEPTS

DO YOU KNOW THE BASICS?

1. How many waiting lines can be encountered during an airline flight?

2. List the most common measures of system performance in a waiting line analysis.

3. Waiting lines can form even when a service system is underloaded. Do you agree?

4. Briefly describe the major cost tradeoff that must be made in managing queuing situations.

5. List the assumptions underlying Queuing Model 1—Single-Channel Waiting Line Model with Poisson Arrivals and Exponential Service Times.

6. Give an example where the first-come, first-service rule would be unfair.

7. Explain what is meant by an exponential service time. Provide an example of an exponential service time and a constant service rate.

8. Give an example of Poisson arrival rates.

9. Distinguish between finite and infinite population sources.

TERMS FOR STUDY

constant service	Poisson distribution
exponential distribution	queue
finite source	queuing (or waiting line) theory
mean arrival rate	single-channel line
mean service rate	utilization factor
multiple-channel line	

PRACTICAL APPLICATION

1. On the average 100 students arrive at the cashier's office each hour; on the average the cashier's office can process 120 students per hour. Assume that arrivals are Poisson-distributed and service times are exponentially distributed.

   a. What is the probability that the system will be idle?

   b. On the average, how many students will be waiting to be served?

   c. On the average, how long will a student wait in line before meeting the cashier?

   d. On the average, how much time will the student spend waiting and negotiating with the cashier?

2. A retailer is evaluating two alternative cash register systems. It is expected that the firm will have about 2,500 customers per hour to service, and that ill will caused by waiting costs is about $2 per hour per customer. The following information is given:

System I	System II
μ = 2,800 per hour	μ = 3,500 per hour
Operating costs: $100 per hour	Operating costs: $125 per hour

Which system should be recommended?

3. Demands on a forklift truck are considered to be Poisson, with an average time of 10 minutes between one arrival and the next $(1/\lambda = 10)$. The length of time a truck is used is assumed to be distributed exponentially, with a mean of 3 minutes $(1/\mu = 3)$.

   a. What is the probability that a person requiring a truck will have to wait?

   b. What is the average length of the queues that form from time to time?

   c. The company will buy a second truck when convinced that an arrival would expect to have to wait at least 3 minutes for the truck. By how much must the flow of arrivals be increased in order to justify a second truck?

4. A company wishes to hire a repairman to service its machines, which break down at an average rate of 3 per hour. Breakdowns occur at random times, which are distributed Poisson. Downtime on any one machine costs the company $30 per hour. The choice of a repairman has been narrowed to two men—one slow but cheap and the other fast but expensive. The slow, cheap repairman will repair the broken-down machines exponentially at an average rate of 4 per hour; he asks for wages of $10 per hour. The fast, expensive repairman will repair broken-down machines exponentially at an average rate of 6 per hour and demands $20 per hour. Which repairman should the company hire to minimize the average costs of downtime and repair on the machines?

5. You are planning to construct an automatic car wash. The traffic count and market study suggest that a mean arrival rate of 6 cars per hour can be expected. You can buy either of two automatic washers: one with a constant service time of 5 minutes (12 washes per hour) and a more expensive one with a constant service time of 4 minutes (15 washes per hour). You have established a criterion that the mean waiting time to get into the wash area should not be more than 2 minutes and will buy the slower machine if it meets this criterion. Which machine should you buy?

6. A community hospital is served by a single ambulance based at the hospital. During peak periods the call rate averages 3 per hour (Poisson distribution) and the average service time is 15 minutes with a standard deviation of 5 minutes.

a. Compute the average number of emergencies waiting during peak demand.

b. Compute the average number of emergencies in the system.

c. Compute the average time waiting for service.

d. Compute the average waiting time, including service.

7. Customers filter into Tour Records at an average of 1 per minute (Poisson) where the service rate is 15 per hour.

a. Determine the average number of customers in the system with 8 servers.

b. Determine the minimum number of servers needed to keep the average time in the system to under 6 minutes.

8. A group of ten machines needs setups every half hour, on the average. Each setup takes an average of 10 minutes, both times being exponentially distributed. There are four mechanics.

a. Find the average number waiting.

b. Find the average number running.

c. Find the average number being served.

d. Find the average waiting time.

e. Find the probability of not waiting.

9. An assembly department has five automatic pieces of equipment which operate for an average of 79 minutes before they must be reloaded. The reloading operation takes an average of 21 minutes per machine.

a. What is the minimum number of servers needed to keep the average downtime per cycle to less than 25 minutes.

b. If one server is used, what percentage of time will the machine be down?

10. The time (rounded to the nearest 10 minutes) between customer arrivals at a small appliance repair center are distributed according to the following frequency distribution:

Time	10	20	30	40	50	60	70
Frequency	20	30	50	40	30	20	10

a. Construct a relative less-than-equal cumulative probability distribution suitable for use in Monte Carlo simulation.

b. Make a table showing the range of two-digit random numbers that would result in the use of each of the seven time values.

c. Simulate the times for a 1-week (7-day) period by using two-digit random numbers from a random-number table, determine which time class they fall into, and record the corresponding number of times. (Use the following random numbers 03, 43, 45, 62, 04, 85, 03 for convenience.)

d. Compare the simulated values with the historical mean.

11. The number of machine breakdowns per day in a large factory can be described by a Poisson distribution with a mean of 2. Simulate the number of breakdowns over a 5-day period, using these random numbers: 728, 202, 205, 927, 589, 473.

ANSWERS

DO YOU KNOW THE BASICS?

1. Waiting lines are possible at baggage check-in at the ticket counter, security check, check-in at gate, at boarding, and baggage pickup.

2. Common system performance measures include the average number waiting (either in line or the system) and system utilization rate. Furthermore, total cost of waiting time and facility expansion are important.

3. Yes. They may form because of variations in service and/or arrival rates that create situations in which demand temporarily exceeds capacity.

4. The tradeoff is between the cost of waiting for service and the cost of providing additional service capacity.

5. The assumptions are Poisson arrival rates, exponential service rates, single-channel–single-phase case, first-come first-served, queue discipline, and mean service rate.

6. The first-come, first-served rule would be the exception rather than the rule in an emergency room at a hospital. This rule would be unfair when a patient with a minor problem is treated before another experiencing severe pain or wounds.

7. An exponential service time implies that most of the time the service requirements are of short duration with only occasional long ones. It also means that the chance that a service will be complete in the next instant of time is not dependent on the time at which it entered the system. Buying an airline ticket at the airport is an example of an exponential service time. Riding a merry-go-round at a theme park is an example of a constant service rate because it has a fixed cycle.

8. In a marathon, the arrival pattern typically shows a few runners arriving "early," the majority arriving in a bunch, and the remainder spreading out along the tail of the distribution.

9. A finite source exists when the system caters to a small, limited number of potential customers. An infinite source model applies when system entry is unrestricted or when the potential number of arrivals exceeds the system capacity.

PRACTICAL APPLICATION

1.

a. $P_0 = 1 - \dfrac{\lambda}{\mu} = 1 - \dfrac{100}{120} = 0.167 = 16.7\%$ of the time

b. $L_q = \dfrac{\lambda^2}{\mu(\mu - \lambda)} = \dfrac{(100)^2}{120(120 - 100)} = \dfrac{10,000}{2,400} = 4.17$, or 4 students

c. $W_q = \dfrac{\lambda}{\mu(\mu - \lambda)} = \dfrac{100}{120(120 - 100)} = \dfrac{100}{2,400} = \dfrac{1}{24}$ hour, or 2.5 minutes

d. $W = \dfrac{1}{(\mu - \lambda)} = \dfrac{1}{(120 - 100)} = \dfrac{1}{20}$ hour, or 3 minutes

2. For System I:

$\lambda = 2,500$ and $\mu = 2,800$ per hour

$W = \dfrac{1}{(\mu - \lambda)} = \dfrac{1}{(2,800 - 2,500)} = \dfrac{1}{300}$ hour, or 0.0033 hours

(0.2 minutes or 12 seconds)

The average hourly cost of ill will = 2,500 (0.0033) ($2) =   16.50

Operating cost =   100.00

    Total System I cost $116.50

For System II: There is no need to calculate the cost of ill will because operating costs alone for System II are already greater than total costs for System I ($130 vs. $116.50). So System I should be recommended.

3. $\lambda = 6$ per hour and $\mu = 20$ per hour

a. The probability of having to wait = Probability of more than zero units in the system:

$$P(w) = 1 - P_0 = \frac{\lambda}{\mu} = \frac{6}{20} = 0.3$$

b. The average number of units in the system, including the one being serviced:

$$L = \frac{\lambda}{(\mu - \lambda)} = \frac{6}{(20 - 6)} = 0.43 \text{ units}$$

c. Given average waiting time of at least 3 minutes or 1/20 hour, solve for λ

$$W_q = \frac{\lambda}{\mu(\mu - \lambda)}$$

$$1/20 = \frac{\lambda}{20(20 - 6)}$$

$\lambda = 10$ arrivals per hour

The arrival rate must increase from 6 to 10.

4.

$\lambda = 3$ per hour = Arrival (breakdown) rate

$\mu_s = 4$ per hour = Service (repair) rate, slow repairman

$\mu_f = 6$ per hour = Service (repair) rate, fast repairman

Wages, fast repairman = $15 per hour

Wages, slow repairman = $10 per hour

Downtime cost, machines = $20 per hour

The average number of units in the system, including the one being serviced:

Slow repairman: $L_s = \dfrac{\lambda}{(\mu - \lambda)} = \dfrac{3}{(4 - 3)} = 3$ units

Fast repairman: $L_f = \dfrac{\lambda}{(\mu - \lambda)} = \dfrac{3}{(6 - 3)} = 1$ unit

Average hourly cost = wages plus downtime

Slow repairman: $10 + 3($30) = $100

Fast repairman: $20 + 1($30) = $50

The fast repairman should be hired to minimize costs of downtime and repair on the machines.

5. For the slower washer, the mean waiting time in the queue will be

$$W_q = \frac{L_q}{\lambda} = \frac{\lambda}{2\mu(\mu - \lambda)} = \frac{6}{2(12)(12 - 6)} = \frac{6}{24(6)} = 0.0417 \text{ hour or 2.5 minutes}$$

For the faster washer, the waiting time in the queue will be

$$W_q = \frac{6}{2(15)(15 - 9)} = \frac{6}{30(9)} = 0.0222 \text{ hour or 1.33 minutes}$$

Therefore, you should buy the faster washing equipment.

6. $\lambda = 3$ per hour; $\mu = 60/15 = 4$ per hour; $\sigma = 5/60 = 1/12$ per hour

a.

$$L_q = \frac{(\lambda\sigma)^2 + (\lambda/\mu)^2}{2(1 - \lambda/\mu)} = \frac{[3 \times (1/12)]^2 + (3/4)^2}{2(1 - 3/4)} = 1.25 \text{ emergencies in line}$$

b. L = Mean number in waiting line = $L_q + \lambda/\mu = 1.25 + 3/4 =$ 2 emergencies in the system

c. W_q = Mean waiting time = $L_q/\lambda = 1.25/3$ hours, or 25 minutes in line waiting for service

d. W = Mean time in system, including service = $L/\lambda = 2/3$ hours, or 40 minutes in the system

(Note also that $W = W_q + 1/\mu = 1.25/3$ hours + 1/4 hours = 25 minutes + 15 minutes = 40 minutes.)

7.

a. $\lambda = 60$ per hour; $\mu = 15$ per hour; $\lambda/\mu = 60/15 = 4$; and $M = 8$. From Table 13.2, we see $L_q = 0.059$.

L = Mean number in system, including the one being serviced = $L_q + \lambda/\mu = .059 + 4 = 4.059$ customers.

b.

M	Average Time in System (minutes)	
8	4.059	
7	4.180	
6	4.570	(6 servers needed)
5	6.216	

8. Note that $M = 4$, $N = 10$, $T = 10$ minutes, and $U = 30$ minutes. Therefore, $X = T/(T + U) = 10/(10 + 30) = 0.25$. From Table 13.3, we see $D = 0.183$ and $F = 0.983$.

a. Average number waiting = L_q = $N(1 - F)$ = $10(1 - 0.983)$ = 0.17 machines

b. Average number running = J = $NF(1 - X)$ = $10(0.983)(1 - 0.25)$ = 7.37 machines

c. Average number being served = H = FNX = $(0.983)(10)(0.25)$ = 2.46 machines (Note that $N = L_q + J + H = 0.17 + 7.37 + 2.46 = 10$ machines.)

d.

Average waiting time = $\dfrac{T(1 - F)}{XF}$ = $\dfrac{10(1 - 0.983)}{0.25(0.983)}$ = 0.692 minutes

e. Probability of not waiting = $1 - D$ = $1 - 0.183$ = 0.817

9. Note that $T = 21$ minutes and $U = 79$ minutes. Therefore, $X = T/(T + U)$ = $21(21 + 79)$ = 0.21.

a. Based on the values of D and F obtained from Table 13.3, we determine W and downtime:

M	D	F	W	Downtime = W + 21 minutes
1	0.713	0.783	27.21[a]	48.21
2	0.211	0.973	2.77	23.77

[a]For $M = 1$,

Average waiting time = $\dfrac{T(1 - F)}{XF}$ = $\dfrac{21(1 - 0.783)}{0.21(0.783)}$ = 27.71 minutes

Downtime is 27.71 + 21 minutes of service time = 48.71 minutes. Two servers are necessary to keep the average downtime per cycle to less than 25 minutes.

b. Average number running = J = $NF(1 - X)$ = $5(0.783)(1 - 0.21)$
$$= 3.093 \text{ machines}$$
Percent of machine down = $(N - J)/N$ = $(5 - 3.093)/5$ = 0.3814
$$= 38.14\%$$

10.

a.

Time	Frequency	Probability	Cumulative Probability
10	20	20/200 = 0.10	0.10
20	30	0.15	0.25
30	50	0.25	0.50

Time	Frequency	Probability	Cumulative Probability
40	40	0.20	0.70
50	30	0.15	0.85
60	20	0.10	0.95
70	10	0.05	1.00
	200	1.00	

b.

Time	Frequency	Probability	Cumulative Probability	Random No. Assigned
10	20	20/200 = 0.10	0.10	00–09
20	30	0.15	0.25	10–24
30	50	0.25	0.50	25–49
40	40	0.20	0.70	50–69
50	30	0.15	0.85	70–84
60	20	0.10	0.95	85–94
70	10	0.05	1.00	95–99
	200	1.00		

c. Using the random numbers 03, 43, 45, 62, 04, 85, 03 provided for convenience,

Day	1	2	3	4	5	6	7	
Random number	03	43	45	62	04	85	03	Total
Time	10	30	30	40	10	60	10	190

d. Note that the mean time (in minutes) from the 7-day simulation is 190/7 = 27.14 minutes. This compares with the mean of the historical data of

$$10(0.10) + 20(0.15) + 30(0.25) + 40(0.20) + 50(0.15) + 60(0.10) + 70(0.05)$$
$$= 36.5 \text{ minutes}$$

11.

From Table 8 in Appendix II, we get the following information:

Number	Cumulative Probability	Corresponding Random 3-digits
0	0.135	0–134
1	0.406	135–405

Number	Cumulative Probability	Corresponding Random 3-digits
2	0.677	406–676
3	0.857	677–856
4	0.947	857–946
5	0.983	947–982
6	0.995	983–994
7	0.999	995–998

Day	Number	Breakdowns
1	0.728	3
2	0.202	1
3	0.205	1
4	0.927	4
5	0.589	2

14
QUALITY ASSURANCE

KEY TERMS

acceptable outgoing quality (AOQ) level average percentage of defectives in lots leaving an inspection station.

assignable causes causes of poor quality that are caused by problems with materials, machines, or operators and that can be remedied.

consumer's risk probability of accepting a bad quality lot.

control chart graphical means of depicting over time sample characteristics such as means, ranges, and attributes that are used for process control.

operating characteristic (OC) curve plot of the probability of acceptance of a lot as a function of the percent of defective items.

producer's risk probability of rejecting a good quality lot.

quality assurance all the activities necessary to ensure that the customer receives satisfactory performance.

In Chapter 1 we discussed the importance of quality and outlined the role of quality assurance in productions/operations management. Designing quality into products or services is an important strategic aspect in OM. Quality assurance involves all the activities necessary to ensure that the customer receives satisfactory performance, including assurance that the product or service is adequately designed and conforms to the design.

Inspection is the major means of determining quality of conformance. In general, sampling, either by variables or by attributes, may be employed in situations that are less critical or where testing is expensive or destructive. Statistical sampling or statistical quality control may be used for acceptance sampling or for process control. Acceptance sampling is used to infer the acceptability of the particular lot or batch from which the sample was extracted. Process control applications are employed to infer whether the process or operations are being performed adequately. In this chapter, we discuss several quality-control techniques and address the operational aspect of quality control.

PARETO ANALYSIS

Pareto analysis is used to differentiate between the *vital few* and the *trial many*. It is based on the concept that about 80% of the problems come from 20% of the items.

We would expect to find a few *vital sources* that primarily contribute to costs rather than the many *trivial sources* that contribute much less to costs. Quality costs are not uniformly distributed. Almost without exception, only a few of the sources account for the bulk of the costs. This "misdistribution" of quality costs is often referred to in quality diagnosis as a Pareto analysis.

Under Pareto analysis, a bar chart is constructed, with bar height representing frequency as a percentage (see Figure 14.1). The bars are arranged in descending order by weight (importance). Pareto analysis shows where process improvements should begin—those problem areas with the greater frequency.

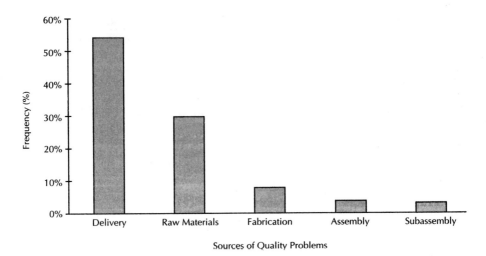

Figure 14.1. Pareto Chart: Occurrence of Errors

STATISTICAL QUALITY CONTROL

The statistical control chart has been developed in the field of statistical quality control (SQC). The control charts use samples as a way of isolating operating situations that need managerial investigation. A control chart is illustrated in Figure 14.2. Assume that average performance for assembling a finished unit is 10.5 minutes, that the upper control limit (UCL) is 13 minutes, and that the lower control limit (LCL) is 8 minutes. The control chart helps distinguish between chance variances (also called *random causes*) and variances that need to be investigated (often called *assignable causes*). The analysis of the latter helps to obtain improvements in products and processes. The identification of chance variances avoids unnecessary investigations of variances and eliminates frequent changes (e.g., machine settings) that may tend to increase rather than decrease the variability of the process.

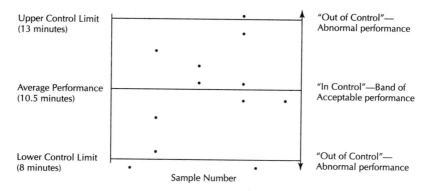

Figure 14.2. Control Chart

Statistical control charts can be used for any repetitive manufacturing or nonmanufacturing operations. Examples include billing, filling containers, boring, turning, stamping, using materials and supplies, printing, examining customer complaints, handling sales returns or orders received, tracking travel expenses, and the like.

Note that the control chart is very crude. The chart suggests that the manager do either something or nothing. It does not tell the manager what to do about the nonrandom variances or how to investigate them.

STATE OF STATISTICAL CONTROL

The control chart helps to decide whether a process (operation) is in a *state of statistical control.* A process is said to be in a state of statistical control if the variation is such as would occur in random sampling from some stable population. If this is the case, the variation among the items is attributable to chance—it is inherent in the nature of the process. There is no point in seeking special causes for individual cases because random variations are beyond management's ability to regulate or eliminate. With a given process and a given state of knowledge about the process, this chance variation is either impossible or impracticable to reduce. If the performance of a process is considered to be unsatisfactory even though it is statistically in control, the only remedy is some change in the process.

The probability that a point will fall outside the control limits from chance causes alone is small, so we conclude that the process is out of control when this occurs. When the process is out of control, it is often possible to locate specific causes for the variation. Removal of these causes improves the future performance of the process.

CONTROL CHARTS FOR MEANS

The sample mean can be an indicator of a shift in the pattern of variations. As long as the sample means remain within the control limits, the process is assumed to be in control. The distribution is continuing to show only the normal variations that result from chance causes.

It is necessary to select a variable to sample that will give the best indication of the effects of an out-of-control condition. The variable selected (usually a specific dimension from among many for a product) is the one that management believes will have the most direct cost relationship to the level of quality. The determination of the frequency and size of the sample is also an important consideration. In constructing control charts for variables, the initial samples used for setting the control limits should be selected at the outset of the run from items produced consecutively. The following samples should be taken at random intervals from items produced consecutively just prior to their selection.

The determination of the control limits is a simple process. The UCL and the LCL can be computed from equations that require little calculation. The equations for the mean or $\bar{X}$ (X bar) control chart follow:

$$\text{UCL}_{\bar{X}} = \bar{\bar{X}} + A_2\bar{R} \quad (1)$$

$$\text{LCL}_{\bar{X}} = \bar{\bar{X}} - A_2\bar{R} \quad (2)$$

where

$\bar{\bar{X}}$ = the grand mean; the mean of the means of the preliminary samples
A_2 = a constant

$\bar{R}$ = the average range of the preliminary samples

The value of A_2, and other applicable constants used for X and R charts are found in Table 14.1.

Table 14.1. Table of Constants for $\bar{X}$ and R Charts

n	A_2	D_3	D_4
2	1.880	0	3.268
3	1.023	0	2.574
4	0.729	0	2.282
5	0.577	0	2.114
6	0.483	0	2.004
7	0.419	0.076	1.924
8	0.373	0.136	1.864
9	0.337	0.184	1.816
10	0.308	0.223	1.777

To illustrate, the data in Table 14.2 are from ten samples of three pieces each. The values are the deviations from a selected dimension of 0.990 inches. From these data, the control limits for this process can be computed, and a control chart can be constructed. The computations follow:

$$\overline{\overline{X}} = 103.00/10 = 10.30$$

and

$$\overline{R} = 88/10 = 8.80$$

Table 14.2. Results of Ten Samples of Three Each Taken from Output (Values in 0.001-inch deviations from 0.990 inch)

Sample	Values			Mean	Range
1	4	6	5	5.00	2
2	9	13	5	9.00	8
3	6	11	15	10.67	9
4	18	10	7	11.67	11
5	19	15	21	18.33	6
6	9	6	19	11.33	13
7	18	12	2	10.67	16
8	9	8	10	9.00	2
9	6	17	7	10.00	11
10	6	3	13	7.33	10
Totals				103.00	88

The control limits for $\overline{X}$ are then

$$\text{UCL}_{\overline{X}} = \overline{\overline{X}} + A_2\overline{R}$$

$$= 10.30 + (1.023)(8.80)$$

$$= 19.30$$

and

$$\text{LCL}_{\overline{X}} = \overline{\overline{X}} - A_2\overline{R}$$

$$= 10.30 - (1.023)(8.80)$$

$$= 1.30$$

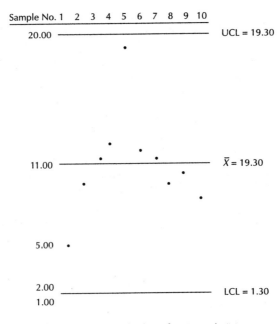

Figure 14.3. Control Chart for Sample Means

It is now possible to draw the control chart for the means of these samples. This control chart is shown in Figure 14.3. As can be seen, at this stage the process is under control. If one of the sample means was outside of the control limits, this would not be true. Note that the control limits in the chart are not the limits permitted by the designer's specifications or tolerances. The control limits established for the mean are narrower than the tolerance limits.

CONTROL CHARTS FOR RANGES

Control charts for ranges can be used to determine any shift in the amount of variation that may take place. The range chart or R chart is used to plot the difference between the highest value and the lowest value in each sample. The plot of the range is made at the same time as the sample mean is plotted on the $\bar{X}$ chart. If the sample ranges stay within the control limits, the process is considered to be in control as far as the variability is concerned. The control limits here are the upper range limit (URL) and the lower range limit (LRL). They are also identified as UCL_R and LCL_R. The LRL is often identified as 0 (zero) because for sample sizes of six or fewer it is always zero. This value results from the fact that the value of the constant used is zero for these sample sizes.

The computation of the range chart control limits is accomplished in a similar fashion to that which was used for the mean chart. The equations are

$$URL = D_4\bar{R} \qquad (3)$$

$$LRL = D_3\bar{R} \qquad (4)$$

The symbols D_3 and D_4 are constants whose values are found in Table 14.1. Note the values for D_3 are zero for sample sizes of six or fewer. This accounts for the zero value of the LRL in such instances.

The computation of the control limits for an R chart and the construction of such a chart can be illustrated with the data found in Table 14.2. The mean range was computed in the illustration for the $\bar{X}$ chart. It is

$$\bar{R} = 88/10 = 8.80$$

The computations for the establishment of the control limits follow:

$$URL = D_4\bar{R}$$

$$= (2.574)(8.80)$$

$$= 22.65$$

$$LRL = D_3\bar{R}$$

$$= (0)(8.80)$$

$$= 0$$

The sample ranges can now be plotted on the control chart in Figure 14.4. The process is also found to be in control with respect to variability because none of the sample ranges is outside the control limits.

These types of process control charts supply instantaneous information about the expected pattern of variation. When a point is beyond the control limits, it is a signal that a problem may be present. Because all the points in the example used were inside the limits for both the means and the ranges, it can be assumed that these limits are suitable for control purposes.

```
Sample No. 1   2   3   4   5   6   7   8   9   10
   20.00   ─────────────────────────   URL = 22.65
   15.00
   10.00   ─────────────────────────   R̄ = 8.80
    5.00
    0.00   ─────────────────────────   LRL = 0
```

Figure 14.4. Control Chart for Sample Ranges

Additional samples can be taken and plotted at the desired time intervals. If there is a change in the processing methods, in the material, in the design specifications, or in some other variable in the system, it would be necessary to compute new limits.

Had there been some points beyond the control limits in these initial samples, it would have been necessary to find the cause. Once found and eliminated (this assumes that they can be eliminated economically), proper new limits would have to be established. Only then can management presume that the process is in control.

ACCEPTANCE SAMPLING FOR ATTRIBUTES

Acceptance sampling for attributes deals with inspection for the purpose of determining whether a unit of output is defective or nondefective. The unit selected may be anywhere from a single item, some portion or component of the item of output, the entire order, the output of some period of time, or a total shipment.

DESIGN OF ACCEPTANCE SAMPLING PLANS

The prime purpose of an acceptance sampling plan is to determine the extent of nonconformity acceptable for the unit of output of concern. This nonconformity is usually expressed as a proportion of defectives in the unit (most frequently, the percent defectives), using the equation

$$\text{Percent defectives} = \frac{\text{Number of defectives}}{\text{Number of units}}$$

A distinction is sometimes made between defectives and defects. A unit is defective if it has one or more defects. When a sampling plan is designed to determine defects, the proportion of nonconformity is stated as the defects-per-hundred units, which is expressed as

$$\text{Defects-per-hundred units} = \frac{\text{Number of defects}}{\text{Number of units}}$$

Any acceptance sampling plan should be designed to avoid two basic errors. The first error to be avoided is the acceptance of output as satisfactory when in fact it is unacceptable. The second error to avoid is the rejection of a lot, which is of an acceptable quality, as unacceptable.

OPERATING CHARACTERISTIC CURVE

We may find the probability of acceptance for every possible value of the true percentage of defective items and plot the curve. This is called an *operating characteristic curve* (OC curve). OC curves are unique for a specific sampling plan and enable us to determine the producer's and consumer's risks. To do this, we need to specify an *acceptable quality level* (AQL) and *lot tolerance percent defective* (LTPD). The AQL is the maximum percent defective that is considered acceptable. For example, a company may be willing to accept lots with 2% defective. The LTPD is the percent defective associated with what is considered to be a bad lot. For example, 10% defective may be considered "bad" for a particular application. Not all lots with AQL values will be accepted, nor will all lots with LTPD values be rejected every time. The producer would like good lots accepted with a high probability. The consumer would like to reject bad lots most of the time; thus the consumer wishes to have a low probability of accepting bad lots.

Suppose a company specifies AQL = 2% and LTPD = 10%. From the OC curve in Figure 14.5, we see that if the percent defective is actually 2%, the probability of acceptance is approximately 0.82. Thus the probability of rejecting this good lot is $1 - 0.82 = 0.18$. This is the producer's risk. On the other hand, if the actual percent defective is 10% (LTPD), then the probability of acceptance is about 0.35. This represents the consumer's risk.

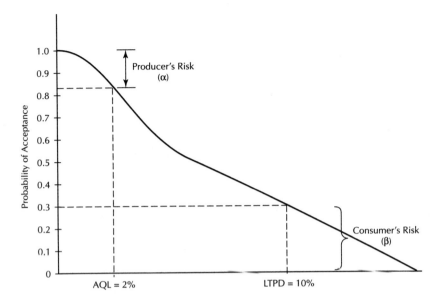

Figure 14.5. Operation Characteristic Curve

The *producer's risk* (α) is identified as the probability that output of the level of AQL will be rejected. The probability that a bad lot of the level of LTPD will be accepted is identified as the *consumer's risk* (β). These two terms and general relationships between them can be seen in the operating characteristic curve illustrated in Figure 14.6.

As AQL decreases, so does α—the probability of rejecting a good lot. Similarly, as LTPD increases, then β—the probability of accepting a bad lot—decreases. The AQL is mutually agreed upon between the producer and the consumer and is a useful negotiating tool in purchase contracts. A smaller AQL reduces the producer's risk but also requires tighter control in manufacturing. Thus economic analysis is important in determining quality specifications and contracts.

How is a sampling plan actually chosen? Note that there is a unique OC curve for every value of the size of the sample (n) and the value of the acceptance number (c). Therefore, to determine an appropriate plan, the quality-control supervisor must choose AQL, LTPD, α, and β. For Figure 14.6, we see that these values specify two points on the graph [i.e., (AQL, $1 - \alpha$) and (LTPD, β)]. There is a unique OC curve that passes through these two points. The value of n and c for this curve determine the sampling plan.

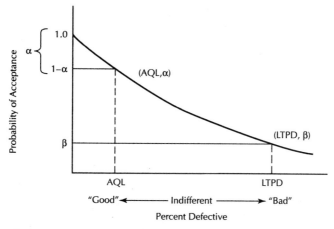

Figure 14.6. Operation Characteristic Curve for Sampling Plan

---

EXAMPLE 1

Suppose that a quality-control manager specifies AQL = 3%, LTPD = 15%, α = 0.25 (1 − α = 0.75), and β = 0.2. Finding the two points (3%, 0.75) and (15%, 0.2) in Figure 14.7, we see that the OC curve corresponding to n = 10 and c = 0 passes through these points. Thus n = 10, c = 0 is the appropriate sampling plan to choose.

Note: Fortunately, there is no need to plot all possible OC curves to select a sampling plan. Published tables are available to choose from. Refer to MIL-STD-105D, Sampling Procedures and Tables for Inspection by Attributes published by the Office of the Assistant Secretary of Defense, 1963 for government contract work.

**Portion of a Cumulative Binomial Distribution Table
(Table 7 from Appendix II)**

	Number of Defectives = c				
Sample Size =10			Sample Size = 15		
p	0	1	p	0	1
0.000	1.000	1.000	1.000	1.000	1.000
0.050	0.599	0.914	0.050	0.463	0.829
0.100	0.349	0.736	0.100	0.206	0.549
0.150	0.197	0.544	0.150	0.087	0.319
0.200	0.107	0.376	0.200	0.035	0.167
0.250	0.056	0.244	0.250	0.013	0.080
0.300	0.028	0.149	0.300	0.005	0.035
0.350	0.014	0.086	0.350	0.002	0.001

Number of Defectives = c

Sample Size =10			Sample Size = 15		
0.400	0.006	0.046	0.400	0.001	0.005
0.450	0.003	0.023	0.450	0.000	0.002
0.500	0.001	0.011	0.500	0.000	0.001
0.550	0.000	0.005	0.550	0.000	0.000
0.600	0.000	0.002	0.600	0.000	0.000
0.650	0.000	0.001			

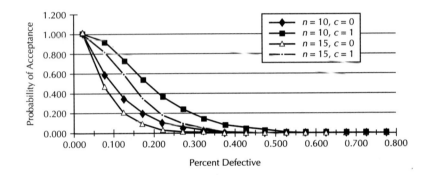

Figure 14.7. Alternate Sampling Plans

The discrimination can be seen by comparing two operating characteristic curves for plans with an acceptance number of two. Figure 14.8 shows one curve for a sample size of 75 and another of 110.

When the acceptance number increases and the sample size remains constant, the probability of acceptance of a given lot percent defective increases. Thus, the curve is less steep and the plan is less discriminating, as can be seen by comparing the family of OC curves in Figure 14.9. In this example, the sample size is equal to 75. Increasing the acceptance number c moves the curve to the right and makes it less steep.

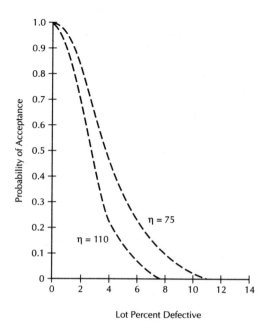

Figure 14.8. Change in OC Curve with Change in Sample Size for $c = 2$, and $n = 75$ or $n = 110$

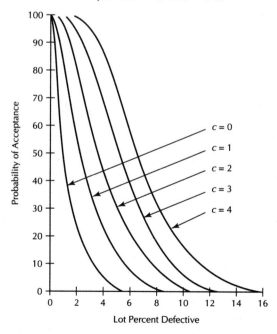

Figure 14.9. Change in OC Curve with Change in Acceptance Number for $n = 75$ and $c = 0, 2, 3,$ or 4

YOU SHOULD REMEMBER

Four important definitions are the bases for specifying a given sampling plan. They are as follows:

AQL = Acceptable quality level. Lots at this level of quality are regarded as good, and we wish to have a high probability of acceptance.

α = Producer's risk—the probability that lots of the quality level AQL will be rejected. Usually, α = 1–5%. If a good lot is rejected, we refer to this as a type I error.

LTPD = Lot tolerance percent defective—the dividing line selected between good and bad lots. Lots at this level of quality are regarded as poor, and we wish to have a low probability for their acceptance.

β = Consumer's risk—the probability that lots of the quality level LTPD will be accepted. Usually, β = 10%. If a bad lot is accepted, we refer to this as a type II error.

The mechanics of actually finding specific plans that fit can be accomplished by using standard tables, charts, or formulas, all of which result in the specification of a combination of sample size *n* and acceptance number *c*, which closely approximate the requirements for AQL, α, LTPD, and β.

AVERAGE QUALITY OF OUTGOING LOTS

An important feature of acceptance sampling is that the level of inspection automatically adjusts to the quality of lots being inspected, assuming rejected lots are subjected to 100% inspection. The OC curve shows that the greater the fraction of defectives in a lot, the less likely the lot is to be accepted.

If all lots have some given percentage of defectives *p*, the average outgoing quality (AOQ) of the lots can be computed using the formula:

$$\text{AOQ} = P \times p \left(\frac{N - n}{N} \right)$$

where P = probability of accepting the lot

p = percentage defective

N = lot size

n = sample size

In practice, the last term is often dropped because it is typically close to 1. The formula then becomes

$$AOQ = P \times p$$

By allowing p to vary, a curve for AOQ can be developed. The curve illustrates the point that if lots are very good or very bad, the AOQ will be high.

EXAMPLE 2

We will develop the AOQ curve for N = 500, n = 10, and c = 1. From Table 7 in Appendix II, we tabulate the probabilities of acceptance P for various values of fraction defective p as follows:

Portion of a Cumulative Binomial Distribution Table (Table 7 from Appendix II)

$n = 10, c = 1$			
p (1)	P (2)	AOQ (3) = (1) × (2)	AOQL
0.0	0.0	0.0	
0.05	0.9139	0.046	
0.1	0.7361	0.074	
0.15	0.5443	0.082 = Maximum AOQ = AOQL	
0.2	0.3758	0.075	
0.25	0.244	0.061	
0.3	0.1493	0.045	
0.35	0.086	0.030	
0.4	0.0464	0.019	
0.45	0.0233	0.010	
0.5	0.0107	0.005	
0.55	0.0045	0.002	
0.6	0.0017	0.001	
0.65	0.0005	0.000	
0.7	0.0001	0.000	
0.75	0	0.000	

The AOQ curve is shown in Figure 14.10.

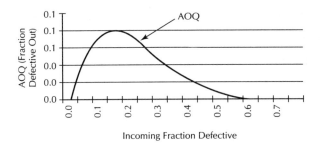

Figure 14.10. AOQ Curve

The maximum point on the curve, often called the *average outgoing quality limit* (AOQL), is 0.082 for $p = 0.15$. Figure 14.9 illustrates that as the percentage of defectives in lots coming into inspection increases, the percentage of defectives in lots leaving inspection deteriorates at first, then peaks at the AOQL, and then improves. The improvement in quality occurs because as the acceptance plan rejects lots, the rejected lots are 100% inspected, and the defectives are replaced with nondefectives. The net effect of rejecting lots is, therefore, an improvement in the quality of lots leaving inspection.

YOU SHOULD REMEMBER

- *AOQ is the average outgoing quality.* In a given case, it depends on the sampling plan and the lot quality.
- *AOQL is the average outgoing quality limit.* It refers to the worst possible outgoing quality and occurs at an intermediate quality level, which is neither very good or very bad.

TYPES OF SAMPLING PLANS

To this point, the examples regarding acceptance sampling plans have dealt with the taking of only a single sample. This is the simplest type of sampling plan because the decision as to whether to accept or reject is made on the basis of what the one sample indicates. When the number of defectives in the sample is less than or equal to the acceptance number, the lot is accepted. If, on the other hand, the number of defectives is greater than the rejection number, the lot must be rejected. It is possible, however, to design sampling plans that use more than one sample. The major objective of such plans is to get the same assurance of quality with a reduction in the amount of inspection. Even though such plans may result in a reduction in inspection time and consequent cost, this is not a certainty. A drawback of sampling plans that require more than one sample is the increased difficulty in designing them. The most frequent types of sampling plans are double, multiple, and sequential sampling plans.

DOUBLE SAMPLING

Double sampling plans provide for the use of a second sample when the first sample is not conclusive enough to make a decision. If the number of defectives in the first sample is less than or equal to the acceptance number specified, the lot may be accepted. As in single sampling plans, if the number of defectives is larger than the rejection number, the lot is rejected. In double sampling plans the range between the acceptance number and the rejection number for the first sample is greater than one. Thus, when the number of defectives in the first sample is between the acceptance and rejection numbers, a second sample must be taken because the results of the first sample in this case are not conclusive.

After the second sample is drawn, the cumulative number of defectives from both samples is compared with the second acceptance and rejection numbers. For the second sample, the range between these numbers is one, as in single sampling plans. The decision to accept or reject is then made as in the case of a single sampling plan.

MULTIPLE SAMPLING

Multiple sampling plans are essentially the same as double sampling plans with the exception that the number of samples required for a decision may be more than two.

SEQUENTIAL SAMPLING

The sequential sampling plan provides for taking an unspecified number of samples. If the lot quality is either very good or very bad, a small sample will suffice. It is only when the quality is between these two levels that a larger sample is required. The range between the acceptance and rejection numbers remains constant and greater than one. The sampling process is carried on until either the acceptance or the rejection level is reached. A sequential sampling plan is illustrated in Figure 14.11. The design of a sequential sampling plan can be accomplished by determining the appropriate acceptance and rejection limits. Tables are available to determine the proper limits for specified values of AQL, LTPD, α, and β.

Double, multiple, and sequential sampling plans should typically result in less inspection than is required for single sampling plans for a given level of protection. However, the amount of inspection required will vary widely from lot to lot.

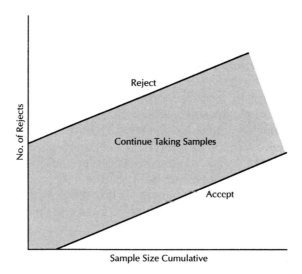

Figure 14.11. Sequential Sampling Plan

CONTROL CHARTS FOR ATTRIBUTES

Control charts can be used in attribute inspection as well as in variable control. The major difference in the control charts is that, in the case of attributes, the unit of measurement used is a distinct value whereas for variables it is a computed measure of central tendency (i.e., mean or range). Control charts are concerned with two types of attributes—the percentage defective (p chart) or the defects per unit (c chart).

PERCENTAGE DEFECTIVE CHARTS

When control is concerned with attributes, a determination is made as to the acceptance or rejection of the output units. For each sample, the percentage of defective units can be determined. The p chart can be used to record the variations in the percentage defective in the lots sampled. Control limits are computed in the same way they are computed for variable control charts. As long as the points remain within the control limits, the quality is assumed to be in control. The control limits for a p chart, based on three standard deviations, are computed as follows:

$$\text{UCL}_P = \overline{p} + 3\sqrt{\frac{\overline{p}(1-\overline{p})}{n}} \qquad (5)$$

$$\text{LCL}_P = \overline{p} - 3\sqrt{\frac{\overline{p}(1-\overline{p})}{n}} \qquad (6)$$

where $\overline{p}$ = the mean of the percentage defective in a series of initial samples.

EXAMPLE 3

ABC City's department of public works is concerned about public reaction to a sewer project that is currently in progress. Each week, a sample of 100 residents are surveyed regarding the project. The department wishes to analyze the survey data using an appropriate control chart to determine if the community sentiment is stable.

	Week								
	1	2	3	4	5	6	7	8	Total
Number Opposed	3	2	4	1	0	5	2	3	20
Fraction Defective	0.03	0.02	0.04	0.01	0	0.05	0.02	0.03	0.2

Because the sample size is 100, the fraction defective is 20/100 = 0.20. Thus, assuming that the average defective percent $\overline{p}$ is 0.11, then $\overline{p}$ = 0.20/8 = 0.025.

$$\sqrt{\frac{\overline{p}(1-\overline{p})}{n}} = \sqrt{\frac{(0.025)(1-0.025)}{100}} = 0.0156$$

The control limits are

$$\text{UCL}_P = \overline{p} + 3\sqrt{\frac{\overline{p}(1-\overline{p})}{n}} = 0.025 + 3(0.0156) = 0.025 + 0.047 = 0.072$$

$$\text{LCL}_P = \overline{p} - 3\sqrt{\frac{\overline{p}(1-\overline{p})}{n}} = 0.025 - 3(0.0156) = 0.025 - 0.047 = 0$$

It appears that the community sentiment is stable.

DEFECTS-PER-UNIT CHARTS

If output is such that defects can occur at a variety of points within the unit of output, the control of the number of defects may be more useful. Examples of processes where this type of control might be valuable are:

Electronics equipment in which a variety of defects can occur.

Textiles that may contain numerous defects per yard.

The number of improper medications issued in a hospital for some unit of time.

The number of incorrect orders sent out by the audiovisual service of a school district.

The cases where this type of control is useful may be generalized as those where the possibility of defects is high, but is in fact small. This condition is found to approximate the Poisson distribution for fluctuations in the number of defects. Using $\overline{c}$ as the average number of defects per unit of output, again based on three standard deviations, the control limits are determined by

$$\text{UCL}_c = \overline{c} + 3\sqrt{\overline{c}} \qquad (7)$$

$$\text{LCL}_c = \overline{c} - 3\sqrt{\overline{c}} \qquad (8)$$

The value of $\overline{c}$ is an estimate, as was $\overline{p}$, based on past accumulated data. The c chart has many uses other than for quality purposes. Examples are found in the area of inventory control for controlling the number of stockouts, in equipment maintenance for the number of breakdowns, and for accident statistics.

EXAMPLE 4

The OK City Transit Authority receives complaints from customers about the way drivers drive, their lack of courtesy, and the like. The manager wants to construct a control chart for defects per unit, c. In this case, a complaint is a defect and a unit of work is 500 fares collected on the bus. The manager intends to post the c chart and complaints reported each week for each group of 500 fares that the driver collected. An average of 28.2 defects per unit occurred before the chart is posted. Control limits on the chart are:

$$UCL_c = \overline{c} + 3\sqrt{\overline{c}} = 28.2 + 3\sqrt{28.2} = 44.13$$

$$LCL_c = \overline{c} - 3\sqrt{\overline{c}} = 28.2 - 3\sqrt{28.2} = 12.3$$

COMPUTER SOFTWARE FOR QUALITY CONTROL

Computer software can relieve most of the tedious calculations formerly required to install and maintain a quality-control system. Some popular packages, developed by TIME/WARE Corporation are listed with a brief description.

- *ML105$*. Determines sampling plan to fit combinations of AOPL, lot size, and the like, and randomly determines which parts to sample according to military standard.
- *MLBIN$*. Evaluates multiple-level sampling plans where users inspect a number of parts from a large lot and accept, reject, or resample based on the number of defectives found (binomial distribution).
- *OCBIN$*. Plots the OC curve. The user supplies the sampling size and number of defectives required to reject the lot.
- *CONLM$*. Determines confidence limits and sample statistics on a process average.

KNOW THE CONCEPTS

DO YOU KNOW THE BASICS?

1. Describe the primary goal of quality assurance.
2. Define assignable causes in quality control.
3. Differentiate between variable and attribute measurement.
4. What is sampling plan, what is an operation characteristic (OC) curve, and how is an OC curve used in sampling?
5. Discuss the concept of in control.
6. Describe the various types of control charts and their applications.

7. Explain the purposes and differences between p charts and $\overline{X}$ and R charts.

8. How does producer and consumer risk relate to errors in statistics?

9. What is the objective of acceptance sampling?

10. Briefly explain AOQ and AOQL.

TERMS FOR STUDY

acceptable quality level (AQL)
acceptance sampling
average outgoing quality (AOQ)
average outgoing quality limit (AOQL)
consumer's risk (β risk)
control chart
lot tolerance percent defective (LTPD)

means
operating characteristic (OC) curve
Pareto analysis
producer's risk (α risk)
ranges
sampling plan
statistical control analysis

PRACTICAL APPLICATION

1. A sample study was made of hand assembly operation on a transistor radio. Samples of the time spent to assemble one unit were taken twice a day, in mid-morning and mid-afternoon. Four units are included in each sample. Observations were continued for 2 weeks so that 20 samples were collected. The results are shown in the following table. Each figure in a sample is the actual time taken to assemble one unit.

Measurement of Time Spent Per Unit
(Two Samples Taken Daily for 10 Days)

Sample Number	Time Spent on Each of Four Items Within Samples				Arithmetic Mean	Range R
1	12	11	10	9	10.5	3
2	10	10	9	11	10	2
3	13	11	10	9	10.75	4
4	10	9	8	11	9.5	3
5	12	11	10	10	10.75	2
6	11	11	14	9	11.25	5
7	10	9	12	10	10.25	3
8	11	12	10	11	11	2

Sample Number	Time Spent on Each of Four Items Within Samples				Arithmetic Mean	Range R
9	13	9	10	10	10.5	4
10	11	9	10	10	10	2
11	11	11	11	10	10.75	1
12	8	14	10	10	10.5	6
13	10	11	9	11	10.25	2
14	12	10	9	10	10.25	3
15	8	10	10	12	10	4
16	11	10	10	9	10	2
17	13	10	9	11	10.75	4
18	11	8	10	13	10.5	5
19	10	9	13	12	11	4
20	13	12	8	13	11.5	5
			Totals		210	66
			Grand Arithmetic Mean		10.5	3.3

a. Compute $\bar{\bar{X}}$ and $\bar{R}$, and then determine the upper and lower control limits for $\bar{X}$ and R.

b. Prepare a control chart for $\bar{X}$ and R.

c. Comment on the charts.

2. The following table shows the length of a new telephone connector, Model T310. Jeannie, an industrial engineer, took a sample of four consecutive pieces each hour for 2 hours and measured their lengths with a micrometer. Based on those eight samples, she wants to construct her control charts. Compute $\bar{\bar{X}}$ and $\bar{R}$, determine the upper and lower control limits for each, and prepare a control chart for $\bar{X}$ and R.

Length of Telephone Connector

Sample Number	Length of Each of Four Items Within Samples				Arithmetic Mean	Range R
1	59.93	60.09	60.01	59.89	59.98	0.2
2	60.11	59.98	60.08	60.15	60.08	0.17
3	59.94	60.11	60.18	60.17	60.1	0.24
4	59.85	60.02	59.92	59.89	59.92	0.17
5	59.98	59.89	60.09	60.12	60.02	0.23
6	60.09	60.02	59.97	60.12	60.05	0.15
7	60.08	60.04	60.09	60.07	60.07	0.05
8	59.9	59.89	60.04	59.93	59.94	0.15
			Totals		480.16	1.36
			Grand Arithmetic Mean		60.02	0.17

3. Jeannie wants to use a *p* chart to control the proportion of defective units coming from Final Assembly. She samples 50 units each hour and tested each unit to see if it works. The number of defective units in her first 8 samples and the proportion defective *p* follow:

Sample Number	n	Number Defective	p
1	50	3	0.06
2	50	2	0.04
3	50	0	0
4	50	1	0.02
5	50	1	0.02
6	50	7	0.14
7	50	2	0.04
8	50	0	0
	Totals	16	0.32

4. Steve Bono, the safety manager, recorded the number of injuries each week and uses a *c* chart to detect changes in the injury rate. Over the next 8 weeks, injuries per week were 6, 5, 3, 8, 2, 6, 9, and 5. Construct the *c* chart and determine if the process is in control.

5. Shipments of bowling balls are sampled before delivery to a warehouse. Lots of 600 balls are checked, using ten observations from each lot. Any lot with more than one defective is rejected. Determine values for the operating characteristic (OC) curve for this sampling plan.

6. Ron Jaffe Industries, Inc., a maker of plastic wrapping material, takes a random sample of 50 items from each lot before sending it to a customer. Lots contain 2,000 items each. Any lot with more than one defective is subjected to 100% inspection, and any defectives are replaced with good ones.

   a. Develop the table for the OC curve for this sampling plan.

   b. Construct the AOQ curve for this plan. What is the approximate average outgoing quality limit?

7. An automobile brake manufacturer buys brake linings in lots of 1,000. Samples of 15 linings are usually tested for defectives.

   a. How would the OC curves appear for acceptance numbers, *c* = 0, 1, and 2?

   b. If the sample size is increased to 20, how do the OC curves in part a appear?

   c. Using a sample size of 20 and AQL = 5% and LTPD = 10%, tabulate the values of α and β for three different sampling plans with *c* = 0, 1, and 2.

ANSWERS

DO YOU KNOW THE BASICS?

1. The primary objective of quality assurance is to ensure that products and services conform to specifications of design and customer satisfaction by preventing defects, detecting them when they occur, and taking remedial action.

2. Assignable causes are causes that are not the result of chance and can be controlled, such as materials, equipment, labor, and personnel.

3. Variables are measured on a continuous scale of measurement such as means and ranges; attributes assume only two values such as good or bad.

4. A sampling plan is a plan that discriminates between lots of various qualities (i.e., percent defectives). An OC curve is the relationship between lot quality (or percent defective) and the probability of lot acceptance given a sampling plan. It attempts to determine the producer's and consumer's risk for a given sampling plan. The curve is used to select a plan having a specified risk profile.

5. In control means that any variation in quality is caused solely by chance; no assignable causes are present.

6. $\bar{X}$ charts are used for averages; R charts are used for ranges or spread; p charts are used for fraction defective; and c charts are used for defectives.

7. p charts are used to monitor the process for attribute data. These are typically binomial "go, no-go" data. An example of a p chart is percent of pieces nonconforming. $\bar{X}$ charts are used for charting population values for continuous measurement. $\bar{X}$ charts are used when the process is too slow to produce enough measurements for an $\bar{X}$ chart. An example of an $\bar{X}$ chart is average time to complete a mile run for one person. R charts are used to compute process ranges for variable data. R charts are used in concert with $\bar{X}$ charts.

8. Producer's risk (consumer's risk) is equivalent to the probability of a Type I (Type II) error.

9. The objective of acceptance sampling is to make a decision as to whether to accept or reject a lot. It is *not* to estimate the quality of a lot.

10. AOQ is the average outgoing quality. In a given case, it depends on the sampling plan and the lot quality. AOQL is the average outgoing quality limit. It refers to the worst possible outgoing quality and occurs at an intermediate quality level, which is neither very good or very bad.

PRACTICAL APPLICATION

1.

    a. For $\bar{X}$: Control limits are

$$\text{UCL}_{\bar{X}} = \bar{\bar{X}} + A_2\bar{R}$$

$$= 10.5 + (0.729)(3.3)$$

$$= 10.5 + 2.41 = 12.91$$

and

$$\text{LCL}_{\bar{X}} = \bar{\bar{X}} - A_2\bar{R}$$

$$= 10.5 - (0.729)(3.3)$$

$$= 1.30 - 2.41 = 8.09$$

For R:

$$\text{URL} = D_4\bar{R} = 2.282\,(0.17) = 7.524$$

$$\text{LRL} = D_3\bar{R} = 0(0.17) = 0$$

    b. See Figures 14.12 and 14.13.

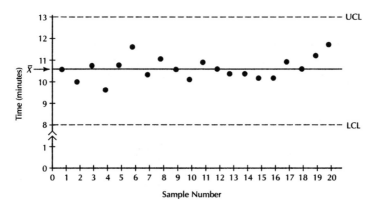

Figure 14.12. Control Chart for $\bar{X}$

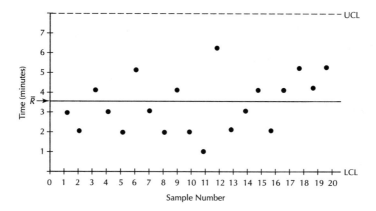

Figure 14.13. Control Chart for $\overline{R}$

c. No observations are outside the control limits so the process is apparently in control as far as the sample means are concerned. The process also seems to be in control as far as the range is concerned. Caution is needed here. Given certain men, materials, machines, and methods, the process or operation may be statistically in control. However, this does not mean that the process or operation is beyond change or improvement.

2. See Figures 14.14 and 14.15.

For $\overline{X}$: Control limits are

$$\text{UCL}_{\overline{x}} = \overline{\overline{X}} + A_2\overline{R}$$

$$= 60.02 + (0.729)(0.17)$$

$$= 60.144$$

and

$$\text{LCL}_{\overline{x}} = \overline{\overline{X}} - A_2\overline{R}$$

$$= 60.02 - (0.729)(0.17)$$

$$= 59.896$$

For R:

$$\text{URL} = D_4\overline{R} = 2.282\,(0.17) = 0.388$$

$$\text{LRL} = D_3\overline{R} = 0(0.17) = 0$$

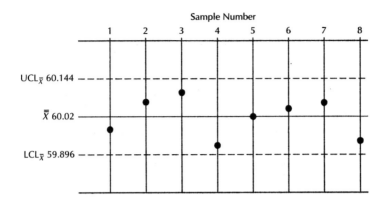

Figure 14.14. Control Chart for $\bar{X}$

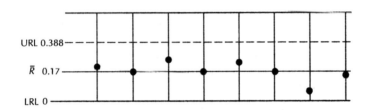

Figure 14.15. Control Chart for R

Every sample is in control on both the $\bar{X}$ and R charts. Both the mean and variation of the process are stable and predictable.

3. See Figure 14.16. The fraction defective is 16/50 = 0.32, so $\bar{p}$ = 0.32/8 = 0.4. The control limits for a p chart, based on three standard deviations, are computed as follows:

$$\text{UCL}_p = \bar{p} + 3 \sqrt{\frac{\bar{p}(1-\bar{p})}{n}} = 0.04 + 3 \sqrt{\frac{(0.04)(0.96)}{50}} = 0.123$$

$$\text{LCL}_p = \bar{p} - 3 \sqrt{\frac{\bar{p}(1-\bar{p})}{n}} = 0.04 - 3 \sqrt{\frac{(0.04)(0.96)}{50}} = -0.043$$

$$= 0 \text{ (because LCL cannot be negative)}$$

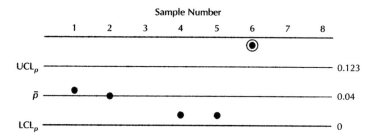

Figure 14.16. Control Chart for p

The defective rate was out of control when sample 6 was taken. The problem must be investigated and the cause eliminated. When the cause is determined and eliminated, she can recalculate $\bar{p}$ and the control limits.

4. The average number of injuries per week is $\bar{c} = 44/8 = 5.5$

$$\text{UCL}_c = \bar{c} + 3\sqrt{\bar{c}} = 5.5 + 3\sqrt{5.5} = 12.54$$

$$\text{LCL}_c = \bar{c} - 3\sqrt{\bar{c}} = 5.5 - 3\sqrt{5.5} = -1.54 = 0$$

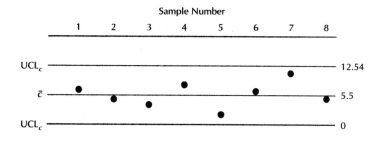

Figure 14.17. Control Chart for $\bar{c}$

All the samples are in control. See Figure 14.17.

5. $n = 10$, $c = 1$. Using Table 7 in Appendix II, we obtain the following information:

Fraction Defective	Cumulative Probability
0.05	0.9139
0.10	0.7361
0.15	0.5443
0.20	0.3758
0.25	0.2440
0.30	0.1493
0.35	0.0860
0.40	0.0464
0.45	0.0233

6. Note that $n = 50$ and $c = 1$. Using Table 8 in Appendix II, we get the following information:

p (1)	$\lambda = np$	Cumulative Probability (2)	AOQ (1) × (2)	
0.002	0.10	0.995	0.00199	
0.004	0.20	0.982	0.00393	
0.008	0.40	0.938	0.00750	
0.012	0.60	0.878	0.01054	
0.016	0.80	0.809	0.01294	
0.020	1.00	0.736	0.01472	
0.024	1.20	0.663	0.01591	
0.028	1.40	0.592	0.01658	AOQ limit = AOQL = maximum AOQ
0.032	1.60	0.525	0.01680	←
0.036	1.80	0.463	0.01667	

7.

a. and **b.** From binomial table, we get the following:

Number of Defectives = c

	Sample Size =15				Sample Size = 20		
p	0	1	2	p	0	1	2
0.0	1.000	1.000	1.000	0.0	1.000	1.000	1.000
0.1	0.463	0.829	0.964	0.05	0.358	0.736	0.925
0.1	0.206	0.549	0.816	0.1	0.122	0.392	0.677
0.2	0.035	0.167	0.398	0.2	0.012	0.069	0.206
0.3	0.005	0.035	0.127	0.3	0.001	0.008	0.035
0.4	0	0.005	0.027	0.4	0	0.001	0.004
0.5	0	0	0.004	0.5	0	0	0

See Figures 14.18 and 14.19.

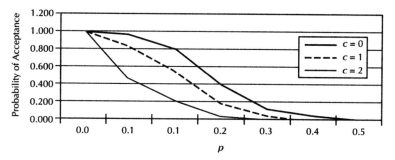

Figure 14.18. The OC Curve for $n = 15$

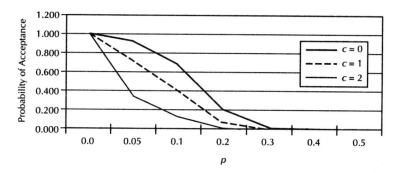

Figure 14.19. The OC Curve for $n = 20$

c. For the sample size of $n = 20$:

	Number of Defectives, c		
	0	1	2
α	0.642[a]	0.264	0.075
β	0.122[b]	0.392	0.677

[a] When AQL = p = 5% = 0.05, the probability of acceptance for c = 0 equals 0.358, which is $1 - \alpha$, so $\alpha = 1 - 0.358 = 0.642$.

[b] When LTPD = p = 10% = 0.10, the probability of acceptance for c = 0 equals 0.012, which is the value of β.

GLOSSARY

ABC analysis inventory control system that divides the inventory into three classes—A, B, and C—depending on the value and importance of the item.

acceptable outgoing quality level (AOQL) average percentage of defectives in lots leaving an inspection station.

acceptable quality level (AQL) quality standard that allows for a prespecified number of defects.

aggregate production planning establishment of aggregate production and inventory levels over a medium-range time horizon.

arrival rate number of customers or units arriving or entering the system in a given period of time.

assembly chart graphical method for visualizing how the various parts and subassemblies flow into the assembly process.

assignable causes causes of poor quality that are the result of problems with materials, machines, or operators and that can be remedied.

assignment problem problem of determining how the assignments should be made in order to minimize total costs.

backward pass calculation procedure moving backward through the network that determines the latest start and latest finish times for each activity.

benchmarking searching for new and better procedures by comparing your own procedures to that of the very best.

beta distribution probability distribution often used to describe activity times.

bill of materials (BOM) structured parts list that shows the manner in which the product is actually put together.

break-even point level of sales revenue that equals the total of the variable and fixed costs for a given volume of output at a particular capacity use rate.

business process reengineering (BPR) approach aimed at making revolutionary changes as opposed to evolutionary changes by eliminating nonvalue-added steps in a business process and computerizing the remaining steps to achieve desired outcomes.

capacity rate at which work is capable of being produced.

capacity requirements planning (CRP) system for determining whether a planned production schedule can be accomplished with available capacity and, if not, making adjustments as necessary.

capital budgeting process of making long-term planning and capital expenditure decisions.

cellular manufacturing groups of machinery that are closely associated with each family of parts.

center-of-gravity method quantitative approach to locating a facility that minimizes the distance or cost of transportation weighted by the volume of goods moved.

channels number of waiting lines in a service system.

chase plan aggregate production plan that adjusts capacity in response to seasonal demand.

classical decomposition approach to forecasting that seeks to decompose the underlying pattern of a time series into cyclical, seasonal, trend, and random sub-patterns.

coefficient of determination proportion of the total variation in the dependent variable that is explained by the regression equation.

computer-aided design (CAD) use of a computer to interact with a designer in developing and testing product ideas without actually building prototypes.

computer-aided design and manufacturing (CAD/CAM) computerized system to both integrate part design, as with CAD, and generate processing or manufacturing instructions.

computer-aided manufacturing (CAM) manufacturing system utilizing computer software that controls the actual machine on the shop floor.

computer-integrated manufacturing (CIM) computer information systems utilizing a shared manufacturing database for engineering design, factory production, and information management.

computer numerically controlled (CNC) machines stand-alone machines controlled by a computer.

consumer surveys method that involves interviewing potential customers to estimate demand relations.

consumer's risk probability of accepting a bad lot.

continuous improvement (CI) also called *Kaizen* in Japanese, never-ending effort for improvement in every part of the firm relative to all its deliverables to its customers.

control chart graphical means of depicting sample characteristics, such as means, ranges, and attributes, over time used for process control.

correlation coefficient measure of the degree of correlation between two variables. The range of values it takes is between −1 and +1.

cost of capital rate of return that investors expect to receive from the firm.

crashing process of reducing an activity time by adding resources and hence usually cost.

critical path longest sequence of activities in a project management network.

cycle time time required to produce one item on an assembly line; length of time between the placing of two consecutive orders.

decision making under risk decision made when the probability of occurrence of the different states of nature is known.

decision matrix also called payoff table; matrix consisting of the decision alternatives, the states of nature, and the decision outcomes.

decision theory systematic approach to making decisions especially under uncertainty.

decision tree graphical method of showing the sequence of possible decision alternatives.

Delphi method qualitative forecasting technique for arriving at group consensus in an anonymous fashion.

deseasonalized data removal of the seasonal pattern in a data series. Deseasonalizing facilitates the comparison of month-to-month changes.

discounted cash flow (DCF) techniques methods of selecting and ranking investment proposals such as the net present value (NPV) and internal rate of return (IRR) methods where time value of money is taken into account.

due date promised delivery date.

dummy activity fictitious activity with zero activity time used to represent precedence or used whenever two or more activities have the same starting and ending nodes.

earliest finish time earliest time at which an activity may be completed.

earliest start time earliest time at which an activity may begin.

economic order quantity (EOQ) amount that should be ordered to minimize the total ordering and carrying costs.

economic production run size amount that should be produced each production run to minimize the total setup and carrying costs.

equivalent uniform annual cost annualized sum of all relevant costs. It is like the amount of an installment loan payment.

exponential distribution probability distribution used to describe the pattern or service times for some waiting lines.

exponential smoothing forecasting technique that uses a weighted moving average of past data as the basis for a forecast.

factor ratings procedure in which each alternative site is rated according to each factor relevant to the decision, and each factor is rated according to importance.

fishbone diagrams often called cause-and-effect diagrams; way of determining likely root causes of a problem.

fixed-position layout layout in which the construction of a large product is accomplished in one place.

flexible manufacturing system (FMS) computer-controlled process technology suitable for producing a moderate variety of products in moderate, flexible volumes.

flow process chart description of the sequence of operations in a production process. These generally are operation, inspection, movement, storage, and delay.

Gantt chart graphical representation of a schedule used to plan or monitor progress.

goodness-of-fit degree to which a model fits the observed data.

GPSS, SIMSCRIPT specially designed computer programming languages used for simulation.

graphical method graphical approach to solving a linear programming (LP) problem. It is limited to the LP problems involving two (or at most three) decision variables.

group layout layout in which machine groups are arranged to process families of parts with similar characteristics.

group technology concept for identifying and classifying part families to efficient mass-production-type layouts. It can be designed for items usually manufactured by a process layout.

heuristic line-balancing technique technique involving the generation of a precedence diagram (technological sequencing requirements) in a particular way, which indicates the flexibility available for shifting tasks from column to column to achieve the desired balance.

independent demand demands for various items are unrelated to each other and therefore determined separately and independently.

internal rate of return (IRR) rate earned on a proposal; the rate of interest that equates the initial investment with the present value of future cash inflows.

inventory status file file indicating how much inventory is on hand or on order.

ISO 9000 certification standards developed by the International Organization for Standardization (ISO) that serve as a basis for quality standards for global manufacturers.

JIT manufacturing manufacturing approach that produces only what is necessary to satisfy the demand of the preceding process (a demand–pull system).

job design determination of specific job tasks and responsibilities, the work environment, and work methods.

Johnson's rule technique that can be used to minimize the completion time for a group of jobs that are to be processed on two machines or at two successive work centers.

just-in-time production approach to manufacturing in which items are produced only when needed in production.

Kanban Japanese information system for coordinating production orders and withdrawals from in-process inventory to realize just-in-time production.

latest finish time latest time at which an activity must be completed without holding up the complete project.

latest start time latest time at which an activity must begin without holding up the complete project.

lead time time between the placing of an order and its receipt in the inventory system.

learning curve effect reduction in labor hours as the cumulative production doubles, ranging typically from 10% to 20%.

least-squares method statistical technique for fitting a straight line through a set of points in such a way that the sum of the squared distances from the data points to the line is minimized.

level plan aggregate production plan that maintains a uniform output rate.

line balancing process of distributing the workloads evenly.

linear programming (LP) mathematical technique designed to determine an optimal decision (or an optimal plan) chosen from a large number of possible decisions.

linear regression regression that deals with a straight line relationship between variables.

loading allocating workloads to specific work.

locational break-even analysis technique that compares potential locations on an economic basis by estimating the variable and fixed costs and then graphing them for a representative sales or production volume at each location.

make–buy decision decision as to whether a given item should be manufactured internally or purchased outside.

manufacturing resource planning (MRP II) integrated information system that steps beyond first-generation MRP to synchronize all aspects (not just manufacturing) of the business.

marginal approach method of inventory analysis that aims at determining the optimal stock level.

master production schedule (MPS) time-phased statement of how many finished items are to be manufactured. It is obtained by disaggregating the production plan and is the primary input to material requirements planning (MRP).

material requirements planning (MRP) computerized data processing system whose function is to schedule production and control the level of inventory for components with dependent demand.

mathematical models quantitative representations of reality.

mean absolute deviation (MAD) mean or average of the sum of all the forecast errors with regard to sign.

mean squared error (MSE) average sum of the variations between the historical sales data and the forecast values for the corresponding periods.

model representation of a real-life system.

modular design design of components that can be assembled in a variety of ways to meet individual consumer needs.

Monte Carlo simulation simulation using a random number procedure to create values for the probabilistic components.

motion study analysis of a manual task in order to improve productivity.

moving average in a time series, an average that is updated as new information is received.

MTM (methods-time measurement) system of predetermined motion-time data used to develop standards for highly repetitive tasks.

multiple regression analysis statistical procedure that attempts to assess the relationship between the dependent variable and two or more independent variables.

multiple-channel line waiting line with two or more parallel identical servers.

net present value (NPV) method method widely used for evaluating investment projects. Under the net present value method, the present value of all cash inflows from the project is compared against the initial investment.

nodes intersection or junction points of a network.

operating characteristic (OC) curve plot of the probability of acceptance of a lot as a function of the percent of defective items.

operation chart often called right-handed, left-handed chart; chart used to describe simultaneous motions of hands when performing a task.

operations set of all activities associated with the production of goods and services.

operations management (OM) also called production/operations management; design, operation, and improvement of the productions/operations system that creates the firm's primary products or services.

operations strategy strategy specifying how the firm will employ its production capabilities to support its corporate strategy.

optimization models prescriptive techniques for finding the best solutions to the problem at hand. Linear programming is an example.

payback period length of time required to recover the amount of an initial investment.

PERT/cost also known as the critical path method (CPM); technique designed to assist in the planning, scheduling, and controlling of project costs.

Poisson distribution probability distribution used to describe the random arrival pattern for some waiting lines.

present value analysis technique used widely to account for the timing of cash inflows and outflows.

priority rules simple heuristics used to select the order in which the jobs will be processed.

process layout layout in which machines or activities are arranged by function.

process planning planning involving a total analysis of the product and its processing requirements, decisions concerning the purchase of items outside versus their internal manufacture, and techniques for selecting among competing processes.

process selection an economic analysis to determine which process should be chosen when operations can be performed by more than one process.

producer's risk probability of rejecting a good quality lot.

product analysis analysis of product assembly. The early phases of product analysis may produce diagrams which "explode" the product into its various subassemblies and parts. These diagrams may be pictorial or schematic.

product layout layout in which equipment is arranged based on the sequence of operations performed on a product or group of products.

production and operations management management of all activities directly related to the production of goods and services.

production design the conscious effort to design for low manufacturing cost.

production system collection of inputs, conversion/transformation processes, outputs, control mechanisms, and managers involved in production and operations.

productivity ratio of outputs to inputs.

quality measure of conformance of a product or service to certain specifications or standards.

quality assurance all the activities necessary to ensure that the customer receives satisfactory performance.

quality function deployment (QFD) system that uses interfunctional teams from marketing, design engineering, and manufacturing to translate the voice of the customer into the design specification of a product.

quantity discount model inventory model that takes into account the price varying with the order size.

queue waiting line that forms wherever there is more than one user of a limited resource.

queue discipline rules that determine the order in which arrivals are serviced.

queuing (or waiting line) theory operations research term for the study of waiting lines.

regression analysis statistical procedure for estimating mathematically the average relationship between the dependent variable (sales, for example) and one or more independent variables (price and advertising, for example).

reliability probability that a product or process will perform satisfactorily over a period of time under specified operating conditions.

reorder point inventory level that triggers a new order.

rough-cut capacity planning analysis of the master production schedule to determine the feasibility with respect to capacity limitations (warehouse facilities, equipment, labor, etc.).

r-squared see coefficient of determination.

safety stock inventory carried to ensure that the desired service level is met.

scheduling assignment of work to a facility and the specification of the sequence and timing of the work.

sequencing determination of the order in which a facility is to process a set of jobs.

service level probability of no stockouts during the lead time.

service rate number of customers or units that can be serviced by one server in a given period of time.

shadow price profit that would be lost by not adding an additional hour of capacity.

simple regression regression analysis that involves one independent variable.

simplex method linear programming algorithm, which is an iteration method of computation, to move from one corner point solution to another until it reaches the best solution.

simulation technique to describe the behavior of a real-life system over time.

single-channel line waiting line with only one server.

slack length of time an activity can be delayed without affecting the project completion date.

SPT (shortest processing time) scheduling rule that chooses jobs in order of shortest processing time first.

supply chain management management of the integration of the functions, information, and materials that flow across multiple firms in a supply chain (i.e., buying materials, transforming materials, and shipping to customers).

systematic layout planning generalized approach to layout that indicates nearness priorities, taking into account factors other than transportation cost.

Taguchi method of quality control method of controlling quality that stresses robust product design and the quality loss function.

tardiness amount by which completion time exceeds the due date.

theory of constraints (TOC) approach seeking to identify a company's constraints or bottlenecks and exploit them so that throughput is maximized and inventories and operating costs are minimized.

THERBLIG one of 17 elementary human motions such as grasp, select, assemble, and so on.

throughput rate at which money is generated by the system through sales.

time bucket term denoting a time period used in the master schedule.

time standard amount of time required to perform a task by a trained operator working at a normal pace and using a prescribed method.

time study development of standards through stopwatch observation.

total fixed costs costs that remain constant in total regardless of changes in activity.

total quality control (TQC) philosophy that aggressively strives for a defect-free manufacturing process.

total quality management (TQM) concept of using quality methods and techniques to strategic advantage within firms.

total variable costs costs that vary in total in direct proportion to changes in activity.

transportation LP problem problem of determining how much to ship from each origin to each destination in order to minimize total shipping costs.

trend analysis special form of simple regression in which time is the independent variable.

unit contribution margin selling price minus average variable cost.

value analysis (value engineering) process of trying to reduce product costs by substituting less-costly materials, redesigning nonessential parts, and the like.

work measurement process of estimating the amount of worker time required to generate one unit of output.

work sampling work measurement technique involving the sampling of the nature of the activity in which the worker is involved; used for the broader problem of determining production standards.

APPENDIX I

AMERICAN PRODUCTION AND INVENTORY CONTROL SOCIETY

Established in 1957, American Production and Inventory Control Society (APICS) is designed to meet the needs of professionals in all areas of resource management, including inventory, materials, information systems, accounting/finance, supply chain, and all other functional areas that contribute to the overall efficiency and productivity of an organization.

APICS is

- an international, not-for-profit organization serving the manufacturing, materials management, resource management, and service industries.

- a source of knowledge and expertise for more than 70,000 professional members representing 20,000 diverse companies worldwide. It is the leading provider of high-quality, cutting-edge programs and materials that advance organizational success in a changing, competitive marketplace.

- a clearinghouse for hundreds of business management publications and educational materials.

- a successful developer of two internationally recognized certification programs, Certified in Production and Inventory Management (CPIM) and Certified in Integrated Resource Management (CIRM), designed to enhance industry professionals' specialized functional and broad-based business knowledge.

- a source of solutions and support for members through local chapters and participation in the international conference and exhibition.

Its goals follow:

- The educational offerings, products, and services of APICS will be market-driven and accessible on demand.

- APICS will be recognized as the source for state-of-the-art information (BOK) in all aspects of integrated resource management.

- Organizations and individuals will find certification of professional expertise available through APICS of value.

- Members will recognize APICS as a provider of value-added services and benefits to support growth and continued professional development.

APICS is located at 500 West Annandale Road, Falls Church, VA 22046, its telephone numbers are (800) 444-2742 or (703) 237-8344, and its Web site is http://www.apics.org.

CERTIFICATION IN PRODUCTION AND INVENTORY MANAGEMENT

The CPIM program was started by APICS in 1973 to provide a common basis for individuals to assess their knowledge of the evolving field of production and inventory management. Since then, APICS has administered more than half a million tests in 40 countries, and CPIM has become recognized as the worldwide standard for those wishing to demonstrate their knowledge of production and inventory management. More than 52,000 people are now certified in production and inventory management, 2,200 of these at the Fellow level.

The CPIM program is the recognized international standard for individual assessment in the field of production and inventory management. The program is designed to test candidates for in-depth knowledge of a variety of subjects specific to this field. The intent of the program is to provide a prospective employer with assistance in recruiting qualified candidates to work in production and inventory management.

The CPIM body of knowledge is composed of the following modules.

- Just-in-Time
- Material Requirements/Capacity Requirements Planning
- Master Planning
- Inventory Management
- Production Activity Control
- Systems and Technology
- Supply Chain Management

CPIM is appropriate for professionals working in or in close cooperation with the following functions:

- Production and inventory management
- Materials management
- Integrated resource management
- Purchasing
- Supply chain management
- Finance and cost accounting
- Manufacturing information systems

PROFILE OF THE CPIM CANDIDATE

All professionals interested in expanding their knowledge of production and inventory management concepts can benefit from the CPIM program.

CERTIFICATION IN INTEGRATED RESOURCE MANAGEMENT

The CIRM program was initiated by APICS in 1991, and more than 3,000 people sat for the first examinations. Since then the program has evolved and is rapidly becoming a requirement for those who wish to be on the cutting edge of management thinking. The intent of the CIRM program is to become the internationally recognized standard for excellence in the field of integrated resource management.

The CIRM body of knowledge is composed of the following modules:

- Customers and Products
- Logistics
- Manufacturing Processes
- Support Functions
- Integrated Enterprise Management

PROFILE OF THE CIRM CANDIDATE

Project managers, team leaders, aspiring managers, operations staff members, consultants, or other professionals in all industries who seek to improve their decision-making abilities can benefit from the CIRM program. Certification is also recommended for individuals who would benefit from a clearer understanding of horizontal management and cross-functional operations within an organization.

APPENDIX II

TABLES

- Table 1—Present Value of $1, $1/(1 + i)^n = T_1(i, n)$
- Table 2—Present Value of an Annuity of $1, $(1/i) [1 - 1(1 + i)^n = T_2(i, n)]$
- Table 3—Normal Distribution Table
- Table 4—Learning Curve Coefficients
- Table 5—Critical Values of Student's t-Distribution
- Table 6—Random Numbers
- Table 7—Binomial Distribution
- Table 8—Poisson Distribution

Table 1. Present Value of $1.00, $\dfrac{1}{(1+i)^n} = T_1(i, n)$

Periods	4%	6%	8%	10%	12%	14%	20%
1	0.962	0.943	0.926	0.909	0.893	0.877	0.833
2	0.925	0.890	0.857	0.826	0.797	0.769	0.694
3	0.889	0.840	0.794	0.751	0.712	0.675	0.579
4	0.855	0.792	0.735	0.683	0.636	0.592	0.482
5	0.822	0.747	0.681	0.621	0.567	0.519	0.402
6	0.790	0.705	0.630	0.564	0.507	0.456	0.335
7	0.760	0.665	0.583	0.513	0.452	0.400	0.279
8	0.731	0.627	0.540	0.467	0.404	0.351	0.233
9	0.703	0.592	0.500	0.424	0.361	0.308	0.194
10	0.676	0.558	0.463	0.386	0.322	0.270	0.162
11	0.650	0.527	0.429	0.350	0.287	0.237	0.135
12	0.625	0.497	0.397	0.319	0.257	0.208	0.112
13	0.601	0.469	0.368	0.290	0.229	0.182	0.093
14	0.577	0.442	0.340	0.263	0.205	0.160	0.078
15	0.555	0.417	0.315	0.239	0.183	0.140	0.065
16	0.534	0.394	0.292	0.218	0.163	0.123	0.054
17	0.513	0.371	0.270	0.198	0.146	0.108	0.045
18	0.494	0.350	0.250	0.180	0.130	0.095	0.038
19	0.475	0.331	0.232	0.164	0.116	0.083	0.031
20	0.456	0.312	0.215	0.149	0.104	0.073	0.026
30	0.308	0.174	0.099	0.057	0.033	0.020	0.004
40	0.208	0.097	0.046	0.022	0.011	0.005	0.001

Table 2. Present Value of an Annuity of \$1.00*, $\dfrac{1}{i}\left[1 - \dfrac{1}{(1+i)^n}\right] = T_2(i, n)$

Periods	4%	6%	8%	10%	12%	14%	16%	18%	20%	22%	24%	25%	26%	28%	30%	40%
1	0.962	0.943	0.926	0.909	0.893	0.877	0.862	0.847	0.833	0.820	0.806	0.800	0.794	0.781	0.769	0.714
2	1.886	1.833	1.783	1.736	1.690	1.647	1.605	1.566	1.528	1.492	1.457	1.440	1.424	1.392	1.361	1.224
3	2.775	2.673	2.577	2.487	2.402	2.322	2.246	2.174	2.106	2.042	1.981	1.952	1.923	1.868	1.816	1.589
4	3.630	3.465	3.312	3.170	3.037	2.914	2.798	2.690	2.589	2.494	2.404	2.362	2.320	2.241	2.166	1.849
5	4.452	4.212	3.993	3.791	3.605	3.433	3.274	3.127	2.991	2.864	2.745	2.689	2.635	2.532	2.436	2.035
6	5.242	4.917	4.623	4.355	4.111	3.889	3.685	3.498	3.326	3.167	3.020	2.951	2.885	2.759	2.643	2.168
7	6.002	5.582	5.206	4.868	4.564	4.288	4.039	3.812	3.605	3.416	3.242	3.161	3.083	2.937	2.802	2.263
8	6.733	6.210	5.747	5.335	4.968	4.639	4.344	4.078	3.837	3.619	3.421	3.329	3.241	3.076	2.925	2.331
9	7.435	6.802	6.247	5.759	5.328	4.946	4.607	4.303	4.031	3.786	3.566	3.463	3.366	3.184	3.019	2.379
10	8.111	7.360	6.710	6.145	5.650	5.216	4.833	4.494	4.192	3.923	3.682	3.571	3.465	3.269	3.092	2.414
11	8.760	7.887	7.139	6.495	5.938	5.453	5.029	4.656	4.327	4.035	3.776	3.656	3.544	3.335	3.147	2.438
12	9.385	8.384	7.536	6.814	6.194	5.660	5.197	4.793	4.439	4.127	3.851	3.725	3.606	3.387	3.190	2.456
13	9.986	8.853	7.904	7.103	6.424	5.842	5.342	4.910	4.533	4.203	3.912	3.780	3.656	3.427	3.223	2.468
14	10.563	9.295	8.244	7.367	6.628	6.002	5.468	5.008	4.611	4.265	3.962	3.824	3.695	3.459	3.249	2.477
15	11.118	9.712	8.559	7.606	6.811	6.142	5.575	5.092	4.675	4.315	4.001	3.859	3.726	3.483	3.268	2.484
16	11.652	10.106	8.851	7.824	6.974	6.265	5.669	5.162	4.730	4.357	4.033	3.887	3.751	3.503	3.283	2.489
17	12.166	10.477	9.122	8.022	7.120	6.373	5.749	5.222	4.775	4.391	4.059	3.910	3.771	3.518	3.295	2.492
18	12.659	10.828	9.372	8.201	7.250	6.467	5.818	5.273	4.812	4.419	4.080	3.928	3.786	3.529	3.304	2.494
19	13.134	11.158	9.604	8.365	7.366	6.550	5.877	5.316	4.844	4.442	4.097	3.942	3.799	3.539	3.311	2.496
20	13.590	11.470	9.818	8.514	7.469	6.623	5.929	5.353	4.870	4.460	4.110	3.954	3.808	3.546	3.316	2.497
21	14.029	11.764	10.017	8.649	7.562	6.687	5.973	5.384	4.891	4.476	4.121	3.963	3.816	3.551	3.320	2.498
22	14.451	12.042	10.201	8.772	7.645	6.743	6.011	5.410	4.909	4.488	4.130	3.970	3.822	3.556	3.323	2.498
23	14.857	12.303	10.371	8.883	7.718	6.792	6.044	5.432	4.925	4.499	4.137	3.976	3.827	3.559	3.325	2.499
24	15.247	12.550	10.529	8.985	7.784	6.835	6.073	5.451	4.937	4.507	4.143	3.981	3.831	3.562	3.327	2.499
25	15.622	12.783	10.675	9.077	7.843	6.873	6.097	5.467	4.948	4.514	4.147	3.985	3.834	3.564	3.329	2.499
26	15.983	13.003	10.810	9.161	7.896	6.906	6.118	5.480	4.956	4.520	4.151	3.988	3.837	3.566	3.330	2.500
27	16.330	13.211	10.935	9.237	7.943	6.935	6.136	5.492	4.964	4.524	4.154	3.990	3.839	3.567	3.331	2.500
28	16.663	13.406	11.051	9.307	7.984	6.961	6.152	5.502	4.970	4.528	4.157	3.992	3.840	3.568	3.331	2.500
29	16.984	13.591	11.158	9.370	8.022	6.983	6.166	5.510	4.975	4.531	4.159	3.994	3.841	3.569	3.332	2.500
30	17.292	13.765	11.258	9.427	8.055	7.003	6.177	5.517	4.979	4.534	4.160	3.995	3.842	3.569	3.332	2.500
40	19.793	15.046	11.925	9.779	8.244	7.105	6.234	5.548	4.997	4.544	4.156	3.999	3.846	3.571	3.333	2.500

*Payments (or receipts) at the *end* of each period.

Table 3. Normal Distribution Table

Areas under the normal curve

Z	0	1	2	3	4	5	6	7	8	9
0.0	0.5000	0.5040	0.5080	0.5120	0.5160	0.5199	0.5239	0.5279	0.5319	0.5359
0.1	0.5398	0.5438	0.5478	0.5517	0.5557	0.5596	0.5636	0.5675	0.5714	0.5753
0.2	0.5793	0.5832	0.5871	0.5910	0.5948	0.5987	0.6026	0.6064	0.6103	0.6141
0.3	0.6179	0.6217	0.6255	0.6293	0.6331	0.6368	0.6406	0.6443	0.6480	0.6517
0.4	0.6554	0.6591	0.6628	0.6664	0.6700	0.6736	0.6772	0.6808	0.6844	0.6879
0.5	0.6915	0.6950	0.6985	0.7019	0.7054	0.7088	0.7123	0.7157	0.7190	0.7224
0.6	0.7257	0.7291	0.7324	0.7357	0.7389	0.7422	0.7454	0.7486	0.7517	0.7549
0.7	0.7580	0.7611	0.7642	0.7673	0.7703	0.7734	0.7764	0.7794	0.7823	0.7852
0.8	0.7881	0.7910	0.7939	0.7967	0.7995	0.8023	0.8051	0.8078	0.8106	0.8133
0.9	0.8159	0.8186	0.8212	0.8238	0.8264	0.8289	0.8315	0.8340	0.8365	0.8389
1.0	0.8413	0.8438	0.8461	0.8485	0.8508	0.8531	0.8554	0.8577	0.8599	0.8621
1.1	0.8643	0.8665	0.8686	0.8708	0.8729	0.8749	0.8770	0.8790	0.8810	0.8830
1.2	0.8849	0.8869	0.8888	0.8907	0.8925	0.8944	0.8962	0.8980	0.8997	0.9015
1.3	0.9032	0.9049	0.9066	0.9082	0.9099	0.9115	0.9131	0.9147	0.9162	0.9177
1.4	0.9192	0.9207	0.9222	0.9236	0.9251	0.9265	0.9278	0.9292	0.9306	0.9319
1.5	0.9332	0.9345	0.9357	0.9370	0.9382	0.9394	0.9406	0.9418	0.9430	0.9441
1.6	0.9452	0.9463	0.9474	0.9484	0.9495	0.9505	0.9515	0.9525	0.9535	0.9545
1.7	0.9554	0.9564	0.9573	0.9582	0.9591	0.9599	0.9608	0.9616	0.9625	0.9633
1.8	0.9641	0.9648	0.9656	0.9664	0.9671	0.9678	0.9686	0.9693	0.9700	0.9706
1.9	0.9713	0.9719	0.9726	0.9732	0.9738	0.9744	0.9750	0.9756	0.9762	0.9767
2.0	0.9772	0.9778	0.9783	0.9788	0.9793	0.9798	0.9803	0.9808	0.9812	0.9817
2.1	0.9821	0.9826	0.9830	0.9834	0.9838	0.9842	0.9846	0.9850	0.9854	0.9857
2.2	0.9861	0.9864	0.9868	0.9871	0.9874	0.9878	0.9881	0.9884	0.9887	0.9890
2.3	0.9893	0.9896	0.9898	0.9901	0.9904	0.9906	0.9909	0.9911	0.9913	0.9916
2.4	0.9918	0.9920	0.9922	0.9925	0.9927	0.9929	0.9931	0.9932	0.9934	0.9936
2.5	0.9938	0.9940	0.9941	0.9943	0.9945	0.9946	0.9948	0.9949	0.9951	0.9952
2.6	0.9953	0.9955	0.9956	0.9957	0.9959	0.9960	0.9961	0.9962	0.9963	0.9964
2.7	0.9965	0.9966	0.9967	0.9968	0.9969	0.9970	0.9971	0.9972	0.9973	0.9974
2.8	0.9974	0.9975	0.9976	0.9977	0.9977	0.9978	0.9979	0.9979	0.9980	0.9981
2.9	0.9981	0.9982	0.9982	0.9983	0.9984	0.9984	0.9985	0.9985	0.9986	0.9986
3.0	0.9987	0.9990	0.9993	0.9995	0.9997	0.9998	0.9998	0.9999	0.9999	1.0000

Table 4. Learning Curve Coefficients

Unit Number	70% Unit Time	70% Total Time	75% Unit Time	75% Total Time	80% Unit Time	80% Total Time	85% Unit Time	85% Total Time	90% Unit Time	90% Total Time
1	1.000	1.000	1.000	1.000	1.000	1.000	1.000	1.000	1.000	1.000
2	0.700	1.700	0.750	1.750	0.800	1.800	0.850	1.850	0.900	1.900
3	0.568	2.268	0.634	2.384	0.702	2.502	0.773	2.623	0.846	2.746
4	0.490	2.758	0.562	2.946	0.640	3.142	0.723	3.345	0.810	3.556
5	0.437	3.195	0.513	3.459	0.596	3.738	0.686	4.031	0.783	4.339
6	0.398	3.593	0.475	3.934	0.562	4.299	0.657	4.688	0.762	5.101
7	0.367	3.960	0.446	4.380	0.534	4.834	0.634	5.322	0.744	5.845
8	0.343	4.303	0.422	4.802	0.512	5.346	0.614	5.936	0.729	6.574
9	0.323	4.626	0.402	5.204	0.493	5.839	0.597	6.533	0.716	7.290
10	0.306	4.932	0.385	5.589	0.477	6.315	0.583	7.116	0.705	7.994
11	0.291	5.223	0.370	5.958	0.462	6.777	0.570	7.686	0.695	8.689
12	0.278	5.501	0.357	6.315	0.449	7.227	0.558	8.244	0.685	9.374
13	0.267	5.769	0.345	6.660	0.438	7.665	0.548	8.792	0.677	10.052
14	0.257	6.026	0.334	6.994	0.428	8.092	0.539	9.331	0.670	10.721
15	0.248	6.274	0.325	7.319	0.418	8.511	0.530	9.861	0.663	11.384
16	0.240	6.514	0.316	7.635	0.410	8.920	0.522	10.303	0.656	12.040
17	0.233	6.747	0.309	7.944	0.402	9.322	0.515	10.898	0.650	12.690
18	0.226	6.973	0.301	8.245	0.394	9.716	0.508	11.405	0.644	13.334
19	0.220	7.192	0.295	8.540	0.338	10.104	0.501	11.907	0.639	13.974
20	0.214	7.407	0.288	8.828	0.381	10.485	0.495	12.402	0.634	14.608
21	0.209	7.615	0.283	9.111	0.375	10.860	0.490	12.892	0.630	15.237
22	0.204	7.819	0.277	9.388	0.370	11.230	0.484	13.376	0.625	15.862
23	0.199	8.018	0.272	9.660	0.364	11.594	0.479	13.856	0.621	16.483
24	0.195	8.213	0.267	9.928	0.359	11.954	0.475	14.331	0.617	17.100
25	0.191	8.404	0.263	10.191	0.355	12.309	0.470	14.801	0.613	17.713
26	0.187	8.591	0.259	10.449	0.350	12.659	0.466	15.267	0.609	18.323
27	0.183	8.774	0.255	10.704	0.346	13.005	0.462	15.728	0.606	18.929
28	0.180	8.954	0.251	10.955	0.342	13.347	0.458	16.186	0.603	19.531
29	0.177	9.131	0.247	11.202	0.338	13.685	0.454	16.640	0.599	20.131
30	0.174	9.305	0.244	11.446	0.335	14.020	0.450	17.091	0.596	20.727
31	0.171	9.476	0.240	11.686	0.331	14.351	0.447	17.538	0.593	21.320
32	0.168	9.644	0.237	11.924	0.328	14.679	0.444	17.981	0.590	21.911
33	0.165	9.809	0.234	12.158	0.324	15.003	0.441	18.422	0.588	22.498
34	0.163	9.972	0.231	12.389	0.321	15.324	0.437	18.859	0.585	23.084
35	0.160	10.133	0.229	12.618	0.318	15.643	0.434	19.294	0.583	23.666
36	0.158	10.291	0.226	12.844	0.315	15.958	0.432	19.725	0.580	24.246
37	0.156	10.447	0.223	13.067	0.313	16.271	0.429	20.154	0.578	24.824
38	0.154	10.601	0.221	13.288	0.310	16.581	0.426	20.580	0.575	25.399
39	0.152	10.753	0.219	13.507	0.307	16.888	0.424	21.004	0.573	25.972
40	0.150	10.902	0.216	13.723	0.305	17.193	0.421	21.425	0.571	26.543

Table 5. Critical Values of Student's *t*-Distribution

Degrees of Freedom	$t_{.100}$	$t_{.050}$	$t_{.025}$	$t_{.010}$	$t_{.005}$
1	3.078	6.314	12.706	31.821	63.657
2	1.886	2.920	4.303	6.965	9.925
3	1.638	2.353	3.182	4.541	5.841
4	1.533	2.132	2.776	3.747	4.604
5	1.476	2.015	2.571	3.365	4.032
6	1.440	1.943	2.447	3.143	3.707
7	1.415	1.895	2.365	3.000	3.499
8	1.397	1.860	2.306	2.896	3.355
9	1.383	1.833	2.262	2.821	3.250
10	1.372	1.812	2.228	2.764	3.169
11	1.363	1.796	2.201	2.718	3.106
12	1.356	1.782	2.179	2.681	3.055
13	1.350	1.771	2.160	2.650	3.012
14	1.345	1.761	2.145	2.600	2.977
15	1.341	1.753	2.131	2.600	2.947
16	1.337	1.746	2.120	2.584	2.921
17	1.333	1.740	2.110	2.567	2.898
18	1.330	1.734	2.101	2.552	2.878
19	1.328	1.729	2.093	2.539	2.861
20	1.325	1.725	2.086	2.528	2.845
21	1.323	1.721	2.080	2.518	2.831
22	1.321	1.717	2.074	2.508	2.819
23	1.319	1.714	2.069	2.500	2.807
24	1.318	1.711	2.064	2.492	2.797
25	1.316	1.708	2.060	2.485	2.787
26	1.315	1.706	2.056	2.479	2.779
27	1.314	1.703	2.052	2.473	2.771
28	1.313	1.701	2.048	2.467	2.763
29	1.311	1.699	2.045	2.462	2.756
30	1.310	1.697	2.042	2.457	2.750
35	1.306	1.690	2.030	2.438	2.724
40	1.303	1.684	2.021	2.423	2.704
50	1.299	1.676	2.009	2.400	2.678
60	1.296	1.671	2.000	2.400	2.660
100	1.290	1.660	1.984	2.364	2.626
120	1.289	1.658	1.980	2.358	2.617

Table 6. Random Numbers

03689	33090	43465	96789	56688	32389	77206	06534	10558	14478
43367	46409	44751	73410	35138	24910	70748	57336	56043	68550
45357	52080	62670	73877	20604	40408	98060	96733	65094	80335
62683	03171	77109	92515	78041	27590	42651	00254	73179	10159
04841	40918	69047	68986	08150	87984	08887	76083	37702	28523
85963	06992	65321	43521	46393	40491	06028	43865	58190	28142
03720	78942	61990	90812	98452	74098	69738	83272	39212	42817
10159	85560	35619	58248	65498	77977	02896	45198	10655	13973
80162	35686	57877	19552	63931	44171	40879	94532	17828	31848
74388	92906	65829	24572	79417	38460	96294	79201	47755	90980
12660	09571	29743	45447	64063	46295	44191	53957	62393	42229
81852	60620	87757	72165	23875	87844	84038	04994	93466	27418
03068	61317	65305	64944	27319	55263	84514	38374	11657	67723
29623	58530	17274	16908	39253	37595	57497	74780	88624	93333
30520	50588	51231	83816	01075	33098	81308	59036	49152	86262
93694	02984	91350	33929	41724	32403	42566	14232	55085	65628
86736	40641	37958	25415	19922	65966	98044	39583	26828	50919
28141	15630	37675	52545	24813	22075	05142	15374	84533	12933
79804	05165	21620	98400	55290	71877	60052	46320	79055	45913
63763	49985	88853	70681	52762	17670	62337	12199	44123	37993
49618	47068	63331	62675	51788	58283	04295	72904	05378	98085
26502	68980	26545	14204	34304	50284	47730	57299	73966	02566
13549	86048	27912	56733	14987	09850	72817	85168	09538	92347
89221	78076	40306	34045	52557	52383	67796	41382	50490	30117
97809	34056	76778	60417	05153	83827	67369	08602	56163	28793
65668	44694	34151	51741	11484	13226	49516	17391	39956	34839
53653	59804	59051	95074	38307	99546	32962	26962	86252	50704
34922	95041	17398	32789	26860	55536	82415	82911	42208	62725
74880	65198	61357	90209	71543	71114	94868	05645	44154	72254
66036	48794	30021	92601	21615	16952	18433	44903	51322	90379
39044	99503	11442	81344	57068	74662	90382	59433	48440	38146
87756	71151	68543	08358	10183	06432	97482	90301	76114	83778
47117	45575	29524	02522	08041	70698	80260	73588	86415	72523
71572	02109	96722	21684	64331	71644	18933	32801	11644	12364
35609	58072	63209	48429	53108	59173	55337	22445	85940	43707
73703	70069	74981	12197	48426	77365	26769	65078	27849	41311
42979	88161	56531	46443	47148	42773	18601	38532	22594	12395
12279	42308	00380	17181	38757	09071	89804	15232	99007	39495

Table 7. Binomial Distribution (Cumulative binomial probabilities)

n	x	0.05	0.10	0.15	0.20	0.25	0.30	0.35	0.40	0.45	0.50	0.55	0.60	0.65	0.70	0.75	0.80	0.85	0.90
1	0	0.9500	0.9000	0.8500	0.8000	0.7500	0.7000	0.6500	0.6000	0.5500	0.5000	0.4500	0.4000	0.3500	0.3000	0.2500	0.2000	0.1500	0.1000
	1	1.0000	1.0000	1.0000	1.0000	1.0000	1.0000	1.0000	1.0000	1.0000	1.0000	1.0000	1.0000	1.0000	1.0000	1.0000	1.0000	1.0000	1.0000
2	0	0.9025	0.8100	0.7225	0.6400	0.5625	0.4900	0.4225	0.3600	0.3025	0.2500	0.2025	0.1600	0.1225	0.0900	0.0625	0.0400	0.0225	0.0100
	1	0.9975	0.9900	0.9775	0.9600	0.9375	0.9100	0.8775	0.8400	0.7975	0.7500	0.6975	0.6400	0.5775	0.5100	0.4375	0.3600	0.2775	0.1900
	2	1.0000	1.0000	1.0000	1.0000	1.0000	1.0000	1.0000	1.0000	1.0000	1.0000	1.0000	1.0000	1.0000	1.0000	1.0000	1.0000	1.0000	1.0000
3	0	0.8574	0.7290	0.6141	0.5120	0.4219	0.3430	0.2746	0.2160	0.1664	0.1250	0.0911	0.0640	0.0429	0.0270	0.0156	0.0080	0.0034	0.0010
	1	0.9928	0.9720	0.9393	0.8960	0.8438	0.7840	0.7183	0.6480	0.5748	0.5000	0.4253	0.3520	0.2818	0.2160	0.1563	0.1040	0.0608	0.0280
	2	0.9999	0.9990	0.9966	0.9920	0.9844	0.9730	0.9571	0.9360	0.9089	0.8750	0.8336	0.7840	0.7254	0.6570	0.5781	0.4880	0.3859	0.2710
	3	1.0000	1.0000	1.0000	1.0000	1.0000	1.0000	1.0000	1.0000	1.0000	1.0000	1.0000	1.0000	1.0000	1.0000	1.0000	1.0000	1.0000	1.0000
4	0	0.8145	0.6561	0.5220	0.4096	0.3164	0.2401	0.1785	0.1296	0.0915	0.0625	0.0410	0.0256	0.0150	0.0081	0.0039	0.0016	0.0005	0.0001
	1	0.9860	0.9477	0.8905	0.8192	0.7383	0.6517	0.5630	0.4752	0.3910	0.3125	0.2415	0.1792	0.1265	0.0837	0.0508	0.0272	0.0120	0.0037
	2	0.9995	0.9963	0.9880	0.9728	0.9492	0.9163	0.8735	0.8208	0.7585	0.6875	0.6090	0.5248	0.4370	0.3483	0.2617	0.1808	0.1095	0.0523
	3	1.0000	0.9999	0.9995	0.9984	0.9961	0.9919	0.9850	0.9744	0.9590	0.9375	0.9085	0.8704	0.8215	0.7599	0.6836	0.5904	0.4780	0.3439
	4	1.0000	1.0000	1.0000	1.0000	1.0000	1.0000	1.0000	1.0000	1.0000	1.0000	1.0000	1.0000	1.0000	1.0000	1.0000	1.0000	1.0000	1.0000
5	0	0.7738	0.5905	0.4437	0.3277	0.2373	0.1681	0.1160	0.0778	0.0503	0.0313	0.0185	0.0102	0.0053	0.0024	0.0010	0.0003	0.0001	0.0000
	1	0.9774	0.9185	0.8352	0.7373	0.6328	0.5282	0.4284	0.3370	0.2562	0.1875	0.1312	0.0870	0.0540	0.0308	0.0156	0.0067	0.0022	0.0005
	2	0.9988	0.9914	0.9734	0.9421	0.8965	0.8369	0.7648	0.6826	0.5931	0.5000	0.4069	0.3174	0.2352	0.1631	0.1035	0.0579	0.0266	0.0086
	3	1.0000	0.9995	0.9978	0.9933	0.9844	0.9692	0.9460	0.9130	0.8688	0.8125	0.7438	0.6630	0.5716	0.4718	0.3672	0.2627	0.1648	0.0815
	4	1.0000	1.0000	0.9999	0.9997	0.9990	0.9976	0.9947	0.9898	0.9815	0.9688	0.9497	0.9222	0.8840	0.8319	0.7627	0.6723	0.5563	0.4095
	5	1.0000	1.0000	1.0000	1.0000	1.0000	1.0000	1.0000	1.0000	1.0000	1.0000	1.0000	1.0000	1.0000	1.0000	1.0000	1.0000	1.0000	1.0000
6	0	0.7351	0.5314	0.3771	0.2621	0.1780	0.1176	0.0754	0.0467	0.0277	0.0156	0.0083	0.0041	0.0018	0.0007	0.0002	0.0001	0.0000	0.0000
	1	0.9672	0.8857	0.7765	0.6554	0.5339	0.4202	0.3191	0.2333	0.1636	0.1094	0.0692	0.0410	0.0223	0.0109	0.0046	0.0016	0.0004	0.0001
	2	0.9978	0.9842	0.9527	0.9011	0.8306	0.7443	0.6471	0.5443	0.4415	0.3438	0.2553	0.1792	0.1174	0.0705	0.0376	0.0170	0.0059	0.0013
	3	0.9999	0.9987	0.9941	0.9830	0.9624	0.9295	0.8826	0.8208	0.7447	0.6563	0.5585	0.4557	0.3529	0.2557	0.1694	0.0989	0.0473	0.0159
	4	1.0000	0.9999	0.9996	0.9984	0.9954	0.9891	0.9777	0.9590	0.9308	0.8906	0.8364	0.7667	0.6809	0.5798	0.4661	0.3446	0.2235	0.1143
	5	1.0000	1.0000	1.0000	0.9999	0.9998	0.9993	0.9982	0.9959	0.9917	0.9844	0.9723	0.9533	0.9246	0.8824	0.8220	0.7379	0.6229	0.4686
	6	1.0000	1.0000	1.0000	1.0000	1.0000	1.0000	1.0000	1.0000	1.0000	1.0000	1.0000	1.0000	1.0000	1.0000	1.0000	1.0000	1.0000	1.0000
7	0	0.6983	0.4783	0.3206	0.2097	0.1335	0.0824	0.0490	0.0280	0.0152	0.0078	0.0037	0.0016	0.0006	0.0002	0.0001	0.0000	0.0000	0.0000
	1	0.9556	0.8503	0.7166	0.5767	0.4449	0.3294	0.2338	0.1586	0.1024	0.0625	0.0357	0.0188	0.0090	0.0038	0.0013	0.0004	0.0001	0.0000
	2	0.9962	0.9743	0.9262	0.8520	0.7564	0.6471	0.5323	0.4199	0.3164	0.2266	0.1529	0.0963	0.0556	0.0288	0.0129	0.0047	0.0012	0.0002
	3	0.9998	0.9973	0.9879	0.9667	0.9294	0.8740	0.8002	0.7102	0.6083	0.5000	0.3917	0.2898	0.1998	0.1260	0.0706	0.0333	0.0129	0.0027
	4	1.0000	0.9998	0.9988	0.9953	0.9871	0.9712	0.9444	0.9037	0.8471	0.7734	0.6836	0.5801	0.4677	0.3529	0.2436	0.1480	0.0738	0.0257
	5	1.0000	1.0000	0.9999	0.9996	0.9987	0.9962	0.9910	0.9812	0.9643	0.9375	0.8976	0.8414	0.7662	0.6706	0.5551	0.4233	0.2834	0.1497
	6	1.0000	1.0000	1.0000	1.0000	0.9999	0.9998	0.9994	0.9984	0.9963	0.9922	0.9848	0.9720	0.9510	0.9176	0.8665	0.7903	0.6794	0.5217
	7	1.0000	1.0000	1.0000	1.0000	1.0000	1.0000	1.0000	1.0000	1.0000	1.0000	1.0000	1.0000	1.0000	1.0000	1.0000	1.0000	1.0000	1.0000

Table 7. (Continued)

n	x	0.05	0.10	0.15	0.20	0.25	0.30	0.35	0.40	0.45	0.50	0.55	0.60	0.65	0.70	0.75	0.80	0.85	0.90	0.95
8	0	0.6634	0.4305	0.2725	0.1678	0.1001	0.0576	0.0319	0.0168	0.0084	0.0039	0.0017	0.0007	0.0002	0.0001	0.0000	0.0000	0.0000	0.0000	0.0000
	1	0.9428	0.8131	0.6572	0.5033	0.3671	0.2553	0.1691	0.1064	0.0632	0.0352	0.0181	0.0085	0.0036	0.0013	0.0004	0.0001	0.0000	0.0000	0.0000
	2	0.9942	0.9619	0.8948	0.7969	0.6785	0.5518	0.4278	0.3154	0.2201	0.1445	0.0885	0.0498	0.0253	0.0113	0.0042	0.0012	0.0002	0.0000	0.0000
	3	0.9996	0.9950	0.9786	0.9437	0.8862	0.8059	0.7064	0.5941	0.4770	0.3633	0.2604	0.1737	0.1061	0.0580	0.0273	0.0104	0.0029	0.0004	0.0000
	4	1.0000	0.9996	0.9971	0.9896	0.9727	0.9420	0.8939	0.8263	0.7396	0.6367	0.5230	0.4059	0.2936	0.1941	0.1138	0.0563	0.0214	0.0050	0.0004
	5	1.0000	1.0000	0.9998	0.9988	0.9958	0.9887	0.9747	0.9502	0.9115	0.8555	0.7799	0.6846	0.5722	0.4482	0.3215	0.2031	0.1052	0.0381	0.0058
	6	1.0000	1.0000	1.0000	0.9999	0.9996	0.9987	0.9964	0.9915	0.9819	0.9648	0.9368	0.8936	0.8309	0.7447	0.6329	0.4967	0.3428	0.1869	0.0572
	7	1.0000	1.0000	1.0000	1.0000	1.0000	0.9999	0.9998	0.9993	0.9983	0.9961	0.9916	0.9832	0.9681	0.9424	0.8999	0.8322	0.7275	0.5695	0.3366
	8	1.0000	1.0000	1.0000	1.0000	1.0000	1.0000	1.0000	1.0000	1.0000	1.0000	1.0000	1.0000	1.0000	1.0000	1.0000	1.0000	1.0000	1.0000	1.0000
9	0	0.6302	0.3874	0.2316	0.1342	0.0751	0.0404	0.0207	0.0101	0.0046	0.0020	0.0008	0.0003	0.0001	0.0000	0.0000	0.0000	0.0000	0.0000	0.0000
	1	0.9288	0.7748	0.5995	0.4362	0.3003	0.1960	0.1211	0.0705	0.0385	0.0195	0.0091	0.0038	0.0014	0.0004	0.0001	0.0000	0.0000	0.0000	0.0000
	2	0.9916	0.9470	0.8591	0.7382	0.6007	0.4628	0.3373	0.2318	0.1495	0.0898	0.0498	0.0250	0.0112	0.0043	0.0013	0.0003	0.0001	0.0000	0.0000
	3	0.9994	0.9917	0.9661	0.9144	0.8343	0.7297	0.6089	0.4826	0.3614	0.2539	0.1658	0.0994	0.0536	0.0253	0.0100	0.0031	0.0006	0.0001	0.0000
	4	1.0000	0.9991	0.9944	0.9804	0.9511	0.9012	0.8283	0.7334	0.6214	0.5000	0.3786	0.2666	0.1717	0.0988	0.0489	0.0196	0.0056	0.0009	0.0000
	5	1.0000	0.9999	0.9994	0.9969	0.9900	0.9747	0.9464	0.9006	0.8342	0.7461	0.6386	0.5174	0.3911	0.2703	0.1657	0.0856	0.0339	0.0083	0.0006
	6	1.0000	1.0000	1.0000	0.9997	0.9987	0.9957	0.9888	0.9750	0.9502	0.9102	0.8505	0.7682	0.6627	0.5372	0.3993	0.2618	0.1409	0.0530	0.0084
	7	1.0000	1.0000	1.0000	1.0000	0.9999	0.9996	0.9986	0.9962	0.9909	0.9805	0.9615	0.9295	0.8789	0.8040	0.6997	0.5638	0.4005	0.2252	0.0712
	8	1.0000	1.0000	1.0000	1.0000	1.0000	1.0000	0.9999	0.9997	0.9992	0.9980	0.9954	0.9899	0.9793	0.9596	0.9249	0.8658	0.7684	0.6126	0.3698
	9	1.0000	1.0000	1.0000	1.0000	1.0000	1.0000	1.0000	1.0000	1.0000	1.0000	1.0000	1.0000	1.0000	1.0000	1.0000	1.0000	1.0000	1.0000	1.0000
10	0	0.5987	0.3487	0.1969	0.1074	0.0563	0.0282	0.0135	0.0060	0.0025	0.0010	0.0003	0.0001	0.0000	0.0000	0.0000	0.0000	0.0000	0.0000	0.0000
	1	0.9139	0.7361	0.5443	0.3758	0.2440	0.1493	0.0860	0.0464	0.0233	0.0107	0.0045	0.0017	0.0005	0.0001	0.0000	0.0000	0.0000	0.0000	0.0000
	2	0.9885	0.9298	0.8202	0.6778	0.5256	0.3828	0.2616	0.1673	0.0996	0.0547	0.0274	0.0123	0.0048	0.0016	0.0004	0.0001	0.0000	0.0000	0.0000
	3	0.9990	0.9872	0.9500	0.8791	0.7759	0.6496	0.5138	0.3823	0.2660	0.1719	0.1020	0.0548	0.0260	0.0106	0.0035	0.0009	0.0001	0.0000	0.0000
	4	0.9999	0.9984	0.9901	0.9672	0.9219	0.8497	0.7515	0.6331	0.5044	0.3770	0.2616	0.1662	0.0949	0.0473	0.0197	0.0064	0.0014	0.0001	0.0000
	5	1.0000	0.9999	0.9986	0.9936	0.9803	0.9527	0.9051	0.8338	0.7384	0.6230	0.4956	0.3669	0.2485	0.1503	0.0781	0.0328	0.0099	0.0016	0.0001
	6	1.0000	1.0000	0.9999	0.9991	0.9965	0.9894	0.9740	0.9452	0.8980	0.8281	0.7340	0.6177	0.4862	0.3504	0.2241	0.1209	0.0500	0.0128	0.0010
	7	1.0000	1.0000	1.0000	0.9999	0.9996	0.9984	0.9952	0.9877	0.9726	0.9453	0.9004	0.8327	0.7384	0.6172	0.4744	0.3222	0.1798	0.0702	0.0115
	8	1.0000	1.0000	1.0000	1.0000	1.0000	0.9999	0.9995	0.9983	0.9955	0.9893	0.9767	0.9536	0.9140	0.8507	0.7560	0.6242	0.4557	0.2639	0.0861
	9	1.0000	1.0000	1.0000	1.0000	1.0000	1.0000	1.0000	0.9999	0.9997	0.9990	0.9975	0.9940	0.9865	0.9718	0.9437	0.8926	0.8031	0.6513	0.4013
	10	1.0000	1.0000	1.0000	1.0000	1.0000	1.0000	1.0000	1.0000	1.0000	1.0000	1.0000	1.0000	1.0000	1.0000	1.0000	1.0000	1.0000	1.0000	1.0000
15	0	0.4633	0.2059	0.0874	0.0352	0.0134	0.0047	0.0016	0.0005	0.0001	0.0000	0.0000	0.0000	0.0000	0.0000	0.0000	0.0000	0.0000	0.0000	0.0000
	1	0.8290	0.5490	0.3186	0.1671	0.0802	0.0353	0.0142	0.0052	0.0017	0.0005	0.0001	0.0000	0.0000	0.0000	0.0000	0.0000	0.0000	0.0000	0.0000
	2	0.9638	0.8159	0.6042	0.3980	0.2361	0.1268	0.0617	0.0271	0.0107	0.0037	0.0011	0.0003	0.0001	0.0000	0.0000	0.0000	0.0000	0.0000	0.0000
	3	0.9945	0.9444	0.8227	0.6482	0.4613	0.2969	0.1727	0.0905	0.0424	0.0176	0.0063	0.0019	0.0005	0.0001	0.0000	0.0000	0.0000	0.0000	0.0000
	4	0.9994	0.9873	0.9383	0.8358	0.6865	0.5155	0.3519	0.2173	0.1204	0.0592	0.0255	0.0093	0.0028	0.0007	0.0001	0.0000	0.0000	0.0000	0.0000
	5	0.9999	0.9978	0.9832	0.9389	0.8516	0.7216	0.5643	0.4032	0.2608	0.1509	0.0769	0.0338	0.0124	0.0037	0.0008	0.0001	0.0000	0.0000	0.0000
	6	1.0000	0.9997	0.9964	0.9819	0.9434	0.8689	0.7548	0.6098	0.4522	0.3036	0.1818	0.0950	0.0422	0.0152	0.0042	0.0008	0.0001	0.0000	0.0000
	7	1.0000	1.0000	0.9994	0.9958	0.9827	0.9500	0.8868	0.7869	0.6535	0.5000	0.3465	0.2131	0.1132	0.0500	0.0173	0.0042	0.0006	0.0000	0.0000
	8	1.0000	1.0000	0.9999	0.9992	0.9958	0.9848	0.9578	0.9050	0.8182	0.6964	0.5478	0.3902	0.2452	0.1311	0.0566	0.0181	0.0036	0.0003	0.0000
	9	1.0000	1.0000	1.0000	0.9999	0.9992	0.9963	0.9876	0.9662	0.9231	0.8491	0.7392	0.5968	0.4357	0.2784	0.1484	0.0611	0.0168	0.0022	0.0000
	10	1.0000	1.0000	1.0000	1.0000	0.9999	0.9993	0.9972	0.9907	0.9745	0.9408	0.8796	0.7827	0.6481	0.4845	0.3135	0.1642	0.0617	0.0127	0.0006
	11	1.0000	1.0000	1.0000	1.0000	1.0000	0.9999	0.9995	0.9981	0.9937	0.9824	0.9576	0.9095	0.8273	0.7031	0.5387	0.3518	0.1773	0.0556	0.0055
	12	1.0000	1.0000	1.0000	1.0000	1.0000	1.0000	0.9999	0.9997	0.9989	0.9963	0.9893	0.9729	0.9383	0.8732	0.7639	0.6020	0.3958	0.1841	0.0362
	13	1.0000	1.0000	1.0000	1.0000	1.0000	1.0000	1.0000	1.0000	0.9999	0.9995	0.9983	0.9948	0.9858	0.9647	0.9198	0.8329	0.6814	0.4510	0.1710
	14	1.0000	1.0000	1.0000	1.0000	1.0000	1.0000	1.0000	1.0000	1.0000	1.0000	0.9999	0.9995	0.9984	0.9953	0.9866	0.9648	0.9126	0.7941	0.5367
	15	1.0000	1.0000	1.0000	1.0000	1.0000	1.0000	1.0000	1.0000	1.0000	1.0000	1.0000	1.0000	1.0000	1.0000	1.0000	1.0000	1.0000	1.0000	1.0000

Table 8. Poisson Distribution

λ\x	0	1	2	3	4	5	6	7	8	9
0.05	0.951	0.999	1.000							
0.10	0.905	0.995	1.000							
0.15	0.861	0.990	0.999	1.000						
0.20	0.819	0.982	0.999	1.000						
0.25	0.779	0.974	0.998	1.000						
0.30	0.741	0.963	0.996	1.000						
0.35	0.705	0.951	0.994	1.000						
0.40	0.670	0.938	0.992	0.999	1.000					
0.45	0.638	0.925	0.989	0.999	1.000					
0.50	0.607	0.910	0.986	0.998	1.000					
0.55	0.577	0.894	0.982	0.998	1.000					
0.60	0.549	0.878	0.977	0.997	1.000					
0.65	0.522	0.861	0.972	0.996	0.999	1.000				
0.70	0.497	0.844	0.966	0.994	0.999	1.000				
0.75	0.472	0.827	0.960	0.993	0.999	1.000				
0.80	0.449	0.809	0.953	0.991	0.999	1.000				
0.85	0.427	0.791	0.945	0.989	0.998	1.000				
0.90	0.407	0.772	0.937	0.987	0.998	1.000				
0.95	0.387	0.754	0.929	0.984	0.997	1.000				
1.0	0.368	0.736	0.920	0.981	0.996	0.999	1.000			
1.1	0.333	0.699	0.900	0.974	0.995	0.999	1.000			
1.2	0.301	0.663	0.880	0.966	0.992	0.998	1.000			
1.3	0.273	0.627	0.857	0.957	0.989	0.998	1.000			
1.4	0.247	0.592	0.833	0.946	0.986	0.997	0.999	1.000		
1.5	0.223	0.558	0.809	0.934	0.981	0.996	0.999	1.000		
1.6	0.202	0.525	0.783	0.921	0.976	0.994	0.999	1.000		
1.7	0.183	0.493	0.757	0.907	0.970	0.992	0.998	1.000		
1.8	0.165	0.463	0.731	0.891	0.964	0.990	0.997	0.999	1.000	
1.9	0.150	0.434	0.704	0.875	0.956	0.987	0.997	0.999	1.000	
2.0	0.135	0.406	0.677	0.857	0.947	0.983	0.995	0.999	1.000	
2.2	0.111	0.355	0.623	0.819	0.928	0.975	0.993	0.998	1.000	
2.4	0.091	0.308	0.570	0.779	0.904	0.964	0.988	0.997	0.999	1.000
2.6	0.074	0.267	0.518	0.736	0.877	0.951	0.983	0.995	0.999	1.000
2.8	0.061	0.231	0.470	0.692	0.848	0.935	0.976	0.992	0.998	0.999

Table 8. (Continued)

λ\x	0	1	2	3	4	5	6	7	8	9	10	11	12	13	14	15	16	17	18	19	20
3.0	0.050	0.199	0.423	0.647	0.815	0.916	0.966	0.988	0.996	0.999	1.000										
3.2	0.041	0.171	0.380	0.603	0.781	0.895	0.955	0.983	0.994	0.998	1.000										
3.4	0.033	0.147	0.340	0.558	0.744	0.871	0.942	0.977	0.992	0.997	0.999	1.000									
3.6	0.027	0.126	0.303	0.515	0.706	0.844	0.927	0.969	0.988	0.996	0.999	1.000									
3.8	0.022	0.107	0.269	0.474	0.668	0.816	0.909	0.960	0.984	0.994	0.998	0.999									
4.0	0.018	0.092	0.238	0.433	0.629	0.785	0.889	0.949	0.979	0.992	0.997	0.999	1.000								
4.2	0.015	0.078	0.210	0.395	0.590	0.753	0.868	0.936	0.972	0.989	0.996	0.999	1.000								
4.4	0.012	0.066	0.185	0.359	0.551	0.720	0.844	0.921	0.964	0.985	0.994	0.998	0.999	1.000							
4.6	0.010	0.056	0.163	0.326	0.513	0.686	0.818	0.905	0.955	0.980	0.992	0.997	0.999	1.000							
4.8	0.008	0.048	0.143	0.294	0.476	0.651	0.791	0.887	0.944	0.975	0.990	0.996	0.999	1.000							
5.0	0.007	0.040	0.125	0.265	0.441	0.616	0.762	0.867	0.932	0.968	0.986	0.995	0.998	0.999	1.000						
5.2	0.006	0.034	0.109	0.238	0.406	0.581	0.732	0.845	0.918	0.960	0.982	0.993	0.997	0.999	1.000						
5.4	0.005	0.029	0.095	0.213	0.373	0.546	0.702	0.822	0.903	0.951	0.978	0.990	0.996	0.999	1.000						
5.6	0.004	0.024	0.082	0.191	0.342	0.512	0.670	0.797	0.886	0.941	0.972	0.988	0.995	0.998	0.999	1.000					
5.8	0.003	0.021	0.072	0.170	0.313	0.478	0.638	0.771	0.867	0.929	0.965	0.984	0.993	0.997	0.999	1.000					
6.0	0.003	0.017	0.062	0.151	0.285	0.446	0.606	0.744	0.847	0.916	0.957	0.980	0.991	0.996	0.999	0.999	1.000				
6.2	0.002	0.015	0.054	0.134	0.259	0.414	0.574	0.716	0.826	0.902	0.949	0.975	0.989	0.995	0.998	0.999	1.000				
6.4	0.002	0.012	0.046	0.119	0.235	0.384	0.542	0.687	0.803	0.886	0.939	0.969	0.986	0.994	0.997	0.999	1.000				
6.6	0.001	0.010	0.040	0.105	0.213	0.355	0.511	0.658	0.780	0.869	0.927	0.963	0.982	0.992	0.997	0.999	0.999	1.000			
6.8	0.001	0.007	0.030	0.082	0.173	0.301	0.450	0.599	0.729	0.830	0.915	0.955	0.978	0.990	0.996	0.998	0.999	1.000			
7.0	0.001	0.007	0.030	0.082	0.173	0.301	0.450	0.599	0.729	0.830	0.901	0.947	0.973	0.987	0.994	0.998	0.999	1.000			
7.2	0.001	0.006	0.025	0.072	0.156	0.276	0.420	0.569	0.703	0.810	0.887	0.937	0.967	0.984	0.993	0.997	0.999	0.999	1.000		
7.4	0.001	0.005	0.022	0.063	0.140	0.253	0.392	0.539	0.676	0.788	0.871	0.926	0.961	0.980	0.991	0.996	0.998	0.999	1.000		
7.6	0.001	0.004	0.019	0.055	0.125	0.231	0.365	0.510	0.648	0.765	0.854	0.915	0.954	0.976	0.989	0.995	0.998	0.999	1.000		
7.8	0.000	0.004	0.016	0.048	0.112	0.210	0.338	0.481	0.620	0.741	0.835	0.902	0.945	0.971	0.986	0.993	0.997	0.999	1.000		
8.0	0.000	0.003	0.014	0.042	0.100	0.191	0.313	0.453	0.593	0.717	0.816	0.888	0.936	0.966	0.983	0.992	0.996	0.998	0.999	1.000	
8.2	0.000	0.003	0.012	0.037	0.089	0.174	0.290	0.425	0.566	0.692	0.796	0.873	0.926	0.960	0.979	0.990	0.995	0.998	0.999	1.000	
8.4	0.000	0.002	0.010	0.032	0.079	0.157	0.267	0.400	0.537	0.666	0.774	0.857	0.915	0.952	0.975	0.987	0.994	0.997	0.999	1.000	
8.6	0.000	0.002	0.009	0.030	0.074	0.150	0.256	0.386	0.523	0.653	0.763	0.849	0.909	0.949	0.973	0.986	0.993	0.997	0.998	0.999	1.000
8.8	0.000	0.002	0.007	0.024	0.062	0.128	0.226	0.348	0.482	0.614	0.729	0.822	0.889	0.935	0.964	0.981	0.990	0.995	0.998	0.999	
9.0	0.000	0.001	0.006	0.021	0.055	0.116	0.207	0.324	0.456	0.587	0.706	0.803	0.876	0.926	0.959	0.978	0.989	0.995	0.998	0.999	1.000
9.5	0.000	0.001	0.004	0.015	0.040	0.089	0.165	0.269	0.392	0.522	0.645	0.752	0.836	0.898	0.940	0.967	0.982	0.991	0.996	0.998	0.999

INDEX